D0712371

GERMAN - HUNGARIAN RELATIONS
AND THE SWABIAN PROBLEM
From Károlyi to Gömbös 1919-1936

THOMAS SPIRA

EAST EUROPEAN QUARTERLY, BOULDER
DISTRIBUTED BY COLUMBIA UNIVERSITY PRESS
NEW YORK

1977

EAST EUROPEAN MONOGRAPHS, NO. XXV

LIBRARY

MAR 2 0 1979

UNIVERSITY OF THE PACIFIC

358344

Thomas Spira is Associate Professor
of History at the University of
Prince Edward Island

Copyright 1977 by East European Quarterly
Library of Congress Card Catalog Number 76-47790
ISBN 0-914710-18-4

Printed in the United States of America

PREFACE

In preparing this book, I have become indebted to many individuals and institutions. Professor Stephen Fischer-Galati encouraged me to write this study. Reginald C. Stuart read the manuscript and provided invaluable suggestions on style and idiom. Michael Foley saw substantial portions of the final draft, and offered helpful insights. Éva Windisch kindly permitted access to her unpublished manuscript. Jon Berlin let me use his research material. Béla Bellér provided valuable insights into Hungary's complex nationality problems. I am grateful to the University of Prince Edward Island stenographic pool personnel, and particularly to Nadeen Robb, who typed the final draft.

I wish to thank the staffs of the West German Federal Archives in Koblenz; the Political Archives of the Foreign Ministry in Bonn; the Austrian State Archives in Vienna; the National Széchenyi Library, the Hungarian National Archives, the Parliamentary Archives, and the Statistical Bureau Archives, all in Budapest; and various other library staffs in Europe and North America. The Kussbach family has kindly given me access to the Franz Kussbach *Nachlass* in the Koblenz Archives. The Interlibrary Loan staff at the U.P.E.I. has been most helpful and understanding.

My work has been facilitated by grants from the Canada Council and the U.P.E.I. Senate Research Committee. For the past five years, my wife Marita and daughter Clara-Maria have patiently borne the burden of my preoccupations. But other people, far too numerous to cite individually, have stamped their influence on this endeavour. Whatever their contributions, all errors of fact and judgment are mine alone.

Charlottetown
Prince Edward Island, Canada
January 1976

T. S.

TABLE OF CONTENTS

INTRODUCTION

The Magyars' peculiar psychological, cultural, and demographic position in Central Europe dictated their attitude towards the other ethnic groups in Hungary. The major problem confronting them since their arrival in the Danube Basin had been national survival. Exposed to the threat of absorption by the culturally superior peoples living in their midst, the Magyars also faced the external menace of their more powerful neighbours. Territorial expansion and the Magyarizing of alien groups in conquered areas were their solutions. They hoped to create an enlarged and homogeneous Magyar state to ensure their dominant position in the region and to defend it against invasion. These plans came to naught. Mongol raids and the Turkish occupation, which decimated the ethnic Magyars, created extensive demographic changes, thus ending the possibility for the emergence of a homogeneous Magyar state. Furthermore, after liberating Hungary, the Habsburgs not only continued the ethnic diversification of the area, they systematically subjected the country to Germanization.

Hungary's desire for an independent Magyar state, stimulated by the nationalistic ideas of the nineteenth century, could not find expression under Habsburg rule. By the time Hungary achieved domestic autonomy as a partner in the Austro-Hungarian Monarchy in 1867, the Habsburgs had adopted a nationality policy which was a departure from their earlier and more obvious Germanizing schemes. Austria now was interested in preserving the Empire through the political hegemony of its heavily outnumbered German elements. By fomenting tensions amongst their minorities and thereby weakening them, the Habsburgs hoped to achieve their objective of *divide et impera*.

In deference to Austria, and also to soothe the non-Magyars, Hungary introduced a nationality law in 1868, supposedly for the protection of non-Magyar minority groups. The statute did little more than offer the same legal protection to individual members of minorities as Hungary's Magyar citizens already enjoyed. Moreover, the government warned the non-Magyars that the protection of the law would not apply to those who engaged in nationalistic agitation. The real intent of the Nationality Law evidently was to provide legal grounds for the unhampered pursuit of the assimilation programme.

But the non-Magyar strains composed a clear majority of Hungary's population, a stumbling block to Magyar domination. In view of the Austrian deterrent, the Magyars had to employ a strategy, therefore, that would prevent overt opposition from their non-Magyar subjects and the Habsburgs. The Magyars found a way to gain control over the non-Magyar youth by the introduction of state supervision of primary education and the passage of compulsory attendance laws in the elementary schools. At the same time, the Magyars also planned to subvert the minority intelligentsia by offering social and professional inducements to those who abandoned their non-Magyar ethnic preferences and adopted the Magyar language and culture instead. In this respect, the Magyars practiced virtually no ethnic, religious, or regional discrimination. Nonetheless, these methods of assimilation during the succeeding fifty years proved to be less than successful, for about half of Hungary's population was still non-Magyar when World War I began. The failure of the supposedly lenient prewar nationality policy influenced profoundly the Magyar consensus on minority treatment after Trianon.

When at the cost of two-thirds of her territory and population Hungary finally became virtually a Magyar state, her leaders determined to eliminate every non-Magyar vestige in the national culture. To justify this policy, the Magyars cited the historic "Magyar Mission" to create a homogeneous Magyar Hungary which would become the bulwark of the civilized, Christian West against the barbaric East. In fact, this policy—though sincerely meant—rationalized the programme of Magyarization already begun in 1868.

These plans encountered new obstacles after the War. The Minorities Clauses of the Trianon Peace Treaty presented little difficulty, however, for their provisions were vague and Hungary evaded them with ease and impunity. Far more serious was the problem of what to do with the Swabians, the largest and most vocal minority remaining in Trianon Hungary. Although determined to eradicate this last serious threat to their hegemony, the Magyars also recognized the possible benefits of a pro-Swabian policy. Germany, which after the War became the only significant power capable of offering economic and political aid, gradually evinced increasing interest in the fate of the Swabians. To resolve the contradictory demands of their internal and foreign diplomacy, the Magyars tried to convince Germany that they would protect Swabian cultural interests if Germany would render economic aid and actively espouse Magyar revisionist aspirations. In fact, the Magyars had no intentions of living up to their promises and they simply adopted a more devious and efficient version of their prewar minority policy.

Over the years, the Magyars promulgated a number of restrictive laws for the minority schools, which in the end virtually destroyed the effectiveness of these institutions. As in the past, an outward show of legal forms and benevolence was maintained, with assimilation aimed primarily at minority youth. This programme was carried out according to a strategy consisting of two steps. First, the government planned gradually to Magyarize Swabian children by building Magyar elementary schools. The regime believed that the Swabians would eventually abandon their own inferior facilities in favour of the attractive Magyar institutions. Furthermore, with minimal use of physical force, but with a great deal of social, economic, and psychological pressure, the government eventually secured the grudging consent of minorities' parents' groups to the establishment of Magyar or virtually Magyar minority institutions. The second stage in the government's strategy was predicated on the maxim, "A minority without an intelligentsia must perish." The government believed that the Swabian villagers would be helpless in the face of Magyar assaults against their ethnic identity if they were deprived of their intellectual leadership. German instruction in the elementary schools was dismal, facilities primitive, and in higher institutions the language was given only sporadically, Hungarian propaganda notwithstanding. The peasant home environment with its tradition of oral culture was not conducive to an appreciation of literary German. Nor did the minority schools impart a proper knowledge of even the Magyar language to the Swabian pupils. Although seemingly contrary to Magyar interests, such a policy had its desired effects. It demonstrated beyond doubt that minority schools, which divided their curriculum more or less evenly between two languages, were inefficient and failed to provide an adequate understanding of either language. As a result, ambitious Swabian pupils were compelled to forsake their own minority schools in favour of Magyar institutions, for only those who were fully conversant with the Magyar language could hope to proceed to a higher institute of learning and to a better station in life. It is no wonder then that most Swabian children became Magyarized; at least to outward appearances, by the time they reached high school.

The influence of Hungarian-German relations on Swabian school policy was direct and obvious. From 1918 to 1920, Hungary courted the minorities in an attempt to discourage their secession. As part of their programme, they published plans for Swabian school reform and for the establishment of German teacher training courses. Most of these plans, however, were not put into effect. In the years 1921-1925, Hungary's chagrin over the Peace Treaty and her shock at being deserted en masse by her peripheral minorities led to the virtual termination of obligations towards minorities. During this period Hungary came very close to the realization of a Magyar nation state. The government began to do away with the pure German minority schools, and it virtually eliminated courses for the training of minority teachers. Minority cultural and fraternal organizations were permitted to function, albeit on a vastly reduced scale, and strictly at the local level. Although these measures represented Treaty violations, the League of Nations failed to rectify the situation. The only potential political deterrent, Germany, was in no position as yet to protest effectively the treatment of the Swabians. It is manifest that barring Germany's subsequent interest in the Swabians and Hungary's interest in German aid, the Swabian minority might soon have been eliminated. True, Germany's postwar recovery in 1925 changed the situation, but only to the extent of slowing down the process of Magyarization among the Swabians.

Between 1926 and 1932, the years which represented the high tide of Hungary's political and economic dependence on Weimar Germany, the government tried to convey the notion that real improvement in Swabian schools and association life were being carried out. In fact, the regime resorted to various types of statistical manipulation and to insignificant, exaggerated improvements. In response to the growing German menace, by 1933, Hungary's apprehensions brought about a reversal in Magyar minority policy. Alarmed over implied threats by Germans and Swabians, especially after the rise of National Socialism, the Magyars feared that the Swabians would be only too willing to play an auxiliary role to abet Germany's expansionist plans in the Danube Basin. More concerned with national security than even with economic or political advantage, the Gömbös government finally revealed its true intentions and began to intimate that Swabian minority rights would be curtailed unless disintegrative activities and National Socialist interference ceased. German threats, cajolery, and protests, merely confirmed the Magyars' determination to deal severely with the suspected Pan-German Swabians and to intensify their efforts to eliminate this last obstacle to the final Magyarization of Hungary.

This was consistent. The motivations for such a policy may be found in the unique position of the original Magyar settlers in the Danube Basin. The contempt of their neighbours, caused by the racial disparity and cultural backwardness of the newcomers, imbued the Magyars with feelings of inferiority. They determined to alter their image by transforming the original Magyar stock through the absorption of Indo-European strains and by adopting the cultural standards of the peoples in their midst. With the customary zeal of proselytes they vied to excel their neighbours and soon made every effort to convert them to the now allegedly superior Magyar culture. Out of this psychological crucible emerged the traditional Magyar policy of contempt for the "inferior" non-Magyar conquered peoples of the Danube Basin and the justification for endeavouring to incorporate them into the Magyar ethos. In fact, this course merely served as a pretext for attempting to ensure the continuing hegemony of the numerically weaker Magyars. In the course of time, this mission gathered more impetus by assuming overtones of a religious crusade. It is no wonder then that security through militant Magyarization became the prime motivating factor in Hungary.

From time to time, the techniques of assimilating the minorities varied to conform to contemporary trends and needs. In contrast to the more overt process of the earlier days, by the time Hungary achieved limited independence in the nineteenth century, Magyarization was carried out by parliamentary means and with purposeful planning. It was in tune with the current centralizing efforts in most Western European nation states. Having attained full sovereignty after World War I, Hungary continued to adhere *pro forma* to the same parliamentary and legal principles as before. But the failure of their Magyarization programme before the War, and feelings of contempt and revenge towards the minorities, impelled Hungary's postwar regimes to adopt measures which exploited the remaining minorities on behalf of the truncated nation's diplomatic policy. It is no wonder that Hungary, although bound by her own laws and by the Peace Treaty, did not feel obliged to respect their provisions concerning the protection of minorities. Moreover, the supposed inferiority of their subject peoples permitted Magyars to ignore any further agreements concluded with them or concerning them. Hence it follows, that the exploitation of these ethnic groups in the service of a higher "State Mission," ostensibly in defense of Western Civilization, in reality on behalf of permanent Magyar hegemony, constituted a basic Magyar national policy.

CHAPTER I
HUNGARY'S MINORITY POLICY BEFORE WORLD WAR I

Asiatic nomadic Magyars burst into the Danubian Plain in the year 896, and within a few decades conquered the area. Ever after, the outnumbered invaders faced the danger of being absorbed by other ethnic groups. In the region they had found a diversified population, mainly Germanic, Slavic and Avar, enjoying a more advanced economic and cultural way of life. While some of the natives fled to the surrounding hills and mountains, the majority remained in the Great Plain (Alföld) as a continual threat for the conquerors, who feared assimilation. In time, the Great Plain now ruled by the Magyars became a sensitive buffer zone, its security endangered by a variety of powerful neighbours. Forming a wedge between southern and northern Slavic groups and unable to overcome them, the Magyars were in danger of being crushed by these two mighty forces. At the same time, by the choice of their new homeland, the Magyars had thrust themselves between the Slavic and Teutonic worlds, and stood in the path of German eastward penetration.

Despite their efforts to consolidate and expand, the Magyar people suffered the effects of repeated war and invasion. The country's population was frequently decimated and new strains were introduced, which further diversified Hungary's ethnic composition. The first crisis was the Mongolian onslaught of 1240-1241, which left the country desolated. The most notable was the Turkish occupation, which began after the disastrous battle of Mohács (1526), and lasted nearly two centuries. During this interval large areas of Hungary were colonized by Serbs and by other Balkan peoples, who accompanied the Turks and pressed northward in great numbers. After the Habsburgs expelled the Ottoman invaders, the recovered Hungarian lands seldom reverted to their Magyar owners, but were usually declared new acquisitions by the Crown. Shortly after the liberation in 1699, the Austrians established large numbers of Serbs as farmer-soldiers on Hungary's southern frontiers to prevent further Turkish intrusions, to weaken the homogeneity of the allegedly unreliable Magyars, and at the same time, to restore the agricultural productivity of the ravaged Hungarian lands.

Most of Hungary's Magyars had embraced Protestantism during the Turkish occupation. The Roman Catholic Habsburgs therefore wished to introduce additional settlers whose religious loyalty would counterbalance Protestant and Orthodox influences in Hungary. In response to attractive inducements, waves of settlers, mostly from Catholic Southern Germany, began to immigrate to the Plain.[1] The Habsburg preference for Germans was also determined by national considerations and by earlier successful ventures with other Germans during the Middle Ages. Before the Turkish occupation Saxon artisans, merchants, and burghers had been invited to take up residence in Hungary's newly built urban centers. Encountering little competition, they soon emerged as the first Hungarian middle class and swiftly assumed control of Hungary's financial and commercial life—a position they continued to maintain well into the nineteenth century. It was hoped in Vienna that the Swabians would achieve the same type of leadership in the countryside as the Saxons had attained in the towns, while also maintaining a devoted attachment to their German ideals. These expectations were fully realized, and the Swabian rural settlers became the backbone of Habsburg support in Hungary. At the same time, however, this Imperial policy laid the foundations for future strained relations between Germans and Magyars.

From the start, Swabian settlers enjoyed Habsburg support in the form of subsidies, grants, and charter privileges. In many instances Swabians were even provided with freshly built and fully equipped villages which were granted tax exemptions by the Crown. Approximately 800 new German settlements were established in this manner between 1711 and 1780 alone. Possessing superior farming skills, the newcomers emerged easy victors in the race for additional land with their Magyar and Serb counterparts. Sober, industrious, and deeply religious, the German colonists developed thriving rural communities possessing superior hygienic and technical facilities. Their special position in Hungarian life imbued Saxons and Swabians alike with something akin to national pride, a sense of superiority over their neighbours, and a deep respect for education. The relatively simple and static society of the seventeenth and eighteenth centuries, as well as generous Habsburg support, encouraged German ascendancy among the several nationalities in Hungary, including Magyars. As a consequence of these migrations, the Magyars constituted less than half of Hungary's population by 1720 and only a little more than one-third by 1778. The high tide of Germanization was reached during the reign of Joseph II, who attempted to consolidate the Empire by establishing uniform administrative methods. In addition to settling still more Germans in Hungary, he also endeavoured to replace Hungary's official language—Latin—with German.

The Germanizing endeavours of Joseph II caused a nationalistic reaction in Hungary which soon flowered into a Magyar renaissance. This rebirth is associated with a number of literary, economic, and political figures, the most important of whom was the great reformer, Count Stephen (István), Széchenyi. In 1825, he founded the Hungarian Academy of Science, and inspired liberal reforms. The Magyar language, partly under his urgings, was soon lifted from vernacular obscurity to literary heights. By the 1840's, Magyar had become the official and mercantile language, while magnificent public works projects in Pest imbued Magyars with new national pride. The 1848 revolution in Hungary was in great measure engendered by the awakening of these nationalistic sentiments, while Hungary's defeat may partly be ascribed to the degeneration of these feelings into selfish chauvinism at the expense of Hungary's sizeable non-Magyar population. During the revolution the Habsburgs apparently supported the ambitions of non-Magyar minorities in Hungary, while the revolutionaries, notably Louis (Lajos) Kossuth, rejected the concept of developing a multi-ethnic ethos in Hungary. On the eve of Magyar semi-independence in 1867 sentiments in favour of Magyarization reached new heights of intensity.

The reaction to Habsburg Germanizing attempts and the Romantic movement of the nineteenth century, which found expression almost everywhere in national rebirths, created the concept of the "Historic Mission of Hungary."[2] According to this doctrine, the small but politically, culturally, and socially superior Magyar race, augmented and voluntarily supported by the inferior polyglot subject nationalities of the Danube Basin, was to form a natural economic and geographic unit in the region. Leadership would devolve not on the most numerous group, but on the "culturally superior Magyar race," whose task was the protection of Western Europe against depredations from the barbaric East. The success of this mission would be assured by the presence of a traditionally strong Magyar central government, which would permit the nonruling races complete freedom and an adequate encouragement in the development of their cultural individualities. The mystical basis of this nationalism elevated the issue of Magyar predominance in Hungary from the level of mundane politics to the realm of a justifiable crusade.

The cold realities of Hungary's ethnic distribution contributed to the intensity of Magyar chauvinism. The majority of Hungary's population was non-Magyar in the nineteenth century, and assimilationist policies, notably in the schools and in public life, did not succeed in reducing the ethnic imbalance even by 1910. (See Appendix I.) Moreover, many among the minorities were impelled by the same degree of nationalistic fervour as their Magyar rulers. This led to widespread feelings in Magyar-dominated Hungary that "the country would not really be safe until every man, woman and child had been Magyarized."[3] Besides, Hungary had obtained both the opportunity and legal justification to create a homogeneous Magyar state, after the Compromise (*Ausgleich*) with Austria in 1867 had freed her hand in domestic affairs. Thereafter, the Magyars felt justified in attempting to realize this end by virtually any means.

In 1867, after the Habsburgs had acknowledged Hungary's sovereignty and granted it equal status in a newly conceived Dual Monarchy, both Austria and Hungary promulgated simultaneous "Compromise Laws," which specifically enumerated both common and separate functions in government. The laws provided for a joint army and navy command, and common foreign policy, while in matters of public law both countries were to be separate and equal. The most significant consequence of these measures for Hungary was the attainment of autonomy in domestic affairs, including jurisdiction over the inextricably linked problems of public education and minority policy. How the Magyars resolved these issues was largely dictated by their geographic, racial, and cultural heritage.

As the Magyars gradually assumed a greater role in the administration of Hungary following the Compromise, the minorities found themselves in a frustrating situation. For example, a German-Hungarian might continue to identify himself as a Swabian. But if his attitude assumed overtones of Pan-Germanism, public opprobrium and social difficulties would beset him. If he wished to embark upon a public career, he had to abandon completely his German ideals. If he failed to renounce his national affinities, he forfeited every hope of achieving his ambitions. Indeed, although not subjected to actual official persecution, he was thereafter stigmatized as a virtual traitor. Such problems made minority life in Hungary difficult and uncertain. Furthermore, in the absence of explicit official regulations, minority matters were frequently subjected to the capricious judgments of local administrators and peer group pressure.[4]

By the time Hungary achieved partnership in the Empire, a clarification of her minorities' rights was therefore long overdue. In 1861 the Hungarian National Assembly had attempted, but failed, to pass a nationality act that would satisfy the clamour of non-Magyars for legal recognition and protection. Only after the Compromise of 1867 did a minority statute finally emerge. The creators of the Nationality Law of 1868 (Law XLIV) were undoubtedly imbued with humanitarian and liberal sentiments, but certain ambiguities in the Act nullified their good intentions. Based on the concept of a unified state and unified political nation, Law XLIV denied legal status to Hungary's non-Magyar nationalities, and proclaimed all Hungarian citizens "Magyar," regardless of their mother tongue. But the meaning of "Magyar" was never clearly defined, while the provision guaranteeing a certain share in higher education to minorities was neither sufficiently elaborated nor clarified. In addition, the government warned Hungary's minorities that nationalist agitators would be prosecuted to the utmost. Reinforced by this threat, the Act enabled the state gradually to weaken the national identity of minorities. Owing to the equivocal phrasing of the Law, even their cultural establishments could be labeled political and hence subjected to treatments ranging from harassment to outright closure. The Act paid lip service, in other words, to minorities' rights.

Once liberated from Austrian control, Hungary was intent on assuming a status among the industrial nations of Europe. The repercussions of this ambition proved to be so devastating for the integrity of Swabian society that the year 1881 may justly be considered a dividing point in Swabian history. In that year, the first Hungarian law was passed for the furtherance of home industry by subsidies, grants, and tax exemptions. Within a decade the industrial population of Hungary increased by 125%.[5] The industrialization took place mainly in those areas where non-Magyar nationalities predominated, since major power resources were situated there. In these urbanized regions the Germans decreased from 180,429 in 1880—29.5% of all Germans living within the boundaries of Trianon Hungary—to only 109,482 in 1910, and they represented only 18.5% of Germans in that area. (See Appendix II.) The paradox is resolved by the fact that in the urban centers the cultural orientation after 1868 became increasingly Magyar, and Swabian immigrants from the countryside adopted it with spontaneous enthusiasm as soon as they had become accustomed to their new milieu. As a result, in the 25 largest Hungarian cities, where originally Saxon elements predominated, the Magyar population increased by 29% between 1880 and 1890. In the 101 smaller towns it rose by 16%. Even in the capital, Budapest, which was 75% German in 1848 with its 120,000 Saxon-Swabians, the proportion declined to only 32% by 1890. Only in a few border towns, such as Sopron and Kőszeg, did the German middle class resist Magyarization. Initially, urban German losses were offset by modest gains in rural areas. For example, 427,156 rural Germans in 1880 increased to 441,729 by 1910.[6]

This poses another seeming paradox, since the exodus of Swabians to the cities should have decreased the rural population. During this period industrialization, urbanization, and immigration had not assumed the intensity they would after the War. As a result, sufficient numbers of marriageable males still remained in the villages to increase the infant population. Owing to the superiority of hygienic and dietary conditions in

Swabian villages, the mortality among children, the aged, and among the population in general, was reduced. Nor did Magyarization reach the villages during those years to the extent it would later. Consequently, although during the decade 1890-1900 the German increase declined to only 10,471, and in the following ten years the German population actually diminished by 95,703, the Swabian villages were still able to maintain a slight gain. After the War, the resiliency of Swabian rural society would be pitted against systematic Magyarization and result in major conflict.

After the Compromise, Hungary's leaders realized that their schools were likely to become the battleground for the youth of the nation, whose population consisted of linguistic and cultural minorities. If they could find a way "to impose the national ideals, language, history, etc., of the majority on all the children, then the de-nationalization [*i.e.,* assimilation] of minorities would eventually become inevitable."[7] Since state-controlled education lent itself to the realization of this goal, the Hungarian government decided to encroach gradually upon the prevailing education system of the nation.

Before 1868 Hungary's primary schools were administered entirely by autonomous religious denominations, composed principally of Catholics, Protestants, Orthodox Christians, and Jews, and by independent parishes. This double role of educators and clergy ensured the virtual domination of the churches over rural minority life before the Compromise, but extreme poverty often prevented their pedagogical effectiveness. The government intended to exploit this weakness and therefore expedite its plans for state control of education. It established Magyar state schools which were well equipped and had access to virtually unlimited official funds. In order to hasten the process of control, it empowered the Ministry of Education to demand high standards in confessional schools concerning equipment and teachers' competence. Failure to live up to specifications resulted in the closing of those institutions, and their replacement by Magyar state schools. In the face of these pressures confessional schools had little choice: in order to survive, they were compelled to accept state subsidies, an action which resulted in the surrender of their freedom. They became subjected to vexing official interference in their internal affairs, consisting of loyalty oaths, disciplinary actions, and arbitrary dismissals of teachers. This was made possible by a series of laws, and most particularly by Count Albert Apponyi's Law XXVII of 1907, which established government control over teachers by declaring them civil servants. Hereafter the government could veto appointments and name teachers over the heads of church-school authorities. Instructors were also obliged to conform to accepted norms of political behaviour and to official standards of instruction. For example, teachers had to satisfy the Ministry that minority students mastered oral and written Magyar by the end of the fourth grade.

The government initiated its drive to submit minority schools to state control at first by arbitrary government interference, and later by a series of education statutes. Although Section 14 of the Nationality Law pledged the continuance of elementary, secondary, and higher education for minorities, it was not long before the government reneged its promises. The first to suffer the consequences of government restrictions was Hungary's Slovak minority, whose relatively weak cultural and political structure provided an easy target. Only seven years after the promulgation of the Act, the government closed the Slovak academy, museum, libraries, and all middle schools, and even confiscated all Slovak institutional funds. Thereafter, Slovak private schools above the elementary level were forbidden.

Arbitrary violations of the Act were shortly followed by legal encroachments. In 1879, a new Law on Primary Education set the legal precedent for state intervention in all minority schools. It made proficiency in Magyar compulsory for all teachers, and in order to assure continuity, in teacher training academies Magyar language qualifications were established for all candidates. The Ministry of Education was empowered to determine the number of hours to be devoted to Magyar language instruction in primary schools and to close institutions which failed to comply. Four years later, the government turned its attention to higher education. The closing of the only non-Magyar college in Hungary, the German law school in Nagyszeben, was one of the results of the Secondary Education Act of 1883, which also placed the fourteen remaining non-Magyar secondary schools still functioning, under strict control of the Ministry of Education. One by one, these were transformed into Magyar institutions, and under various pretexts the establishment of new minority secondary institutions was denied. In the state gymnasia all instruction was to be given in Magyar, while Magyar language and literature became compulsory subjects in all secondary institutions. Having almost entirely Magyarized primary and secondary schools, the government next promulgated the Kindergarten Act of 1891. This was a prelude to the virtual Magyarization of primary schools eleven years later, when the Ministry obliged all such institutions to provide between 18 and 24 hours of Magyar instruction in all subjects weekly. The Education Act of 1907 completed the process of state encroachment and Magyarization in Hungary's public school system by destroying the autonomy of denominational and parochial schools.

As a result of these measures, the relative number of primary schools was far greater among Magyars than among other nationalities. In the 1910-1911 academic season Hungary's minorities, who comprised jointly 45.5% of the population, possessed only 22% of these facilities. The Slovaks, for example, whose primary schools diminished from 1,921 in 1869 to only 429 in 1910, suffered the greatest relative losses. By 1910 there were no longer any kindergartens, kindergarten training schools, industrial and commercial institutes, middle schools, academies of law, or theological seminaries, in which they could receive instruction in their own language.[8]

In contrast, due to Hungary's close affiliation with Austria, as well as to Hungary's desire for good relations with the German Empire, the educational position of German-Hungarians before the War remained, if not privileged, at least tolerable. But they, too, began to feel the pressures of Magyarization when Article 18 of the 1907 School Law transformed all their continuation schools for ages 12 to 15 into Magyar institutions. Since these functioned chiefly in Hungary's villages and rural towns where the majority of Hungarian Swabians lived, the regulation signified *de facto* termination of German instruction above the elementary school, or sixth grade, level.

The government's zeal in the Magyarization campaign of the minority schools is demonstrated by the fact that during those years it became government practice to neglect the education of rural Magyar children in favour of non-Magyars. It was believed that exposure to Magyar culture and language would help to assimilate them. One way to gauge the effects of this policy is to examine the steadily diminishing number of German elementary schools in the forty-year period following the Compromise. In 1869, there were 1,232 pure German-language elementary schools in Hungary. By 1890, nearly half of these had been abolished, and by 1905, on the eve of the 1907 school law, Swabian attendance was limited to only 272 German primary schools throughout Hungary. The situation in mixed-language primary schools was only a little better. Another way to appraise the extent of decline in Swabian lower education is to consider the school-pupil ratio. By 1913, Hungary's other major nationalities, Rumanians, Serbs, and Slovaks, had each outstripped the Swabians insofar as proportional numbers of minority schools were concerned. The Rumanians were in the most favoured position in this respect, since 255,000 Rumanians in two Hungarian counties (Temes and Torontál) had 168 minority schools (1507:1), whereas 521,000 Germans in three counties (Temes, Torontál and Bács-Bodrog) possessed only 49 pure German schools (10,630:1). Even the Slovak elementary school system, which had suffered the greatest relative decline during these years, was in a far better position than the Swabian.[9] Yet even these figures are misleading, since most rural Swabians attended tiny one-room village schools with small attendance; consequently, the 49 school units ascribed to the Swabians could not have accommodated a significant number of pupils. This meant, of course, that the overwhelming majority of Swabian students attended mixed-language and pure Magyar-language schools. It is evident that the Germans were not doing this voluntarily, but were compelled to do so by the Magyar authorities, and in far greater numbers—relatively—than any other national group in Hungary. This policy was designed to rend the ethnic ties between the Swabian youngsters and the German-oriented Swabian village environment and to Magyarize them in a systematic, organized manner. In the opinion of a contemporary Hungarian observer, Hungary's educational system before the War constituted an instrument for the aims of Magyarization, "which served almost with religious fervor the supreme dogma of National unity."[10]

The assimilative process in Hungary's minority schools had a drastic effect on the development of an ethnic intelligentsia before the War. The distribution of educated classes among minorities was considerably below their percentage representation in Hungary. (See Appendix III.) These statistics suggest that the Swabians enjoyed broader higher educational opportunities than any of Hungary's other ethnic groups, although they had far fewer graduates than the Magyars. In fact, the figures obscure more than they reveal. Many graduates listed as Germans were not Swabians at all but Jews who had been listed in the census as Germans. Conversely, many individuals listed as Magyars were assimilated Swabians, who, in the fashion of converts, would no longer tolerate even the presence of German culture on Hungarian soil. Consequently, these statistics, although accurate, do not fully reflect the lack of Swabian participation in the realm of higher education.

Despite administrative centralization, Magyarization in Hungary was in many ways only skin deep. Some "Magyarized" youths turned into the most ardent champions of their respective minorities. This resulted from the Magyarization techniques practiced in the schools, which ignored the personal feelings and convictions of the pupils and were limited to the superficial transformation of minority children into Magyar-speaking individuals. Such practices embittered many of the minority peoples against the Hungarian state itself, in which they saw the source of forcible homogenization. As C.A. Macartney observed:

> A bitter hatred came to reign between the Magyars and many of the nationalities. Those whose national consciousness had once become active—most particularly the middle classes and intelligentsia—resented most deeply the alternative laid before them of either renouncing their nationality or else abandoning any prospect of public or even social advancement.[11]

In view of these undercurrents of hostility between government and minorities and growing Pan-Germanism in the Reich, it is surprising that the Swabians did not turn to political activism to attain their ends. Before World War I, only the Transylvanian Saxons showed any indication of opposing the regime by pursuing an independent course of German political action. Outside Transylvania, their efforts came to naught. In 1901, the Saxon political leader, Edmund Steinacker, tried unsuccessfully to introduce a German-oriented programme in Nagykomlós. Five years later, he founded a secret political organization, the *Ungarländisch—Deutsche Volkspartei*, which organized two meetings in the Bánát and Bácska regions of southern Hungary the following year. Despite protests to King Charles, the meetings were banned by local police. In 1910, Steinacker's party fielded five candidates, including himself. All of them were defeated, thanks partly to Magyar interference with the electoral machinery. In 1913, another Saxon, Rudolf Brandsch, founded the *Deutscher Bauernbund,* an association devoted to the joint interests of Swabian and Saxon peasants. The organization soon ran afoul of Magyar opposition, even though Prime Minister Stephen (István) Tisza went through the motions of negotiating with it and the *UDV.*

On the whole, then, German parties were not successful in prewar Hungary. This was mainly because they did not truly represent Swabian public opinion. As a result, indignation against Magyar interference never gathered momentum. In addition, the Swabians were restrained partly by their loyalty to the Habsburg dynasty, whose ultimate protection they believed they enjoyed; and partly by the erosion of a dynamic Swabian village intelligentsia through assimilation. Also, Swabian educated classes, especially clergymen, teachers, and notaries, frequently became converts to the Magyar cause, and in their neophyte zeal exceeded the enthusiasm of even the most nationalistic Magyars.[12] The Magyars welcomed these proselytes with open arms, and practiced no discrimination against them. This shrewd generosity was a mixed blessing for the minorities who, although assured equal treatment legally and economically, had to stand by helplessly while their potential leaders were transformed into Magyars through assimilation and enticement. In this respect, the Swabians suffered greater dilution than the other minorities. Whereas Hungary's Slovaks, Rumanians, and Serbs possessed their own autonomous Protestant and Orthodox church organizations, the Swabians belonged overwhelmingly to the Magyar-dominated Roman Catholic faith, and hence could not pursue an independent German ethnic course.[13] In sum, the Swabians, who boasted the largest intelligentsia among the non-Magyars, both proportionately as well as in absolute numbers, experienced the most assimilation of Hungary's ethnic minorities.

The authors of the 1868 Nationality Law had envisioned the adoption of a tolerant cultural policy toward non-Magyar citizens, but it was never really put into practice; it remained merely a constitutional show-piece. Hungary's real nationality policy was characterized not by the Nationality Law, but through subsequent legislative and administrative measures between 1868 and 1918. All the resources of the state were mobilized to Magyarize the nationalities in violation of the spirit and letter of the Law. R. W. Seton-Watson summed up the situation thus: "The internal policy which has dominated the ruling classes of Hungary since 1867 may be summed up in one word: Magyarization."[14]

CHAPTER II
MINORITIES "CONCILIATED"—EDUCATIONAL
AND CULTURAL POLICY 1918-1919

Postwar Magyar minority policy remained dominated by the same spirit of Magyarization which had characterized it ever since 1868. Indeed, when the framers of the Peace Treaty of Trianon deprived Hungary of most of her minorities, they unwittingly encouraged an old Magyar dream for the creation of a mononational state. Postwar Hungary's leaders responded by intensifying their Magyarization campaign against the remaining minorities. The execution of this programme became a leitmotif in Hungarian postwar praxis which, notwithstanding apparent deviations, was followed by every government, and after Trianon became the Magyar *idée fixe* in both private and public life.

From shortly before the end of the war until the ratification of the Peace Treaty of Trianon in June 1920, a period of apparent reconciliation prevailed with the minorities; but by 1917, nationalist agitation made it evident that a Magyar-dominated Hungary was impossible. On the eve of Hungary's disintegration in the Fall of 1918, King Charles IV attempted to arrest the growing disaffection and irredentism among Hungary's minorities by adopting what seemed a more lenient policy. This vague and belated gesture failed to convince them that the government was acting in good faith.[1]

The period just after the war also became one of apparent rapprochement with the minorities. The Magyars made cultural, political, and educational overtures, but the consequences were nugatory. Nearly everywhere the story was the same. As the Austro-Hungarian Empire crumbled, large enclaves containing Hungary's sundry minority peoples proclaimed their solidarity with newly formed or reorganized nations across Hungary's shrinking frontiers. Slovaks and Ruthenians in the north and northeast joined Czechoslovakia; Rumanians in the east defected to the Kingdom of Rumania; and Serbs in the south joined the Kingdom of Serbs, Croatians, and Slovenians (Yugoslavia). Croatia, heretofore an integral part of

Hungary, followed suit. Over two million Germans became—with the possible exception of Transylvania's Saxons—unwilling captives in the newly created successor states. Especially galling was the additional loss of some 3½ million Magyars. Hungary herself seemed to be crumbling along with the Imperial parent. As a result, Hungary's population suffered drastic reductions, and its postwar security became seriously compromised. The remaining Rumanian and Slavic population was small and harmlessly dispersed. The Swabians, however, emerged as a relatively numerous and formidable, though fickle minority. Their proximity to sensitive new national frontiers contributed to Magyar unease. The fears of political heterodoxy were added to those of ethnic suspicion.

Swabian prospects were dim. In the closing days of the war, Austria seemed suitable as a new fatherland, at least to the Swabians in Burgenland. But when the conflict ended, Austria's Socialist regime offended the predominantly ultra-conservative rural Swabians. Nor did they relish the prospect of falling under the domination of the allegedly culturally inferior peoples in the Successor States. Remaining with Hungary was at best an uncomfortable third alternative, particularly in view of past Magyar persecutions. The situation was not likely to improve in the postwar era, since the protective aegis of the Habsburgs was gone. Although Magyar domination seemed to be the least of many evils at the time, it was quite apparent the Swabians would never be bound to Hungary by sincere ties of affection but only by the iron laws of political and economic necessity.

Since the Magyars had few, if any, illusions about the loyalty of their German citizens, they were concerned lest even the remaining Swabians desert the storm-tossed ship of state. Magyar anxieties were particularly aroused by the presence of substantial and strategically disposed Swabian enclaves near Hungary's unstable frontier regions. Only about 16% of this population was scattered harmlessly in small fragments throughout Hungary; the remainder was concentrated not only in the Baranya, Pécs, Bács, and Bodrog areas near the Yugoslav frontier, and in Burgenland adjoining Austria, but in and around Budapest as well, the security of which was already precarious because of its proximity to the new Czechoslovak frontier. In effect, the Magyars found themselves caught on the horns of a dilemma. If they persecuted or harassed the Swabians, they might eventually succumb to alluring propaganda from abroad—especially from Austria or Germany. If the Magyars pacified the Swabians—at the cost of far-reaching political, cultural, and lingual concessions—they might in time become too powerful and prevent the realization of a pure Magyar state. Before the war, Swabians had been loyal citizens, even though assimilationist practice had diminished their intelligentsia, and endangered their long-term ethnic survival. In the nationalistic postwar period the Swabians were unlikely to tolerate continuing mistreatment. With considerable justification many Magyars feared that their patience was at an end to the point of seceding, if Hungary insisted on becoming an ethnocentric Magyar state. Growing national consciousness, born of cameraderie with Germans during the late war, caused Swabians to be more self-assertive, which only served to intensify Magyar suspicions that they would not submit to any further overt Magyarization without a struggle. To make matters even worse, Magyar statesmen knew that Hungary stood in the direct path of traditional German eastward penetration, and the possibility that Swabians might at some future time become "fifth columnists" filled the Magyars with great alarm and uncertainty.

Hungary's precarious position forced Magyar leaders to develop an opportunistic minority policy to achieve an integral Magyar nation state. In the immediate postwar era, assimilationist objectives had to be disguised as much as possible in order to try and rescue Hungary's rapidly dwindling ethnic empire. Thanks to their unique demographic distribution and political situation the Swabians temporarily assumed an importance that was totally out of proportion to their normal position in Hungarian life. Within a two-year period, four different Hungarian regimes, led respectively by Count Michael (Mihály) Károlyi, Béla Kun, Julius (Gyula) Peidl, and Stephan (István) Friedrich, were to pursue an elusive and subtle minority policy within the fragile interrelationship of converging and conflicting Magyar-Swabian aspirations. Although the ideological composition of these governments spanned a broad spectrum from extreme left to extreme right, their fundamental approaches to the Swabian problem were surprisingly similar. Each adopted what appeared to be a conciliatory stance and each practiced its evasions with such skill that the Swabians were constantly suspended between hope and despair.

The crucial struggle between Magyars and Swabians occurred principally in the thousands of rural classrooms in Hungary's German districts. The Magyars considered the liquidation of the Swabian problem an educational task, a contest between themselves and the older Swabians, to capture the allegiance of the new generation. It would be useful, therefore, to cast a brief glance at conditions in Swabian education at the beginning of the postwar era.[2] By then, German higher education was dead. All that remained of the former extensive German educational organization was the predominantly rural six-year primary school. Attendance figures for the 1918-1919 academic year indicate that in the territories still held by Hungary at the time there were 281 supposedly pure German schools, attended by 32,827 pupils and staffed by 543 instructors, so that a pupil-teacher ratio of about 61:1 prevailed. The following year the number of German schools rose slightly to 287, the number of pupils to 33,682, and the number of teachers to 571. The pupil-teacher ratio thus stood at 59:1. These figures, though fairly accurate *per se,* tell only part of the story. Superficially, the quality of Swabian elementary education appeared to be satisfactory, even though life patterns and vital services were extremely chaotic and inadequate in Hungary right after the war. Yet, during the same period Magyar school children were considerably better off. In Magyar elementary schools the pupil-teacher ratio stood at 54:1 in 1918-1919 and 49:1 the following year. Superior Magyar educational practice may be only partially ascribed to the fact that Magyar schools were mostly urban institutions while Swabian education was almost exclusively rural. Furthermore, German schools accommodated only a fraction of eligible Swabian pupils. According to official statistics elementary school pupils professing to be Germans in 1918-1919 numbered 81,851. Their numbers rose to 83,861 in 1919-1920, due to the influx of refugees from the severed territories. But even if every single pupil in the Swabian school system was German, about six out of ten Swabian children attended not German but Magyar schools. This proportion is significant since most German-Hungarians lived in homogeneous ethnic clusters, where they presumably exercised some control over the education of their children. Finally, we must pose the question: Did Swabian children obtain a satisfactory German education, even in the so-called minority schools? According to statistics, most of the Swabian children, even those attending German schools, were not taught in the German language and certainly not in the German cultural spirit, since the vast majority of their teachers were Magyars. In the 1918-1919 school year only 273 teachers of German origin functioned in all of Hungary. Several were engaged in Hungary's Magyar regions, while others taught above the elementary school level. Official figures unfortunately conceal just how many of the 273 teachers taught in German elementary schools, but we may safely assume that their number could not have been very large.

To round out this picture, a glance at higher education among the Swabians is illuminating. In 1918-1919, only 46 Swabian gymnasium students graduated out of a Swabian student body totalling 1,191. This was still the highest Swabian attendance figure during the entire interwar period. The unusually low graduation figures suggest that the drop-out rate among Swabian gymnasium enrollees was inordinately high. Only 207 Swabians frequented upper commercial and industrial schools, and the number of Swabian gymnasium professors never exceeded the 41 of the 1918-1919 academic year. It is surprising that only 2,181 Swabians attended urban schools (*Bürgerschule, polgáriskola*), since most trades drew their journeymen from these institutions, and many Swabians made their living as artisans. It goes without saying that even if other sensitive issues had not intruded to complicate Magyar-Swabian relations, the disappointing condition of Swabian education alone was the gravest obstacle to an understanding between the two peoples.

Unfortunately for the Magyars, their minority problems became entangled with external affairs after the war, when a dispute with Austria exacerbated already strained Magyar-Swabian relations. The controversy, involving Burgenland, became an intensely bitter territorial question.[3] The struggle embroiled not only Hungary, Austria, and the Swabians, but eventually even Germany and the Victorious Powers. This incident, more so perhaps than any other, laid the foundation for the mutual distrust that stigmatized Magyar-Swabian relations ever after in the postwar era.

The Burgenland question seemed uncomplicated. Until 1647, when it was ceded to Hungary by Emperor Ferdinand III, Burgenland had belonged to Austria. At war's end, Burgenland's 1,514 square miles contained nearly 345,000 inhabitants, of whom about 75% were Swabians. The remainder of the population comprised Magyars and a sprinkling of Croatians and Slovenians.[4] No sooner had hostilities ended, when Austria began to agitate for the return of Burgenland.[5] On 20 July 1919, the Peace Treaty of St. Germain awarded most of the region to Austria. The Magyars, however, refused to vacate on the grounds that the Austrian Peace Treaty did not apply to Hungary. Although on 22 November 1919, Austria pledged not to occupy the area by force, she would not relinquish her claim in principle. Gradually, relations between Austria and Hungary drifted to the edge of armed conflict, as regular troops and irregulars from both sides began to terrorize the population. Italy's intervention finally settled the controversy through the Venice Protocols of 13 October 1921. During this time, four Hungarian regimes, devoted to differing political philosophies each, had the opportunity to demonstrate whether it could settle the crisis, and cope with the Swabian minority.

Hungary's first postwar regime endured from 31 October 1918, to 21 March 1919. It was led by the Social Democrat, Count Mihály Károlyi, a man no less dedicated to the preservation of Hungary's multi-ethnic empire than his predecessors had been, albeit his plan vouchsafed concessions to the minorities. As Károlyi had phrased it shortly before war's end: "My programme: peace and agreement with the nationalities. . .and a policy recognizing the principle of self-determination for all peoples."[6] Once in power, Károlyi departed from this promise. In his second fact-finding report for the Allies from Budapest in January 1919, Professor A. C. Coolidge noted that "on the burning question of the day, the integrity of

Hungary, there are almost no differences [among Magyars] except a greater or lesser insistence on the principle of a fair plebiscite. . ."[7] On 25 October 1918, one week before his accession to power, Károlyi met with members of the Independence Party (*Függetlenségi Párt*), and together they formed a National Council (*Nemzeti Tanács*), whose task it was to seize the reins of government.[8] On the same day the National Council released its Twelve-Point Programme, in which the sections dealing with the minorities were prominent. Unfortunately, the programme drafted by Oscar (Oszkár) Jászi, Károlyi's Minister of Nationalities, was ambiguous if not contradictory. Point V favoured the well-known Wilsonian formula of national self-determination for Hungary's peoples, and Point X announced Hungary's recognition of the newly formed successor states on the basis of mutual respect. On the other hand, Jászi assumed that Hungary's minority peoples had no wish to jeopardize Hungary's territorial integrity, and would be content "with the most far-reaching cultural and administrative autonomy," on the basis of brotherly equality with the Magyars (Point V).[9] Jászi admitted later that his programme was contradictory indeed. This he explained on the grounds that "Károlyi made it clear that he was concerned [only] with territorial integrity in an economic sense."[10] As the fortunes of three successor states—Czechoslovakia, Rumania, and Yugoslavia—depended on whether Hungary's minorities would defect to them, Jászi's plan left a hollow ring and augured ill for the resolution of Hungary's disintegration, because minorities entertained hopes for full independence among their own kindred, while Jászi promised only vague intimations of autonomy in a traditionally hostile Magyar environment.

Because Jászi's scheme, though undoubtedly motivated by sincere concern for the welfare of all, was less than practical, the Károlyi regime could not but encounter grave difficulties in dealing with the nationality problem. Various ethnic groups, mainly Rumanians and Slavs, had already defected, taking millions of unwilling Magyars and Germans with them. These minorities somehow had to be wooed back into the Magyar fold. About ¼ million others, mainly Rumanians and Slovaks, still remained in truncated Hungary. These minorities were for the most part culturally and economically deprived and leaderless peasants, who were harmlessly intermingled among Magyars and Swabians. Finally, about ½ million Swabians, some residing in large ethnic clusters near sensitive frontier areas, constituted a potential menace the Magyars could not afford to ignore. Consequently, Károlyi's primary task was to regain the nationalities already lost and to pacify the minorities still remaining—the Swabians in particular. Despite offers of far-reaching political and cultural concessions to the minorities within a federated Hungarian state—a virtual "Eastern Switzerland"—

Jászi's scheme foundered. After extensive negotiations the defected nationality leaders refused to return to the fold.[11]

Among Hungary's nationalities only the Ruthenians and Swabians remained firmly under Hungarian political control. Of these, only the Swabians commanded sufficient influence to merit special consideration from the Magyars. Unfortunately, the regime proceeded ineptly to consolidate its control over the Swabians. Károlyi's belief that an accommodation with them was possible proved to be false. His actions were based on two erroneous assumptions. One had to do with past experience. Before the war, the Swabians had been loyal, if not model, Hungarian citizens. To all appearances, their allegiance had not changed with the disintegration of the Dual Monarchy; but astute observers detected signs of disaffection towards the end. Swabian notables, such as Johannes Huber and Joseph Kath, perceived the growing disaffection in Burgenland. Ethnic, cultural, and economic considerations impelled more and more Swabians towards Austria. Diplomats also noted this tendency. According to one such observer, no sooner was the war over when the Swabians' national consciousness emerged as from a long dream. Within two months of the armistice, a number of officials in Burgenland's Swabian communities, led by the mayor of Fürstenfeld, begged Vienna for Austrian protection or intervention. About this time, the Austrian army began to smuggle small arms into Hungary at the request of dissident Swabians. The number of these dissatisfied elements mounted each day.[12] The growing Swabian preference even for Social Democratic Austrian rule had serious repercussions for Austro-Hungarian as well as Swabian-Hungarian relations.

In addition to misjudging the loyalties of Hungary's Swabian citizens, Károlyi also misunderstood Austria's politico-economic aims and involvement in the region. Károlyi assumed that starving Austria would maintain a strict hands-off policy and gladly forfeit Burgenland in return for desperately needed food staples and favourable Hungarian trade concessions. Károlyi also believed that the Austrian Socialists would not disturb relations with a fraternal Socialist government over an issue which he thought the Austrians deemed unimportant.[13] Károlyi erred on both counts. Officially as well as quasi-officially Chancellor Renner stirred up rebellion in Burgenland in order to acquire the region for Austria. The Austrian press and Renner's Christian Social coalition partners also clamoured for the liberation of Burgenland with its allegedly captive Swabians. The small but influential Pan-German Party was the most vocal in this respect, but even the more moderate Christian Socials, particularly the latter's spokesman in the Austrian Parliament, Alois Heilinger, agitated ceaselessly for annexation. Their arguments were based on territorial, ethnic, and economic considerations. Renner's Socialists were embarrassingly suspended between Austrian annexationist demands and the requirements of a prudent foreign policy. Renner hesitated to offend Károlyi at a time when he needed Hungary's cooperation in solving Austria's food shortage. Renner therefore failed to advocate radical measures lest he risk a Hungarian food embargo. Officially he urged, therefore, that the formula of self-determination be applied in the Burgenland dispute.

Austria's other political parties were not committed to Renner's cautious course. On 22 November 1918, the Provisional National Council claimed three Hungarian counties (Moson, Vas, and Sopron), and part of another (Pozsony-Pressburg).[14] Even more serious for Hungary was the role of Burgenland emigrés in Vienna. It is indicative of Renner's annexationist intentions that these zealots were not only not discouraged, but secretly aided and abetted. At least two expatriate groups functioned in Vienna at the time, the *Verein zur Erhaltung des Deutschtums in Ungarn,* and the *Zentralstelle für die Organisation der Deutschen in Westungarn.* The former had so much influence with the government that when the Austrian peace delegation left for Paris in the spring of 1919, it was accompanied by a Dr. Ernst Beer, a West Hungarian Swabian "expert." The second group's involvement with the Renner regime was even more intimate. Hungary accused Austria of providing the *Zentralstelle* with physical facilities, moral support, and even secretarial help. Allegedly, Austria failed to prevent extremists from inundating Burgenland with Austrian newspapers critical of Hungary, with propaganda leaflets printed in Austrian State printing presses, and with political agitators to stir up the Swabian population.[15] The Hungarian government offered proof that *Zentralstelle* agents had penetrated into Burgenland in Austrian military vehicles, which roamed throughout the region with impunity. *Zentralstelle* agents had urged Swabians to proclaim an independent German republic. Swabians were to have received weapons from the Austrian army when the time was ripe. Hungary resented the fact that the *Zentralstelle* operated under the protection of the very same Austrian regime which publicly claimed to favour a peaceful solution through a plebiscite.[16] Austria failed to deny these allegations.

In addition to penetrations by Austrian interests, Burgenland also spawned a fairly strong annexationist movement led by Géza Zsombor, the controversial editor of the Sopron journal *Grenzpost.* Zsombor probably used the secession threat merely as a means of securing autonomy for Burgenland and an important position for himself. Nonetheless, secessionists within and sympathizers outside of West Hungary failed to discern the fine points of Zsombor's miniscule *Realpolitik.* The editor's political stratagem only fed the flames of secession in the discontented province.

Had it not been for a common peril confronting Austria and Hungary towards the end of 1918, the Burgenland dispute might easily have erupted in violence. Both disputants concluded a tacit but temporary truce in response to Czechoslovakia's abortive Corridor Plan. Under it, all of Burgenland and the area immediately to the south would have become a narrow corridor linking Czechoslovakia with Yugoslavia, thus sundering the two former members of the Dual Monarchy. The Corridor Plan, placed on the Peace Conference agenda on 5 February, was rejected on 5 March 1919. The Austro-Hungarian "truce" did not survive the latter date. The Austrians renewed their drive to secure Burgenland, and confront the Peace Conference with a *fait accompli*. The *VEDV* swung into action with mass meetings in Vienna on 2 March. Its resolution was extremely provocative to Hungary since it exceeded demands for Burgenland. It called for the establishment of a united front comprising all Central European Germans living in areas contiguous with Austria and Germany. This new German supra-national imperium would constitute a virtual homeland and refuge for all Germans throughout the world.[17] The emotional impact of such an appeal was well-nigh irresistible for the Swabians living in close proximity to Austria, especially since their national consciousness had been aroused after a sleep of many centuries.

Suffused as it was with an attractive aura, Austria gradually loomed larger on the horizon of Hungary's Swabians. There were emotional as well as economic reasons for this development. The Swabians feared losing their traditional Austrian markets and sources of seasonal employment in Lower Austria and Styria. These fears by far outweighed the Swabian peasants' delight about the additional land they hoped to acquire under Károlyi's projected (but unfulfilled) agrarian reforms.[18] Károlyi's radicalism and his choice of Socialist and Jewish officials to execute reforms in Swabian areas further alienated Hungary's well-meaning but naive leader from his Swabian subjects. The immediate postwar period must be viewed therefore from the perspective of this first unsuccessful effort by a fully independent Hungarian government to effect a satisfactory settlement with its major non-Magyar nationality group. For all its good will, the Károlyi regime laid the foundations for future acrimony between Magyars and Swabians. It only required a leader of some stature to capture the imagination and allegiance of the Swabians, who would challenge Hungary's sometimes cynical handling of the Swabian problem.

Such a man was waiting in the wings. Until his premature death in 1933, Jakob Bleyer became the most important and influential Swabian leader. Bleyer was a man of the people, a devout Roman Catholic of peasant origin from occupied Bácska. When the Dual Monarchy collapsed, Bleyer was already known, both as professor of philology at the University of Budapest and, since 1917, as a leading exponent of Swabian aspirations. In December of that year Bleyer, together with his friend and collaborator, the Roman Catholic canon Johannes Huber, founded the ultra-conservative daily *Neue Post*, his official publication until it was superseded in January 1921 by the weekly *Sonntagsblatt*. During the war, Bleyer published a series of articles in various Hungarian journals, in which he propounded his views on the appropriate Swabian role in Hungarian life. In one of his most important articles Bleyer hailed the Magyars as Hungary's leading nationality and consequently entitled to assimilate all non-Magyars, including even the Swabians. Magyarization was not only a question of self-preservation for the outnumbered Magyars, it was part of the natural process of urbanization and assimilation through acculturation. It was foolhardy and futile to block the gradual Magyarization of the Swabian urban intelligentsia, for the process could not be arrested. Swabians attending institutes of higher learning had been adopting Magyar cultural standards as a matter of course for many years. These proselytes were bound to become enthusiastic supporters of the Magyar ethos. It was otherwise in the villages. Swabian peasant children should not be Magyarized, but given a sound, practical education in the Magyar language in elementary schools that were purely German in all other respects. Bleyer fretted about the fate of scattered Swabians residing in Slavic and Rumanian environments. They were isolated from Magyars and Germans alike and risked being absorbed by these hostile nationalities. This would injure both Swabians and Magyars, because the Swabians were—and always had been—the Magyars' natural allies against these other peoples. They had always lived in perfect harmony with each other, and it would be deplorable to jeopardize this wholesome relationship through forcible Magyarization in the Swabian villages. Above all, Magyars would have to relinquish their idle dream of creating a pure Magyar state, whereas Swabians would have to resist the temptations of autonomy, such as the Saxons of Transylvania possessed. Even if the Magyars limited German exclusively to private use, the Swabians would still retain their rural culture, provided the German village school remained a vigorous reality. Summing up, Bleyer predicted that the Magyars

Shall never succeed—and never can—in assimilating the large masses of German villagers, whether linguistically or ethnically; the current Magyar school policy can only weaken and alienate the Swabians. Would the Magyar majority really suffer if a few hundred thousand simple farmers and honest tradesmen were to speak German, while in their hearts they continued to feel like Magyars?. . .Even if Hungary's Germans wished to be counted as a separate people, they would always rally to the Magyar cause in case of a conflict, and always against the same common enemy, whether from within or from without.[19]

In the closing days of the war, Bleyer's views still reflected his 1917 plan. In a *Neue Post* editorial, Bleyer repudiated Transylvanian Saxon leader Rudolf Brandsch, who urged Hungary's Germans to press for full autonomy. Bleyer conceded certain legitimate grievances, but dismissed autonomy out of hand on patriotic grounds. Restoration of German elementary schools was the only really important Swabian demand, and even this only in total harmony with the Magyars.[20] When, on 1 November 1918, Károlyi officially recognized Hungary's first Swabian administrative organization, the *Deutschungarischer Volksrat*,[21] its programme was announced by its founder, Jakob Bleyer. The Swabians would at all cost and under all circumstances support Hungary's integrity. Although the *Volksrat* rejected Swabian autonomy, it did lay claim to all the privileges already possessed by other non-Magyars.[22]

Bleyer despised the Károlyi regime both for being weak and for being radical, and he swiftly became far more intransigent. Bleyer had ceased being the platonic ideologue of 1917, and was now the political leader of an ethnic minority beset with myriad practical and difficult problems. One other circumstance must have influenced Bleyer's increasing militancy. On 10 November Brandsch challenged Bleyer's hegemony for the allegiance and leadership of Hungary's Swabians by founding a rival organization in opposition to Bleyer's group, the *Deutscher Volksrat für Ungarn*. The leadership consisted mainly of radicals, such as the Jewish Social Democrat Heinrich Kalmár (or Kalmár-Kohn, as the *Neue Post* called him), and the Swabian Social Democrat Viktor Knaller. Despite its apparent affinity to the Károlyi regime, the new group embarrassed the Hungarian state from the very start. Cultural autonomy and the right of self-determination were only minimal aspects of the Party's programme. Most startling of all was the *DVU*'s refusal to swear unconditional allegiance to Hungary. Its leaders merely proclaimed ambiguously that the *DVU* would endeavour to maintain Hungary's integrity as long as possible.

The *DVU* gathered support with surprising alacrity, especially among Transylvania's Saxons and among Germans in seceded Slovakia and southern Hungary. But Swabian Social Democrats, ostracized by Bleyer's *Volksrat*, flocked into the *DVU* by the tens of thousands. Bleyer had to respond vigorously to this challenge. In the *Neue Post*, he and his associates tried to discredit Brandsch by casting aspersions on his patriotism and loyalties. Indeed, they were correct. Within less than two months, Brandsch was to default from the leadership struggle by defecting to the Rumanians, thus leaving the field uncontested to Bleyer. In the interim, however, Bleyer had had to adopt a sufficiently vigorous programme to convince Swabians that he was no less tough and demanding than Brandsch.

It is not surprising that only one week after founding his *Volksrat* Bleyer also began to toy with the idea of Swabian autonomy. In his 7 November *Volksrat* speech, Bleyer announced that under the prevailing difficult circumstances cultural concessions no longer sufficed; for the sake of self-protection the Swabians also had to have political power. As an addendum Bleyer now suggested:

> Our pledge of allegiance to the political Hungarian State stands only so long as it is not limited to the Magyar people alone, and only if the integrity of the Hungarian State can be maintained in its entirety. In all other instances we reserve our right of unconditional self-determination.

Bleyer also spelled out in greater detail the terms of an earlier demand:

> We desire for German-Hungarians all those rights in politics, administration, justice, economics, education, and culture, which the newly constituted Hungary has already vouchsafed for all its other non-Magyar peoples.[23]

In addition to combatting Brandsch's challenge to his own authority, Bleyer also defied the government by attempting to extort concessions exceeding by far his earlier demands. In effect, Bleyer threatened the Károlyi regime in the hour of its greatest peril. The subject peoples were deserting Hungary *en masse,* and the military might of the Entente stood at the gates. While professing loyalty and fidelity to Hungary and solidarity with the Magyars, Bleyer in fact undermined the country's security by demanding the right of self-determination. Although there was nothing intrinsically wrong with such a claim, in the diplomatic lingua franca of the immediate postwar world "self-determination" was a euphemism for "secession." By insisting on the right of self-determination at that juncture Bleyer served *pro forma* notice that the Swabians had joined the ranks of Hungary's other dissatisfied minorities. Although in an article entitled "Deutschungarn, rasche Organisation!" Franz Bonitz, one of Bleyer's colleagues in the *Volksrat,* urged Swabians vaguely to "march shoulder to shoulder with Magyardom," at the same time he also urged "a united [German] front to the public both at home and abroad, with respect to our cultural, linguistic, political, and economic aspirations."[24]

Pressures of this sort had their short-term effects. On 16 November 1918, the Swabians were granted the right to terminate Magyar language instruction in the first two grades of elementary schools located in predominantly Swabian regions. The Swabians rejoiced. Apparently, the new government had honest intentions towards German-Hungarians after all, exclaimed the *Neue Post*. This was a good first step for the future. In an emotional outburst, Bleyer characterized his feelings for Hungary as love for mother, those for Germandom as love for father. The easily won victory only prompted new demands. On 20 November 1918, the *Volksrat* insisted on German schools and on German as an official language in the courts and in the administration of predominantly Swabian areas. The *Volksrat* also urged that non-Germans be barred from participating in any way in Swabian affairs. As the *Neue Post* phrased it, "we wish to be represented in public life only by men who stand close to us."[25]

Amid these demands Bleyer and his associates maintained their air of patriotism. They steadfastly urged Burgenlanders to remain loyal to Hungary. Lest anyone misunderstood their meaning and intention, however, they predicted that the loss of 300,000 West Hungarian Germans to Austria would weaken the German cause in Hungary, because the remaining few Swabians would be fatally enfeebled by being totally disconnected from the German-speaking world.[26] Apparently the Bleyerites were far less interested in Hungary's territorial integrity than in preserving the effective might of Germandom.

In order to gratify Swabian demands the Minister of Education and Religion, Martin (Márton) Lovászy, issued a regulation on 21 November 1918, that exceeded the concessions granted a few days earlier. Henceforth, German would be the mandatory language of instruction in the first and second Swabian elementary grades. Magyar would be taught only as a subject from the third grade upward. Moreover, the regulation would be effective not only in state schools but in church-run institutions as well.[27] This was a major concession, since nearly 86% of Swabian schools were confessional. Normally, any order affecting only state schools would have had only minimal impact on Swabian education. As it turned out, the new ordinance proved to be a gift of Danae. In the interim, however, the Swabians were overwhelmed with additional "favours." In his telegram of 24 November to Bleyer, Lovászy promised German instruction in Swabian kindergartens, and in all Magyar middle schools situated in Swabian-inhabited regions. Lovászy's offer was meaningless. All Swabian schools suffered from a critical shortage of teachers, and German instructors in particular were in short supply. German was currently a compulsory subject in all middle schools throughout Hungary.

Signs of Swabian disenchantment with Károlyi appeared toward the end of 1918. Obviously, new laws had to be enforced, but the Károlyi government had neither the means nor perhaps any strong desire to implement them in a meaningful way. Soon complaints began to filter into *Volksrat* headquarters that local officials were violating the education ordinances, and thus the government's stratagems became revealed. Even under normal conditions village and county officials enjoyed considerable latitude in the exercise of their authority, and frequently countermanded or ignored central government directives. In the disturbed postwar era conservative notaries, teachers, school principals, and clergymen in particular, assumed greater importance and influence than ever before. Since most of them were patriotic Magyars or fervent proselytes, they effectively blocked all attempts by the unpopular Socialist regime to introduce German instruction in the schools. The government certainly knew this. Yet Károlyi and his men could claim with some justification and self-righteousness that they made serious attempts to come into closer contact with the needs of the Swabian minority. It was not their fault if Budapest was powerless to intervene vigorously in the affairs of what were, after all, autonomous church and county administrations. The Swabians discovered that the adoption of German in the schools was nothing but a cruel hoax because Apponyi's 1907 minority school law was still in effect. Under it, German elementary school textbooks were forbidden. Hence Swabian pupils were worse off than before. Magyar instruction was curtailed for them, while the means towards an effective German education were barred.[28]

The government's cynical avoidance of its own laws rapidly terminated the brief Swabian honeymoon. On 27 December 1918, Geza Zsombor announced that failing immediate autonomy, Burgenlanders would proclaim an independent German Republic. The crisis deepened when on 2 January 1919, the Transylvanian Saxons, led by Brandsch, defected to Rumania.[29] To the Magyars, Brandsch's betrayal was proof that all Germans were opportunists and potential traitors. To the imprudent Swabians, however, the incident drove home the mistaken lesson that they were in the driver's seat. Unless the Magyars met their full claims, they too would threaten secession. On 11 January 1919, the *Volksrat* escalated its demands by seeking middle schools and teacher academies of their own, and German primary education on demand, even in predominantly Magyarspeaking areas.[30] On 20 January 1919, Swabians in Sopron demanded immediate autonomy, otherwise Burgenland would secede and either proclaim its independence or join Austria.

The government was hard pressed. In deference to the Swabians, Károlyi commissioned several Germans, notably Peter Jekel, Guido Gündisch, and Otto Herzog, to draft a new statute embodying extraordinary Swabian privileges. The gesture might have been a step in the right direction but it was not, because a Magyar, Ödön Berinkey, and the Jewish Heinrich Kalmár, participated in the preparation of the document. Even the final draft had to be modified and approved by the Minsterial Council. Despite the Cabinet's misgivings and Jászi's protest that the Swabians did not merit special treatment, Law VI of 29 January 1919, granted cultural and political autonomy to Swabians in predominantly German-speaking areas of Hungary. This included administration, justice, education, and religion. Although autonomy would be centered in *Deutschwestungarn* (West Hungary), the entire Swabian community became a distinct corporate body. In addition, the Swabians received a National Assembly, a German Ministry, district councils, and commissioners. With János Junker's designation as Minister of German Affairs, and Zsombor's nomination of Governor of Burgenland, Jászi's involvement in the Károlyi regime terminated, signifyingthe bankruptcy of his ideas for solving the nationality question.[31]

The new law failed to satisfy German aspirations. It was not a voluntary gift, but had been extorted from Károlyi by threats. It was frankly designed to forestall further German defections—as in Burgenland—and to lure back already seceded Germans—as in southern Hungary and Transylvania. Although the concessions were generous, they actually exacerbated the conflict. In a surprising about-face, the unpredictable Bleyer announced that he scorned the new law because Swabian political autonomy conflicted with his own views on loyalty to the Hungarian nation. The issue must be resolved by the peace conference, hence autonomy was premature. Finally, Bleyer declared, cultural autonomy was all the Swabians ought to accept.[32]

Bleyer's reasons for rejecting autonomy were far more complex than his statement implied. He shared conservative Swabian misapprehensions that the Károlyi regime was evil. Moreover, the autonomy statute was inoperable and belated. The Swabians also pondered why their cherished political goals should have been achieved so easily and rapidly. The Károlyi regime had hoodwinked them before, and they suspected further treachery. The Magyars would revoke the concessions just as soon as stability had been restored in Hungary, leaving the Swabians worse off than before. Conservative Swabians like Bleyer were mortified when Heinrich Kalmár, as Károlyi's State Secretary for Swabian affairs, had a major role in drafting the Swabian autonomy statute.[33] They objected no less to Kalmár's Judaism than to the government's impudence in foisting an alleged outsider on them. A similar stigma clung to Ödön Berinkey, another non-Swabian architect of the law. The Bleyerites desired only Christian Swabians to be involved in their affairs. Diehard Swabian nationalists objected no less strenuously, therefore, when Géza Zsombor, whom they considered to be an ethnic

Magyar, became governor of Burgenland, this most sensitive and German-conscious region in all of Hungary.

The *Neue Post* fulminated. Károlyi tried to sabotage his own autonomy law. He attempted to subvert Swabians by introducing Social Democratic officials and ideas into their midst.[34] An editorial pilloried the radical Minister of Education, Zsigmond Kunfi, for having forbidden religious instruction in the schools and because he planned to nationalize education. Swabians feared this would give the government ideological control over the education of German youth.[35] The Swabian press campaign raged with great intensity, when Bleyer unexpectedly resigned from the *Volksrat* and terminated all contact with the government. On 12 March 1919, the *Neue Post* hinted at possible secession in Burgenland. Swabians in West Hungary had grown very skeptical about the manner in which autonomy was being administered. Home rule had not brought economic security for Burgen-landers, who needed the Austrian market for selling their produce, while Swabian workers usually obtained well-paying jobs in Austria. The *Neue Post* urged the government not to isolate Austria from Hungary by erecting tariff barriers or by imposing excessively strict criteria in the granting of border passes. Autonomy was unworkable because Zsombor, being a Magyar, staffed his office with Magyars and Magyarized Swabian fellow travellers. The government must rectify this unbearable situation at once.[36]

In the final weeks of Károlyi's political tenure secessionist activities increased in number and intensity. The mayor of Fürstenfeld continued his annexationist campaign. Otto Bauer failed to intervene when Austrian agitators infiltrated West Hungary, provided they did so as private individuals. Oscar Charmant, Hungary's envoy in Vienna, reported that anti-Magyar propaganda in Burgenland went merrily along. He singled out *Fremdenblatt* as the chief culprit in this respect.[37] At the end of March 1919, the Károlyi regime fell on a multitude of issues, not the least of which was the unresolved minority crisis. Károlyi's moderate government, contemptuously labeled "Hungary's Kerensky regime,"[38] now yielded to the volatile 133-day interlude of Béla Kun's Communist Republic of Councils.

When Kun acceded to power on 21 March 1919, only the Ruthenians and Swabians remained firmly under Hungarian rule. Before long, even the Ruthenians seceded, and joined Czechoslovakia. Bleyer, together with his conservative entourage, went underground to plot the overthrow of the Marxist regime. They left the Swabians' fate in the hands of radical Social Democrats and Marxists, many of whom were Magyars and Jews. The Marxist leaders at first ignored the minority situation entirely. Soon, however, foreign policy considerations—principally Austrian intrigues in Burgenland—prompted a reappraisal of the Swabian problem after all. The

Communists' initial ventures into minority politics were confusing, their diplomacy unskillful. Consequently, they fared even worse in attracting widespread Swabian support than the Social Democrats had before them.

Kun considered nationality problems as such a major nuisance, a bourgeois affectation, and hence just another obstacle to Communism. Far from entertaining seriously the Swabians' ethnic and cultural aspirations, he wished to conduct Hungarians of every race, nationality, or creed, into a Communist nirvana. Such a state would no longer need minority legislation, since the capitalist system, which in his view had exploited and persecuted minorities, would have melted away. Astute Swabians knew therefore that Kun had no interest in their survival in the ethnic sense. They perceived that concessions merely meant that for reasons of his own, Kun courted their support, or that he sought to counter Austrian and other diplomatic measures detrimental to the integrity of Hungary. It is within the framework of this complex Marxist *Realpolitik* that the government's highly erratic sallies into Swabian minority policy must be surveyed.

From the time of its founding on 20 November 1918, to its rise to power, the Hungarian Communist Party had no nationality programme of its own. Only a few months earlier, in the spring of 1918, Kun had tried to evade the entire issue by proclaiming that political boundaries would become meaningless after the establishment of the dictatorship of the proletariat.[39] Several days before assuming the helm of Hungary's government, Kun even repudiated Hungary's territorial integrity.[40] These policy statements sowed confusion in the minds of Swabians and other non-Magyars. On one hand, they were urged to be loyal to a state whose political boundaries were soon to be abolished, while at the same time the Communists seemed to encourage them to explore possibilities of uniting with their brethren across Hungary's frontiers. Kun's muddled political philosophy thus contributed to many misunderstandings between the Soviet Republic and its Swabian citizens.

Kun's undistinguished approach to Hungary's nationality problems obscured the fact that he recognized the nature of its difficulties. At the end of 1918, for example, he accurately predicted that Károlyi was doomed because the nationality problem eluded him.[41] When it was Kun's turn to unveil Soviet Hungary's nationality policy, he mouthed bland generalities. His message "Mindenkihez!" ("To All!"), appealed "to the proletariat of the world." Kun called upon all nations, but especially the seceded peoples of the former Monarchy to follow the recent revolutionary example of Hungary's proletariat. In his proclamation he said not one word about the projected fate of Hungary's own minorities.[42]

What was the source of Kun's inconsistency on the nationalities question?

Evidently, Kun believed that a bolshevik uprising was just around the corner in Central Europe and hence nationality laws would be superfluous. He was convinced, for example, that Austria would soon become a Soviet Republic, the third of many yet to come. His judgment was also deeply influenced by what appeared to him to be massive popular support in Austria. When the news of Kun's accession reached Vienna on 21 March, tens of thousands of Austrian sympathizers paraded through the streets. Kun failed to consider that many of the demonstrators celebrated not a bolshevik victory in Hungary but a blow struck against the arrogant Entente.[43] Kun's erroneous judgment was reinforced when the Austrian Communist Party, in a message on 28 March, implied that within three to four weeks Austria, too, would join the ranks of Soviet republics. A few weeks later a similar message, delivered on Hungarian soil by an Austrian Communist speaker, timed the impending revolution to occur within days, even hours. In Graz and elsewhere in Austria the Social Democrats broke ranks with their ruling Party, with its conservative coalition bedfellows, and joined the Communists. In joint communiqués they expressed solidarity with the Hungarian Soviet regime.[44] There were also tangible evidences of practical support from radical circles. Throughout this period a steady stream of Austrian recruits and smuggled arms found their way to Hungary. Renner made only half-hearted attempts to arrest this traffic. His behaviour was guided by two considerations. He wanted to express his solidarity with what was, after all, a fraternal Socialist regime. Even more likely, however, he wished to bolster Hungary's defences. At the time, Czechoslovakia had still not relinquished the idea of a common frontier with Yugoslavia by driving a wedge between Austria and Hungary. Hungary no less than Austria would have been the loser in such an arrangement.

Kun misunderstood the significance of these events with tragic consequences. Although many Austrian Social Democrats sympathized with Kun, a bolshevik revolution was not imminent in Austria. When Renner failed to intervene in the arming of the Magyar Soviets, Kun jumped to the wrong conclusion that Renner had lost control over his party, just like Károlyi, and that Austria's Socialists and Communists would overthrow Renner and establish a Soviet republic. But Renner had no intention of forming a coalition with the Communists, and his policy was not prompted by weakness. Indeed, his lenient Hungarian diplomacy came to a speedy end. On 2 May 1919, Austria was invited to attend the Peace Conference, and Renner was determined to woo the Entente. It is important to remember that Hungary was then reeling under Allied military attacks, which had brought Rumanian detachments to within 65 miles of Budapest. Since Austria sought a favourable decision in Burgenland, relations between

Austria and Hungary grew worse each day.

About this time Austria found herself under increasing pressure by conservatives at home and by the Entente abroad to join the Allied effort against Hungary by occupying Burgenland.[45] On the eve of his departure to Paris, the Chancellor told a delegation of Burgenland Swabians that he hoped for a determination in their favour, and Austria's, through a plebiscite. Coolidge reported on his fact-finding tour that Renner went so far as to advocate the occupation of Hungary by the Entente as the only certain means of getting rid of Kun. If Hungary's communist rulers had any remaining illusions about Renner, these were quickly dispelled in the following months. On 2 June the Peace Conference failed to award Burgenland to Austria, and Renner lodged an immediate protest, accusing the Victorious Powers of ignoring the wishes of Burgenlanders.

In the meantime, Austrian involvement in Burgenland continued, even intensified. In an evident attempt to demonstrate to the Peace Conference that Kun could not maintain order in Hungary, Renner encouraged Austrian nationalists and Hungarian emigrés to infiltrate that nation. In the early June days, these forces fomented a crippling railway strike in West Hungary, followed by armed rebellions in as many as thirty localities. Unconfirmed reports said the dissidents were led by Austrian army officers. Both Cnobloch in Budapest, and Burgenland's Swabian peasants, appealed to Austrian authorities to intervene in Hungary at once.[46]

Although publicly the Austrian Social Democrats pledged not to intervene in Hungary unless Kun fell, their subversions filled Hungary's leaders with apprehension. No wonder that Kun's nationality policy was designed not to grant the Swabians minority rights in the generally accepted sense of that term. Kun was far more interested in staffing West Hungarian posts with reliable Marxists than with Swabian patriots, who might please the population but who would not protect the Soviet republic from the mortal dangers besetting it from all sides. The rationale of Kun's German nationality policy becomes far clearer if these considerations are kept in mind.

Understandably, Kun hesitated even to broach the nationality question, and tried with all his might to subsume ethnicity under the heading of class struggle. When the nationality question emerged for the first time in the official Party newspaper *Vörös Ujság,* the author claimed only a proletarian revolution could solve the nationality question once and for all. Hoping to banish the issue into thin air, the writer asserted that society contained only classes, not nationalities. In another attempt to disparage the nationality question, József Pogány, a radical Communist official, stated: "Where there is proletarian rule, the proletariat finds its fatherland immediately, even if it speaks a different tongue."[47] Evidently, ideology transcended all, even reality.

The Communists had expected supra-national bolshevik uprisings to erupt all over Europe and solve their nationality problems. These ambitions came to naught. The few coups occurring, such as in Bavaria and Slovakia, were brief and abortive. In view of these dashed hopes, Hungary's Soviet leaders had to cashier their nationality policies as counterproductive and resort to more orthodox nostrums to restore the confidence of the minorities and re-establish the Hungarian state to its former prominence. Whatever, there can be little doubt the Communists dreamt of a new soviet-style Hungarian imperium, in which the nationalities—one way or another— would have to assume their rightful dialectic niche.[48]

The Communists had inherited from the defunct Károlyi regime a slender framework from which to construct a nationality formula more suitable, and perhaps more realistic, than the one they had entertained in the first few weeks in office. The Marxists dared not retract even the few illusory Swabian gains under Károlyi. Not to be outdone, almost immediately they established a Hungarian Federal Soviet Republic with two provisional autonomous jurisdictions—one for Ruthenia and one for Trans-Danubia (Burgenland). *Deutschwestungarn,* the German region, was to be governed by a Commissar attached to the Ministry of German Affairs. Still another stopgap regulation involving Swabian autonomy was published on 30 April. Although it contained certain attractive features, the projected law failed to please the Swabians. A powerful *Gaurat für Deutschwestungarn* (District Council for West Hungary), was designed to arrest annexationist threats. The *Gaurat* negotiated trade treaties with foreign powers, especially with Austria; established a separate German Red Army; and reorganized the German school system.[49] A number of counterproductive measures undermined these seemingly splendid achievements. The government failed to clarify the constitutional status of Swabians residing outside *Gaurat* jurisdiction. Decision on this point was postponed until an unspecified later date, causing severe Swabian anxieties. Although the government hinted the Swabian jurisdiction would be expanded later on, the Revolutionary Governing Council's Law 139 on 17 July 1919, finally limited Swabian autonomy to Burgenland. The government blundered again by deferring to the wishes of Burgenland's Magyar minority. Bowing to the nationalistic Magyar press of Sopron, and to a self-styled action committee, the "Propaganda Office for the Maintenance of the Integrity of Hungary," the government removed Sopron from the *Gaurat's* jurisdiction. The Swabians naturally resented this because Magyars comprised only 44% of Sopron's population.

The Swabians were even more aghast when they learned the identities of their new leaders. Sándor Kellner, enjoying only the most casual acquaintance with Burgenland's problems, became *Gaurat* head. For the Swabians, Kellner's nomination represented a triple error. Kellner was co-founder of the Hungarian Communist Party, he was a Magyar, and not even a native of Burgenland. Adolf Berczeller and Miklós Lazarovits, his two deputies, were also Magyar Marxists. Géza Zsombor was dismissed as governor and replaced by Heinrich Kalmár as Commissioner.[50] He was also entrusted with the *Deutsches Volksamt* (German Peoples' Bureau), with largely cultural tasks, and of its official journal, the *Volksblatt*. Lesser executive positions were also tendered mainly to Magyar Marxists, whereas petty officials, for lack of reliable Marxists, were recruited from the ranks of the former German Ministry and kept under close surveillance. The Social Democrats had only recently incurred Swabian wrath by appointing Magyar and Jewish officials to high Swabian positions. The Communists, who had lived through this experience and should have known better, chose to travel the same perilous road.

To demonstrate its concern for minority rights, the Communist regime maintained the fiction of a *bona fide* Swabian cultural association. Brandsch's *Deutschungarischer Volksrat* was dissolved, and Bleyer's *Deutscher Volksrat* became reorganized as *Deutscher Kulturbund für Ungarn,* but it functioned along strictly Marxist lines. The government also published a decree, enjoining all authorities "to accept any official request framed in any of Hungary's languages and to respond to it in the language of the appellant."[51] This regulation hoped to allay the fears of non-Magyars who viewed the regime with the same jaundiced eye as all previous Magyar-dominated governments. Indeed, the new regulations were largely paper decrees and nobody, the government included, really took them seriously.

As May approached, Austrian secessionist plots in Burgenland and widespread disaffection among Swabians compelled Kun to reconsider some of his uncompromising minority policies.[52] At the end of April 1919, the government began very cautiously to modify its earlier stubborn stand. This ushered in an era of experimentation, confusions, and contradictions. Order No. LXXVII of 29 April, issued by the Revolutionary Governing Council, is the most significant and telling contemporary document in this respect. Paragraph 1 deplored the oppression of non-Magyars in Hungary; yet the framers again blandly sidestepped the nationality issue: "The Hungarian Soviet state rests on the principle that it represents a fusion of multi-ethnic proletarians with equal rights, and hence it does not recognize that a nationality problem exists in the ordinary sense."[53] The Council also ordered immediate elections for both Ruthenian and German National Councils, which were to enjoy an exclusive privilege. They were to represent their peoples at the conference of the committee that would draft the final version of the Constitution of the Hungarian Soviet Republic. This might have been a felicitous step for these nationalities in their struggle for self-determination. Unfortunately, the National Council represented only the proletariat (*i.e.,* Communists), and hence it spoke for only a tiny minority of the total ethnic population. The regulation was also clearly designed to keep the Ruthenians and the Swabians from seceding and to lure back the nationalities already defected. The Marxists were deluded into thinking that, given a free choice, all the former peoples of Hungary would choose autonomy within a Hungarian Communist state rather than union with their co-nationals in the Successor States.

The Communists' overconfidence was boundless. Their belief in the class-consciousness and Marxist orientation of the peoples of the former Dual Monarchy prompted Kun to adopt a somewhat modified approach to the nationality problem, one which deprecated the importance of ethnicity and emphasized the significance of class. Heretofore the regime had blandly denied even the existence of an ethnic problem, except on a few rare occasions. In mid-May the regime renounced the principle of self-determination of nationalities in favour of self-determination of the proletariat. For the Hungarian Communists this was a deviationist course, which pitted them against Lenin. Through circuitous reasoning that fooled no one the Hungarian Soviets sought to convince the non-Magyars that their own interests were consonant with this approach.

Though belabouring the point once again that the nationality question *per se* was unimportant, Kun at last began to show greater concern for the outrage the nationalities felt in the face of paper decrees and continued oppression by local Magyar officials. By his 15 May speech on the occasion of the modification of the Party programme, Kun declared that in his own view self-determination of nationalities was a bourgeois concept and hence invalid. Nevertheless, Magyars must treat non-Magyar proletarians with consideration. Kun also felt that the Magyars should deal gently with Hungarians speaking "oppressed" languages in order to banish the charge that Magyars had still not jettisoned their chauvinism. Kun's unwarranted optimism that an international bolshevik revolution was imminent prompted him to declare a few days later in Sopron, his readiness "at any moment to create a federative state with the proletariat of Austria," provided, of course, that it proclaimed an Austrian Soviet Republic.[54]

Needless to say, Kun's attempts to solve the nationality problem on the basis of proletarian self-determination and class struggle fell on deaf ears among Germans both at home and abroad. If anything, Kun's doctrinaire and shortsighted tactics deepened the growing Magyar-Swabian gulf and sealed the fate of any further meaningful cooperation. As well, by appealing to foreign peoples over the heads of their own governments, Kun invoked the enmity of all the Successor States. Austria's Socialist regime in particular intensified its efforts to rescue the by now quite willing Swabian Burgenlanders from enforced Soviet captivity.

The government's questionable educational and religious policies contributed to the feelings of malaise in Swabian society. In education, for example, the government introduced a string of regulations which—although not specifically designed to benefit Swabians alone—ultimately might have raised Swabian educational standards. On 29 March 1919, the government nationalized Hungary's school system. The following day, Kunfi centralized Hungary's educational plant. One of the felicitous provisions of this regulation eliminated the one-room village school, where frequently one teacher taught grades one through six.[55] Such schools were especially prevalent in the overwhelmingly Swabian agricultural milieu and caused the rural Swabians' inordinately high semi-literacy. On the whole, the educational system was placed on a more progressive and humanitarian basis, designed to benefit children through the expansion of more practical subjects and the elimination of corporal punishment.[56] Furthermore, teachers were to be paid extremely high salaries, in order to attract only the most competent and dedicated. In addition to their normal teaching duties teachers would have to devote their after hours to instruct adult illiterates and perform other similar public services without additional remuneration.[57]

Promotion into higher education free of charge was assured every child without regard to his religion, race, or creed; those who showed great talent were passed.[58] The government also improved German lower education by importing kindergarten teachers and German textbooks from Austria and Germany, and by establishing schools for Swabian illiterates. Plans were under way to create 47 German elementary schools in the Budapest area alone, and some 400 additional ones in Burgenland. These changes struck at the very heart of Swabian educational deficiencies and augured well for the eventual enrichment of Swabian cultural life.

Religion, the Achilles heel of Swabian-Magyar relations, must be discussed simultaneously with education, for in Hungary most Swabian schools were confessional. Swabian peasants were mostly conservative and devout, and cherished the system of religious control over education, a tradition dating back several centuries. On 29 March 1919, all schools and training institutes were nationalized, a gesture scarcely designed to reassure the Swabian faithful. Furthermore, within three months all teachers—the clergy included—would have to pass an examination designed not only to test their knowledge but their social understanding as well. Swabians were dismayed when they learned that in the interim teachers would remain on probation.[59] In rapid succession, the Soviet regime published new school regulations, each more offensive than the last. On 19 April 1919, *Fáklya,* the Commissariat of Education official organ, announced that the teaching of history would have to be modified drastically in order to attune it to the Socialist New Order.[60] This merely heralded far greater changes yet to come. During summer vacation teachers were ordered to read Marx, Engels, Bukharin, and Edvin Szabó, in order to understand and be able to explain the basic tenets and goals of Communist society. Presumably, there would be little room for traditionalist or clerical teachers in the new world of Communist education. As Kunfi declared, "Henceforth our schools, thanks to the efforts of our teachers, shall become the most essential means of training [the people] for Socialism."[61]

The Swabians fumed when these measures were also coupled with an anti-religious campaign, both in the schools and in public life. Though the Soviet Constitution guaranteed all citizens freedom of religion and considered violations as treason, Communist authorities allowed their zeal to overwhelm their judgment. In Budapest, prayers were forbidden in all public schools. Crucifixes were to be removed from churches throughout Hungary, and in the National Congress of Councils accusations were leveled that hothead revolutionaries were desecrating the host in village churches and planned to turn houses of worship into cinemas.[62]

Indeed, it was disheartening news for the Communist regime when reports began to reach Budapest that local Magyar officials sabotaged the minority laws. Complaints of every kind poured into the capital daily. Magyar instructors in Swabian areas allegedly refused to establish German instruction programmes; German meetings were being banned by local officials; Magyar agitators were infiltrating Swabian regions and stirring up trouble. The *Deutscher Kulturbund* complained further that even in purely German areas political power continued to reside exclusively in the hands of Magyar proletarians who had no sympathy whatever for Swabian aspirations. The situation was so bad that on 15 April 1919, the *Kulturbund* pleaded with Kun to intervene personally against chauvinistic Magyar elements. Anti-Swabian sentiments began to surface even at public gatherings of the Marxist governing authorities. The Executive Committee of the Workers' and Soldiers' Council of Pest County, for example, inveighed against the influx of German teachers from abroad. The Council must prevent the *Deutsches Volksamt* from Germanizing Hungary by terminating the influx of alien teachers.[63] In view of these threats to their accustomed way of life, soon even Swabian supporters of the regime lost their enthusiasm. In the villages priests and teachers—the two most influential members of Swabian society—repudiated the Soviet regime. Without their active support, a communist educational and social transformation was doomed.

On 23 June 1919, the Kun regime, still soliciting Swabian support, unveiled its long-heralded final Constitution, which contained certain favourable provisions for the minorities. Unfortunately for the Communists it was too late. Swabian public opinion had definitively spurned the regime. Clause 84 vainly proclaimed, that

> Every nationality may use its own language freely and cherish and develop its own culture, and even if it does not reside on a continuous territory, may form a National Council for the development of its culture.[64]

Hungary's Marxist masters now conceded expanded cultural privileges to all Swabians, not only Burgenlanders. At the same time, however, they did not elucidate how administrative autonomy would apply to the rest of the scattered Swabians. As one writer put it,

> The clauses in the constitution dealing with the rights of nationalities were eclectic and ambiguous. Austro-Marxism, Leninism, traditional units of government, and new units were combined but not made consistent with one another. Provisions which, by themselves, seemed just became unworkable when juxtaposed with other clauses. And some statements were, from the very beginning, unclear. The difficulties within the constitution were disastrously magnified when the soviet government dealt on a practical level with its nationality groups.[65]

In view of such an abundance of confusing directives, together with a regime of Red Terror in Burgenland against secessionists, Kun could not hope to maintain himself in power much longer. Reeling under the impact of domestic disaffection, converging Entente armies, and Allied refusal to negotiate with a Communist government, the Kun regime fell on 1 August. One of Kun's last official acts was to register his disapproval on 21 July of the provision of the Treaty of St. Germain which had allocated Burgenland to Austria the previous day. At first, Kun steadfastly clung to the concept he had so despised in Magyar bourgeois statesmen, namely, the inviolability of Hungary's territorial integrity; but yielding to sheer practicality, he decided to demand a plebiscite. Thereupon the Soviet Council empowered Kun to negotiate with Otto Bauer. The meeting never materialized. A few days later, Kun had to resign, bequeathing to Julius (Gyula) Peidl, his Social Democratic successor, an aggravated Burgenland crisis, a Swabian nationality policy that was close to disastrous, and a totally disenchanted Swabian minority.

At a cursory glance, Peidl's Trade Union government appeared bent on somewhat the same course as its two left-wing predecessors. Closer scrutiny, however, betrays certain differences. Peidl did not retain separate ministries for each minority. Instead, one Ministry of Nationalities served all non-Magyar ethnic groups. Viktor Knaller, Kalmár-Kohn's former deputy, headed the consolidated Ministry. Kalmár was retained as State Secretary, supposedly at the request of West Hungarians. On the whole, the cast of characters responsible for minority policy had scarcely changed since the end of the war. Nonetheless, Burgenlanders feared that a single nationality Ministry might jeopardize their autonomy and demanded the restoration of their own separate German branch. On 5 August 1919, Peidl soothed the Germans that their autonomy would not be curtailed and promised to issue a decree "in the very near future."[66] It was never published, however, because the next day Peidl was overthrown in a bloodless coup.

With Peidl's departure, ultra-conservative forces under a renegade Social Democrat, István Friedrich, assumed control of Hungary's government. Friedrich became Prime Minister, a post he maintained through three turbulent cabinet changes. Jakob Bleyer emerged once more as a prominent and influential Swabian spokesman—at least for a time. Bleyer had literally clawed his way to the high councils of the new regime by having been one of the chief anti-left conspirators. Indeed, Bleyer, supported by a goodly crowd of other Swabian and quasi-Swabian counterrevolutionaries, such as Haller, Schnetzer, Huszár, Peyer, Grunn, Heinrich, and Gömbös, enjoyed so high a prestige at that moment with Magyars and Swabians alike that he was tendered the choice between two important cabinet posts. He was first offered the portfolio of Education and Religion. This he refused, probably because one of the other cabinet posts was promised to Jenő Polnay, a Jew. The issue was settled to Bleyer's satisfaction when archconservatives blocked Polnay's candidature. On 15 August 1919, Bleyer accepted the portfolio of Minister of Nationalities in Friedrich's second cabinet.[67]

Several days later Bleyer issued a position paper, which summarized recent Swabian history and outlined his own prescription for their wellbeing. In Bleyer's view, Communism had injured the Swabians because it exacerbated nationalistic passions in Hungary. His Ministry would heal these wounds. Swabians should integrate themselves into the totality of the Hungarian State, but simultaneously also maintain their national identity within the framework of linguistic and ethnic boundaries. Bleyer also demanded an effective German elementary school and cultural programme immediately, and an extremely modest political action plan as well. The use of German in all official transactions was an essential goal; but Bleyer remained discreetly silent on Swabian autonomy. His New Course would convince Magyars that the Swabians' loyalty for the Hungarian fatherland was true and tried, and thereby restore the somewhat tarnished Swabian image.[68]

At the same time Bleyer was extremely eager to reassure the other minorities that they would obtain proper treatment. His Ministry personnel would be chosen proportionately from Hungary's remaining ethnic groups. It took until 28 August 1919, when Friedrich began his third Ministry, to choose state secretaries for the Ministry of Nationalities. His promises to the contrary, Bleyer surrounded himself mainly with Magyar or Magyarophil Swabian officials, mostly members of his own intimate circle. As a reward for having resisted Bolshevik blandishments, Zsombor was created State Secretary. Georg Steuer, a Magyarized Swabian, became administrative State Secretary and chief of the Swabian section. The only non-Swabians of any importance were Michael (Mihály) Kutkafalvy, and Zoltán Szviezsényi, chiefs of the Ruthenian and the Slovak Section.

Bleyer addressed himself vigorously to the task of recapturing the loyalties of Hungary's seceded nationalities. It was a convenient way of proving to the skeptical Magyars that the Swabians were Hungarian superpatriots who wished above all else to restore Hungary to her former greatness. There were growing indications, however, that Bleyer no longer thought in terms of Hungary ruled by the Magyars alone, as he had when Hungary was still part of the Dual Monarchy. Although motivated by sincere patriotic sentiments, this complex man was riven by two loyalties— the one to Hungary, the other to Germandom. He wished his country well, but at the same time he desired far greater prominence for the Swabians than they had enjoyed hitherto. Out of the crucible of these two contradictory allegiances Bleyer arrived at a new synthesis, one of joint Magyar-Swabian hegemony in Hungary. Bleyer believed naively that if the Swabians outdid even the Magyars in their patriotic fervour, then cultural as well as certain political concessions would materialize as a matter of reward. All of Bleyer's assumptions rested on false premises, of course. Neither the seceded non-Germans, nor the dominant Magyars, were inclined to heed Bleyer's utopian blueprints.

Under Bleyer's direction, the Swabian Section performed prodigious feats, at least on paper. Bleyer and his aides tried to stem the tide of anti-Magyarism sweeping embittered Swabian public opinion. Under Steuer, the Swabian Section sought to restore a *modus vivendi* of sorts with the Magyars. They tried to persuade Burgenland's Swabians to remain true to Hungary and agitated among Yugoslavia's German citizens to demand annexation by Hungary. Another important task of the Swabian Section was to erect an ideological cordon sanitaire to separate Swabians and the politically more sophisticated Pan-German Transylvanian Saxons. The safeguarding of Swabian cultural interests was yet another task entrusted to its care.[69]

The Swabian Section's task of reconciling Swabians and Magyars was wrought with contradictions. If the Swabians were to be offered inferior concessions to those they had enjoyed before, then they would scarcely accept an accommodation with the present regime. If, on the other hand, they were granted concessions which equalled or surpassed those of the radical era, then the Swabians would have to face an outraged Magyar public. Caught between Scylla and Charybdis, Bleyer emerged with what he hoped would be a fair compromise. At the end of August 1919, he unveiled a statute that in spirit resembled the Nationality Law of 1868. Its fairness would attract the minorities, whereas its moderation would not offend the Magyars. Hungary would derive still another benefit from such a law. The peace treaty was still pending, and consequently Hungary's territorial boundaries were still *de facto* and hence negotiable. For the Magyars it was a matter of life and death to persuade the Entente that they had repudiated their prewar oppression and Magyarization, and that Hungary encouraged the concept of self-determination currently in vogue. By stressing the rights of individual citizens rather than those of minority groups as an entity, the framers sought to compromise between the two extremes of Magyar elitism and of ethnic separatism.

The statute (Law 4044.1919 M.E.) was drafted under the personal direction of Bleyer and promulgated on 20 August 1919.[70] Although the law stopped short of recognizing ethnic groups as corporate structures, it did designate non-Magyar ethnic groups as national minorities. It thus went beyond the 1868 statute, which merely acknowledged the existence of racial distinctions. The point may be moot, but the issue sparked a heated controversy as to Bleyer's motives in recognizing non-Magyars as national minorities. According to traditionalists, only the Magyars qualified as a nationality; non-Magyars would have to become Magyarized before being admitted to the ranks of the only nation in Hungary. The Magyars obviously distrusted Bleyer, for this was his plan. It can be seen how wrong Bleyer was to believe that the Magyars would agree to an *Ausgleich* with their Swabian minority even on terms of quasi-equality. At all events, the Law, although stopping far short of even hinting at autonomy for non-Magyars, later provided the Swabians with a convenient legal argument for escalating their demands. Just as its Magyar critics had feared, the Law established the Swabians as a national minority with distinct privileges not only under

Hungarian law but under the League of Nations Charter.

What did the Nationality Law accomplish? Every citizen was vouchsafed the right to address all the Ministries, courts of law, local assemblies, and even Parliament in his own mother tongue (Par. 2). Authorities had to respond in the language of the applicant (Par. 8-10), and all the laws had to be published in every language spoken in Hungary (Par. 3). Unfortunately the law failed to provide proper mechanisms to ensure its successful execution. As well, many provisions, although seemingly solicitous of the political, educational, and administrative requirements of non-Magyars, were not clearly articulated and hence ineffective. A local assembly, for example, might choose German to be the official language in that locality. In that case, the protocols would have to be maintained in German. A parallel Magyar translation would have to accompany the Germany text. While there is nothing intrinsically wrong with such an arrangement, serious complications and ethnic strife were certain in the wake of this law in a multi-lingual society such as Hungary's. Many communities had mixed Magyar-German-Rumanian populations (or other combinations). If one-fifth of the local assembly desired the adoption of still another language, then the protocol had to be published in as many languages as desired (Par. 4-7). Unfortunately, non-Magyar minority leaders, in the true sense of that word, seldom served in local assemblies, or anywhere else, for that matter. The few who did were subjected to pressures brought upon them by Magyar and Magyarized colleagues. Under the circumstances, these provisions of the Law had little more than publicity value.

With respect to religion and education, the Law appeared to grant the minorities a great deal of responsibility and discretion. Ecclesiastic authorities had the right to determine the official language of their congregations and schools (Par. 12). The framers expressed the pious hope that all non-Magyars would find their ethnic aspirations fulfilled at all educational levels. The Law also held out exaggerated hopes for minority teachers' institutes, academies, gymnasia, lycea, and even for chairs in the universities for each minority (Par. 13). Non-Magyars were led to believe that private individuals and secular organizations could establish schools of all types (Par. 14). Observers acquainted with conditions in Hungary discounted these promises. It was common knowledge, for example, that in the course of the previous few generations the ethnic clergy had become thoroughly Magyarized and that it vied with the Magyars in patriotic fervour. Especially Roman Catholic clergymen had become steadfast opponents of minority education in the ethnic tongue and the staunchest advocates of inculcating minority youth with the Magyar language ethos. These priests naturally insisted on maintaining pure Magyar schools in their dioceses and districts, to the detriment of minority education as suggested by the Law. There were no legal resorts to enjoin them from these acts, since they enjoyed total autonomy and immunity in such matters. With respect to private schools, individuals and secular organizations had encountered financial difficulties even before the war. They tried in vain to live up to the demanding standards set by the central authorities. Since these institutions received no subsidies from the government, they had either to cease operations or conform. There were no indications of a reversal in this established pattern in the postwar period. Clearly, private secular schools were no match for the State-run and financed schools and the massively subsidized Church-directed institutions. The new law was mere window dressing.

The government also wished to assure the minorities that their districts would be staffed only with judges, notaries, and other administrators belonging to their own ethnic groups (Par. 15). This provision invited misunderstandings and disappointments. The Law failed to make clear, for example, that the government was not compelled to appoint dedicated minority leaders to these positions. In fact they were reserved for Magyars and "reliable" Magyarized individuals almost without exception. The government tried very hard to convince the minorities that it really had their interests at heart. The Law stipulated, for instance, that all public officials in areas inhabited predominantly by minorities would be obliged to learn the language of the resident minority group within two years (Par. 15). This provision, too, led to exaggerated hopes and disillusionments. Experience both before and since this occasion has indicated that such an approach does not work. Undermining the morale and security of civil servants by compelling them to learn an objectionable language merely aggravates rather than palliates ethnic conflicts. In Hungary, whose polyglot population frequently consisted of as many as three-four mixed groups within a single community, the law had to be a dead letter from the start. In one observer's view, the Nationality Law was a mere manoeuvre, designed to persuade the minorities and the Entente that Hungary had decisively broken with her oppressive prewar nationality policies and hence was worth preserving.

Whereas Friedrich appeared to have no intentions of living up to the provisions of the Nationality Law, Bleyer and his followers took the statutes very seriously indeed. Their rationale rested on firm grounds. The traditional Hungarian State could be saved only if the Magyars discharged their legal and moral obligations towards the minorities. Once more, Bleyer and the government found themselves at opposite poles on a fundamental issue. Should Hungary's minorities be given the far-reaching cultural and moderate administrative concessions the Nationality Law vouchsafed, or should the Law be ignored and the ethnic groups subjected to Magyarization? As on previous occasions, the Hungarian government—whether dominated by conservative monarchists, enlightened Social Democrats, Marxist radicals, Trade Unionists, or arch-Conservatives—clung tenaciously to the concept that the frontiers of the Crownlands of Saint Stephen were unalterable and sacred and the domination of the Magyars exclusive and paramount. An irreconcilable conflict arose between Bleyer, who stressed the need for cultural and ethnic diversity in a supranational Hungarian State under a joint Magyar-Swabian partnership, and Hungary's Magyar leaders, who with equal tenacity clung to the notion that Hungary must achieve a Magyar-dominated cultural, ethnic, and political unity. Under the latter system non-Magyar Hungarians would have enjoyed only second-class citizenship, and their language would have been relegated to private use only.

The Hungarian government's intransigence toward the minorities imperiled Bleyer's cherished wish—the retention of Burgenland. Since the overthrow of Hungary's leftist regimes Bleyer's ambition in this respect was no longer as utopian as before. With a conservative government ensconced in Budapest once more, the attraction of radical Austria began to fade for the traditionalist Swabians. An Allied observer noted at this time that Burgenland's population was still largely undecided between Austria and Hungary. Conservative and religious Swabians feared Austria because it was radical, but they also feared Hungary because it had a tendency not to keep promises. The Hungarian government did nothing in a practical sense to swing Swabian public opinion to its side. Fortunately, however, thanks to a timely intervention, the Friedrich government barely averted the annexation of Burgenland in the fall of 1919.

Austria's Social Democrats had refused to take drastic action against Hungary as long as that nation was under Socialist rule. Thus far, Renner had successfully restrained his conservative coalition partners from embarking on a military venture that would have brought Austrian troops into direct confrontation with Hungarian garrison troops in West Hungary. On 2 August, for example—during the last few days of the Peidl regime— Renner, who was in Paris negotiating with the Entente, wired his Secretary of War, Julius Deutsch, and urged him to secure permission from the Anglo-Italian mission then in Vienna for the occupation of Burgenland by *French* troops.[71] Only a few days later, after the coup which brought Friedrich into power, Deutsch began to urge Renner to occupy Burgenland immediately with Austrian troops, because the Friedrich regime supposedly lacked the military strength the Communists had wielded. In an understandable turnabout they now demanded an instant to arms in order to grab Burgenland from conservative Hungary. On this occasion their coalition partners stopped them. The Christian Socials in particular refused to embarrass Hungary's new conservative masters through a military intervention.[72] It was a curious twist of events that Burgenland—at least for the time being—was saved for Hungary not due to the benevolent actions of its government towards the Swabians, nor owing to the Germans' loyalty to the Hungarian State, but because of supranational Austro-Hungarian ideological considerations.

For a brief interval after the demise of leftist radicalism Bleyer rode the crest of popularity with both Swabians and Magyars.[73] The former expected Bleyer to throw his prestige behind the Nationality Law; the latter misjudged Bleyer's motives, believing him to be a pure Magyar patriot, his nationality law mere window dressing, his German sentiments a mere sham. Bleyer's honeymoon with the Magyars did not endure. Soon, Bleyer showed evidence of disillusionment. At the Ministerial Council session on 20 September he complained that the Nationality Law was being systematically violated by Magyar officials. The situation was particularly serious in the Budapest area, in Tolna County, and in West Hungary. Swabian officials wishing to introduce the statute in their jurisdictions were scorned by their Magyar colleagues, who accused them of entertaining Pan-German sympathies. In some instances, these law-abiding Swabian officials found themselves behind bars. Bleyer pilloried the government for not having lifted a finger to effect a more equitable ethnic distribution of civil servants in Hungary. The Ministerial Council agreed with Bleyer and even pledged to arrest the wave of abuses.[74] Little was accomplished, in fact, due partly to a legal technicality. In Hungary a law remained invalid until the requisite Ministry issued an enabling act to implement the statute in question. As Minister of Nationalities Bleyer could issue such acts only to a limited degree; for the rest, he had to depend on his various colleagues.[75] But to Bleyer's chagrin they refused to release these orders, and hence Germanophobe Magyar officials stood on firm legal ground when they refused to put the various provisions of the Nationality Law into effect. Further, they had every right to restrain those officials who wished to implement it.

Less than two weeks later, Bleyer resorted to a forceful device to bend his colleagues to his way of thinking. At the next meeting of the Council he circulated a memorandum to all the cabinet members, demanding that they release the enabling decrees at once. In his message Bleyer shrewdly observed that unless the Magyars improved the condition of their minorities, they could scarcely expect those living in the still disputed occupied regions to believe that Hungary entertained a due regard for their ethnic aspirations. The time was ripe to make the Nationality Law a reality; not merely to satisfy the aspirations of Hungary's minorities and prevent the development of a dangerous irredenta inside Hungary, but in order to ensure the viability of a vital aspect of Hungarian foreign policy. Bleyer opined that Hungary's seceded minority peoples could be prevailed upon to opt for Hungarian rule in any plebiscite, but only if the government henceforth pursued a benevolent and indulgent nationality policy, in theory as well as in practice.[76]

In his heavyhanded "carrot-and-stick" fashion, Bleyer tried to propel his recalcitrant colleagues towards a favourable disposition of the Nationality Law. On one hand he implied continued abuse of the non-Magyars might induce even Hungary's remaining minorities (he meant Swabians) to consider secession; on the other hand, he led the Cabinet to believe that hopes for the recreation of a Greater Hungary were not extravagant dreams, provided that the terms of the Nationality Law were dutifully executed. Bleyer's pleas fell on deaf ears, partly because the Friedrich regime was only a caretaker government and lacked a broadly-based mass support. Consequently, Friedrich and his associates, with the exception of the ambitious Bleyer, preferred fence sitting to problem solving on delicate issues, the most troublesome of which was the nationality question. Thus, as of 16 November 1919, when Admiral Horthy rode into Budapest at the head of his troops, soon to become regent of Hungary, the minority problem was still as acute and unresolved as ever.

CHAPTER III
THE EARLY HORTHY ERA: SWABIANS, AUSTRIANS,
AND GERMANS—THE SEEDS OF A DILEMMA (1919-1922)

During a conservative political reaction under Prime Minister Friedrich, Admiral Nicholas (Miklós) Horthy's military legions and ultra-conservative political forces began their sweep towards the capital in November 1919. Thus far, the Whites like the Social Democrats and Communists before them, had largely failed to solve either Hungary's ethnic problems or any other ills. After Horthy's arrival in Budapest, the Magyars acceded to Entente demands by ousting Friedrich, and prepared for their first postwar election. Karl (Károly) Huszar, a lacklustre conservative politician, became Prime Minister *pro tem* on 25 November to be followed in rapid succession by Alexander (Sándor) Simonyi-Semadam (15 March 1920-19 July 1920) and Paul (Pál) Teleki (19 July 1920-15 April 1921). Not until the advent of Count Stephen (István) Bethlen as Prime Minister (15 April 1921-19 August 1931) would Hungary achieve anything resembling stability. Meanwhile, on 1 March 1920, Admiral Horthy became regent of Hungary and imposed his right-radical views on the course of both domestic and external affairs.

In addition to the usual postwar dislocations and confusions Hungary faced a growing nationality crisis. The Swabian problem had by then become imbedded in foreign policy, and the Burgenland question had progressively laced the Swabian predicament. These twin problems had become indistinguishable, and would compound almost with each passing day over the next two years.

Hungary's interaction with the two important German-speaking nations—Austria and Germany—revealed the intricate links between the Magyars' minority and foreign policies. At the end of 1919, when Hungarian minister Gustav Gratz's negotiations with Austria miscarried, Admiral Horthy, at the time only Minister of War but in reality the power behind the throne, began to plot the overthrow of the Renner regime. This conspiracy had two simultaneous thrusts. One scheme called for the forcible removal of Renner through a secret alliance with conservatively-minded Austrian officers and with certain rightwing Austrian Christian Socialists. Hungary's price for helping these dissidents, according to Horthy, was renunciation of Burgenland in favour of Hungary. Of course, Burgenland's Swabians would be liaison between the Magyars and their Austrian confederates.[1]

A parallel plan in the Austrian putsch entailed right-wing Bavarian politicians and paramilitary forces. Horthy's contacts with these circles, notably the *Bayrische Volkspartei*, commenced as early as the end of 1919. Bavarian Magyar sympathizers not only provided favourable publicity for the Magyars in Southern Germany, but also procured munitions and funds for anti-Austrian activities in Burgenland. Even more important was the Magyars' connection with General Ludendorff. Although the General distrusted Hungary's Bavarian allies, he was not averse to dealing with the Magyars, and even envisioned a joint Hungarian-Bavarian frontier. Ludendorff's scheme emerged in a letter addressed to Horthy and his intimate circle about an anti-bolshevik conspiracy. To make the plan work, Austria's Socialist regime would be forcibly removed. Ludendorff projected a virtual partition of Austria, West Hungary going to Hungary, and the Alpine regions to Bavaria. Austrian right-wing elements were to be drawn into the venture as accomplices. Its success would be assured by Hungarian funds and food supplies.[3]

This scheme, partially masterminded in Budapest, was not merely a momentary lapse in the suspension of normal diplomatic practices by Hungary. Except for a brief period in the fall of 1920, Horthy and his associates wanted to establish forcibly a friendly regime in Austria. This was only one act of a grandiose Magyar scenario, to create a supra-national anti-bolshevik bulwark in Europe, stretching from the White armies in Southern Russia to Bavaria, where a rightist regime held momentary power. Besides Hungary and Bavaria, this federation was to have encompassed Poland, the Ukraine, and Austria.

These intricate plans misfired because of confusion, misunderstanding, and mutual suspicion. In the fall of 1920, Chancellor Mayr's Christian Socials proved no more amenable to a Hungarian solution in West Hungary than had the Social Democrats under Renner. Hungarian leaders had hoped that with their growing influence, the Christian Socials would make the desired changes in Austria's foreign policy without armed coercion by Hungary. At the end of 1920, the Magyars adopted a wait-and-see attitude, only to plunge back to their conspiracy in early 1921.

Hungary's hesitation at this crucial juncture was a great blunder, because later both the Austrian and the Bavarian conspirators changed their minds. Despite their continued plottings with Austrian royalist military circles and with dissident right-wing Christian Socials such as Mgr. Ignaz Seipel, the

Hungarians to their chagrin could not make headway with their grandiose blueprints. In March 1921, Seipel reneged on his earlier secret agreement with the Magyars, in which he had promised to adopt a pro-Hungarian policy in the event of election victory. The Seipel plan foundered when it became clear that the Christian Socials would be thrown out of office and replaced by the Social Democrats, should they vo through with their plan. Even before this, the Magyars saw their mistake and concluded that the shortest road to Vienna still led through Munich. In December 1920, they dispatched two unofficial envoys—Bleyer and Huber—to the Bavarian capital to prod their friends into action. Unfortunately, the Bavarians changed their minds. They could no longer support Hungary against Austria, which had discarded Socialism for a more congenial regime.

In desperation, Hungary once more turned to Bleyer and Huber. In February 1921, the two were dispatched to Germany to convince highly placed German officials in the Foreign Ministry to abandon Germany's unbendingly pro-Austrian policy. but the Swabian envoys never saw anyone above the rank of press attaché.[3] They had thus permitted themselves to be used twice in a scheme that was really none of their business. By representing the Magyar viewpoint, they risked alienating many of their followers and earning the contempt of most Austrian and Reich Germans. The only concession they might secure was the possibility of eventual Swabian cultural self-determination. The Swabians' abortive Berlin missions capped a whole series of Hungarian diplomatic fiascos. For the time being, any thought of active military intervention in Austria and in Burgenland had to cease.

Clearly, Hungarian leaders considered the Swabian problem an important adjunct to external diplomacy, not merely an isolated domestic concern. It is also clear why Hungary's relations with Austria took such a poor turn when the Burgenland issue intruded. It was not just a matter of territory or even economics. Hungary wished to instigate a change of government in Austria, a regime that would not only be ideologically compatible, but also willing to relinquish its claim to West Hungary. Previous Austro-Hungarian talks had transpired in an atmosphere of suspicion, which negated Gratz's suave and skillful negotiating. Now, thanks to the Hungarian conspiracy to overthrow the Austrian government, suspicion turned to fury.

As soon as Hungary's conspiratorial plans became known in Vienna early in 1920, the Austrians became intransigent and began counter-measures. Gratz consequently had even less success than before. The Austrians assured him that their slogan "so weit wie die deutsche Zunge reicht" (As far as the German language reaches) was expansionary, aimed exclusively at Cze-

choslovakia's German-inhabited Sudetenland and at West Hungary, not—
as the Magyars feared—at the Swabian hinterland east of Burgenland. Since
both the Sudetenland and the Burgenland had at one time or another
belonged to Austria, the explanation, though unacceptable to the Hungarians, seemed logical enough.

But the Austrians were unscrupulous in the pursuit of this self-proclaimed
policy. Even while reassuring Hungary that their western boundaries were
secure, Austria's provisional head of state, Carl Seitz, and Chancellor Karl
Renner, responded favourably to Czech overtures for secret negotiations at
Hungary's expense. The Czechs sought a corridor which would create a
joint Czechoslovak-Yugoslav frontier. The plan would have clearly in-
fringed on Hungarian territory, thus contradicting Austrian assurances. As
soon as this manoeuvre came to light in December 1919, Gratz retaliated
against what appeared to be a developing Czech-Austro-Yugoslav conspiracy. He immediately initiated economic negotiations with the Czechs, the
most formidable of the trio. Gratz hoped to divide Austria and Czechoslovakia, two fledgling industrial nations competing for the potentially lucrative,
war-starved Hungarian consumer market.

But Gratz failed. The international forces arrayed against him were
overwhelming. Although the corridor plan evaporated, due mainly to
Allied objections, on 12 January 1920, Czechoslovakia and Austria reached
an understanding aimed—at least partially—against Hungary. The two
countries decided to pool their military resources in the event of Hungarian
aggression, and pledged to prevent a Hungarian-inspired putsch in Austria.
This encircled Hungary, which continued barren and desultory talks with
Czechoslovakia for several more months.[4]

The Magyars managed to derive some benefit from this Austrian policy.
With justice they could claim that they had every reason to fear a forcible
Austrian usurpation in Burgenland, buttressed by Czech armed forces
stationed in nearby Bratislava. Hungary's Swabian press hammered away at
this theme, aligning Burgenlanders temporarily with Hungary. The Swabians were only annoyed with the Magyars, but they feared and despised the
Czechs.[5]

It was at this juncture, early in 1920, that France launched an intense
diplomatic offensive in Central Europe. Peace negotiations with Hungary
were scheduled for the Spring; and consequently, French statesmen tried to
lever that country into signing a favourable treaty. France began secret talks
in January, hoping to persuade Hungary to exchange France's economic
protection for a more lenient territorial settlement. French foreign policy
here was really aimed at solidifying the cordon of steel already formed
around Hungary. Under French auspices, Czechoslovakia undertook com-

prehensive military, political, and economic negotiations with Rumania and Yugoslavia. These led to an anti-Hungarian Little entente. Worse still for Hungary, France urged Austria to expand her newly-formed relationship with the Czechs to embrace the other two partners, Rumania and Yugoslavia.[6] While unwilling to go quite that far, Austria recognized the benefits of French friendship in the Burgenland controversy. Backed by France and the other Victorious Powers, Austria felt both justified and secure in exerting increasing pressure on Hungary to cede the disputed region. It is clear that whereas Hungary's nationality problem before the War was strictly an internal affair, its ramifications could not be kept within domestic bounds after 1918. The minority problem had gradually merged into the Burgenland dispute, and from there it had spilled over into the larger international political arena, including even the Versailles peace settlement.

Despite Hungarian attempts to subvert the Austrian government, and despite Austrian counter-measures, conversations between the two nations continued, albeit in an hostile atmosphere. In January 1920, the Christian Socials had urged Austria to establish closer economic links with Hungary as a means of forestalling food shortages. But Bauer rejected the idea and assailed the Hungarian regime as a ruthless enemy that was attempting to subvert political order in Austria.[7] There was more than a grain of truth in Bauer's assertions.

As the months wore on, both the pace and the spirit of discussions between Austria and Hungary became more perfunctory and plodding. In February 1920, the Magyars made a proposal they knew Austria would reject. They suggested that a plebiscite be held in Burgenland and promised to grant autonomy if the vote favoured Hungary. Austria naturally refused and consented to negotiate with the Magyars only to implement Burgenland's surrender. In the Summer of 1920, the Austrians definitively rejected the principle of territorial compromise with Hungary. They drew up detailed and elaborate plans for the administrative incorporation of Burgenland, with Ödenburg (Sopron) as its capital, into the Austrian Federal Republic. This infuriated the Magyars because the plan had been hatched not by the hated Social Democrats but by the supposedly friendly Christian Socials. No wonder that the Magyars thereafter increasingly interlaced their diplomacy with threats of violence.[8]

Deteriorating Austro-Hungarian relations even emerged in parliamentary debates in Hungary. Count Kuno Klebelsberg, representative from Sopron, and future Minister of Education and Religion in the Bethlen regime, took Austria—more so than the Entente—severely to task for deceiving an old trusted ally, which in the recent war had shed copious blood for the preservation of the Austrian Empire. He contrasted Magyar fidelity with Austria's deceitful attempts to impose German standards on Hungary during its 400-year domination. He warned that the Magyars were now as skilled bearing their Austrian yoke as they were adept at casting it off; West Hungary would be no exception, for the Magyars would gladly fight for it.

> If after transgressing against us for four centuries Austria should now top it all by robbing us. . .then the Magyars will become so alienated from Austria that nothing could ever heal the breach.

Although partially of Austrian parentage, the Count felt certain that

> . . .not one of us would fail to consider it his sacred duty to cultivate a spirit of revenge against Austria if she should tear Burgenland from us.[9]

Klebelsberg, a potential Swabian leader, rallied to the Magyar cause instead, and his example was characteristic, not exceptional. In the heat of the occasion the Count had dredged up traditional Magyar grievances against imperialistic Austria. At a time when the pro-Habsburg Bleyer and his supporters tried to encourage Magyars to cultivate a pro-German orientation, Klebelsberg's essentially anti-German note soured Magyar-Swabian as well as Austro-Hungarian relations. Even Gustav Gratz's elevation to the ambassadorship in Vienna failed to arrest the declining relations of the two former partners. As usual, talks foundered on Austria's insistence that Hungary surrender Burgenland unconditionally.[10]

Amid the prevailing impasse, mutual recriminations involving the Magyars, the Austrians, and even the Swabians, became quite common. The *Neue Post* complained bitterly because Austrian and German papers branded Bleyer and his supporters as "Magyarones." It cited the ultra-nationalist German *Vossische Zeitung,* who saw Bleyer as a "German Herostrates, who oppressed Hungary's Germans in the worst way." *Neue Post* dismissed the authors as "German fanatics" and reaffirmed Bleyer's righteousness.[11] Evidently, the Magyars succeeded in splintering an incipient Pan-German movement by creating internal dissension. The Magyars were in the habit of sending Swabian emissaries to Austria and Germany, in order to ensure support for a Hungarian solution in Burgenland. As unofficial ambassadors the inexperienced Swabians failed, but their principal value lay in their downright clumsiness. Everywhere they went, these emissaries unwittingly sowed discord which could benefit only the magyars.

Another empty round of negotiations with Austria commenced in February 1921. Near the end of 1921, animosities reached such intensity that limited armed conflict appeared inevitable. When the Allied Council of

Ambassadors ordered Hungary to evacuate Burgenland by 27 August 1921, the Bethlen regime began to organize "volunteer" bands under the leadership of Hungary's future Minister of War and later Prime Minister, Julius (Gyula) Gömbös. They were to seize West Hungary when the Hungarian army evacuated to keep Austrian forces out. While disavowing any connection with these irregulars, the government continued to support them at least until the beginning of October, when one of the guerrilla leaders, Paul (Pál) Pronay, proclaimed West Hungary an independent province called *Lajtabánsdg.* The conspirators intended to go through the motions of an election, and then unify the province with Hungary. Angry Entente protests prompted Bethlen to jettison the insurgents, whose enthusiastic "support" had proved an embarrassment. Despite this, irregular bands continued to plague Burgenland long after the plebiscite, apparently with impunity and at least with tacit Hungarian government aid.[12]

Even direct intervention by the Entente failed to curb mutual animosities. In October 1921, Italy's mediation resulted in an uneasy compromise entailing the partition of Burgenland. The Entente awarded most of the disputed region, with its predominantly German-speaking population, to Austria. In December, Sopron, with its immediate vicinity, was to hold a plebiscite, its fate to be decided by a simple majority vote. Both parties endorsed the plan, yet both flouted the conditions of the plebiscite by intimidations. For example, Sopron's mayor Thurner charged that prior to the referendum Austria had established election headquarters in Agendorf (Ágfalva), on Hungarian soil. Austrian agents had allegedly warned its inhabitants and of Harkau (Harka) that should they vote for Hungary, the Austrian army would storm the two communities and burn them to the ground. The Austrians reinforced their threat. Throughout the election incessant machine-gun fire could be heard from across the Austrian frontier. Female voters were particularly intimidated. Thurner ventured that had it not been for this, the vote would have favoured Hungary far more than it did. Indeed, in the two communities in question the Austrians won overwhelmingly, by a majority of 83% and 91% respectively.

Austria suffered a crushing blow to her prestige by losing Sopron by a margin of 72:28. The Austrians at first refused to accept the results. They objected to the presence of both Hungarian regular troops and irregular bands in the election zone, who countered Austrian propaganda by electioneering through the persuasive voice of the bayonet. Further, Hungarian officials, whom the Entente permitted to remain in the plebiscite zone before, during, and after the balloting, allegedly imported hundreds of Magyars into Burgenland for the election and forged their names on voters' lists. Thus both sides sought new results. As late as March of the next year, persistent rumours circulated about an impending Magyar putsch in the ceded regions. This uprising was to be led by irregular bands financed by the Hungarian government.[13]

Whether the Bethlen regime did in fact support the insurgents remains a moot point. Be that as it may, these irregulars created much chaos in West Hungary at the time of the plebiscite. Their interventions not only estranged Magyars and Austro-Germans, they strained the Swabians' fidelity to the Hungarian cause, and imperilled their tenuous co-existence with Magyar-dominated Hungary. The plebiscite left some 70,000 West Hungarian Swabians under Hungarian jurisdiction. The Magyars considered the prospect of harbouring so many disillusioned Swabians, imbued as they were with Pan-German sentiments, a great danger for the internal security of Hungary. Years of cultural abuse, capped by the notorious anti-Swabian exploits of the dreaded paramilitary units, had driven Burgenland's small but militant Swabian minority emotionally far closer to the seven million Austro-German brethren across the Leitha (Lajta) than to the alien Magyars to the east. These Swabians thus threatened to become a dangerous irredenta connecting German influence from the west with their Swabian co-nationals in the east. The Magyars rightly feared that someday they might infect hungary's other Swabian citizens with Pan-German *völkish* ideas, and imperil the economic and political sovereignty of the Hungarian State.

Austro-Hungarian venom in the Burgenland affair profoundly affected German-Hungarian relations. Germany's defeat did not dismiss the Magyars' giant western neighbour as an economic, even military, menace. Hungarian diplomacy thus sought to keep Austria and Germany separate, sovereign, and hopefully unfriendly states. The Magyars thought this would prevent a calamitous *Anschluss*. The Magyars therefore tried everything in their power to create friction between the two Germanic nations. Burgenland, where the fate of over ¼ million Germans was at stake, offered the Magyars an excellent opportunity to apply their divisive tactics.

The chaotic nature of postwar German politics assisted the diplomatically skilled Magyars in exploiting the situation. At first, German politics were dominated mainly by the Socialists, who had proclaimed a republic in November 1918, and by the moderate Centrists. Not so in Bavaria, where the pressure of a strong nationalist-conservative and Wittelsbach monarchist movement created a tension between Munich and Berlin which the Magyars exploited. After Horthy's rise, South German, and especially Bavarian newspapers, had begun to support Hungary's claim in Burgenland.[14] These papers all praised the Magyars for their bravery and for their fidelity to Germany in the late war. German readers were told not to abandon Hungary, a former trusted ally, in her hour of need, and that the

Entente had given Burgenland to Austria in order to divide the Magyars and the Germans, thus dashing any chances of a future German-Hungarian alliance. Burgenland's Swabians were urged to prove their loyalty to Hungary and blunt the Entente's evil intentions.[15] These stories were so similar to Hungarian propaganda releases that they were no doubt planted by Magyar officials. These conservative journals, not to mention many South German public figures, were certainly driven by greater loyalty to the right-radical Hungarian government than to German *völkisch* ideals, as long as these were represented by either the German or the Austrian Socialist regimes. In contrast, the Social Democratic governments in Vienna and Berlin were ideological bedfellows, both of whom detested Hungary's rightist regime. Thus it came about that many ultra-conservative Pan-German Bavarians paradoxically supported Hungary's claim in Burgenland—at least for a while—even though such a policy threatened to consign many Germans to permanent Magyar rule. For the time being, ideology smothered nationalism in both camps.

During this period Hungary's diplomatic relations with Germany were stormy and complex. Aware that they were not likely to arouse the sympathy of Germany's left wing regime, the Magyars resorted to various stratagems designed to embarrass the Germans and prevent the formation of a Swabian-Austrian-German entente. In this diplomatic game the Magyars were in their element. At the beginning of 1920 they launched an offensive. In a note to Count Fürstenberg, Germany's Consul General in Budapest, the Hungarian Foreign Ministry accused Germany of encouraging Austria's intransigence in the Burgenland affair, and charged that German leaders were planning an early Austrian *Anschluss* to acquire Burgenland without effort. Fürstenberg was not intimidated and counselled Berlin to maintain strict neutrality.

The Magyars' next broadside against Germany was slightly more conciliatory but still laced with veiled threats. In April 1920, Baron Kálmán Kánya, Hungary's future German envoy, dismissed Germany's professed neutrality as inconsequential, since Austrian policy was largely determined in Berlin. If Germany should persist in taking Austria's part in Burgenland, then German-Hungarian relations would be greatly compromised. Kánya demanded that Germany support Hungary against Austria. The stakes were high because should Hungary lose Burgenland, Germany would be blamed by Magyar public opinion. The Hungarian government would then have no choice but to seek an economic and political accommodation with France. German support for Hungary's claim in Burgenland would lead to close collaboration between Germany and Hungary. Eventually, a strengthened Germany would be able once again to banish French influence in the Danube

Basin and reimpose her own dominance. Kánya finally argued that only if she followed his advice could Germany ever hope to implement Naumann's *Mitteleuropa* plan.

Another diplomatic flurry followed Hungary's realization that Austria's Christian Socials had no intentions of accommodating Hungarian demands in Burgenland. In November of that year Foreign Minister Imre Csáky once again solicited Germany's support, arguing that this would benefit German unity, because Burgenland's sizeable Swabian population would link the German world to the west with Hungary's Swabians residing east of Burgenland. The German government was not impressed. About the same time, Furstenberg secretly assured his Austrian colleague that Germany would never entertain a settlement in Burgenland that did not fully accord with Austrian views. Undeterred by German rebuffs, Csáky persisted, albeit more moderately. He still hoped, however, to enlist active German support over Burgenland. Csáky requested that Germany mediate the dispute between Austria and Hungary, but Fürstenberg avoided the trap. Germany would not consider mediation unless also requested by Austria, but Fürstenberg tried to avoid antagonizing Hungary beyond recall. Hungarian-German relations in the future might become irreparably poisoned if Germany ignored Hungary's needs. He, therefore, recommended that his government not support Austria publicly, and even suggested that for the sake of Hungary's Swabians, an autonomous Burgenland under limited Hungarian sovereignty might not be a bad idea.[16]

Fürstenberg's conciliatory report leaked out to the German press, which loosed an indignant barrage at the Foreign Ministry. The *Vossische Zeitung* excoriated Fürstenberg for stabbing Austria in the back.[17] Germany's envoy in Vienna, Rosenberg, agreed. He considered it an outrage that Germany should permit a friendly nation, Austria, to be deprived of territory to which it was legally entitled. Rosenberg also pointed out shrewdly that no matter which side should win, the loser would inevitably blame Germany for its defeat.

The Entente Note of January 1921 underscored the urgency of the Burgenland problem and sharpened differences between Germany and Hungary. This divergence surfaced even before year's end, when the semi-official *Pester Lloyd* assailed Germany. In Fürstenberg's opinion, the anonymous article in *Pester Lloyd* was written by Foreign Minister Kánya, who accused Germany of imperialistic ambitions in the Danube Basin. Fürstenberg scornfully rejected the charge, called the Hungarian government perfidious, and recommended that Germany in some way punish Hungary for her insolence. He concluded that traditions and gratitude meant nothing to Hungary. She was motivated exclusively by egoism.[18] Although Fürstenberg usually was the more cautious of the two German diplomats in the region, on this occasion Rosenberg was conciliatory. In a confidential report he conceded that the manner in which the Burgenland crisis would be solved was bound to have far-reaching consequences for Hungarian-German relations. Germany should stay out of the Austro-Hungarian dispute. Therefore, the German government, public, and political parties must exercise utmost restraint. Over the centuries, Magyars and Austrians had learned how to deal with one another. Leaving them to settle the controversy without outside interference would be best for all the parties concerned. Yet Rosenberg was far from pleased with Magyar behaviour and performance. He remarked that no matter how favourable the Burgenland settlement might be for Hungary, the Magyars would sooner or later break their promises to the Swabians. He considered Hungary an unstable influence in the Danube region and urged Berlin not to permit that unreliable and volatile nation to enlarge its territory.

Fürstenberg had even greater qualms about the Magyars than his Vienna colleague. Influential Hungarian government circles, especially those in the Foreign Ministry, were planning to deceive Germany by reorienting Hungarian foreign policy to favour the Entente. Allegedly, these forces even contemplated a rapprochement with hated Rumania. Thus the Magyars hoped to gain Allied support for the retention of Burgenland. The Magyars were insincere, since they had shown not a shred of evidence in their various proposals to the Austrians that they truly desired an equitable settlement. With respect to the Swabians, the Magyars were plainly hoodwinking Bleyer with promises they never meant to keep. Chauvinistic Magyar officials violated Swabian privileges with impunity. Fürstenberg cornered Count Sigray, Burgenland's Hungarian Commissioner, during a dinner given by Prime Minister Teleki. Sigray's arrogant allusion to Sopron—originally and until recently a purely German community—as a Magyar city with a few German inhabitants, was offensive. He boasted that the Magyars would defend Burgenland to the very limit, that France no longer required Hungary to evacuate Burgenland. Since Sigray was a high-ranking and greatly trusted public figure, Fürstenberg naturally concluded that his views corresponded with official government policy.

The Magyars realized, of course, that their German offensive endangered future relations between the two countries, and might also antagonize Burgenland's Swabians, who looked askance at any insult of Germany. Hungary could hardly expect to prevail without their active support. Consequently, the Magyars tried to give some evidence of good will. Fürstenberg believed that recently Burgenland's Magyar authorities had been attempting to curtail the atrocities of Hungarian troops. Further, many

Hungarian Christian Socials regarded Germany as the key to Hungary's security and well-being, and hence refused as a matter of principle to join the shrill anti-German chorus then in progress. Surprisingly, they even demanded restoration of Bleyer's virtually defunct Ministry of Nationalities. Fürstenberg also noted that Gratz was every bit as influential in Hungary as Sigray, but Gratz was a devoted champion of a powerful German movement in Hungary.

Having lost any hope of attracting France's support in Burgenland, Hungarian statesmen curbed their anti-German inclinations. Instead of leveling threats, they decided to feign concern for Germany's interests. The Magyars announced that Germany stood in mortal peril of French encirclement. Hungary would perforce join France, unless Germany actively sought a solution in Hungary's favour in Burgenland. German newspapers printed alarming variants on this theme. If we offend Hungary, wrote the *München-Augsburger Abendzeitung,* France will make a scapegoat out of Germany and turn Hungary against us. Some day, Hungarian troops might well march into Vienna, and even beyond. Hungary also sent Bleyer on a mission to Germany. The Swabian leader was to lay Hungary's case before high-ranking German government officials. Both phases of Hungarian diplomacy misfired. The Germans were as unintimidated by Hungary's threats as they were unmoved by Magyar promises. Bleyer's reception in Berlin had been less than enthusiastic, and indicated that German officials set little store by his visit and his prestige. Bleyer's mission did convince the Magyars that the Germans were not seriously interested in Hungary's friendship or— mistakenly—in the welfare of Hungary's Swabians. Thus it seemed futile for Hungary to continue her current policy of Swabian conciliation. Once the Burgenland crisis was out of the way, the Magyars believed they might revert to a policy of total neglect with impunity. On a negative side, Bleyer's German trip also promoted the mistaken belief among the Austrians that Germany favoured the Magyars in the Burgenland controversy. All in all, Hungary's initiative seemed a resounding failure.

Only in one respect did Hungary's diplomacy achieve the Magyars' avowed aims and purposes. The Germans could not forgive Bleyer's apostasy in championing the Magyar viewpoint to the apparent detriment of the Swabian minority. They felt that Bleyer also disregarded Germany's economic and political interests in the Danubian area. The Magyars saw with great satisfaction that a gulf yawned between Bleyer, and his only possible future source of material and ideological support. The Magyars erroneously assumed that Germany's disenchantment with Bleyer was total and permanent. On this premise they proceeded to insult him in later years, with regrettable consequences.

During the remainder of 1921 until the plebiscite, Hungarian diplomacy forged ahead undeterred. The Magyars began to "suggest" that in the event of an expected Austrian *Anschluss,* Germany should "naturally" let Hungary keep Burgenland, as a magnanimous gesture from a former ally. Fürstenberg considered this suggestion naive. When these manoeuvres failed, the Magyars tried to persuade France to permit Hungary to keep Burgenland, lest the province fall into Germany's hands. Worse, the government let it be known that Germany was dangerous because its massive Pan-German propaganda in Burgenland. This ploy was designed both to alarm the Entente and to embarrass Germany in the eleventh hour into abandoning her neutrality in Hungary's favour. Such heavy-handedness merely attracted the opprobrium of German officials. Germans, by and large, had come to consider their former ally an opportunist bereft of all sense of proportion and character. A casual observer might conclude that Hungarian diplomacy had suffered a major setback. While it is true that the Magyars had incurred Germany's wrath and contempt, and their Austrian diplomacy had seemingly collapsed, they had also succeeded in fragmenting the alleged Pan-German menace by sowing suspicion and disunity among Germans, Austrians, and Swabians.

No study of this early phase in German-Hungarian relations would be complete without an account of the growing tensions besetting Swabians, Austro-Germans, and Reich Germans. The Swabians, at the time perhaps the least politicized German group in Europe, generally inclined to be German-Hungarians rather than *volksdeutsch.* Indeed, Germandom, especially the efficiently organized and politically and ethnically conscious Transylvanian Saxons, disdained the Swabians as a people not quite German; certainly indifferent to the prevailing German *Volksgeist.* The Swabians' Hungarophil sentiments at War's end explains why nationalistic firebrands, such as Brandsch, received short shrift from most Swabians. Loyalty to the Hungarian State, coupled with a certain fidelity to German cultural ideals, were concepts advocated by Bleyer and accepted by most Swabians. At first, Bleyer's formula suited them, and the Swabian leader, with his small elitist entourage, spoke for nearly all the Swabian rural—though not all urban—masses.

But Magyar persecutions and broken promises, as much as Pan-German agitations and Great-German blandishments from abroad, slowly and inexorably eroded Magyar credibility, and with it, Bleyer's semi-assimilationist policies. By the end of 1921, events had long since outstripped Bleyer and his followers, who still pursued their original aims in splendid isolation. Bleyer now found himself deeply compromised and vulnerable. Although an enthusiastic champion of German *Kultur,* he was nonetheless one of the very few German leaders not unreservedly dedicated to *gross-deutsch* objectives. Moreover, Bleyer favoured intimate German-Hungarian economic and political ties. His goals corresponded with the aspirations of Pan-Germans, albeit only coincidentally. In fact, Bleyer believed that Hungary would greatly benefit from associating with Germany, and entertained extravagant visions of a prosperous Hungary reunited with her lost territories thanks to her German connection. Unfortunately, Bleyer could not convince the nationalistic German public that a Swabian might reconcile two loyalties: one to his native land and one to the German *Volksgeist*. Most Germans only saw irreconcilable differences where Bleyer envisioned compromise and a fusion of interests. No wonder that the Germans distrusted him. They condemned Bleyer for having betrayed Germanism both at home and abroad. Most of the calumny arose from the Burgenland dispute, that great virus of German relations. The Hungarian government was alert to the opportunities for disturbing German unity. The Magyars exploited Bleyer's philosophy of restraint and compromise by using him as an intermediary in the Burgenland dispute. Far from contributing to the pacific settlement of the issue, Bleyer's amateurish efforts merely created an atmosphere of ill feelings and recriminations in the German camp.

By the middle of 1920, Bleyer's Hungarophilism had brought him into sharp conflict with German nationalists. The *Vossische Zeitung,* who saw Bleyer betraying the Swabians, clashed with the *Neue Post,* which dismissed such accusers as "German fanatics."[19] Bleyer fell under more suspicion after his Bavarian visit in December 1920, when he sought the aid of German sympathizers on behalf of Hungary's claims in Burgenland. He was rebuffed, but the Germans feared that his junkets might shake German unity. Bleyer next attempted to meet with high-ranking Foreign Ministry officials. Unfortunately, his efforts coincided with the Entente Note of 28 December 1920, a document which ordered Hungary to evacuate Burgenland for Austria. Bleyer's request seemed particularly inopportune in such a highly charged atmosphere and the Foreign Ministry peremptorily rejected it.

A few days later, Rosenberg dispatched his personal appraisal of Bleyer, a report which undermined Bleyer's good sense, if not his motives. Bleyer apparently believed that the loss of Burgenland would sound the death knell for isolated Germans in East-Central Europe. But Rosenberg believed that under Magyar rule Burgenland would never develop into a mighty bastion of Germandom. The West Hungarians would never obtain their promised political and cultural rights. As for Bleyer's assertion that Burgenland's unification with Austria would prejudice Hungary's remaining Swabians, they might suffer temporarily, but it was far more important for Germany to support her Austrian friend than to please Hungary and a few Swabians, if Germany wished to maintain the loyalty of all those Austrians who supported Germany's annexationist plans. Rosenberg urged the Ministry to exhort all German groups and politicians whom Bleyer had approached to demonstrate the greatest restraint and caution.

Fürstenberg seemed to regard Bleyer with greater favour, but a report of 19 January 1921 betrayed skepticism. Fürstenberg's "conversion" stemmed from a conversation with Gratz. Although Gratz was a native of Moson (Wieselburg) County and hence a Swabian, his upbringing was Transylvanian. To Fürstenberg, Gratz's Saxon background enhanced his German reliability. Fürstenberg particularly admired Gratz's handling of the Burgenland problem. The ambassador seemed malleable and willing to modify Hungary's rigid stand. Gratz had also expressed the need for a "strong German movement in Hungary...whose prerequisite [must be] the presence of a conscious German leader." Fürstenberg must have inferred from Gratz's conversation that he disapproved of Bleyer, who was Swabian-born and Swabian-bred.

> Gratz's statement brings to mind the old controversy between the Transylvanian Saxon deputies and the Swabian orientation of Bleyer and his adherents, who have never been considered 'full-fledged Germans' by the Saxons.[20]

Many Reich Germans apparently hoped for a change in Swabian leadership, with the mantle passing from the unreliable Bleyer to the more trustworthy shoulders of a *volksbewusst* "Saxon" such as Gratz.

The German government continued to treat Bleyer almost like a pariah. Fürstenberg informed his superiors that Bleyer had begged a consulate official to convey a private letter, addressed to Hugo Stinnes, a German industrialist, through diplomatic channels. The plea had been so urgent and insistent, that a flat refusal would have been tantamount to an overt insult. Bleyer urgently requested a brief interview for himself and his two confidants, Huber and Protestant bishop Scholtz. The object of the meeting was to solicit private German funds for the founding of a Swabian daily newspaper in Budapest and for the establishment of a Swabian economic organization. Bleyer tried to forestall the creation of a journal by German monied interests. Bleyer had heard about this, and it would have bypassed the Swabians entirely. He asserted that the Hungarian government knew and approved of his plan to contact Stinnes. Presumably, Fürstenberg ventured, the Magyars hoped that Bleyer would exhort German capitalists to influence the German government in Hungary's behalf. Although

Fürstenberg had no objections, he urged that the industrialist be advised in strictest confidence either to avoid Burgenland as a topic entirely, or to explain the futility of expecting German intervention. Berlin followed Fürstenberg's advice to the letter. On 3 March 1921, Fürstenberg dispatched a telegram to the Foreign Ministry:

> In a surprise move early today, at the instigation of the [Hungarian] Foreign Ministry, Bleyer, Ertus, and Scholtz, departed for Germany [to discuss] the Burgenland question, despite our warnings to them and to the Foreign Ministry that their mission was senseless and inopportune.[21]

It is no exaggeration to say that Bleyer and his companions invited censure by both Swabian and *reichsdeutsch* circles. They represented Swabian interests only in the most tangential manner, since their chief objective seemed satisfying the demands of the Hungarian government. Argue as they might that their good offices would earn Magyar confidence and engender a Magyar-Swabian rapprochement, the Bleyerites merely evoked both Magyar and German distrust.

Bleyer's German trip convinced Fürstenberg that Bleyer and Hungary spoke with one voice. He resented Hungary's encouragement of the pro-Magyar German press and Bleyer's embarrassing attempts to secure interviews with Germany's Foreign Minister through the rightist Dr. Zahnbrecher of Munich. Bleyer's choice as an intermediary was not surprising, because the Magyars had every reason to trust him. Bleyer's stand on the nationality issue as Minister of Nationalities defied German interests, undermined German education in Hungary, and endangered Swabian survival. Bleyer's influence with Austrian and German nationalists might dash Burgenland's unification with Austria.

For some inexplicable reason, nearly everyone assumed that Bleyer wielded influence with powerful German circles. This largely erroneous assumption accounts for much of Bleyer's vilification. Those threatened called him a Magyarone, a renegade, a "15% German," a throttler of German consciousness in Hungary, and a false leader who had re-Magyarized Hungary's German schools.[22] In a top-secret dispatch, Fürstenberg delivered the most devastating critique to date. Bleyer's insistence to secure Burgenland for Hungary was born of fanatic conviction and self-interest. His supporters he dismissed contemptuously—and inaccurately—as individuals scared of coming into conflict with the Magyar criminal judge, should they fail to support their "leader" unquestioningly. Fürstenberg revealed details of Bleyer's alleged secret plan: Selected Magyar-trained Swabian shock troops would resist Austrian forces after Hungarian forces had departed, seize Burgenland and annex it to Hungary. Fürstenberg was outraged by Bleyer's apparent plot for fratricidal strife among Germans. It would threaten German unity. Bleyer was a dangerous man indeed, because thanks to his eternal machinations he fomented schism between Magyars and Germans.[23]

The evidence strongly suggests that the Hungarian government succeeded in creating friction among the Germans, who felt uneasy lest they permanently alienate the troublesome and unreliable but strategically essential magyars. As a result, the Germans rendered only lip service to the Austrians, and even that in secret. Magyar diplomacy concentrated on keeping the two powers off balance and wrought internal havoc among the Germans. They alienated conservatives and socialists by persuading right-wing elements to support Hungary's claim against Austria. Austrian and German Social Democrats detested Horthy's Hungary, a circumstance the Magyars skillfully exploited in order to confound the Germans. Finally, by enlisting their own naive Swabian leaders in a pro-Hungarian campaign in return for nebulous concessions, the Magyars ensured that most Germans would regard them as traitors to the German cause.

Austro-Hungarian commercial relations reflected the tensions arising from the Burgenland controversy. Hungary exploited her advantageous position as a major food producer by extorting territorial concessions in West Hungary in exchange for provisions desperately needed by the Austrians. Right after the war trade was at a virtual standstill. Most transactions were conducted regionally on an *ad hoc* basis. Frequently, both sides resorted to smuggling. Hungary's first postwar commercial agreement with Austria was negotiated in April 1919, and ratified within one week, on the principle of simple exchange. In return for scarce consumer items, Hungary pledged to deliver 200 wagons of corn and over 300 heads of livestock to replenish Vienna's empty larder. Although Kun mistrusted Austria's friendly intentions, he hoped that feeding Lower Austria in return for manufactured products would create a better atmosphere for settling the Burgenland dispute in Hungary's favour. Unfortunately, the flow of material under the treaty never amounted to more than a trickle, due mainly to the imposition of an Allied economic blockade of Hungary. This draconic measure was designed to force Hungary to the negotiating table. Austria joined the blockade, partly because the Entente demanded it, and partly because the Austrian Socialists believed that if Hungarian bolshevism was not weakened, the dangerous ideology would soon spread into Austria.

Poor communications had surprisingly little to do with the breakdown of the treaty. In fact, the Austrians secretly preferred chaos, hoping to acquire Hungarian provisions through smuggling, greatly in evidence in Burgenland at that time. By the end of April 1919, all commercial traffic had terminated. Andor Fenyő, Hungary's Viennese envoy, said the American Military Mission was partly to blame for the impasse. It prohibited wine shipments from Hungary into Austria, while paper destined for Hungary was stalled in Marchegg, on the Austrian side of the frontier. In mid-May 1919, the Austrians attempted virtually to legitimize smuggling operations from Hungary. Austria's official foreign commerce clearinghouse, the *Warenverkehrsbüro,* had begun to conclude private—and illegal—agreements with Hungarian producers' associations, thus infringing on the Hungarian government's constitutional perquisites. (The Communist regime had given permission to Burgenlanders to negotiate trade agreements with Austria, but only within the framework of legally constituted autonomous trade delegations designed for that purpose). The Austrians had allegedly pledged to guarantee the flow of goods in both directions, at a time when traffic was officially completely stalled.[24]

The Kun regime made one more try to normalize commercial relations with Austria. This met with superficial success because on 12 June 1919, the two nations concluded a trade agreement resembling that of 3 April. Unfortunately, the second treaty turned out to be as ineffectual as the first. For all practical purposes, insignificant *ad hoc* arrangements and the by now familiar smuggling operations predominated. Austria clearly sought to convince Burgenlanders to entrust their economic future not with Hungary but with Austria, and it forced kun onto the offensive against the Swabians of Burgenland. Smuggling operations seriously undermined the prestige of his government, and it resorted to severe measures to arrest the abuse. However justified Kun might have been to maintain order in territories under his jurisdiction, these policing actions served to alienate West Hungary's swabians.

Austro-Hungarian economic relations remained strained even after Kun's ouster by conservative elements. Austrian Socialists feared right-wing radicalism nearly as much as they dreaded Communism. These fears, as well as the repercussions of the Burgenland dispute, compromised the establishment of normal trade relations. The first serious attempt at anything like a rapprochement occurred on 10 November 1919, the same day Gratz presented his credentials as ambassador to Renner. Trade relations, among other pressing matters, came under scrutiny. Gratz established the ground rules for Hungary's handling of the Burgenland dispute. Hungary would henceforth employ her sole trump card—Hungary's bountiful food supply, to preserve Burgenland. Renner saw Burgenland's importance to Austria in terms of foodstuffs. Gratz retorted that Austria needed the food surplus of all of Hungary. Should Austria take possession of West Hungary, it might well create an atmosphere between the two countries that would exclude Austria's access to Hungary's surplus food supplies. In his conversation with Austrian President Dr. Carl Seitz two weeks later, Gratz reiterated this stern warning. In the coming months it became only too clear that Hungary meant to fulfil Gratz's threats.

In view of Gratz's threats it is surprising that Hungary should have proffered a new solution favouring Austrian capital and discriminating against Hungary's infant native industries. Gratz's idea was to create an Austro-Hungarian free trade zone encompassing all agricultural and industrial commodities. At the time, this plan was roundly condemned by Hungary's industrialists, and more recently, by Marxist historians. Hungary's manufacturers felt threatened by the competition of efficient Austrian rivals, whereas the Marxists have accused Horthy of trying to abort Hungary's industrial development, curtail the growth of the proletariat, and nip a Communist revolution in the bud. At the time, however, Gratz's scheme seemed to be the only plausible alternative for bringing the Austrians to the conference table. On the eve of the Trianon Peace Conference the Magyars were trying desperately to settle with the Austrians, and if possible overcome their determination to acquire Burgenland.

As the new year of 1920 dawned, the Huszár regime became willing to resume normal trade relations with Austria, especially when the Hungarian delegation in Trianon received the Entente's peace terms. The Magyars lost vast territories and population groups in the North, East, and South; confirming a galling provision of the Treaty of St. Germain with Austria, Hungary was compelled to cede Burgenland. thenceforward, until the Hungarian Parliament's ratification of the peace instrument on 15 November 1920, Hungarian foreign policy aimed to persuade Austria to exchange Burgenland for a favourable Hungarian commercial policy. As Count Somssich, Hungary's foreign Minister asserted to Gratz, the government was prepared to make great sacrifices to achieve a friendly arrangement concerning West Hungary, even if it meant free trade or a customs union with Austria.[25] Consequently, immediately after Trianon, Gratz offered Austria unlimited free trade in exchange for West Hungary, or at least, for advance acceptance of the Burgenland plebiscite results.

The Austrians refused since they believed that the Peace Conference, sanctified through two separate Treaties, had clearly established Austria's claim to the disputed region. They refused to entertain any plan that contained restrictions and also declined to sign a long-term agreement. In the end, Hungary bowed to the seemingly inevitable and consented to a six-month trade agreement with provisions reminiscent of the abortive trade treaty of the previous year. As before, the pact turned out to be ineffective, largely because both countries lacked the requisite material resources to deliver meaningful quantities of merchandise. Hungary also hoped to convince the Austrians to exchange Burgenland's vegetable plots, vineyards, and Swabian peasants for bountiful deliveries of Hungarian wheat and livestock. Renner saw through Hungary's transparent manoeuvres and declared unequivocally that under no circumstances would he use West Hungary's Swabians as pawns in a commercial deal with Hungary. He called on the Magyars to settle the Burgenland issue once and for all on the basis of Entente demands and withdraw their forces from the region.

After Trianon, Hungary's Austrian strategy was to try and thwart the Treaty by concluding a bilateral agreement, under which Austria would renounce its gains in return for massive commercial and other concessions by Hungary. Magyar persistence in the face of past failure may be ascribed to the fact that on this occasion Austria wavered, owing to her greatly diminished food reservoirs. Hungary had one other reason for pursuing a commercially-oriented diplomacy. Socialist influence was waning, and new Austrian elections in October 1920 portended a Christian Social victory. Eagerly anticipating this change, the Magyars hoped to derive great advantages from a politically congenial regime in Vienna. A prudent Austrian policy now would facilitate normal relations with the new regime and predispose the Austrian public to concessions. As the current treaty would lapse in January 1921, the Magyars offered to renew it, even to improve it with a most-favoured-nation clause. The Socialists insisted on a six-month extension of the existing agreement. Certain of a Christian Social victory, the Magyars paid little heed. Behind the government's back they negotiated secretly with Christian Social leader Seipel. The Magyars promised to support the prelate and his Party fully if they won the impending election, in return for a pledge to renounce Austria's claim to West Hungary.[26]

The latest agreement with the Austrian Socialists was perfunctory and a decided failure. By harvest time, Hungary paradoxically faced a major food shortage, thanks to Austrian machinations. As Baron Frigyes Villani, Hungary's delegate to the Inter-allied Mission for West Hungary in Sopron, indicated to Foreign Minister Teleki,

> In inspecting the borders between the county of Sopron and Austria, I found that smuggling assumed frightful proportions. Unless we double at once the frontier and customs guards, it is to be feared that the greater part of the harvest will be smuggled out into Austria and, in consequence, Western Hungary will face a serious food shortage.[27]

Budapest failed to arrest this trend, convinced that a Christian Social victory in October would stop Austria's collusion with smugglers.

Christian Social successes at the polls justified Magyar expectations. By the end of the month, the Mayr regime had been swept into power in Austria, prompting a flurry of activity by Austrian and Hungarian officials alike. Austrian Minister of Commerce Edward Heinl offered to resume negotiations with Hungary at once. Gratz dispatched a jubilant telegram to Foreign Minister lmre Csaky. The psychological moment seemed to have arrived when economic negotiations between Austria and Hungary could be seriously considered. He proposed to invite Heinl and his entourage to Budapest, and hoped that ways and means would be found to extend the expiration date of the existing treaty. He also suggested that the forthcoming agenda contain the question of facilitating Hungarian food exports to Austria.

Hungarian hopes for a speedy and favourable settlement of the Burgenland controversy now rose, underscored by the continuing deterioration in Austria's food situation. During his sojourn in Vienna, Csáky obtained ample proof of the Austrians' desperate plight. Richard Weisskirchner, a highly-placed Christian Social, appealed for at least 300 carloads of flour and for the immediate resumption of potato shipments. In responding, Csáky blundered. Whether food shipments would be resumed or not, and whether the trade agreement would be renewed or not, depended entirely on Austria's willingness to resolve the Burgenland issue in Hungary's favour. Weisskirchner capitulated and agreed to a plebiscite as a precondition for further Hungarian food deliveries. Hungary appeared victorious. Weisskirchner, however, had evaded the trap by stipulating that in view of the extreme importance of the issue he would first have to seek the concurrence of the Christian Social Party caucus. Momentarily, the fate of Burgenland and its Swabians seemed to rest on the slender reed of Weisskirchner's stipulation.

Austria smouldered with indignation at the tactlessness, if not cynicism, of the Magyars. While the Hungarian Foreign Ministry invented complex fiscal and procedural arrangements for the delivery of provisions, the Austrians formulated a policy that would disavow Weisskirchner's pledge without an outright refusal. By 11 November 1920, Gratz despaired with vague Austrian promises for a speedy reply. He wired Csáky that

> The present situation did not seem promising, and simple stylistic changes in the assurances heretofore given would not represent a tangible concession.

Csáky's response was similarly somber:

The Christian Socialist leaders must be told that without a prompt and satisfactory solution of the question of Western Hungary, lasting good relations between the two countries either in the economic or in the political field were inconceivable.[28]

As a result of indignant Hungarian demarches, each more bitter than the last, the Austrians finally lost faith in bilateral talks. Mayr informed Gratz that negotiations would continue only if the initiative came from a member of the Sopron Allied Mission. As expected, the Magyars considered Mayr's new tactic a betrayal of a faithful wartime ally into the hands of their former enemies. Csáky unsuccessfully insisted on continuing bilateral negotiations, without involving the Entente, and he advised Gratz accordingly.

As the end of 1920 drew close, the situation became increasingly more acrimonious. In a conversation with Felix Parcher, Hungary's chargé d'affaires in Vienna, Mayr admitted that Austria found Hungary's oft-stated prerequisites for friendly commercial relations unthinkable. Many reasons explained why Austria could not part with Burgenland. The Austrians bolstered this diplomatic rebuff with another slap at Hungary. On 1 December 1920, A. Grunberger, Minister of Austria's Public Food Supplies, backed by Mayr and the Christian Social Party, informed Gratz that Austria considered the pending flour agreement null and void unless the Magyars agreed to certain changes. The price must be reduced from the stipulated 80 crowns per kg. to the prevailing world market price of only 67 crowns. Austria currently could purchase wheat abroad at normal prices and hence no longer depended on the inflated Hungarian market. Furthermore, overpayment would in all likelihood create anti-Hungarian feelings in Austria. The Magyars had been thoroughly outmanoeuvred. On 3 December 1920, Hungary consented to deliver 300 carloads of flour under Austrian stipulations. After additional exchanges, the wheat agreement was finally ratified by both parties. This may have been a relatively minor episode, but it dramatized Hungary's inability to pursue her Austrian "wheat diplomacy" effectively. This ended any chance to deal with the offended Austrians.

Relations deteriorated further at the end of December, when the Entente confronted Hungary with the peremptory demand to surrender Burgenland to the Allied mission in Sopron. The allies would thereupon turn over the territory to Austria. Foreign Minister Teleki strongly suspected that this move had been made upon the initiative of Austria with a view to precluding the possibility of direct negotiations. The Magyars were shocked to learn that the Entente request had been prompted by three separate Austrian notes demanding the possession of West Hungary. The next day Teleki was furiously considering whether to refuse signature of the commercial treaty recently negotiated with Austria. He urged Gratz to obtain a clear statement from Austria on this question. Mayr told Gratz that he had no knowledge whatever of the decision of the Conference of Allied Ambassadors and that he was in no way responsible for their decision. He admitted, however, that after taking office he had instructed his diplomats to insist on Austrian rights in West Hungary, although direct negotiations with Hungary under Allied mediation might be feasible. Mayr also conceded making a similar declaration personally to Pietro Torretta, Italy's Envoy Extraordinary to Vienna, just before Christmas. Gratz thereupon demanded that Mayr negotiate directly immediately, with or without Allied sanction. Mayr evaded by pleading for more time. Even at best, the Austrian government could only discuss frontier rectifications such as, for instance, those in connection with the village of Nagyczenk. Wanting a satisfactory Austrian reply, Gratz delivered a strongly worded note concerning the utmost gravity of the catastrophic shift in Austro-Hungarian relations. Certain irresponsible elements in Hungary would forcibly resist any Austrian occupation and he feared the consequences. Instead of serving as a bridge, Burgenland would become a wall separating Austria and Hungary, and all hopes for close economic relations would be dashed forever. With Burgenland lost, the Magyars would refuse to maintain protective laws for Hungary's few remaining Swabians; this, too, would irretrievably poison Austro-Hungarian relations. In the end, Hungary reluctantly signed the commercial treaty, but it never went into effect. Prime Minister Teleki suppressed it after obtaining further evidence implicating Mayr in continuing West Hungarian intrigues, a policy continued by Schober.

After Teleki's demission in April 1921, Bethlen continued Hungary's wheat diplomacy. He dangled attractively priced food deliveries before the eyes of Austria's new Chancellor Schober. Bethlen engaged in horse-trading. Would Schober be content with a certain portion of Burgenland and be willing to defer occupying the region to be ceded indefinitely? At first, Bethlen offered to part with two-thirds of West Hungary, later with three-fourths of it. Schober insisted on all of it immediately. Matters became even more complicated when the Allies made Yugoslavia's evacuation of the Pécs-Baranya region conditional upon West Hungary's cession to Austria. Before Italy's intervention in October 1921, Austria and Hungary had become totally alienated and reached a complete impasse. Talks had terminated, guerrilla fighting had erupted, and official trade was at a standstill. Until 1922, after the plebiscite had settled the Burgenland issue, no further Austro-Hungarian negotiations took place on any level.

Hungary's commercial relations with Germany, the other German-speaking nation, developed along somewhat more favourable lines than with Austria. At least until the mid-twenties, trade was extremely modest, due mainly to distance, disrupted communications, and Germany's impoverishment. Hungary enjoyed two initial advantages. Firstly, by tacit agreement, Germany's commercial pact of 1906 with the Austro-Hungarian Empire continued in force. There, both parties had enjoyed most-favoured-nation privileges. In addition, as a special benefit to Hungary, Germany had waived the usual stringent hygienic inspection standards generally imposed on imported livestock and meat products, which enabled Hungarian producers and packers to compete in the German market. Hungary's other advantage accrued gradually as a consequence of the German inflation, which enabled the Magyars to reap considerable benefits.[29]

The first noteworthy German-Hungarian contact occurred only after Kun's demise. In November 1919, Hungary established a consulate in Berlin, with orders to seek a commercial agreement. Conditions seemed to favour an understanding. Whereas Hungary desperately needed a market for her agricultural surpluses, Germany sought to recapture her former dominance in the Balkans.[30] Germany offered Hungary a great variety of badly needed consumer products at reasonable prices. The Hungarians thought that Germany would soon become Hungary's most dependable purchaser of agricultural products and a major supplier of consumer commodities. The Magyars were understandably shocked and disappointed, therefore, when in February 1920 Germany renounced the 1906 trade pact. Since the Dual Monarchy had ceased to exist Germany could no longer maintain the fiction of a treaty with its former members. Indeed, Germany simultaneously terminated similar agreements with Austria and Czechoslovakia. To cushion the shock, the Germans suggested that they immediately launch new talks to conclude a provisional trade treaty on vital commodities. The Magyars tried to convince the Germans to restore the 1906 arrangement with Hungary alone, or at least to conclude a most-favoured-nation agreement. But the Germans refused, and the Magyars had to accede. On 1 June 1920, Germany and Hungary concluded a short-term compromise agreement on the basis of most-favoured-nation principles, involving the exchange of all types of Hungarian food products and a great variety of badly needed German consumer items and industrial commodities at reasonable prices. As a gesture of reciprocal good will both parties agreed to exchange essential raw materials.[31]

The pact disappointed high Magyar expectations. Firstly, it would not commence until 1 January 1921. Secondly, during 1920 Germany concluded similar agreements with Austria and Czechoslovakia, Hungary's chief antagonists. The Magyars realized they had been overly optimistic about Germany as a favoured trading partner. The Magyars' disappointment rivaled their chagrin because they had been unable to woo German support for their position in Burgenland, in exchange for preferential treatment in food shipments. Thirdly, although trade between the two countries improved steadily until 1923, the volume was never sufficient to please the Magyars.

Despite this, the agreement proved beneficial to both Hungarian agriculture and industry. Hungary found an outlet for her agricultural and livestock surpluses, and it placed essential raw materials at the disposal of Hungary's infant industries. Thus, modest though it was, Germany's contribution to Hungary's postwar economic revival was sufficient to merit prolonged debate among the Magyars. They agonized about tying Hungary's humble economic potential to the formidable German political-economic bandwagon. A favourable argument arose as early as April 1921, when Germany's uncooperative attitude in Burgenland annoyed Hungary. At the time, Germany relaxed its export regulations on various strategic raw materials indispensable for Hungary's industrial recovery.[32] This concession was Germany's way of salving the thoroughly discouraged Magyars.

The trouble with the trade agreement was, of course, that the Germans' main intention was not helping Hungary but to pursue their own long-range economic aims in the Danube Basin. After the first few euphoric months the Germans began to curtail imperceptibly the import of Hungarian agricultural commodities at a time when they were increasing their shipments of industrial products into Hungary. The Germans began to find convenient pretexts. Hungarian wheat was considered poor compared with grain from the Americas; produce of equal or better quality was available from France, Spain, and elsewhere at a lesser price; an essential Hungarian export item such as paprika was barred for nearly eighteen months on some technicality.[33] Other Hungarian export items encountered similar difficulties. Germany's caprice was far from erratic. It rested on sound psychological principles. The Germans wished to infiltrate Hungary economically and pursued a policy of confusion to conceal their aggression. Before long, the Magyars hardly knew whether to consider the Germans as benefactors or as exploiters. At all events, Hungary needed (or thought it did) Germany's good offices with Austria in Burgenland, and neither Teleki nor Bethlen wished to offend Germany by revoking the agreement. Bethlen did introduce a limited import ban on all industrial products—a policy he applied with vigour only to Austria and Czechoslovakia, but to Germany hardly at all. As a result, Hungary's trade balance with Germany failed to improve. Although the volume of overall trade increased by nearly 50% between 1920 and 1921, Hungary's imports from Germany exceeded exports by 48% in 1920, and by nearly 51% by 1921.[34]

Germany's policy generated increasing debate and controversy among the Magyars. They wondered whether Hungary's interests could be reconciled with the dynamic and aggressive aims of Germany's diplomacy and commerce. Hungary's agriculturalists generally favoured the German connection, whereas the fledgling industrialists opposed it. The largely agricultural Swabians enthusiastically endorsed any movement, be it ever so slight, that augured a Germanophil orientation. They hoped to gain more than mere material recompense, seeing Germany as their champions against Hungary's de-Germanizing policies.

Considering the situation from the vantage point of harmonious Magyar-Swabian relations, the immediate postwar era was a dismal failure. Hungary's dealings with her two German wartime allies also languished. Magyar-inspired interventions by Swabian intermediaries in Austria and Germany failed to engender friendly feelings for Hungary, save among special interest groups with an axe to grind. With Austria, Hungary was sharply at odds over Burgenland, a bitter territorial dispute which poisoned relations for years. With Germany, Hungary never collided, as with Austria, but fundamental political and philosophical differences effectively separated the two nations. Hungary could not even achieve significant economic accommodations with her former allies. Despite a clever and ruthless diplomacy—perhaps because of it—Hungary stood alone after the war. She was abandoned, isolated, or encircled not only by her foes but even by her former confederates. The Magyars neither forgot nor forgave alleged Austro-German perfidy. This is of the utmost importance, for it determined Hungary's subsequent opportunism and cynicism. It also sheds light on the reasons for the Swabians' cavalier treatment. Having expected the moral, political, and economic support of their former Germanic allies in vain, the Magyars were disillusioned to learn that they had no interest whatever in compensating Hungary for her wartime sacrifices. Austria was willing and eager to cannibalize Hungarian territory in conjunction with the victorious French, an action considered outrageous by the Magyars, yet unopposed by the Germans. Germany was no better, for it concluded commercial deals with hostile Czechoslovakia, on terms no less favourable than with the Magyars. Further, Hungary had a long-range security problem. A potentially powerful Germany threatened the integrity of a small nation such as Hungary. The peril was magnified by popular Austrian sentiments for an *Anschluss* with Germany, which conjured up nightmares of a mightily augmented German empire ensconced on the very doorsteps of defenseless

Hungary.

Under these circumstances the Magyars decided to minimize their risks by at least eliminating the incipient internal German menace. It may be true that even had Austria and Germany shown greater consideration for Hungary, her Swabians would still have been persecuted as a distinct ethnic group. Their long-range survival might still have been seriously compromised, for Hungary was determined to become a homogeneous nation state. But in view of their former allies' apparent unconcern even for Swabian welfare, the Magyars proceeded to Magyarize the remaining Swabians swiftly and resolutely. In effect, this was merely a continuation of official policy at least since 1907, if not 1868. It was to permeate Magyar public and official thinking, and with the exception of minor aberrations, set the tone for Magyar-Swabian-German affairs for the remainder of the interwar period.

CHAPTER IV

THE EARLY HORTHY ERA; THE SWABIAN MINORITY PROBLEM BEGINS (1919 - 1922)

When Huszár relieved Friedrich as Prime Minister in November 1919, Hungary's external and domestic difficulties seemed wellnigh insurmountable. Neither Huszár nor any of his immediate heirs could cope with them. Hungary was thoroughly isolated. No diplomatic gambit had any chance of success. Huszár had been unable to solve Hungary's dispute with Austria over West Hungary. Even Gratz, Hungary's most astute diplomat, could not brighten his nation's bleak prospects. Hungary's leaders had to look elsewhere to resolve existing problems, since it appeared unlikely that surrounded Hungary might influence events in Central Europe. Huszár, as well as Simonyi-Semadam and Teleki in the months to come, had little choice but to change tactics. For the time being, it appeared far more profitable to influence events by applying domestic remedies where they might do the most good.

The Burgenland controversy was one external problem which might lend itself to such an indirect solution. The Swabians, especially those residing in West Hungary, fretted because Law #4044, a statute they had greeted with so much hope and enthusiasm, turned out to be a dead letter. Bleyer's pleas to activate the Law through enabling decrees had fallen on deaf ears. Nothing could breathe life into the inanimate statute, because Friedrich had ignored Bleyer's appeals. Huszár therefore resolved to eliminate what seemed to be a mere technical obstacle to a Hungarian-Swabian entente—or at least the semblance of one—because such an understanding gained importance as Hungary's hopes for an amicable settlement with Austria and the Entente faded.

It is far from surprising, therefore, that the very first of these enabling acts aimed to assuage the Swabians' greatest complaint, the school problem. The regulation issued by the Ministry of Education and Religion embraced minority kindergartens, elementary, and the continuation schools, constituting the backbone of the predominantly rural Swabian educational system in Hungary. Unfortunately, the new ruling attempted to please everyone, at once promising too much and too little. Casual observers were led to believe that henceforth every non-Magyar child in Hungary could be educated in his own mother tongue until his sixteenth birthday. In fact, the new statute was emasculated by hidden caveats and complexities. Minority schools were not mandatory. At least twenty parents in each community had to demand instruction in a given non-Magyar tongue. Further, only state and community schools were obliged to obey the law. Once a school board accepted the parents' recommendation to adopt a non-Magyar language, then reading, writing, arithmetic, religion, singing, and spelling had to be taught in the pupil's mother tongue. The language of instruction in all other subjects was to be optional, except that Magyar had to be a compulsory subject past second grade. Where the majority of the population spoke Magyar, or even where only twenty Magyar-speaking school children could be found in the community, any or all subjects could be taught optionally either in any number of non-Magyar languages (technically up to five); or in both Magyar and the non-Magyar language or languages, depending on the wishes of the local school board or parents' conferences. Where insufficient numbers of non-Magyars resided, arrangements were to be made for parallel classes in both or more languages. Where there was only a scattering of non-Magyars, a few hours of instruction in the minority language were to be provided each week. Controversies were to be settled by specially appointed deputy school inspectors with full powers to dispose of all minority education cases. Only the Minister of Education would have the right to overrule them.[1]

In theory the law seemed fair and enlightened. Children in ethnically mixed communities might have as many as five different school systems, instructing in as many languages. None of these schools had to be Magyar, if fewer than twenty Magyar children of school age resided in the community. In practice, these multiple school systems seldom functioned properly, due to a lack of adequate financial and physical resources in typical Hungarian village environments. Furthermore, most of Hungary's educational system was confessional. Hence the new law, which did not extend to church schools, had very little practical impact. Even in the few instances where the statute might have been partially applicable, it was a dead letter. Taking advantage of a loophole in the law which permitted non-Magyar children to attend Magyar schools if they so desired, Magyar or Magyarized officials all too often by-passed parents' groups to influence children directly.

Within a very short time complaints, both of a general and a specific nature, began to pour into Bleyer's Ministry of Nationalities and to the editorial offices of the *Neue Post*. A reader complained because clerics, teachers, and other Swabian leaders boasted that thanks to their efforts entire Swabian communities had become thoroughly Magyarized.[2] Nothing documents the complaint more graphically than the events in Törökbálint. The predominantly Swabian parents' conference had voted to establish German instruction in the elementary school. The village priest denounced the parents' decision. The school principal supported Weichert and stated that Bleyer was no teacher and therefore unfamilar with local conditions. Apparently, the Swabian parents cheered Bleyer, defied their local officials, and continued to insist successfully on German instruction for their children.[3]

Bleyer intervened personally with the Minister of Education on at least one occasion, when distraught parents sought his assistance. The Swabians in Elek complained that under Rumanian military occupation they had established a German elementary school at their own expense. When the Magyars reoccupied Elek, they at once transformed their school into a Magyar institution. Complaints were unavailing. Bleyer thereupon demanded that the Minister restore the German school and that the inspector responsible for the violation be transferred to a purely Magyar region. This was one of the few instances where Bleyer successfully redressed a violation of the law.

The enabling laws issued by the other Ministries took over ten months to materialize in some instances. None brought the Swabians close to their desired goals. In every case the Ministries attempted to create the illusion that a major reform was in the offing. In fact, they engaged in thinly disguised subterfuge. One by one, the various Ministries released regulations governing the use of non-Magyar languages in official life, as well as rules relating to the employment of non-Magyar personnel by government agencies.[4] The latter allowed no Ministry to refuse employment to a Hungarian citizen of non-Magyar background. This was redundant since laws already protected every Hungarian citizen's civil rights. The new regulations further stipulated that regional Ministry officials would have to learn the predominant non-Magyar language or languages in their respective jurisdictions within two years. This ruling was ineffectual. Senior officials might either request transfers, or else engage junior personnel conversant with the minority language of the region. As a direct result, the number of temporary translators employed by the various Ministries grew in number, especially in Burgenland. One of the provisions, that minority regions be adequately staffed with personnel familiar with the local language was thus satisfied, but the spirit of the law was subverted. The Magyars excelled in the art of legal deception. Their laws frequently expressed exalted sentiments but little else. They knew how to execute the laws when pressed to do so, but in such a manner that the would-be beneficiaries were worse off than before. The enabling laws are good examples in this respect.

Most of the enabling acts were ignored, while others were introduced but submerged or left to languish. The Hungarian government apparently had no intentions of inaugurating an era that might threaten the primacy of the Magyar language and culture. Much to the Swabians' chagrin, the Magyars refused to agree with their oft-repeated plaint that Hungarian patriotism had nothing to do with proficiency in the Magyar language but rather with observing the supra-national spirit of St. Stephen, Hungary's medieval Westernizer.[5] The Magyar counter-argument emerged in the wording of one of the enabling acts: "We cannot be totally unbending and must permit a certain degree of permissiveness [in granting linguistic privileges], but we must make certain we do not commit ourselves irrevocably for the future."[6] The evidence suggests that neither Huszár nor his predecessors cared to promote effective minority laws. As one observer noted, all the enabling acts shared one common characteristic: none was put into effect.[7] Reluctance at the highest level of government filtered down to the lower echelons of the various executive arms. Tacitly encouraged from above, lesser officials obstinately refused to establish linguistic practices that could be construed as precedents by the various nationalities. Nationwide opposition to any concessions to the minorities grew so that by October of that year the Praesidium was ready to consider the terms of Law #4044 in the more conservative spirit of the 1868 Nationality Law.

In view of the growing hostility toward the minorities in general and to himself in particular, Bleyer had no choice but to resign his portfolio as Minister of Nationalities.[8] Before relinquishing his post on 16 December 1920, Bleyer issued a position paper on the nationality question, a document notable for its illuminating candour. It would be sheer folly for Hungary to revive her repressive prewar nationality policies. The war, the revolutions, the various peace treaties, no less than the ethnic policies of Hungary's neighbours, had combined to create a new national awareness among the minorities. Consequently, it was no longer possible to pacify them with mere bagatelles. The concessions granted Hungary's remaining minorities should relate solely to their own aspirations. The Magyars had to evaluate their own desires to regain lost territories and peoples. Bleyer claimed to balance the poles of the 1868 Nationality Law, which had not gone far enough, with Jászi's autonomy law, which had gone too far.

The steady growth of Magyar ill-feelings toward their minorities derived from two major sources. When the war ended, vast stretches of Hungarian soil with large non-Magyar populations were left in enemy hands. The

Magyars believed that their former subjects were being held captive, and that given the opportunity, they would eagerly rejoin Hungary. As the months passed and the fragmented nationalities showed no signs of revolting against their new masters, the Magyars began to be plagued with doubts as to their fundamental integrity. In June 1920, when the Peace Treaty of Trianon confirmed Hungary's territorial and population losses, Magyar suspicion against the allegedly faithless non-Magyars turned into anger, even hatred. Now living across Hungary's frontiers, they became targets of Magyar verbal venom; but the remaining non-Magyars still on Hungarian soil were the whipping boys against whom the Hungarian state apparatus vented its spleen. To a certain degree the Swabians—but not the seceded Transylvanian Saxons—escaped Magyar indignation. But Trianon was a turning point in Magyar-Swabian relations as well. Never again would the Magyars trust a non-Magyar ethnic group residing within Hungary. Right after Trianon, when the Burgenland crisis grew and Swabian support was crucial, the Magyars embarked on a self-defeating course of action. Extravagant promises became ambiguously worded ineffectual nationality laws. When abuses evoked Swabian protests, Magyar apprehensions grew that even their "reliable" Swabians were not to be trusted any longer. A state of paranoia came to grip the Magyars. Intensified oppression merely speeded the deprivation the Magyars feared most after Trianon—that of Burgenland. In almost classic style, the tragedy spun itself out. After this loss, with its approximately 225,000 unprotesting German-speaking inhabitants, the Swabians were to lose whatever shred of credibility they still had with the Magyars. Driven by lust for revenge, no less than by feelings of insecurity at the thought of harbouring a still relatively large and potentially dangerous minority, the Magyars throttled their irksome German minority in every possible way. It is no exaggeration to say that the disappointments of Trianon and Burgenland laid the foundation for subsequent ethnic mistreatment of the Swabians. It reflected the psychological frustration of the Magyars that this occurred even when Hungary's political and economic interests should have dictated a far more lenient Swabian policy. The threatened Magyars preferred to risk material impoverishment, even extinction, at the hands of powerful Slavic and Germanic adversaries, rather than surrender their claim to the principle of Magyar supremacy in the Danube Basin. The supranational character of the Crown of St. Stephen was to be sacred, as was the righteousness of their own dominance of the alleged lesser peoples inhabiting that realm.

In order to salvage from the shambles of war whatever little they could, the Magyars adopted certain countermeasures just before Trianon. Although they had lost about 90% of their non-Magyar population, not to mention millions of Magyars, the prevailing situation was only *de facto* and hence still subject to recognition and affirmation by the Peace Conference. In the interim the Magyars made every effort to gain time by postponing a confrontation as long as possible, and persuade their former subjects and remaining minorities to remain true to the Crown of St. Stephen. To execute this plan, the government instigated widespread "spontaneous" outbursts of indignation against the victorious occupying powers.[9]

One of the first of these protest meetings took place on 31 December 1919 in Gólyavár, where delegates representing all of Hungary's nationalities assembled to protest against the Entente's anti-Hungarian designs and acclaim Bleyer's minority policies.[10] Every speaker had only one cherished aim—to remain with Hungary—but only if the government provided effective assurances that minority rights would henceforth be protected. Johannes Huber blamed Hungarian Liberalism for all the current nationality strife. Until 1867 there had been no ethnic problems in Hungary. After that, the Liberals introduced the Nationality Law, which churned up national emotions and engendered ethnic strife. Huber recommended that the nation return to the hallowed supra-national Christian ideals embodied by Stephen the Saint.

The surprise speaker at the meeting was the Transylvanian Saxon delegate Printz, who made a startling allegation. The Transylvanian Saxon secession to Rumania took place at the town of Mediasch (Medgyes) some months back. Printz claimed this had been nothing more than a swindle engineered by Brandsch and a small group of inexperienced youngsters. The bulk of the Saxons still longed to return to the Hungarian fold. Daniel Erlemann, representing southern Hungary's Swabians, many of whom lived under provisional Yugoslav rule, reaffirmed the loyalty of his people to Hungary, provided they would receive a just administration from the Magyars. Indeed, the delegates, assembled chiefly for the purpose of pledging allegiance to Hungary, focused their attention on extorting concessions instead. Their chief resolution insisted that the Hungarian government unequivocally declare its intention to render the nationalities their traditional rights, and provide the administrative machinery whereby these privileges would be assured. Finally, the conference requested a greater share in public life for the minorities. These resolutions were conveyed to Count Albert Apponyi, chief delegate to the Peace Conference, and to Prime Minister Huszár.

Undoubtedly, the Conference enjoyed government encouragement, even its blessing. The Magyars could not foresee, of course, that the enterprising Bleyer would usurp the proceedings for his own ends, simultaneously purporting to serve Hungary's interests. He apparently sought to forge an entente comprising all of Hungary's minorities, an association representing nearly one million non-Magyars in Hungary alone and many millions more abroad. Bleyer had demonstrated his influence in minority circles by producing a large retinue of faithful spokesmen to do his bidding, including a loyal Saxon favouring reunion with Hungary. It was no doubt Bleyer's eventual intention to head an all-Hungarian minority movement. Then, at the price of securing ironclad guaranties, he would lead them back to a reconstructed supra-national Greater Hungary. Far from being soothed, the Magyars branded Bleyer as potentially dangerous. This stigma was to dog his footsteps until the end of his days. The Magyars could hardly ignore this determined and influential man, so they used him whenever they could. At the same time, however, they were mindful never to conclude meaningful agreements with him.

When Bleyer proposed an amalgamation of all minority groups, the government had no choice but to encourage it. On 8 January 1920, an all-Hungarian minority association was formed.[11] Although intimately involved in its planning, Bleyer avoided the limelight. Ferenc Jehlicska, the Slovak leader, became President. The Praesidium was to comprise one elected member for each Hungarian minority—Swabian, Ruthenian, Slovak, Rumanian, South Slav, and Zips German from northeastern Slovakia. The new association had two major goals: to preserve Hungary's integrity, and to ensure equal rights for her minorities. Only a few weeks later, the group held its giant rally at Gólyavár to protest against continuing Entente pressure to deprive Hungary of her seceded territories.[12] One of the most ambitious of these protest meetings took place in Hungary's Upper House, attended by representatives of all the minority groups. On 30 January the delegates dispatched a note to the Victorious Powers, deploring the separation of the various ethnic groups from Hungary and demanding plebiscites to be held in the regions ceded to the Successor States. The delegates particularly resented the fact that their co-nationals would become citizens of countries with inferior cultures and thus risk the loss of their cherished national traditions.

About the same time, there were other protests involving Swabians. The Union of South-Hungarians, South-Hungarian Germans, and Catholic South Slavs circulated a joint memorandum protesting the cession of their respective regions to Yugoslavia. Similar complaints arose from the West Hungarian counties of Moson, Vas and Sopron. Although the Treaty of St. Germain had assigned parts of these regions to Austria, the mixed Swabian, Croatian, and Magyar population strenuously opposed the cession, at least according to the Hungarian government. The Magyars stressed that a unanimous declaration of loyalty by Mosonites was the more significant since that county was inhabited almost exclusively by Swabians.[13] Although the texts of these representations were strongly reminiscent of Hungarian Foreign Ministry propaganda releases, and although the lists were carefully "supervised" by the Hungarian gendarmerie, there can be little doubt that the Swabians, if not the other nationalities, were eager for a time to avoid coming under the jurisdiction of nations and regimes they considered odious.

All of these meetings—some undoubtedly spontaneous, others elaborately staged by the panicky Hungarian government—had but one purpose: to persuade the wavering non-Magyars to reject the uncertainties of life under regimes as yet untried and to cast their lot with the Magyars. It is so much more puzzling that when Hungary's peace delegation at Trianon had the opportunity to appeal to the former minorities over the heads of their new masters, they failed to do so. Worse still, the Magyars literally went out of their way to convince the former subject peoples that they had exercised prudent judgment by seceding. In an ill-advised oration to the Supreme Council on 16 January 1920, Count Apponyi endeavoured to implant the notion that Hungary's former subjects were unable to assume self-determination because of their cultural and political backwardness. At the same time, he wished to convey a favourable image of Magyar culture. After declaring that Hungary's non-Magyar nationalities were socially and politically inferior to the Magyar population, Apponyi proceeded to introduce statistical evidence to support his contention. He pointed out, for example, that 80% of the Magyars, as distinct from only about 60% of the Serbs, and 33% of the Rumanians, were literate. Those who had passed the equivalent of the French baccalaureat examination, numbered 84% among the Magyars, who represented only 54.5% of the population. The proportion of Rumanians was only 4%, even though they constituted 16% of the total population. In the case of the Serbs, their high school graduate population came to only 1%, even though one out of every four Hungarian citizens was a Serb. This detraction by comparison made Hungary's postwar minority problem clearly evident.

It is interesting to note that the Count shrewdly separated Hungary's German minority from the group of "inferior" peoples. Apponyi alluded in his statistics to the fact that the Germans' literacy rate was superior even to that of the Magyars. In prewar Hungary apparently 82% of the German population knew how to read and write. This, of course, included the more highly developed Jews and Transylvanian Saxons. Apponyi neglected to mention, however, that out of the total prewar German population of about 12%, only 7.8% were high school graduates and that no more than 4.3% managed to graduate from universities.[14] Apponyi might have gone even further to explain the poor performance of the various minorities, including the Germans with their spectacular literacy figures. The truth was that when a non-Magyar child in prewar Hungary reached higher education, he almost invariably became Magyarized, at least to outward appearances. Henceforth, the statistics would list him not under the rubric of mother tongue, but under the heading of the language he prefers and knows best to use. Even in their hour of total defeat, the Magyars sought to pursue a divisive Machiavellian policy with their nationalities, alternately courting and rebuking them. Apponyi had no hope of reversing the territorial decisions of the Victorious Powers, and consequently he did not mind offending the seceded Slavs and Rumanians. The Germans were a different story entirely. They were the most numerous minority left in Hungary; they held the key to West Hungary; and they must be available to cooperate with expatriate Magyars in the Successor States to spearhead a drive to rejoin Hungary.

In view of the need to court the Germans of Hungary and the Successor States, the Magyars went to great lengths to devise impressive programmes. It even became necessary to outdo the Swabians in their zeal for some sort of self-government, efforts which only served to further complicate Magyar-Swabian relations. One of the more sensitive and recurrent themes during this period was the question of autonomy for Burgenland. By the end of 1919, most Swabian West Hungarians tended to favour self-government if not outright annexation by Austria. These aspirations found expression as far back as 26 August, when Bleyer's Swabian opponents, led by Guido Gündisch, demanded autonomy for Burgenland under the terms of the still valid Law VI.1919. Bleyer rejected autonomy because he still advocated only cultural, administrative, and economic reform in the disputed province. The *Neue Post* termed Swabian proponents of self-government unpatriotic. It soon became evident that scant communication, if any, existed between Minister Bleyer and the rest of the cabinet. This included the Prime Minister who released an autonomy plan of his own. On 14 February 1920 Huszár proposed that a plebiscite be held in Burgenland. If the Swabians chose to remain with Hungary, they would be given the most far-reaching opportunities for self-government. Huszár's statement was inadequate and ill-timed. Few Burgenlanders believed his promises, the Austrians scoffed, whereas Bleyer, who firmly opposed autonomy, was left dangling. In fact, he began to appear more Magyar than even the Magyars themselves, a circumstance that did not escape the attention of German diplomats. Indeed, Bleyer became more and more the target for slurs and epithets from German nationalistic quarters.

Huszár's clumsy move thus left both the government and the Bleyerites in a difficult tactical position. On 29 July 1920, on a day devoted to loyalty declarations by minority representatives in Parliament, Huber demanded that a plebiscite be held at once in West Hungary. Three days later Huber delivered a speech in Parliament, an oration which tried to convey a Christian Social *Weltanschauung*. He also tried to rescue Swabian desiderata from a welter of confusing claims and counterclaims. According to Huber, unilingualism was not a prerequisite for a viable state. A common economic and historical heritage was a more important consideration by far, having had great success in Hungary from St. Stephen's time until the coming of Deák in 1867. In Huber's view there had to be a half-way point of moderation between the extremes of a *Pesti Hirlap*, whose editors would deny the vote to anyone not fluently Magyar, and Jászi's autonomy plan, which was outright nationalistic agitation. Turning to more practical matters, Huber served notice that the united Christian parties in the government coalition supported lingual and cultural rights for minorities, as well as the use of their mother tongue in local administration and politics. He ended with an emotional appeal:

> The seceded peoples are longing to return to Hungary. Do we have the right to stand in their way by not providing them with these rights?[15]

Huber's speech did him and the Swabian cause more harm than good; however, the fault was not all his. Ever since the signing of the crushing peace document in June the Magyar public, the press, and officialdom had been venting their spleen against the Swabians. In the cabinet, Bleyer was totally isolated. His enemies demanded the dissolution of the Ministry of Nationalities. His friend Huber endured bitter attacks in Parliament. There were even insistent calls for Huber's ouster from the government coalition.

It was at this inauspicious moment in November 1920 that Huber, supported by his Swabian Christian Social colleagues in Parliament, unveiled his autonomy plan for Burgenland. According to Fürstenberg, Huber's move represented a last desperate gamble to secure West Hungary before the imminent ratification of the peace treaty by the Hungarian Parliament.[16] The proposal failed to embody any new approaches or accommodations. In brief, under the plan Austria and Hungary would negotiate a settlement on the basis of an autonomous Burgenland, in which the province would remain an integral part of Hungary; Austria's economic interests in the region would be safeguarded; and in deference to the sensitive strategic position of Vienna, only local militia would be stationed in the province.[17] The plan had absolutely nothing to recommend it from the Austrian point of view. Austria's position was clear. Having had Burgenland assigned by the Entente, Austria was merely waiting for Hungary to ratify the treaty and vacate the area. At any rate, Huber's assurances on military and commercial affairs were inadequate and vague. But the main fault of the proposal lay with its source and its method of propagation. Huber and his colleagues were not cabinet ministers and hence could not speak for the government. Further, the popular daily press was hardly the place for launching a new plan on a sensitive issue during a period of crisis. Bleyer was also embarrassed. He did not sign the manifesto, and merely remarked that he approved the plan if only because his trusted friend Gratz found the proposal acceptable.

Reactions to the West Hungarian parliamentary group's autonomy scheme were mixed. One Swabian association, the *Westungarische Landsmannschaft,* endorsed the proposal, whereas another, the more prestigious *Westungarische Liga* opposed it.[18] Magyar nationalistic circles, especially the *Területvédő Liga,* an organization devoted to the recapture of Hungary's prewar territories, were vehemently against any scheme that would diminish the hegemony of the ruling Magyars.[19] Austria had no choice but to reject the proposal, if only because acceptance would have meant the immediate collapse of the Mayr regime. Magyar official circles and the public ignored Huber's manifesto entirely. This prompted Fürstenberg to remark that the Magyars were obviously not really interested in an honest understanding with Austria on Burgenland.

In April 1921 came the last of many schemes to secure Burgenland for Hungary under the guise of autonomy. The author of this elaborate plan, which enjoyed tacit government support, was none other than Bleyer. It came upon the heels of further galling setbacks for both the Magyars and the Swabians. A Habsburg restoration by ex-King Charles IV had been only recently averted, leaving the Little Entente and Austria more suspicious than ever about Hungary's aims and purposes. Bleyer's late German visit, which had explored possibilities of Swabian aid in Reich circles, had been unsuccessful. A delegation composed of Hungary's Swabian parliamentary contingent came home with empty hands from Vienna after a discussion about the fate of Burgenland with Mayr. The Chancellor politely rejected any solution that would have left Burgenland under Hungarian control. Bleyer's plan called for the immediate political indoctrination and organization of West Hungary's population in time for the parliamentary elections in the fall of 1921. The people would hopefully vote for candidates (having been handpicked by Bleyer and his associates) who would vote for the return of Burgenland to Hungary. Since it would not be prudent for Hungary to violate the peace treaty agreement with the Entente, regular Hungarian troops would duly vacate West Hungary on schedule, but their places would be taken by native Burgenland detachments, to be equipped and financed by Hungary. These "civic guards" would prevent Austrian forces from entering and seizing West Hungary. Burgenland would then be incorporated into Hungary, and subsequently the population could proclaim it a German autonomous region. Important Magyars, in and out of government, supported this scheme, the most noted being Count Bánffy, the Foreign Minister, Gratz, and Bethlen. It is interesting to note that official Hungarian communiques at the time rejected the concept of West Hungarian autonomy.

It would appear that Bleyer and his associates entertained a double-barreled plan whose contradictory terms they found perfectly harmonious. The Swabians were trying to restore Hungary to her prewar greatness, but not on the basis of prewar Magyar hegemony. Whereas the Magyars insisted that they had earned their right to rule Hungary by virtue of prior conquest, the Bleyerites wanted to introduce what seemed to them a more plausible scheme. They wished to reestablish Hungary on the basis of a supra-national Christian elitist imperium, in which the Magyars and themselves would be coequals. The Bleyerites expanded much energy trying to convince the Magyars that their plan had merit. They also kept insisting *ad nauseam* that they were loyal patriotic Hungarians and they no doubt meant every word of it. The Swabians outdid even the Magyars, plotting and scheming to retain Burgenland for Hungary. They hoped to demonstrate their loyalty to Hungary, not to Austria, a foreign—and German—state. These efforts were all in vain. The times were against the establishment of a supra-national state. The nationalistic waves sweeping Europe since the nineteenth century prohibited its success. Furthermore, the Magyars wished to be masters in their own house, and besides they distrusted the Swabians as a potential vanguard of a German *Mitteleuropa* plan. If the Swabians were to become shareholders of power in Hungary, then the weight of revived German economic power must soon tip the balance in their favour. The Magyars might yet become the hewers of wood and the drawers of water in their own hard-won homeland. As much as the Magyars desired Burgenland for Hungary, they were suspicious of Swabian support. Was the acquisition meant to enhance Hungary's power or was it designed for the benefit of German influence in the Danube Basin? Bleyer himself had supplied the answer by emphasizing in no uncertain terms that the acquisition of Burgenland was a matter of life and death for the survival of all Germandom in East-Central Europe.[20] The divergent aims of the two Hungarian peoples—Magyar and Swabian—thus profoundly affected their relations in the postwar era. No sooner did the Swabians pursue aims and purposes that were not in harmony with Magyar aspirations, than serious conflicts arose to poison their relationship. Bleyer enjoyed great popularity during his early Ministry because the Magyars believed him to be engaged in activities beneficial to their own interests. When it became apparent that Bleyer considered himself to be more of a loyal German-Hungarian than a loyal Magyar, there was an instant change in attitudes.

One of the watersheds separating the era of good feelings and the period of tension in Magyar-Swabian relations appeared around the beginning of 1920. Nor was this turn of events fortuitous. It related to the New Year's decision of the Peace Conference to deprive Hungary of all her seceded territories. To cushion the shock, the Magyars sought a scapegoat. Their non-Magyar minorities, to some extent even the Swabians, fitted such a role perfectly. Had we Magyarized all our minorities before the war, ran the typical Magyar argument, then our lost territories and peoples would be with us still. The Magyars came to the ineluctable conclusion, on the basis of this reasoning, that all the remaining minority peoples must henceforth adopt total Magyarization without reservation. Only thus could Hungary prevent a possible future Trianon, in which additional chunks would be torn from Hungary's ethnic body.[21] The other watershed in Magyar-Swabian relations came nearly one year after Trianon, when the Peace Conference affirmed the loss of Burgenland. For the next two years, thanks to these and other lesser shockwaves in Hungarian political life, Magyar-Swabian affairs developed along extremely unstable and unpredictable lines.

At the beginning of 1920 an unwritten Magyar-Swabian entente was still in evidence. As news of the unfavourable Peace Conference decision spread, there were outpourings of pro-Hungarian (though scarcely pro-Magyar) sentiments and sympathies in West Hungary. In an official statement, Mayor Thurner of Sopron responded to the cession by reminding his people that under Austrian rule we would atrophy and die. We could not separate ourselves from Hungary, and we wished no part of Austria. We desired to remain Germans, but only in Hungary. On the practical side, the Mayor pointed out that, economically, Burgenlanders would suffer hardship under Austrian rule because they could not compete with the more efficient producers across the Leitha. A few days later in Sopron a demonstration took place. A large crowd burned the Austrian flag while singing the Hungarian national anthem. In the Swabian border village of Wandorf (Bánfalva) authorities turned a local referendum into an unofficial plebiscite on the Burgenland question. According to election officials the balloting indicated near unanimity to remain with Hungary. Only two dissenting votes were cast, both by resident Austrians. There were other indications of support for a Hungarian Burgenland. In Steinamanger (Szombathely), people reacted with sorrow to the news about West Hungary. Black flags appeared and all entertainment ceased. While these reports undoubtedly reflected the truth, one must remain cautious. Both Sopron and Szombathely were urban centers with large Magyar and Magyarized Swabian populations and hence did not necessarily reflect the feelings of Swabians in general. Indeed, in the course of the subsequent plebiscite in Sopron, three out of four people elected to remain with Hungary. In the case of Bánfalva, the election results may be suspect. If the balloting had been conducted in secrecy, how could the election officials have known the identities of the two dissenters?

As the weeks passed, pro-Hungarian and anti-Austrian expressions continued. Common adversity and possibilities of common danger made temporary bedfellows of Burgenland's Magyar and Swabian inhabitants. As early as January rumours began to circulate that Czech troops, stationed only a few miles away in Bratislava, were ready to occupy Burgenland on behalf of Czechoslovakia's new Austrian ally. The Czechs were held in great fear, but it was the Austrians who reaped the opprobrium of Burgenlanders for exposing Hungary to a possible invasion. This never materialized, but the occasion temporarily united West Hungary's Magyar and German-speaking populations in righteous anger against the "godless" Austrian "half-Communist" regime, and its leader, the "anti-Christ"Renner.[22]

Continuing the pro-Hungarian "offensive," on 11 February 1920, Burgenland's newly-elected parliamentary contingent of eleven men issued a joint manifesto protesting the fate of their region. About two weeks later, Sopron once again captured the spotlight. On 4 March two Austrian negotiators arrived in the city and were given a hostile reception. There were no official welcoming ceremonies, but about 10,000 hostile demonstrators at the railway depot threatened physical violence. Bloody events in Yugoslav-held South Hungary, the so-called Bácska, further helped to rally the Swabians around Hungary. In contrast to Hungary, where during the conservative era repression was often subtle and indirect, seldom brutal or violent, in Yugoslav territories relations between the military authorities and the largely Swabian inhabitants were extremely strained. For reasons that will probably be never known, Yugoslav troops opened fire on a group of allegedly unarmed Swabian demonstrators. Pitched battles were subsequently fought, in which many dozens of Swabians were killed and wounded.[23]

Amid all these events, many changes were also gradually occurring in the Magyar political arena. Each change tended to strengthen the Magyars and hence contributed to their cherished determination to become autonomous. The Swabians soon began to feel the impact. After the elections, on March 3,

Huszár resigned. Simultaneously, Admiral Horthy, a Magyar nationalist with a large chauvinistic entourage, became regent designate. Thereafter, Hungary's government was surrounded by men such as Gyula Gömbös, Hungary's future Prime Minister of partly Swabian descent who, as a typical proselyte, became the most outspoken advocate of energetic Magyarization. In the same month the hated Rumanians left Hungary, allegedly "taking everything with them that is not nailed down."[24] At last the Magyars could concentrate their energies on eliminating whatever alien influences still survived.

The sudden chill in official temperatures toward the Swabians began to assert itself by the middle of March. Although the new government won at the polls with the aid of the united Christian Social parties, among whom the Swabian *Integritätspartei* commanded some influence, the minority issue had not even been broached in Parliament. This lapse was challenged by Huber, who complained indignantly that the new session did not have the nationality problem on its agenda. He reminded his colleagues that all the current minority regulations were merely provisional, awaiting parliamentary action. Even the existing statutes had not yet been introduced, thanks to laggard local officials. Huber railed that the Swabians had been very patient, aware that the government had myriad worries. But now,

> We demand a speedy and proper solution, otherwise Bleyer cannot continue as Nationality Minister and we Swabians can no longer support the government. We demand these rights also for Hungary's other minorities. The government's response will be a sure sign whether the repressive policies of the past forty years are forever abandoned.[25]

This constituted a clear warning to Simonyi-Semadam, who became Hungary's Prime Minister on 15 March 1920, to show concern for the minority issue. After four months of inaction, Huber reiterated his demand during the next cabinet crisis, which ultimately led to the Ministry of Count Paul (Pál) Teleki. Huber threatened that the Swabians would no longer support a government that failed to carry out the injunctions of Law 4044. By then, the Swabian *Integritätspartei,* charter member of the united Christian Social parties, had lost a great deal of prestige, due mainly—and undeservedly—to the almost certain loss of Burgenland, a prospect that hung like a thundercloud over the heads of all Hungarians.

Despite its disadvantageous position, by dint of persuasion that remains a mystery, the Party was able to rouse itself and force the adoption of Bleyer's nationality programme upon its two Magyar partners in the Christian Social coalition. This victory turned out to be a master-stroke in timing, for only two days later, as the cabinet crisis deepened and the old government coalition began to disintegrate, future Prime Minister Bethlen called a meeting of all parties, with the aim of forming a new government. Fresh from its victory, the Integrity Party aggressively made its position known. Swabians would under no circumstances support a government that did not embody their ethnic demands as an integral part of its programme. Essentially, the desiderata concerned the use of German in lower education, administration, and justice. Astoundingly, most Magyar parties present at the meeting accepted this platform and promised to make it their own. When on 13 July 1920, the new coalition, *Egységes Keresztény Kormánypárt (Christnationale Vereinigung),* unveiled its platform, it was a considerable tactical and moral victory for the Swabians. Point 9 responded to their wishes by pledging to fulfill the cultural and linguistic aspirations of the national minorities; to assure their participation in national politics and administration, naturally within the framework of Hungarian national unity.

Although the platform fell far short of autonomy, hardly exceeding the limits of the Nationality Law of 1868, the Swabians were confident that such a manifesto would eventually produce the desired results. Indeed, the Swabians were to all appearances in an excellent position and had every reason to feel optimistic. Not only had they won a smashing political victory under adverse circumstances, but a month earlier a formidable and distinguished opponent, Count Apponyi, had issued a startling statement on the nationality issue, a declaration completely at odds with all his previous views. In a speech in Jászberény the Count, author of the repressive minority school bill of 1907, admitted to having been one of the most intransigent representatives of the former spirit of Magyar national unity. He went on to say that Hungary had to break with such a policy once and for all and

> adopt a cultural and administrative self-government for the minorities, who must honour the unity and interests of the [Hungarian] State. . . .We must do this if we are ever to be united with our seceded non-Magyar fellow citizens.

Apponyi concluded by saying, "I herewith recommend this new approach because it is a prerequisite for the reestablishment of Hungary within the framework of the new world order."[26] One might argue that the Count merely wished to give Hungary's seceded ethnic groups food for thought in order to hasten their return to the fold. Be that as it may, his speech actually went beyond Swabian demands. It clearly indicated that Hungary's minorities should obtain some sort of autonomy. In view of the great prestige Apponyi enjoyed both at home and abroad, the Swabians did not doubt for a moment that his talk must mark the auspicious beginning of a new era for them. Teleki's inaugural speech was far less spectacular than Apponyi's, but at least he promised, as his minimal task, to implement the provisions of Point 9.[27]

The Swabians' expectations were high and their disappointment was so much the more crushing. Far from being carried out, the existing nationality laws continued to be flouted. Clearly, Teleki did not intend to introduce new minority legislation to satisfy the impatient Swabians. On the contrary, only a few weeks after his speech, Pest County, boasting a most Magyar-conscious political organization, shook the very foundations of Hungary's slender nationality structure. At an unprecedented public meeting on 10 August 1920, a special Pest County commission demanded that Parliament abolish Bleyer's Ministry of Nationalities and the minority school inspectorships. The Ministry was allegedly wasteful, created chaos in the various executive branches, and engendered German nationalism among Swabians and other national groups, even in areas where Magyar reigned as the exclusive language in public life. The critics saw Pest County as a case in point. Hungary had just lost 3½ million Magyars because they had been interspersed among non-Magyar ethnic groups. In times like these, the Ministry of Education, at the instigation of the Ministry of Nationalities, was trying to introduce German schools into Swabian and Slovak communities, even where Magyar was the accustomed language. At this rate, Hungary would soon suffer the fate of eighteenth-century Poland: its neighbours would carve it up. Next, the Committee repudiated all the nationality statutes since 1868. Magyars should not be asked to learn seven or eight foreign languages; Hungary's "visitors" should learn Magyar. Nobody had the right to live in Hungary and expect to use the voluntarily abandoned language and culture of his former homeland. Visitors must accept Magyar ways, or return.

Pest County's resolution was adopted and emulated by other counties throughout Hungary. Various revisionist organizations, such as the *Nemzeti Ligák Szövetsége* and *Tevél,* joined the fray against the Ministry. Attacks against the Swabians continued in Parliament as well. Gyula Rubinek, Minister of Commerce and member of the hostile Independent Smallholders' Party, demanded the abolition of Bleyer's Ministry, assailed Huber in particular, and attacked Swabian participation in the government coalition in general. In a stormy session on 2 December 1920, Aladár Balla, another *ISP* member, confronted Bleyer with charges of treason. In 1919, the Swabian leader was alleged to have written a note to then Prime Minister Károlyi, offering to "support the Revolution with all our soul."[28] Other charges, too numerous to mention, but all in a similar vein, were leveled at the Swabians by nationalistic Magyars and the jingoist press. It was apparent that the last hour of the Ministry of Nationalities had struck.

The Swabians defended themselves vigourously. Bleyer accused Pest County of unwarranted charges. The Ministry fulfilled an essential function on behalf of frontier revision. It demonstrated Hungary's determination to keep faith with the seceded nationalities. Remove the Ministry, said Bleyer, and these promises become a hollow shell. Pest County's allegations that Bleyer fostered secession in Burgenland were also indignantly refuted. A few days later the *Neue Post* lashed out against Pest County's liberal politicians, who were spreading malicious rumours. The newspaper cited an unnamed government spokesman to the effect that there were no intentions of terminating Bleyer's valuable portfolio. In fact, if Hungary had no such office, one would be essential. Huber also struck back at his tormentors, threatening to resign from the Christian Social Party and leave the government coalition if Rubinek ever became party leader, or if his nationality policies ever prevailed in the government. In Parliament, Bleyer defended himself brilliantly against Balla's accusation of treason, pointing out that the quoted passage qas totally out of context. The parliamentary consensus appeared to favour Bleyer.[29]

Encouragement came from unexpected sources for the Swabians during these difficult weeks, when Bleyer's popularity among Burgenland's Germans reached a low ebb. A number of Magyar statesmen—formerly ill-disposed towards the nationalities—now reversed their views and adopted Apponyi's recent position on the issue. The Prime Minister became another surprising "ally." On 16 November Teleki declared in Parliament that the minorities would be given both opportunities for cultural development and administrative autonomy. According to this unexpected plan, there would be three levels of ethnic autonomy: communal self-government with unrestricted use of the mother tongue in villages and towns with non-Magyar majorities (this type of autonomy would apply anywhere in Hungary, even in small ethnic enclaves); district (*járds*) self-government in jurisdictions containing "sufficient numbers" of unilingual non-Magyar communities; and county self-government, wherever non-Magyars enjoyed a clear majority of the population. Of course, the proposed law was far from perfect. It was in many respects vague and vulnerable. It failed to regulate conditions in communities with more than one non-Magyar language; and it had no administrative safeguards. Yet under the Swabians' straitened circumstances the present plan was still welcome news. The Prime Minister's other gesture was equally surprising. By 26 November Bleyer could no longer tolerate Rubinek's unceasing attacks and insults. He therefore tendered his resignation. Teleki refused to accept and begged Bleyer to reconsider. Surprised, Bleyer decided to remain, only to find himself quietly dropped from the cabinet when the second Teleki Ministry was formed on 16 December 1920.

It is plain to see why Hungary's elder statesmen, as well as Teleki, became so solicitous of the needs of Hungary's Swabians, even as attacks against them by Magyar nationalist extremists mounted in intensity. The Peace Conference had still not fully decided Hungary's status in Burgenland. Although the outlook for the Magyars was bleak, they still hoped a plebiscite might favourably decide the fate of their westernmost province. Naturally, they wished to put their best foot forward for the benefit of the minorities. They hoped to convince West Hungarians that a vote in favour of Hungary would mean self-government and freedom. No wonder, therefore, that the central government coolly ignored the Magyar national-istic agitation rampant throughout Hungary. It also explains why the various Magyar political parties, where sober heads prevailed, were willing to tolerate the Swabians and their demands in the government coalition, at least for the time being. It is clearer now why Bleyer's resignation from the Ministry was not accepted at first and why Rubinek was made to issue a joint statement with Teleki, in a way an apology to Bleyer.[30] The sad but true fact remained, nonetheless, that the Swabians were unable to obtain an honest settlement from their government. The latter preferred to use the German minority group as a pawn to achieve its own political and diplomatic objectives.

Bleyer's plaintive letter addressed to Dr. F. X. Zahnbrecher, a conserva-tive Bavarian politician and member of German Parliament, revealed the Swabians' gloom and pessimism. Bleyer painted an apocalyptic picture, not only about the projected fate of Swabians in post-Burgenland Hungary, but also about the prospects of all Germans east of Hungary. In Bleyer's view they were all doomed. He reasoned that if Austria had the ill judgment to take away Burgenland, relations between Magyardom and Germandom would be thoroughly poisoned and the Magyar national spirit would rise in hatred against Germandom, an enmity more unbridled and elemental than that unleashed against any other country. This breach would have two major consequences. Firstly, no Swabian leader would be permitted to function, for

It is natural that. . . .Magyar nationalism, after many bitter experiences during the past few years, would flare up brighter than ever before, and little Hungary would attempt at all cost to become a unified nation state. This would result in the Magyarization of Germans with as much force and determination as the history of Magyarization has ever known.[31]

The second major result would be the eventual withering of German groups in Yugoslavia and Rumania. Germans there would be truncated from the German homeland. If Burgenland remained with Hungary, it would receive autonomy, and would be strong and full of German consciousness. Under such conditions the Swabians would be able to act as a cultural bridge between Germans to the east and west. Bleyer wanted to enlist Zahnbrecher's good offices with German nationalist circles in the forlorn hope that they would intervene for Hungary with Austria.

In the last few feverish weeks towards the end of 1920, before the final Allied decision on Burgenland became known, the Hungarian government took a desperate gamble and dispatched Bleyer and Huber to Bavaria on a semi-official mission. The Swabian leaders were to seek out sympathetically inclined nationalist politicians such as Ludendorff, Kahr, and any others willing to listen, and solicit their support against Austria. Although the Germans expressed a great deal of polite sympathy, in the end they proved to be adamantly opposed to any plan that would deprive Austria of the West Hungarian province. The isolation of the Swabian leaders was now complete.

During the first week of the New Year, 1921, the expected blow fell. The Magyars were ordered to hand over Burgenland to Austria without any further delays. The Allied note had a sobering effect on Magyar-Swabian relations. Fürstenberg sent a number of dispatches to the Wilhelmstrasse, apprising his superiors about the course of events in Hungary. According to Fürstenberg, the Hungarian government's recent persecutions had created a great change of heart among the Swabians. Formerly loyal to Hungary, Burgenland's parliamentary representatives now favoured Austria and even expressed concern for those of their compatriots who would have to remain with Hungary. According to the Austrian Legation in Budapest, Swabians now hoped for an *Anschluss* with Austria in order to become German citizens. Burgenlanders apparently expected a momentary German-Austrian fusion. Fürstenberg believed Bleyer had reached a point of such despair that he seriously contemplated leaving Hungary for good and returning to his native Bácska. Fürstenberg exaggerated. No doubt the Swabians were deeply depressed and from time to time contemplated giving up. It is doubtful, however, whether they meant to abandon Hungary except during moments of despair. Fürstenberg's analysis is nonetheless valuable because it captured the spirit of the Swabians' disappointment and disillusionment with the Magyars. Moreover, the Swabians' pain was compounded by the realization that they were being pilloried for the sins of others.

Genuine bitterness welled up among the Magyars against the Austro-Germans for their allegedly coldblooded determination to feast on Hungary's corpse in the company of their former common enemies. These sentiments surfaced in the weeks following Hungary's receipt of the Entente Note in January 1921, which demanded the immediate evacuation of Burgenland by Hungarian forces. The Swabians shared the consequences of this embitterment in Magyar public opinion, which tended to lump together all Germans indiscriminately. Fürstenberg remarked that the Swabians failed to derive any benefits despite their faithful support of Magyar policies. He wrote that naturally—as it was pointed out in Budapest constantly—thanks to the Burgenland settlement in Austria's favour, the Swabians were finished in Hungary as a political force. Under the present circumstances no Swabian leader would dare to demonstrate on behalf of his *Volkstum*.

The entire year 1921 was thus marked by a steady deterioration in Magyar-Swabian relations. The gradual dismantling of the Ministry of Nationalities was one of the major features of this trend. Although its operations were not formally terminated until February 1922, the Ministry ceased functioning effectively about the time when the plebiscite of 14-16 December 1921 defused the Burgenland crisis.[32] Clearly, it was being kept alive only because a last-minute reprieve might yet throw Burgenland into Hungary's lap. Indeed, during the last months of its existence the Ministry spent most of its time, funds, and energy on pro-Hungarian propaganda aimed at the minorities at home and abroad rather than on protecting their ethnic interests.

Numerous other signs in the course of 1921 also pointed to deteriorating Magyar-Swabian relations. On 15 April 1921, Bethlen became Hungary's Prime Minister, a position he was to maintain for the next decade. Although an ardent proponent of a rigorous Magyar course, Bethlen was not considered to be hostile to German culture, which he professed to admire. The new Premier took good advantage of his well-publicized teutonic bent to convince the gullible Swabians that his promises regarding their cultural ambitions were sincere. On 1 June 1921 Bethlen delivered a major minority policy statement in Parliament. While obviously responding to Bleyer's speech of the previous day on the same topic, the Prime Minister ostentatiously ignored the former Minister's remarks. Bleyer had argued in favour of better treatment for Swabians in Hungary. He also came out strongly for the adoption of a Germanophil orientation in Hungary's foreign policy. In his own speech Bethlen tacitly admitted the presence of grievances by stating that before the War Hungary had known neither nationality problems nor national oppression. The War, in his view, had changed everything. Currently, Hungary was greatly diminished in territory, and although ethnically the country was nearly homogeneous, it paradoxically still retained a fair number of minorities. Bethlen deemed it essential for the sake of Hungary's own vested interests that the legitimate demands of these peoples be granted. Hungary had to create a nationality policy that would preserve Hungary's integrity without encouraging the development of an artificially engendered nationality problem. In Bethlen's opinion the problem was principally cultural.

> We have to see to it that in our nation anyone who cannot speak Magyar should be able to obtain an education in his own mother tongue from the lowest grade to the highest. Our nation's error has been the neglect of such facilities in the past.[33]

Bethlen also declared in his speech that wherever minorities resided in compact blocks, they should not only enjoy linguistic rights but that indigenous officials be permitted to administer their affairs. In conclusion, Bethlen explained that he did not advocate a Jászi-type regimen; his plan was more in keeping with Hungary's semi-autonomous constitutional approach taken with the Transylvanian Saxons before the War.

Bethlen's speech, although apparently logically conceived and reasonable, was never seriously entertained. At the time, Bethlen still hoped for a miracle to occur in West Hungary that would enable him to influence Burgenland's Swabians to elect Hungarian rule in the event of a hypothetical plebiscite. Barely one month elapsed before Bleyer took the government severely to task for failing to implement the Prime Minister's greatly touted programme. Bleyer reiterated that a Gleichschaltung of Hungary's foreign policy with that of Germany was an inescapable historic necessity. He further demanded that Bethlen's fine words be translated into action without any further ado. Hungary's Magyar press ostentatiously ignored Bleyer's speech.

Dissatisfaction with prevailing conditions was underscored shortly before the plebiscite by eleventh-hour demands for reform. Swabians were disturbed by press reports describing gross neglect in minority schools. According to one such report, education in Swabian villages had come to a virtual standstill since the war, in defiance of existing school laws. Officials seemed not to care. According to Sonntagsblatt, as a result of such malpractices—a trend in evidence at least since 1907—the Swabians had begun to turn out functionally illiterate children who knew a hybrid German-Magyar but neither language properly. Pupils like that were not fit candidates for higher education and consequently the number of Swabians attending middle schools had decreased dramatically since shortly before the War. For decades the Swabians had led Hungary intellectually, having had the fewest illiterates and the highest proportion of the intelligentsia issuing from their ranks. This hegemony was now clearly in danger.

Impelled by these and other reasons, a deputation consisting of forty Swabian leaders from the plebiscite area paid a call on Bethlen. They assured him that fundamentally they were loyal to the Hungarian State. At the same time, however, the spokesmen expressed profound chagrin over the frustrating position and dim prospects of Hungary's Swabians. They demanded the immediate implementation of the existing minority laws, especially in education, administration, and justice. The deputation also solicited the Premier's protection against the arbitrary obstructions of lesser officials, who sabotaged the minority regulations not only in Burgenland but everywhere in Hungary. In his reply Bethlen pointed out that he was an alumnus of a German gymnasium in Vienna and hence a devotee of German culture. This being the case, his guests' wishes were as good as fulfilled.[34]

The plebiscite, held one week later, turned out to be a partial victory for the Magyars. They acquired the city of Sopron and several surrounding villages besides, but it was a distinct loss for the approximately 70,000 West Hungarian Swabians remaining with the Hungarian State. A good portion of the Swabians thus left Hungary were in fact members of the Magyarized urban intelligentsia, whose German-oriented rural brethren could scarcely hope to hold their own against the inroads of their more sophisticated cultural betters. Indeed, the Swabian history of the succeeding two decades may be constructed around the struggle between the German-conscious but culturally weak rural masses on the one hand, and the thoroughly Magyarized Swabian triumvirate—clergyman, teacher, and notary—on the other.[35]

The years 1922-1926 roused futile expectations for Swabians. Magyar indignation boiled after most non-Magyar subjects defected and because Hungary lost territory and population to the Victorious Powers. The forfeiture of most of West Hungary rankled, and engendered a sullen atmosphere for dealing with the remaining minorities. Even the minor concessions extended to the non-Magyars before and shortly after the war seemed harmful and based on erroneous principles. Magyars believed that had all the nationalities been assimilated, there would have been no basis for the dismemberment of Hungary. Magyar resentment intensified because Trianon imposed an obligation that severely curtailed Hungary's sovereignty. The minorities were placed under League protection, while Hungary had to satisfy their cultural and linguistic aspirations. Although the nationality law of 1868 had been as demanding, and the regulations bore with equal weight on surrounding states, the Magyars resented external interference. After Trianon, the Magyar public branded all minority legislation as morally not binding.

The Swabians felt this chill immediately after the Burgenland plebiscite. Their education system suffered first. Although Article 59 of the Peace Treaty obliged Hungary to maintain minority elementary schools, pure German schools were vastly reduced in number shortly after the signing of the Peace Treaty. They shrank by 68% between 1919-1920 and 1920-1921.[1] Most of these schools were located in West Hungary; the remainder became mixed Magyar-German institutions. In 1919-1920, only 40% of German grade school pupils attended German minority schools of any kind.[2] Next year, 22,072 pupils were transferred to newly created mixed-language schools, together with 7,427 other Swabian children from pure Magyar institutions. The transaction was pedagogically unsound but served propaganda purposes. It enabled the government to advance the claim that German educational facilities for over 7,000 additional Swabian children had been found. In fact, even the government admitted subsequently that mixed-language schools were minority institutions in name only. Hence over 22,000 Swabian children were deprived of an education decreed by the Peace Treaty, statistical obfuscation notwithstanding.

In the 1921-1922 school year the government reduced the number of German schools. Ninety-two institutions accommodating 11,610 pupils dwindled to 58, with only 7,506 pupils. This left only still disputed Burgenland with pure German schools. In the ensuing two-year period Hungary's minority school system become nearly extinct, a blow from which it never entirely recovered. In 1922-1923, German schools were reduced to 53, in which only 825 pupils were taught. But the government "improved" the situation by creating sixteen new unspecified types of bilingual schools for 5,380 children. This was more statistical juggling, however, because the number of students in previously established Magyar-Swabian schools was reduced by over 20%.[3] In 1923-1924, pure German schools diminished to nine, accommodating but 239 pupils, while the number of schools of other types and students remained unchanged until the 1925-1926 school year.

Hungary thus obeyed the letter of the Peace Treaty minority provisions, but only insofar as they accommodated her own educational philosophy. The Magyars exploited the ambiguities of Article 59, embodied in Hungarian jurisprudence by Law 33 of 1921, and denied minorities the substantive benefits which the Treaty intended them to have. Phrases such as

an equitable share of public funds shall be provided for educational purposes of members of minorities who constituted a considerable proportion of Hungary's nationals,[4]

weakened rather than strengthened the effect of the Article, while the threat of "proper and effective action in case of infractions" was too vague and constituted virtual encouragement for ignoring them. The Magyars justified violations on the grounds that they enjoyed a more highly evolved cultural level than any of the minorities and hence were entitled to impose their own standards, and eventual assimilation, upon them. To camouflage their intentions the Magyars curtailed, but never abolished, minority schools, and thereby superficially fulfilled the demands of Article 59 and of the minorities. They also succeeded in weakening the quality of Swabian minority education by diminishing the amount of German instruction and by arbitrarily shifting minority pupils from one type of school to another. The government deemed this action appropriate in the light of Article 59, that this proviso shall not prevent the Hungarian government from making the teaching of Magyar language obligatory in the minority schools. Moreover, the Treaty imposed neither a floor nor a ceiling on the amount of non-Magyar instruction minority youth were to receive. The Magyars naturally stretched the point by reducing German instruction in the schools to an irreducible minimum. They knew very well that Swabian nationalists had few defences against such a policy, especially since Swabian parents frequently insisted on Magyar instruction for their children for practical purposes. The Magyars also shrewdly recognized that if they neglected German instruction in the minority schools, and German *Kultur* should disappear in this strategic Danubian region, the Entente, especially the French, would not be overly upset.

The first domestic public outcry about the schools arose in the pages of Bleyer's weekly *Sonntagsblatt*. From its inception, it editorialized on behalf of German *Selbstbewusstsein* and the need for German education. After the war Hungary's German people became inwardly transformed and remodelled, boasted the first issue. They now had new demands and requirements, new hopes and aspirations. They hungered for more culture and education. In a subsequent issue the editor underscored the importance of practical education, which had languished in recent years. For many decades the Swabians had excelled all other ethnic groups intellectually, possessing the fewest illiterates and the largest intelligentsia in Hungary. With the introduction of the 1907 School Law, the number of Swabian illiterates rose sharply ever thereafter. Worse still, the most undesirable uneducated type made its first appearance: the semi-literate who knew only a hybrid German-Magyar, but neither language properly.

This intellectual crisis prompted a delegation of forty West Hungarian Swabians to demand that Bethlen introduce the Nationality Law of 1868 and 1919 without further delay. They also desired better treatment for Swabians in administration and justice, and protection against the machinations of arbitrary lower administrators who sabotaged the laws in Burgenland and elsewhere in Hungary. Bethlen soothed his visitors by assuring them that he would do all he could to prevent further violations.[5]

Next month a second delegation hailing from formerly Yugoslav-held Hungary visited Bethlen, who promised to rectify their admittedly dismal minority school situation, a predicament he attributed to old thinking by local officials. The deputation also called on Minister of Education Vass. During the Serbian occupation, they recounted, most Swabian villages had established German schools at their own expense. The newly arrived Magyars closed them and introduced Magyar instruction. Vass ventured that this action was the work of overzealous lower officials and promised immediate remedy, for he believed it essential for elementary school pupils to receive instruction in their own mother tongue. Vass then divulged that a new school law was being contemplated. In the first two grades non-Magyar children would receive instruction in their own mother tongue; thereafter Magyar would be gradually introduced. He also hinted that the establishment of greatly sought German teacher academies would soon be established. The delegation departed content.

Subsequently, the Wilhelmstrasse complained that after nearly one year following these promises, not one Swabian grievance had been rectified in eleven Baranya County communities. In Pécsvárad, elementary schools were being Magyarized by Magyarone Swabians. A privately owned Magyar *polgáriskola* alienated many Swabian children from German culture. Similar conditions prevailed in Feked and Geresd, where Swabian pupils were forbidden to exchange greetings in German. In Kisbüdmér children had their names entered in a "Book of Shame" (*Schandbuch, szégyenkönyv*) for speaking German. In Véménd, German instruction was poor; in Sómberek, the people were coerced to terminate German instruction; in Püspöklak, a little German was being taught in the overwhelmingly Magyar school system; and in Németboly, the Magyarone clergy tried its utmost to introduce Magyar instruction.

In March 1922, Alfred von Schwartz, a prominent Swabian, wrote a pamphlet accusing the Magyars of gradually dismantling German cultural establishments, such as middle schools, teachers' lyceums, and even the elementary schools. Swabian children nowadays merely parroted Magyar phrases and no longer comprehended even the simplest religious abstractions in either language. Thanks to the Magyars' unkept promises and unmitigated terror, and their destruction of the German cultural niveau through Magyarization, Swabians could no longer maintain their German status. The government confiscated the pamphlet and sued von Schwartz for having slandered the Hungarian nation. *Sonntagsblatt* was suspended for three weeks (27 June through 18 July 1922) for printing excerpts from the offending publication. The ban was lifted, however, when the minister of the Interior realized that Schwartz's harsh critique had been motivated by patriotic concern and on 11 November a Sopron court exonerated him. It was a rare moral victory, not only for the Swabians, but for the government. Notwithstanding it disapproval of a non-Magyar ethnic ethos in Hungary, the government nonetheless refused to suspend freedom of speech for a non-Magyar citizen or his right to a fair trial.[6]

Even so, the German press severely criticized Hungary's persecution of von Schwartz. The *Deutsche Allgemeine Zeitung* complained not only about the seizure of pamphlets but also inveighed against the closure of German cultural associations in Hungary, the persecution of loyal Swabians, and the termination of all German schools. It could not comprehend such a diplomacy by a former comrade-in-arms. The Magyar anti-German *Szózat* indignantly rejected the German newspaper's charges as outright lies. The Swabians were caught in the middle, for they could not openly criticize their government in the von Schwartz episode without appearing to be Pan-Germans. *Sonntagsblatt* tactfully thanked *Szózat*, a newspaper not exactly friendly, for having called the critical article to their attention and thereby helping German-Hungarian relations.[7]

Despite the temporary furor created by the von Schwartz incident, Swabian education remained the principal source of friction. One problem entailed the general decrepitude of physical facilities. The notary of Mosonszolnok (Zanegg), publicized the deplorable condition of the German village school system. Elementary schools were terribly neglected. Most had no fuel, window panes were broken, doors would not shut properly, and stoves gave only smoke, not heat. Teachers did their best but could make no headway. Often school had to be suspended indefinitely and learning was negligible.

Bleyer published several letters written by West Hungarians. One, by a Roman Catholic priest, posed a rhetorical question: Would anything ever come of the minority law in German regions? In the writer's view, Swabian children ought to study both Magyar and German for practical reasons, and for comprehending religious studies with greater ease. But Swabian children would learn Magyar properly only if they had a thorough grounding in German. If current conditions continued, children would learn neither German nor Magyar and their cultural, economic, and confessional life would be brought into dire peril.

A second letter, written by a Swabian peasant, revealed the methods local officials employed to discourage German instruction:

> On 4 February 1923 we had a meeting in which we chose our elementary school teacher. The school board's choice won (he knows no German), but we (ten of us) were not satisfied and went to see the *Obergespan*. He called us Pan-Germans.

The peasant feared arrest and sought Bleyer's help. But his response betrayed disillusionment, even cynicism:

> Both writers ask what we have to say? The answer is: nothing. What can we do? Nothing. What can we promise? Nothing, except what they [the government] give us constantly: promises. I just wish to add that both writers are represented in Parliament by German deputies. These made pretty

promises to their constituents before the election but what do they do after the elections? Nothing.

Still, we should not permit our hopes to sink entirely. If we do not give up we will see things through.[8]

Two weeks later Bleyer published a third letter, written by the other side in the teacher-election dispute. The informant claimed the teacher in question knew German, but not too well, because few Swabians knew German perfectly any longer. Under the circumstances, the only valid criterion for a teacher's qualifications should be his ability to make himself understood. This underscored a fatal flaw in Hungary's German minority school system. At any given time during the interwar period it would have been difficult to find more than one hundred qualified elementary school teachers who knew the German language sufficiently well to teach it.

The Swabian problem, including the school situation, became a topic in Parliament. Franz Neuberger declared that the Swabians desired only two things: competent German elementary schools where their children might also learn Magyar properly; and to communicate with officials in their own language. He urged Magyars not to distrust the Swabians, as they would always remain true Hungarians. *Sonntagsblatt* noted that Neuberger was the first Swabian in Parliament daring to defend his people. But Bleyer also saw that Bethlen ignored Neuberger, and this contributed to Swabian alienation.

Gratz joined the chorus of Swabians offended by government delay. The Peace Treaty had bestowed a new, legal character upon minorities. What happened to them now was of international concern. Thus far, Hungary had either ignored its obligations or had paid them only lip service. The government should not take the matter lightly, lest Hungary's former subjects in the Successor States suffer grievous injury in retaliation. Bleyer claimed he heard Gratz expound these views in cabinet, where they made a deep impression.[9]

By failing to discharge their obligations on minority protection effectively, the Magyars also courted the opprobrium of the Reich. Germany's apparent non-concern in the Burgenland affair had led the Magyars into the mistaken belief that Germany lacked interest. They were chagrined, therefore, when the Reich began to show active concern for the Swabians' well-being. In a verbal note addressed to the wilhelmstrasse, the Magyars struggled to clear the air. They denied the Swabians suffered either economic or cultural oppression. Hungary had 49 pure German and 370 mixed Magyar-German elementary schools, as well as fourteen Swabian members of Parliament. But Swabian protection was strictly an internal affair. The Magyars claimed favouritism, citing the example of Josef Wild, who had defeated Bleyer in the recent election. Until recently, Wild had been a German citizen who spoke Magyar imperfectly; yet he encountered no hurdles because of his background. This was typical. The Magyars preferred a man like Wild, whose ideology suited them, rather than a man like Bleyer, whose Magyar was perfect, but whose German cultural *Weltanschauung* was objectionable.

A Wilhelmstrasse dispatch of 8 September addressed to Fürstenberg left no doubt about Germany's vexation.

> We do not doubt the Prime Minister's good will, but we are under the impression, reinforced by your own reports, that he is not only weak but that he feels himself to be weak; and in the German question . . . he tends to limit himself to friendly and encouraging conversation.

Furthermore, recently Bethlen had not been exactly a man of his word. Aware that his moderation irritated Berlin, Fürstenberg vigourously denounced the Bethlen regime. It took unfair advantage of Germany's current weakness in order to destroy the Swabians. Fürstenberg offered no reason for this unexpected and decisive change. Perhaps the Magyars exploited the touchy Erzberger extradition case to settle the score with the Swabians. Regarding Swabian education, the Magyars had partially fulfilled their obligations. Hungary's 47 pure German and 370 mixed elementary schools corresponded almost exactly with the number of German communities. The danger of irredentism in Burgenland might have played a part in the retention of the pure German schools. Yet he was not pleased with the overall situation. Odenburg (Sopron) and Güns (Kőszeg), two traditionally German towns, had lost all their pure German schools; in all higher educational institutes, instruction was given exclusively in Magyar. Furstenberg also cautioned that his statistics might no longer be accurate. Nobody knew for certain whether the pure German schools remained. Outside of Burgenland and recently recovered southern Hungary only six such schools survived. Even there, the language was taught ineffectively. Everywhere, Swabian children lacked German texts and the authorities refused to order them. In the Hungarian Parliament, only one Swabian deputy, the Social Democrat Viktor Knaller, concerned himself with the welfare of his people in any way. Furstenberg excoriated Bethlen for reneging on his promises. Germany should not interfere in Hungary's internal affairs, but Germany could not vouch for the attitude of its public if persecutions continued much longer. Fürstenberg's note was relatively mild, his appraisal lax. He apparently saw official Hungarian school statistics but neglected to investigate first-hand whether minority schools still existed, how many students were enrolled, and whether instruction even in so-called pure schools merited the name. Fürstenberg failed to pursue German and Swabian interests in Hungary vigourously, a circumstance that possibly hastened his removal shortly after.

During the next few months, the Swabian issue continued to predominate. Hungary's Minister in Berlin complained that the German press exaggerated Swabian grievances. New regulations designed to remedy certain evils were being contemplated. Where many Swabians resided, schools would soon be established having either predominantly German instruction or German-Magyar parallel classes. This was a vague promise to perpetuate the existing system, nothing more. A similar proposal surfaced when Bethlen received Germany's new minister, Count Welczek. The Prime Minister reiterated his determination to provide effective protection for the Swabian minority, that would remove the only apparent stumbling block to German-Hungarian friendship. Swabian aspirations would soon be honoured, for a new law was imminent, providing protection for the development of Swabian cultural growth.

The Hungarian school offensive continued unabated. In March 1923, von Mutius, German envoy and minister plenipotentiary, submitted a report concerning his conversation with Hungary's Baron Szterényi. Szterényi was in Berlin on a secret and confidential mission on Bethlen's behalf to unveil Hungary's impending minority law. His information was so privileged, he claimed, as to be unknown to the Hungarian minister in Berlin. According to Szterényi, Bethlen decided to issue a new regulation resembling the 1868 Nationality Law. It would be effective in all communities with minority populations of 20% or more per nationality; compliance by local authorities would be mandatory; all administrators would perforce learn the language (or languages) of a minority region within two years; every citizen's mother tongue would be recognized as a legal medium of communication. There would be two types of minority schools: those where Magyar was taught only as a subject; and those where Magyar would be the language of instruction, excepting religious studies, reading, writing, and arithmetic, which would be also taught in the minority language. Special courses for minority school teachers would be established; German parallel classes would be organized in one boys' and one girls' *polgáriskola,* and in one gymnasium. But Mutius doubted seriously whether Bethlen— even with the best of intentions—could prevail with such a liberal programme in view of the chauvinistic wing of his coalition government.

Shortly after Szterényi's visit, Hungary's minister in Berlin reiterated Bethlen's wish not to permit misunderstandings to obstruct German-

Hungarian friendship. Bethlen had not forgotten his promises. The Magyars would not object if Reich Germans interested in minority affairs established contact with their Swabian counterparts, provided they did not attempt to destroy "the Hungarian national state."[10] Even when extending the hand of friendship, the Magyars could not resist a veiled insult.

In addition to education, German-Hungarian relations were exacerbated by a number of other vexing disputes. Hungary's conservative regime clashed with Germany's Social Democratic system. Relations became deeply compromised, therefore, when on 29 August 1921, right-wing extremists murdered Germany's Minister of Finance, Matthias Erzberger. The assassins allegedly fled to Hungary, whereupon Germany accused the Horthy regime of complicity in the crime and of shielding the fugitives. The culprits were common criminals and should be extradited under international law. The Magyars maintained the offenders were political fugitives and hence the criminal code did not apply. The incident shook the fragile German-Hungarian friendship to its foundation.

Hungary's evasions embittered the Reich. In an interview with Furstenberg, Bethlen unwittingly betrayed his flimsy position, and the normally mild-mannered Count struck back angrily. Germany had waited patiently for many months for a reply to its extradition demands. But Bethlen argued the question was academic since both murderers had fled Hungary. Fürstenberg sarcastically demanded why Bethlen had not produced this information before. Perhaps he had just found out about it that very day. The embarrassed Bethlen thereupon tried to change the subject. Fürstenberg warned Bethlen that German-Hungarian relations were precarious and his attitude would vanquish remaining German confidence in Magyar promises. Despite firm commitments, Hungary had steadfastly refused to arrest and extradite Erzberger's murderers. Bethlen protested his innocence; his friendship for Germany was sincere. Undaunted, Fürstenberg pressed the attack, demanding an accounting of Hungary's connections with Reich rightist radicals. Bethlen replied evasively. He deplored these connections, but they were, after all, private contacts involving right-wing extremists in both countries. Bethlen vowed to carry out all his promises, especially to the Swabians, and pledged to instruct Count von Emich, Hungary's minister in Berlin, to convey Hungary's position on all these matters to the German Chancellor. Fürstenberg was unconvinced. In his secret report he denounced Hungarian agencies, especially the police and passport bureaus who shielded common murderers and fraternized with right-wing dissidents in Germany. In the long-run, German-Hungarian relations would be shattered beyond repair, and convince Germans that Hungary conspired to destroy German unity.

The German Chancellor responded personally. Hungary's succour to the Reich's enemies now amounted to internal intervention. Bethlen's excuses were insufficient, and the Chancellor alerted Fürstenberg that he might be recalled shortly. In the meantime, he was to seek an interview with Bethlen to announce the impending crisis. Though firm in tone, Fürstenberg's verbal note fell short of accusing Hungarian officials of outright complicity with Erzberger's assassins. Nevertheless, Hungarian soil was being used as a sanctuary by German political desperadoes against the security of the German State. Bethlen's statement that the murderers had fled Hungary proved conclusively that the culprits had indeed sojourned there for a long time. He demanded energetic steps to end the machinations of these undesirables. Afterwards, Fürstenberg had second thoughts. His superiors' aggressive tactics might miscarry; Bethlen might find himself in a precarious position and his recent promises might have to be sacrificed to political expediency.

Fürstenberg was correct in one respect at least. German pugnacity evoked a Magyar response in kind. Hungary refused to entertain Germany's extradition theory, and it questioned its validity in international criminal theory. Germany's refusal to extradite Béla Kun, not to hand over the assassin of Prime Minister Count István Tisza, remained alive in Magyar memory. The Magyars also indignantly refuted German contentions about internal interference, labelling such charges as "monstrous." On the contrary, after Vienna, Berlin was the chief haven for Communist fugitives from Hungary. While Hungary's press was pro-German, German newspapers engaged in a systematic anti-Hungarian hate campaign, based on fabrications and downright horror stories, and obviously designed to tarnish Hungary's international reputation.

Two weeks later, a reply to Fürstenberg's own dispatch of 26 August arrived from the Wilhelmstrasse. Geheimrat Rumelin lectured the Count in the art of diplomacy. Fürstenberg should not be swayed so easily by the Magyars. A little energetic conversation in Budapest had never done any harm, and it is thus in the present affair. Bethlen was in a weak position, and had no sympathy for Germany in the Erzberger case; his general friendliness was mere pretense, masquerading behind an engaging turn of speech. Count Emich, whom Bethlen was to have instructed to visit the German Chancellor immediately had not only failed to do so but had gone on a leisurely holiday instead. So much for Magyar promises. Fürstenberg was advised to tell Bethlen that the Erzberger case was very close to the Chancellor's heart and that Hungary would gain absolutely nothing by dragging her feet.

The offended Fürstenberg fired off an angry and defiant reply. A rift had developed between the pliant and impressionable Fürstenberg and his inflexible superiors. He insisted that intractability in Hungary was not always desirable, as the present situation suggested. Had his own advice been followed in the past, there would be far fewer difficulties now; the Foreign Ministry was ignorant and paid little attention to important situations. He knew more about Hungary than they, because they were in Berlin, while he was in Budapest. An eight-page report accompanying this broadside conceded that overwhelming proof from all sides had convinced Fürstenberg after all that Bethlen's promises were hollow. Strangely enough, however, he pointedly ignored the Erzberger case, one of the most important issues separating Germany and Hungary. Fürstenberg's outburst cost him his diplomatic post. On 23 September he was ordered to take a furlough and then return to Berlin for consultations. He was shortly replaced by Count von Welczek.

Not before the new year did von Emich finally visit Germany's chancellor, fulfilling a six-month promise. Even so, it only exacerbated hard feelings. Emich curtly repudiated Germany's extradition claim as invalid and evaded the issue further by pleading that personal contacts between individual Hungarian and Bavarian factions should not be permitted to be used for political intrigues. Only with respect to the condition of the Swabian minority did von Emich hold out vague promises of improvement.

In the meantime, Welczek succumbed to Bethlen's suave charms. Welczek characterized the Prime Minister in a dispatch as a calm, considerate, serious man, more Anglo-Saxon than Magyar. His mind was sober, evidently due to his upbringing among the Transylvanian Saxons. His programme, considering Hungarian conditions, was relatively liberal. Concerning the rightist menace, Bethlen allegedly assured Welczek that it would be a catastrophy for Hungary if the Gömbös-Héjjas-Prónay clique ever came to power. Bethlen had labeled these right-wing radicals as political illiterates, but could not guarantee that they could be kept out of office indefinitely. Bethlen clearly wished to arouse German fears of an imminent rightist coup in Hungary. The new regime would certainly argue that German Social Democracy had to go. For better or for worse, Germany should cooperate with Bethlen, for the alternatives were too unpleasant. Bethlen had yet another trump card to play. He planned to visit various Entente capitals in search of funds for Hungary's fiscal reconstruction. If Allied economic and financial blandishments proved to be sufficiently attractive, might not Hungary abandon even a pretense of a pro-German orientation? It was a tempting thought. Bethlen left the Germans guessing.

Several months later, Emich paid yet another visit to the Wilhelmstrasse, pursuing the same harsh line as before. According to Undersecretary of State Köpke, the minister engaged in mere generalities, contributing nothing new to the solution of the triple Gordian knot confounding German-Hungarian relations: the Erzberger case, Magyar-German right-radical connections, and the plight of the Swabians. Emich merely admitted that connections between Magyar and Bavarian right-wing groups undeniably existed. Köpke offered no further comment. The Magyars evidently benefited from Germany's apprehensions about a possible rightist coup in Hungary.

The Germans were indeed preoccupied with the possibility of a Hungarian putsch. Only a few days after Emich's visit a telegram reached the German Foreign Ministry stating that Bethlen's overthrow by a group representing a chauvinist-reactionary Gömbös orientation was imminent. For the sake of German interests, Bethlen's hand should be strengthened. German newspapers in Rumania, for example, should be persuaded to write flattering accounts of Bethlen, extolling his sympathetic views on minority problems, and excoriating Gömbös chauvinism. Whether or not Bethlen faced deposition is moot. Welczek fueled speculations about Bethlen's political demise by writing that at first he doubted the imminence of a right-wing coup; recently he obtained concrete proof that a wide-spread conspiracy involving Gömbös' *Ébredő Magyarok,* a secret extremist patriotic organization, existed. It had intimate links with Fascists in other countries, including Hitler's people in Bavaria. Whether Bethlen deliberately circulated alarms to jettison constant German harassment is another question. Be that as it may, the situation benefitted him and his clever policy of restrained Swabian repression.

For a time Germany exercised greater caution than before in dealing with the Magyars. The German legation dissuaded Karl von Loesch, dynamic president of the ultra-nationalistic *Deutscher Schutzbund,* an organization devoted to the protection of German interests abroad, from delivering a scathing denunciation of Hungarian minority policies when he visited Budapest. Instead, von Loesch limited himself to flattering remarks, which emphasized Hungary's glorious past and traditional German-Hungarian friendship. He closed prophetically that Germany and Hungary would either sink together or rise together. In a subsequent interview with *Új Nemzedék,* a Budapest paper, Loesch none too delicately raised the question of Magyar involvement with German rightist elements. The Bavarian separatist movement was supported principally by France, which sought to destroy German unity by creating a separatist Rhineland state stretching all the way to Vienna. It was astounding that Magyars misinterpreted French intentions. Instead of dealing with Munich, they ought to be negotiating with Berlin. Loesch carefully avoided any construction that might be misconstrued as a slur against Hungary. If the aim was to enlighten the

Magyars about the implications of a fractured Germany, and if he hoped to draw them back from the abyss, Loesch was greatly mistaken. The Magyars desired a divided Germany. From every point of view an independent southern German state would be a boon to Hungary. A moderately powerful, predominantly Roman Catholic, politically kindred, conservative nation would depend on Hungary for its food supply, and would buffer an aggressive, Protestant, Prussian-oriented German imperium, paradoxically serving Social Democracy.

The question of private and quasi-official rightist collusion, including the Erzberger case, remained unresolved and poisoned German-Hungarian relations for years. Even as late as in 1925, when Germany and Hungary began a cautious rapprochement, the German press kept it alive, agitating not only on extradition, but also against Hungary's alleged anti-Semitism and her Swabian persecutions. Welczek appealed for a cessation of anti-Magyar attacks, since they impeded a German-Hungarian understanding.[11] Hungary emerged triumphant in the extradition "war" but it proved to be a pyrrhic victory. Progressively more conservative, Germany cared less and less about Erzberger's killers. At the same time, the Germans recognized that the Magyars drove a hard bargain. They were relentless adversaries, uncertain friends, and crass opportunists. Growing German might rendered Hungary's short-term egocentric strategy extremely hazardous for the Magyars in the long-run.

On 22 June 1923, after many months of hints, promises, and top-secret sneak previews Bethlen unveiled his minority legislation in Parliament. Actually, there were two laws: one dealing with minority elementary (six-year) schools, the other with the official status of minority tongues. Bethlen cited Hungary's obligations under the Trianon Peace Treaty as the chief reason for the promulgation of the new statute. This was a bad omen. In his previous statements, particularly to the Swabians and the German government, the Prime Minister had implied genuine concern for the cultural welfare of the minorities. Everyone acquainted with Magyar sensibilities after Trianon knew that promulgating a law which rested on the hated peace treaty was bestowing it with a kiss of death.

In theory, the new school law merely perpetuated existing conditions. The original pure minority schools corresponded with a newly-established A institution; mixed minority-Magyar institutions resembled the new B schools; while C establishments supplanted the original Magyar schools where pupils learned their mother tongue only as a subject. Before the law could be carried out, a number of technical, legal, and practical hurdles had to be overcome. At first glance, the new law failed to live up to expectations aroused by various previews and promises. German parallel classes above grade school level were not mentioned at all, and teachers' courses were not being contemplated. C schools were so watered down that they did not qualify as minority institutions. Decisions regarding school types to be adopted in each community were to be left to the discretion of parents and school boards. Local officials had ample opportunities for coercing parents' conferences[12]. In all, Swabians and Germans had little cause for rejoicing.

In a series of articles, *Sonntagsblatt* publicized the new law. Swabians were told that the 1868 and 1919 nationality laws were still binding, although frequently cast into doubt by government neglect and abuse.[13] All citizens were to be equals in every respect and could use their mother tongue both privately and in official life. This aspect of the law corresponded faithfully with the draft presented to the German government a few months earlier, but it provided nothing new in the way of minority protection. On the whole, if the wording alone could have determined its effectiveness, the language provision of the 1923 minority statute would have been a great success. Paragraphs 20 and 21 clearly stipulated that officials in minority districts would be disciplined, even pensioned, if they failed to learn the minority language within two years. Perhaps the only flaw, concealed in paragraphs 13 and 14, was that minorities would have to specifically petition that the language of protocol in their region be other than Magyar. Since most county, municipal, and village officials were Magyar patriots, such requests would receive short shrift.

The weaknesses of the new law became apparent immediately. Confessional, association, and private schools retained their privilege of determining the language of instruction. Since only 22% of Hungary's elementary schools were under state control the law had only marginal significance. Even in state institutions it was by no means certain that a minority language would be introduced automatically. According to paragraph 18, it all depended on the sympathetic consideration of local school and administrative organs. The designation was vague, the procedure only dimly spelled out. Swabians were likely to encounter serious difficulties in establishing minority schools under these circumstances. Similarly vague was the provision that higher schools, universities excluded, might establish parallel classes in minority languages. This was never put in operation. Paragraph 19 laid the foundation for the creation of minority cultural and economic organizations, a measure that would soon be introduced, though far from satisfactorily.[14]

As the second step in its publicity campaign, *Sonntagsblatt* attempted to convince Swabian parents that the success of the school law rested on their frail shoulders. The editors claimed to have discovered certain peculiarities in the new regulations, which the adherents of minority education might use to good advantage. In the past, whenever Magyar instruction was introduced, it could never be abolished; continuation schools (two years past elementary level) could be conducted only in Magyar; and the Minister of Education could arbitrarily demand that confessional schools introduce Magyar in certain specific subjects on pain of losing their substantial government subsidy. These harsh provisions of the 1907 School Act were now rescinded. Swept away with his own enthusiasm, the editor rhapsodized that parents might become instruments of an instant renaissance in minority education, provided they seized the initiative. He even suggested that *Bürgerschulen* and teachers' academies also qualified as *Volksschulen* under the new regulations, and hence they might commence teaching all their subjects in German at once. "We will be temporarily satisfied with the present arrangement," wrote *Sonntagsblatt,* with euphoric disdain for the stark realities of Hungarian minority life. It evidently did not occur to the editor that the Magyars might consider such premature hopes by Germans as insolent gloating.

Sonntagsblatt stressed loopholes that clever Swabian parents might exploit. Minority regulations applied only in districts where at least 20% of the population was non-Magyar, and only a few communes fell into this category. However, Swabians could easily outmanoeuvre the law. Confessional schools did not have to await ministerial releases before the new law could be introduced. Swabians could take immediate action since clergymen were not always as hostile as Magyar officials in government-run secular institutions. Swabian parents' conferences would have little impact here, but in Protestant schools, for example, the church council had to decide the language of instruction. Parents were obliged to convey their wishes either to their pastor or priest or to the community church inspector. Although many clergymen admittedly were Magyarones, they might find it difficult to resist the energetic and concerted demands of their parishioners. Protestant church councils could resist expressions of the popular will even less. Thus, the Swabians had some reason to believe they might outwit the authorities by concentrating on the possible Achilles heel of minority education, the confessional schools.[15]

In Hungary, the new law was surprisingly well received. In Parliament it was hailed by both Left and Right. The Magyar-language press supported it nearly unanimously. This runs counter to Magyar hostility after Trianon, but the Magyars desired favourable publicity abroad since they needed foreign aid desperately. Bethlen had only recently made a questing tour of Entente capitals. This may be the reason why *Pester Lloyd,* Hungary's widely read and respected newspaper abroad, published the most extensive coverage of the school law. Szterényi remarked in *Pester Lloyd* that the government would have to observe the statute in order to maintain favourable opinions of Hungary abroad. *Népszava,* the Social Democratic Party organ, gave the law its blessing, but doubted seriously whether the government would really carry it out. *Magyarság,* the influential opposition leader Count Gyula Andrássy's paper, argued that the law should have been passed in Parliament, not issued arbitrarily as an executive decree. Andrássy feared reversal of existing assimilationist trends. The Swabians might subvert the law by demanding concessions detrimental to the unity of Hungary.

At first, the Swabians and Germans were pleased and surprised; in time they grew more cautious. Anton König, a Swabian leader, wrote that

> at least there were no two ways about the law—it would either be observed or not. Officials had no way out, regardless of their own feelings or opposition to the law. Previously, they could always argue that the Apponyi law superseded all others. No longer.

Bleyer hoped the new law would be administered honestly, throughout the administrative structure of the country. He prophesized that failure would have dire consequences.

But Bleyer was even more concerned about the efficacy of the provisions than with the government's performance. He felt that feature for feature the law was rather poor. Yet at long last the government had formally promised to sponsor minority education, even though kindergartens and continuation schools were to remain purely Magyar institutions. In principle, Bleyer endorsed A and even B schools. C institutions, however, were not minority schools at all, since children would not learn how to count in German. Bleyer fretted because even if parents should vote in favour of A or B schools, they would be initially introduced only in the first grade. In other words, even at best, it would take at least six years to transform the school system in each community. Bleyer also worried because the Ministry of Education failed to issue hourly schedules for minority schools; study plans would have to be devised *ad hoc* by unsympathetic local school administrators. German curricula, even in A and B schools, could be easily subverted under these circumstances. Obviously, this was one of the weakest links in the minority education system. The only silver lining was that parents could demand German reading and writing in all six grades simultaneously. On the whole, Bleyer feared the law would be ineffective and create a poor impression among Germans in the lost areas.

Reich Germans echoed Swabian skepticism. Count D. Bernstorff, president of the *Deutsche Liga für Völkerbund* and member of the Reichstag, felt it was essential for Hungary to grant school and association rights to the Swabians, since they were faithful Hungarian patriots without a trace of irredentist sentiments. He doubted, however, whether the Magyars would live up to their promises. Swabian indifference, no less than Magyar pressures, would soon nullify the new regulations. The only hope was that Hungary and Germany were bound together, thrown into each others' arms, as it were, by the common Slavic menace and by their postwar dissatisfactions.[16]

The two-month period between the issuing of the law and school-opening day should have been spent in feverish preparation by the government. To Bleyer's chagrin, however, nothing happened. Usually, when the government issued a new regulation or a ministerial decree, Hungary's official machinery swung into efficient action. Not so with Law 4800. Although it was effective on the day of its promulgation, as usual with minority laws, the government dragged its feet. Bethlen had a good explanation, however, and Bleyer sadly discovered what it was. The penultimate paragraph stipulated that the individual releases in connection with this statute will be issued by the relevant Ministries in cooperation with the Prime Minister. This threw responsibility for implementation squarely into the laps of the various ministries and Bethlen, who blamed each other for the delays. In the meantime, the Swabians had no minority schools for yet another year. Bleyer was indignant. Two months ought to have been enough to resolve any bureaucratic technicalities.

> The fact that the announcement came as late as 22 June was already suspicious. More time than that is needed to initiate German schools. There are no German texts! Old ones are few and dated. As well, organizing an entire school system takes time. Most teachers do not know German and these would have to be exchanged for German-speaking instructors—yet even those know only dialects and should have to be retrained.

The government pursued a game of cat-and-mouse with the Swabians, alternately raising and dashing their hopes. Bleyer expressed cautious hope a week later:

> The ministerial decree has appeared! The Minister of Education released it on 24 August, he published it on 28 August and on 31 August in the newspapers. Under it, school boards, in agreement with parents of school-age children, must decide what types of schools are desired—but [it must be accomplished] no later than 9 September![17]

knowing the ways of bureaucracy, Bleyer doubted that anything would be accomplished by the deadline. His own readers would not even know about the new release until too late. Hungary earned few laurels for tantalizing the Swabians. Toying with peoples' sensibilities is bound to have disastrous long-range consequences, as the Magyars were to find out later to their sorrow.

Governmental duplicity became fully evident later that month. In no Swabian community had officials even received word about the new school decree and the September extension. Even where parents knew the situation, they often lacked either the will or the courage to remind functionaries. In some communities meetings did take place at the behest of parents, most of whom voted overwhelmingly in favour of A schools. Some desired B institutions, but almost none wanted C schools. In many places, disagreements poisoned amicable relations between parents and authorities. In view of this anarchic situation Bleyer demanded that the deadline be extended until the end of October.

The law sharpened latent cleavages in Swabian society between assimila-tionists and nationalists. The dispute began even before the school law was published. When the Ministry of Nationalities was abolished in the Spring of 1922, the government named the assimilationist Swabian Georg Steuer to be German commissioner. Steuer, formerly an *Obergespan (föispán)* in Baranya County, was a notorious pro-Magyar, at least from the nationalist Swabian point of view. His denunciation of German schools in Torontál County during the war on the grounds that they were a Pan-German menace ingratiated him with the Magyars but earned him the hatred and contempt of *volkisch* Swabians. In a scathing article, Bleyer assailed assimilants by labeling the commissioner an opportunistic, self-seeking sycophant. Bleyer scarcely hoped to gain the government's trust because by attacking Steuer, he automatically derided the government. It was a foregone conclusion that decisions entailing the minorities would henceforth reflect assimilationist philosophy rather than cultural nationalism.

Yet once the law was issued, it suited neither side. The nationalists complained that Swabian officials in the villages almost invariably sabot-aged the law and hence deceived their own people. The assimilationists attacked the law on pedagogical grounds. An Evangelical cleric wrote, for example, that mixed-language instruction harmed and confused both teachers and pupils. He suggested that only reading, writing, and arithmetic be taught to Swabian children in their own language. Gratz adopted a middle of the road position. In his view, lower officials probably misinter-preted the new minority law. He feared that resentful Swabians might turn bitter and repudiate the interests of the dominant Magyar ruling majority.

For the sake of Hungary's foreign policy, therefore, local officials should be made aware of changed conditions and be induced to obey the law.[18]

The extremist anti-Swabian fringe also entered the fray. The Roman Catholic teachers' association of the deaconate of Máriakeménd asserted at its Püspöklak meeting that it was the duty of every patriotic Hungarian to transform all the schools into Magyar institutions within two years, the only exception being that reading, writing, and arithmetic be also taught in the pupil's mother tongue. Another resolution condemned *Sonntagsblatt's* editors as Pan-Germans propagating treason under the guise of Roman Catholicism. In general, both Magyar and Magyarophil ecclesiastic authorities in Baranya County conducted a hate campaign against Bleyer and *Sonntagsblatt* for their espousal of German education. The anti-Swabian Church campaign extended throughout Hungary. Only in Vasvár (Steinamanger) County in West Hungary, where Bishop Count Mikes permitted German instruction, was the law fully obeyed. Out of seven communities, six chose A schools, while one selected a B institution. *Sonntagsblatt* observed that Mikes was the only Magyar bishop who took the law seriously.[19]

Wishing to embarrass the government, two Social Democratic deputies, Knaller and Rothenstein, raised the school issue in Parliament on the eve of the arrival of a League of Nations delegation intent on examining Hungary's financial position prior to granting aid. Knaller complained that none of the previous minority laws had ever been observed and he saw no reason why this one should be an exception. Rothenstein contemptuously posed a rhetorical question: Would Swabians or Slovaks in Hungary *dare* to use their mother tongue, law or no law? Stung to the quick, Bethlen countered the following day that even before the war Hungary's minorities were better off than anywhere else, and cited copious statistics to support his contention. Regarding the present law, it was true that in some respects it had not been carried out, but this was because the law had come too late in the season. He promised it would be in effect by the 1924-1925 school year. Even currently, the Prime Minister insisted, the situation was not so bad. Hungary had 400 communities in which Swabians numbered at least 20% of the total population. Of these, 240 had at least partly German schools. In fact, schools in two Burgenland communities, Wandorf (Banfalva) and Brennberg (Brennbergbanya), did not offer Magyar even as a subject before the third grade. Bethlen urged Members to call all violations to his personal attention and the government would do its duty. Bethlen's remarks were not confined to Parliament. He made similar promises to a distinguished European minority leader, Ewald Ammende, who cautioned that the school law was in danger of remaining a paper fiat. Bethlen assured Ammende that this was to be no show-window law. A few officials might oppose it, but as soon as he returned to Hungary he would immediately take up the matter personally. If need be, a few officials would have to be suspended if they obstructed the law too energetically.[20]

Performance fell far short of promises. Towards the end of the 1923-1924 school year, *Sonntagsblatt* reminded complacent Swabian parents that German education languished and that certain legal loopholes might yet defeat them. According to Ministry regulations, parents desiring to change the prevailing system had to petition many months before the beginning of the following season. By 1 July of each year, communities had to make the required changes, otherwise the prevailing system would continue until the end of the following year. According to *Sonntagsblatt,* thus far, very few communities had adopted German instruction. Parents were urged not to delay, for they had only one more month left. The paper despaired because even if parents should force through German instruction, the gesture would be useless. Too few teachers spoke the language in Swabian areas and texts were not available. The government was urged to do something at once.

The article triggered a cascade of mail. Some parents merely made inquiries, while others lodged complaints of various types. An ugly picture emerged, justifying the Swabians' worst fears. Apparently, local officials refused to obey the law, and would not convene parents' conferences. Parents had to initiate proceedings on their own hook. Without the support of local officialdom, however, their efforts were in vain. Faced with concerted opposition by the Magyars, how could the Swabians prevail? They were confused. There seemed to be an inexplicable gap between high government decree and local action. A fragment of Bethlen's recent speech in Parliament seemed to cast the contrast into bold relief:

> Before the war, we frequently confused language with patriotism. We believed that whoever spoke good Magyar was a patriot, whoever did not was no patriot. This was a great error. We have to realize this and make it possible for our minorities to receive instruction in their mother tongue if they desire. This does not negate Magyar patriotism.[21]

But the situation did not improve by the beginning of the 1924-1925 academic year as Bethlen had promised in Parliament. Parents' conferences were still frustrated by obstinate local administrators. No A schools were introduced that year and only a few B institutions were launched. "Progress" was limited to C schools, in which instruction in German reading and writing would not commence until the third year.

The fiasco of the first month in the 1924-1925 academic season convinced Bleyer that the entire minority school system was built on erroneous principles. The conferences were a poor device, since with three school types from which to choose, conflict developed between parents and officials. C schools were not minority schools at all. Bleyer concluded that ideally, all subjects ought to have been taught in German to begin with, with one hour each day devoted to the Magyar language. In this manner pupils might have learned Magyar slowly and gradually, but perfectly. At the very least, Swabian pupils ought to learn history and geography in their own language, not only for pedagogical, but for psychological and patriotic reasons. He saw in his approach a road to Magyar patriotism.

The government of course ignored Bleyer's proposal and violations continued. The Swabians, no less than Reich Germans, exercised great caution lest they embarrass Bethlen politically. They knew that the alternative to Bethlen's non-violent repression might very well be a chauvinistic reaction under Gömbös. Consequently, for the time being, Bethlen escaped the blame for school and other violations. Local administrators earned the concentrated opprobrium of their Swabian critics instead. In Parliament, for example, Neuberger stated that Swabian rights and wishes were greeted with good will in many places, especially from Prime Minister Bethlen. In contrast, Neuberger lashed out at local administrators who broke the law, citing several flagrant examples. In one instance, a Magyar school inspector reversed the decision of a parents' conference at Somberek to continue German minority schools established during the Yugoslav occupation. Another case entailed the reversal of a nearly unanimous decision by Swabians in a Komárom County community. The village board had voted to compel the authorities to communicate in the german language with citizens whose Magyar was imperfect. The *Vicegespan* vetoed the decision. Neuberger demanded more honest laws, not ones that merely pulled the wool over peoples' eyes.

Without mentioning Bethlen by name, Bleyer echoed Neuberger's sentiments. Magyar statesmanship must abandon a one-sided racial policy and readopt the noblest features of a traditionalist national philosophy. He vowed that Swabians would never submit to one-sided Magyar racial policies. Neither the Swabians' colonist ancestors, who were summoned to bring culture to Hungary, nor the succeeding generations had any intentions of submitting to such a policy. In a more practical vein, Bleyer repeated his plaint of one year earlier. Nothing had been done to expedite Swabian minority schools. Only three days were left before the deadline of 1 July, yet nowhere had preparations been made to convoke parents' conferences. He noted sadly that the school law had driven a wedge between the Swabian people and their Magyarone intelligentsia. Bleyer hoped that Bethlen and Klebelsberg would create a new, better law for the next academic year.

Bleyer's expectations were boosted once more a few days later when he discovered that the government had extended the deadline for parents' conferences until 15 August. This seemed to him a patent display of Bethlen's good will and willingness to deal fairly with the Swabian community.

Bleyer was euphoric again one month later, when the government delivered its oft-promised final and definitive minority school study plan on 14 August, in time for the 1925-1926 academic year. Bleyer found it far from perfect, but it did incorporate certain improvements, such as a business-like approach to regulate relations between parents and officials. Both were informed unequivocally of their duties and what minority instruction must accomplish as to method, content, and language. The new directive also implied that one of the three minority school types would be introduced with or without the formal convening of parents' conferences. Bleyer considered this the most felicitous proviso and hoped that there would be no chicanery. He also rejoiced that the deadline was extended once more, to 15 September. Moreover, the Minister promised to publish an official roster of all Swabian communities and their school types. Bleyer hailed a pedagogical change in B schools. Henceforth, geography, history, and composition would be taught in German in the first three grades, and in Magyar the last three grades. He believed pupils would master these subjects more readily this way. Bleyer recognized the flaws as well as the progress. The C schools had not been improved. The new regulation applied only to fully divided schools, in which each class had a different teacher. Unfortunately, nearly all Swabian schools were either partially or totally integrated, that is, teachers taught either all or several classes simultaneously. Bleyer feared that this would serve as yet another pretext for not introducing the school law in Swabian institutions, but he reaffirmed his faith in Bethlen: The Prime Minister and Klebelsberg would enforce the law in state schools and ecclesiastical institutions alike. Bleyer's confidence was further strengthened by Bethlen's speech at the League of Nations. Bethlen attempted to minimize the perils of an alleged Pan-German menace in Hungary. In an obvious allusion to Hungary's Swabians, Bethlen rejected the antiquated ideologies of those who considered patriotism dependent on language only, and promised to enlist his government's power and prestige behind the drive for German schools in Hungary.[22]

As the Swabian minority school system limped along, the government placated the unhappy minority on 15 June 1923, with the right to form a nationwide cultural association, the *Ungarländischer Deutscher Volksbildungsverein (UDV)*. Since obtaining such a permit in Hungary was difficult, this concession may be fully appreciated. Even after the formal granting of its charter, but prior to its public organization, many Swabians feared that the permit would be yet another stillborn affair. The right of association was so severely limited in postwar Hungary that any ill will by national or regional authorities could kill a chartered organization. Baron Szterényi alerted Swabians that despite the assurances in paragraph 19 of the school law, the right of association was not regulated by statute, but by the Minister of the Interior. The Ministry meticulously examined the by-laws of all would-be organizations, and if they were not deemed to be in the public interest, law or no law, a permit would not be granted. Under prevailing government policy, moreover, national associations were considered to be undesirable unless proved otherwise. Szterényi hoped that the government's permit was not merely a way station to further disappointment.

Indeed, the government deferred its final permit for over a year, until 3 August 1924. Soon, the reason for the delay became apparent. The government wished to dominate the organization. For over a year, the government bargained with the Swabians, demanding the right to nominate half of the UDV's functionaries, including two-thirds of its executive triumvirate (Gratz, Wild, and Bleyer). Only after the Swabians acquiesced, did the government grant its final permit. Eager to smooth the way, Bleyer painted a somewhat more attractive picture:

> It took the government this long to approve most of our constitution, alter a
> few provisions, and suggest additional members for our directorate, namely,
> people of German ancestry who also played a confidential role in Hungarian
> public life.[23]

It speaks well for Bleyer that he accommodated Wild, a political adversary. His tactful euphemisms could not obscure the fact that the UDV was little more than a government puppet. Though cooperating with it to some extent, most Swabians and Reich Germans branded the association for what it was—a creature of the regime.[24]

In order to "reassure" the UDV and the Swabians of its support and good will in the face of vociferous Magyar nationalist opposition, Bethlen issued a rescript confirming that the UDV's programme corresponded with the government's wishes. All the existing minority statutes were meticulously surveyed and the Swabians advised that they would be introduced and maintained. It was an ominous sign, however, that Bethlen ascribed the rationale for all these laws, the one dealing with the UDV included, as "arising from Hungary's obligations incurred by the Treaty of Trianon."[25]

The UDV's programme was modest, limited to strictly cultural matters. Politics were taboo. The association was to issue newspapers, periodicals, and books, arrange lectures, courses, exhibits, patriotic and ethnic folk festivals, establish libraries, museum exhibits, schools, bursaries, and prizes. It was also to nurture the non-political aspirations of Hungary's Swabians, including their ethnic peculiarities, traditions, language, Christian standards, and not least, their loyalty to the Magyar fatherland. The *UDV* was even charged with the responsibility of bringing minority school infractions to the attention of the Prime Minister personally. The latter promised to advise county executives not to hinder *UDV* operations.

Despite Bethlen's virtual sponsorship, a veritable storm of slander and insinuations arose almost from the moment the *UDV* launched its membership drive. Its efforts were labelled Pan-German, anti-Magyar, for home consumption, and *völkisch*-antisemitic for the benefit of the Reich public. Magyar detractors, especially in the Budapest area, objected to *UDV* recruitment on patriotic grounds. At a Pest County general assembly a speaker considered it bizarre that foci of German influence should be permitted to flourish so near the capital. Nor was this an isolated incident. In the Buda region, a judge told a would-be *UDV* recruit that the association was designed only for Germans from abroad, not for Swabians. There were also cases of indirect persecutions. Faul-Farkas, editor of *Sonntagsblatt,* purchased a piece of ground in Törökbálint, near Budapest. The authorities refused to honour the deed because the owner was deemed politically unreliable.[26]

When the government, in response to these and other similar incidents, quietly shifted *UDV* operations southward and westward, the shrill chorus of disapproval intensified. In Baranya County a Roman Catholic priest claimed the *UDV* circulated books inimical to the Hungarian nation, spread the Protestant faith, and coerced Swabians to join the organization. The secular authorities used every possible device to throttle *UDV* operations. In Somberek, the police chief called *UDV* organizers *büdös svábok* (stinking Swabians) and suspended their first meeting. In Nyomja, the authorities threatened to prosecute *UDV* stalwarts for spreading German propaganda. In Mohács, a would-be *UDV* organizer incurred a heavy fine. In most other communities, *UDV* promoters fared no better. Chauvinistic Magyar administrators and clergymen enjoyed the enthusiastic support of Magyarones, who resented *UDV* encroachments in existing local Swabian cultural and religious organizations. These were widespread, and had hitherto operated unimpeded. In West Hungary, the predominantly Swabian Roman Catholic clergy stigmatized Bleyer and his friends as Pan-German blood poisoners. In Baranya, Bleyer was accused of trying to infiltrate and seize a local German religious organization, the *Katholischer Volksverein.* A teachers' group threatened to boycott it should Bleyer gain control.[27]

It was Swabian fighting Swabian. So concerted were these attacks that the very existence of the *UDV* was soon at stake. This was precisely the gist of an article written by Deputy George (György) Perlaki in *Pesti Napló*. Perlaki, whose Magyar name belied his Swabian origin, argued that there were ample German associations already, and hence the *UDV* was superfluous. Perlaki obviously wished to see the demise of all German associations, because in 1924 he launched the rival *Faluszövetség* in Baranya County. It was a Magyar counterpart of the *UDV*, functioning with apparent government permission, if not outright support. Consequently, the *UDV* in Baranya County could not organize chapters or seek members for at least two years.

Bleyer and his circle challenged their Magyar and Swabian detractors, in the hopes that Bethlen, who was after all the *UDV*'s self-proclaimed champion, would rally to their aid as a matter of personal prestige. Bleyer concentrated his ire on two adversaries. One was Bethlen himself. In a confidential letter to Gratz he complained:

> Attacks in the Magyar press continue, and have assumed the rudest forms. . . .
> A decisive, open word from Bethlen would put an immediate end to all this. If his word is delayed much longer, the damage will be immeasurable.[28]

The other object of Bleyer's wrath was the Magyarone Swabian establishment, which intrigued to discredit and isolate the Swabians with both the Magyar and the German public. Bleyer blamed this harmful propaganda mainly on "assimilated people. . .who are willing to surrender their *Volkstum* in favour of another. . .who coin slogans against us, calling us Great-German agitators, anti-Semitic agitators, ultramontane conspirators, or Protestant heretics, as the case may be, to ingratiate themselves with this or that Magyar faction."[29] Franz Bonitz, one of Bleyer's lieutenants, pursued the same line of reasoning. he pointed out also that the *UDV* was essential for Swabian unity since it was a nationwide organization binding both regions and people. Besides, he claimed, the government, from Bethlen down, heartily endorsed it.

It was one thing for the government to sponsor the *UDV*, quite another to permanently keep the wolf from its door. The Bleyerites' efforts to stir Bethlen into action failed. Indeed, for all its protestations of support, the Bethlen regime conveyed just the opposite impression when it forbade the Swabian-born chief of staff of the Hungarian army, Heinrich Werth, to join the *UDV*. In view of the government's indifference, if not sabotage, the *UDV*'s enemies found encouragement and maintained unrelenting pressure on the organization.

In a way it is astonishing that the *UDV* met such a solid wall of resistance.

Although "blessed" by the Hungarian government, there was little to suggest that it would ever justify the apprehensions of its detractors. Over one year elapsed between the foundation of the UDV and its formal organization. Swabians had ample time to prepare to join it. Yet on opening day only fifty communities sent delegates while fifty others sent messages of solidarity. Three-hundred Swabian villages and towns evidently ignored the affair entirely. Initial gains were also modest. During the first year, one-hundred fifty communities were visited, after the government intervened with recalcitrant county executives. In nearly one-third of these, local chapters were established. In addition, by the end of the year, seventy-five villages had memberships exceeding fifty persons each, which qualified them to establish local chapters. In all, the UDV was active in 200 communities, with 8,000 members at year's end. Faul-Farkas maintained that in view of the numerous obstructions the UDV encountered, these figures were satisfactory. But neither the hullabaloo of the opening ceremonies, nor the impassioned, optimistic speeches and greetings from Magyar notables such as Bethlen and Horthy, could dispel the impression that the UDV was a relatively minor enterprise. It was hardly likely to shake the security of the Hungarian state, because even by 1932, its heyday, 180 localities mustered only 27,517 members. Of course, the peril for the Magyars was potential rather than immediate. They feared the octopus-like growth of the UDV, its alien tentacles reaching into schools, libraries, fields, shops, and even into Germany.[30]

These apprehensions surfaced at a conference summoned by Bethlen in the Spring of 1925. The Prime Minister was resolved to terminate the bitter controversies surrounding the UDV. Most of the Magyar participants—mainly county chief executives and parliamentary representatives from Swabian districts—objected strenuously to the UDV as a matter of principle. Others resented its recruiting methods, which they believed were overly aggressive. Pleading for moderation, Gratz and Wild (Bleyer was not invited) complained that the authorities offered passive resistance and warned that this would encourage Swabian extremists. Bethlen declared that carrying out the provisions of the minority laws was not only a matter of prudent internal policy; Hungary's foreign diplomacy, the success of its revisionist dreams, depended on it. He ordered all officials to observe the minority regulations faithfully, and established guidelines to prevent misunderstandings.[31] Bethlen's intervention had little effect. As before, local prejudice transcended the dictates of prudence and official policy.

The UDV's tribulations offer an excellent insight into the complexities of Hungary's internal and external diplomacy. Bethlen was indifferent to Swabian welfare, except as a useful tool of foreign policy. Whether minority regulations were carried out properly or at all meant little, as long as appearances were maintained. At the time, Bethlen wished to restore German-Hungarian commercial contacts, and sweeping the Swabian dust under the carpet seemed to be the appropriate thing to do.[32] This opportunism characterized Magyar-Swabian relations. In public, Bleyer affirmed his confidence in Bethlen; in private, he had serious misgivings about the man who promised so much and delivered so little. An honest broker with modest demands, Bleyer expected Bethlen to honour his pledges to the last tittle. The discrepancy in the character and basic aims of the two leaders augured ill for Magyar-Swabian harmony for the remainder of the decade.

During this period, Bethlen's foreign policy had two major goals: reconstruction and revision. In view of conflicting big-power interests, neither programme could be carried out without doing violence to the other. Hungary's most cherished goal was revisionism; reconstruction was merely a means to an end. Only the West could provide the wherewithal to put Hungary on the road to fiscal health, and only this could assure Hungary's leadership in Central Europe, which could in turn lead to restoration. Bethlen's *Realpolitik* would not only convince the Entente of Hungary's peaceful intentions, but would also keep Hungary independent. Simultaneously, Germany, Hungary's greatest hope as a potential revisionist ally, had to be cultivated as a future confederate, without running the risk of alarming the West. As Hungary's position improved, the West would be gradually phased out, Germany phased in. Bethlen's policy was tantamount to a great balancing act.

It served Hungary well that Bethlen never confronted the Entente head-on, not even in the Burgenland crisis. He drew back from the abyss, as in the case of disowning the irregular bands in West Hungary. His compliance with Western interests had its desired effects. Hungary signed a humiliating peace treaty with only a dignified murmur. In September 1922, she was rewarded by becoming the first vanquished nation admitted into the League of Nations. Germany was not permitted to join until four years later. In 1923 came Bethlen's successful trip to Western capitals, which paved the way for a League of Nations inquiry into Hungary's fiscal problems and its subsequent reconstruction loan of March 1924. By 1926, Hungary had gained the trust of the Entente and declared financially solvent. Her treaty-making powers and competence to conclude commercial agreements were transferred from the League to the Bethlen regime.

Bethlen's wooing of the West represents one of the cleverest public relations achievements in postwar Europe. It was capped by his panegyric of Hungary in *Foreign Affairs*. Bethlen knew exactly what his readers in the Western democracies wished to hear. He enunciated three major goals of

Hungarian policy. Economic and financial reconstruction came first. He also wanted democratic reorganization on the basis of the principle of a gradual and sound evolution. A number of backward practices existed in Hungary, but a nation with a democracy nearly as old as England's would surely find its road to a more representative system under settled conditions. Bethlen also publicized the organic linking up of Hungary and all Hungarians with Western culture, and in connection therewith a settlement of the minority question. He referred only obliquely to Hungary's fervent desire for a total restoration of lost lands and populations. As his masterstroke, Bethlen appealed to the avarice of Westerners, swelled with war profits. He alerted Entente capital, especially American investors, to exploit Hungary's practically unlimited industrial, commercial, and agricultural possibilities. On the whole, the Prime Minister stressed Hungary's peaceful and cooperative nature, and did not demand anything beyond a definite stabilization of all outstanding minority issues in Central Europe. Few individuals in the West could disagree with Bethlen's reasonable formulations.[33]

Bethlen's simulated pro-Allied policy exacerbated German-Hungarian relations. While Bethlen sought to recruit Western capital to rebuild Hungary's economy, Germany had other plans—the energetic pursuit of an economic, cultural, and political *Ostpolitik,* inspired by Naumann's *Mitteleuropa* plan. Germany's recent defeat had postponed, but by no means cashiered this design. The frightening feature from the Hungarian point of view was that the Reich planned to utilize German minority groups in the East in the attainment of their *Drang nach Osten.*

The Magyars had been nervous for some time about growing evidences that Reich Germans were interested in more than vouchsafing cultural concessions for their fellow nationals abroad. A professor and deputy in the German Parliament addressed himself to this topic at a meeting of the *Deutschnationale Volkspartei.* He demanded German foreign policy that encouraged and sustained *Auslanddeutsche,* or Germans living outside the Reich:

> Our own destiny is being undermined each time a *Grenzdeutscher* or *Auslanddeutscher* is unable to prevail against oppression or submersion and is thus subsumed by other peoples. The Great-German concept for us is a matter of realistic German foreign policy.[34]

Although the Magyars should have been grateful for any support on behalf of cultural autonomy for their own nationals in the Successor States, at times the price was too high. In November 1924, German minority leaders from twelve European nations attended a three-day conference in Berlin.

Bleyer represented Hungary's Swabians. They agreed unanimously that German cultural standards abroad needed strengthening. To this end, other minorities had to be vouchsafed the same privileges the Germans sought for themselves. Consequently, at the very least, all minorities in every nation must attain cultural autonomy, centring in separate ethnic school systems, where they might function unimpeded by the state. The greatest beneficiaries would be the Germans, whose minorities stretched from Belgium to the Volga. The Magyars would also benefit with their nearly 3½ million brethren in the Successor States. Although Hungary would have been overjoyed to gain such privileges for the Magyars in the diaspora, they were determined not to grant similar rights to their own minorities, certainly not to the Swabians, whom they suspected, rightly or wrongly, of Pan-German inclinations.

The Magyars had reasons for distrusting the motives of Germany and its clients, the German national minorities, whose role was to be far from innocent. An exhaustive Wilhelmstrasse memorandum, circulated by Foreign Minister Stresemann, left little doubt that the Reich expected *Volksgenossen* in the European diaspora (overseas Germans, Swiss and Luxembourg Germans were exempted) to play a vital role in Germany's foreign policy. Politically, they were to influence their governments to adopt policies beneficial to the Reich. Culturally, they were to spread German ideals and *Weltanschauung*. Economically, their task was to be more than purchasers of German goods and procurers of vital raw materials for Germany: they were to be focal points for German economic propaganda abroad. This was essential, since most Germans outside the Reich lived in areas such as the Baltic and the Danube Basin, where Germany's economic and political life and death questions must be decided. Stresemann warned that the nation states bordering Germany and Austria knew of the auxiliary role of their German minorities and consequently they would try to destroy them. Due to their extreme importance for Germany's cultural, political, and economic survival, these minorities had to be succoured and preserved from extinction at all cost, even if the effort seemed futile, and even if it took too long. Since applying power politics or providing financial help were impracticable at the moment, the German minorities had to be supported for the time being strictly through cultural means. German culture in the diaspora could survive only if the minorities were given schools and taught the German spirit in the proper language. The ultimate goal of German foreign policy was

the creation of a nation, whose political frontiers encompassed all the German national groups living in contiguous settlements in Central Europe and who wished to be annexed by the German Reich.[35]

In view of the prevailing mixed population patterns in Central Europe, it was unavoidable that eventually others would have to come under German rule. Stresemann pledged that Germany would provide full cultural freedom to all non-German groups residing within the Reich.

A contemporaneous Wilhelmstrasse draft gives an illuminating insight into Hungary's plight and Germany's reluctance to aid her troublesome "ally." The most important problem was Hungary's encirclement by a ring of enemies, all determined to keep the rich territories they had appropriated. Germany's recent arbitration agreement with Czechoslovakia discouraged Hungary. Previously, many Magyars had valued Germany as a potential ally that would someday help regain Hungary's lost territories. But unfortunately sundry difficulties and dangers awaited a German-Hungarian alliance. Hungary's advantage would be so overwhelming that Germany could not afford the risk. In fact, Germany might compromise her relations with Hungary almost to the limit with impunity, because Hungary's traditional role as a strategic stepping stone to the Middle East was finished. For the time being, Germany ought to pursue a peaceful, economically oriented policy in the East. Though Hungary's wartime losses pained Germans, her revisionist efforts were of no more than passing interest. Even the fate of Hungary's former Yugoslavian and Rumanian German subjects could not justify an aggressive pro-Hungarian German policy, since Hungary's friendship was based not on pro-German sentiments but on a desire for a new conflagration in Europe, especially in the Balkans. Reich diplomacy, therefore, must serve German, not Hungarian interests. Germany had to avoid fighting a war the Magyars desired. Should a war occur, however, then of course the situation would be changed, because then Hungary would be fighting for German interests. But to suggest that German interests were identical with a Hungarian war of liberation was absurd.[36] Although only a draft, prepared by Köpke, this fundamental formula was largely adopted. For the next fifteen years, a German-Hungarian formal alliance that would enlist Germany squarely on Hungary's side became a much-sought plum by Hungary but was skillfully avoided by Germany.

In view of numerous conflicts of interest, German-Hungarian relations were understandably strained during the period 1922-1925. The Erzberger extradition affair and the mistreatment of Swabians occasioned shock waves extending into other areas that sowed dissension. A number of less dramatic but nonetheless thorny incidents also arose to confound amity. The Germans were indignant, for example, when a Hungarian verbal note sharply attacked visits by noted Hungarian politicians in Berlin, individuals known to be sharply opposed to the Hungarian government, as for example Baron Szterényi and Bleyer. Fürstenberg pointed out the perfidy of the charges. The two had in fact engaged in diplomatic missions for Hungary: Szterényi explored a German-Hungarian commercial agreement, Bleyer represented his government's view in the Burgenland case. The German Foreign Ministry lectured the Magyars:

> The Royal Hungarian government cannot deny that Baron Szterényi and Professor Bleyer happen to be two individuals in Hungarian public life about whose loyalty to their own state—whether they belong to the opposition or not—there can be no doubt.[37]

Germany's special envoy, Baron von Stumm, humiliated Bethlen with the same intelligence during a face-to-face encounter. Bethlen was visibly amazed and taken aback, admitted that Bleyer and Szterényi had indeed been under government orders, and apologized for the insulting tone of Hungary's verbal note of August.[38]

No sooner had this affair died down, when the Germans were up in arms again. Hungary's envoy in Paris, von Praznovszky, had authored a pro-French article in *Pesti Hírlap*[39] almost immediately after his resignation from the Hungarian Foreign Ministry. This was a particularly inappropriate gesture, because Praznovszky attempted to justify France's reparations policies and Ruhr occupation, two sensitive issues with Germany. Praznovszky may have been paving the ground for Bethlen's projected Paris visit later that spring. The Germans felt he was bribed by the French and complained. The episode left a bitter taste, especially since the Hungarian Foreign Ministry refused to give a satisfactory explanation. Count von Kánya, Hungary's envoy to Germany, merely stated that Hungary could not be held responsible for the actions of former employees.

A few months later, while Bethlen sojourned in Paris soliciting Entente aid to reconstruct Hungary, the Germans' suspicions grew to certainty that Hungary pursued a ruthless *Realpolitik,* completely oblivious of Germany's welfare. The German legation in Budapest bristled at a report in *Pester Lloyd*[40] depicting Bethlen as an opportunist par excellence at Germany's expense. *Pester Lloyd* publicized an article circulated in *Action Française,* in which Bethlen was to have exclaimed that the Entente ought to provide credit to Hungary but not to Germany. Hungary was allegedly a better risk, having proved her willingness to economize and to reach an accommodation with its neighbours. That Bethlen committed certain indiscretions in the French capital seems perfectly clear. He could hardly expect to cement

German-Hungarian relations in this way. Of course, whether Bethlen was guilty or not is immaterial; the Germans believed he was. They had little reason to doubt the report since Hungary greeted it with silence. The Germans chafed at their own unpopularity in France, in contrast to Hungary's sympathetic reception in Paris—as a Hungarian diplomat boasted to a German colleague.

German-Hungarian relations were also exacerbated by fundamentally disparate political philosophies. Nothing demonstrated this better than an interview granted to *Jövő*, a Hungarian left-wing emigrant paper published in Vienna, by the president of the German Reichstag, Löbe. Löbe declared that evidently Hungary had lost every vestige of political judgment. He assailed her as Horthy-land, the nation of pogrom-heroes such as Héjjas. Implying that he spoke not merely as a private individual, but on behalf of his government, Löbe declared that the continual political sensations in Hungary made him indignant. No wonder Germany could not cooperate with a regime that maintained close comradeship with people like Héjjas.

Anti-Hungarian attacks in the German press also irritated the Magyars. They reached such proportions by 1925 that Welczek feared they might impair eventual German-Hungarian cooperation. Indeed, the Hungarian government expressed deep concern lest the press campaign undermine traditional Magyar-German friendship. Not even the chauvinistic French and Little Entente press equaled in ferocity and vehemence the German attacks, from the conservative *Kreuz-Zeitung* to the Social Democratic *Vorwärts*. Most articles dealt with familiar bones of contention: the Erzberger extradition case; the treatment of Swabians; Hungary's so-called reactionary internal policy, especially anti-Semitism. A Magyar spokesman complained that Hungary had become the whipping boy of the German press. He cited a few cases. The *Berliner Tageblatt* had published such an insulting article about Admiral Horthy that Emich was ordered to write an Open Letter in the same paper to explain Hungary's position. The *Reichspost,* a Viennese paper, had published a similar diatribe about Horthy, but the Austrian authorities immediately deprived it of its mailing privileges. Nothing of the sort occurred to the *Berliner Tageblatt.* Welczek explained that Germany had no press control, but he did promise to intercede with the editors of the *Berliner Tageblatt* and the *Vossische Zeitung* (the two most outspoken anti-Magyar papers), whom he knew personally. Yet the German public would never accept the fact that Hungary refused to settle the Erzberger case. Nevertheless, Germany would have to do something about arresting the worst excesses by the German press, which did everything it could to denigrate Hungary's image in world opinion. In response to Welczek's advice, a Wilhelmstrasse official wrote "nonsense" in the margin of the dispatch.[41] Obviously, Hungary had few friends in Berlin at that time.

In view of these conflicts, a Hungarian-German rapprochement languished, though the roster of those who, for one reason or another, desired an accommodation, was both long and diverse. The Swabians, of course, who had the most to gain from an entente accentuated this theme incessantly. Swabian leaders used it as their leitmotif in nearly all their speeches and writings. Hungary's large landowners desired intimate economic ties with Germany, in whom they saw a steady and generous customer for their surpluses. Horthy was convinced, for example, that only Germany could absorb most of Hungary's agricultural output. As much as Hungary wished to attract Germany, in the early postwar years this was not always possible. Germany had little to offer in recompense, and furthermore, Bethlen was more interested in attracting the West. Hungary resorted to *Realpolitik,* alternately dangling collaboration or flaunting a host of rivals before Germany's eyes. In 1923, for example, when the Magyars sought Entente aid, they did not wish to appear as if they had any interest in Germany. In a conversation with Fürstenberg, Apponyi ventured that although Hungary's place was indubitably at Germany's side, this could not be publicized at the moment. Another important Hungarian statesman, Count Andrássy, also believed in an eventual German-Hungarian entente; but at the present they had to bide their time. Fürstenberg misconstrued these messages and concluded that in Hungary, many important personages considered German-Hungarian collaboration as next to impossible. Fürstenberg's appraisal was erroneous. This was demonstrated in the course of a secret trip to Germany by Bethlen's personal plenipotentiary, Baron Szterényi. Among numerous other issues, Szterényi raised the possibility of limited Hungarian-German collaboration. He suggested that Apponyi might represent Germany's interests during his impending American propaganda journey, and urged the Germans to establish contact with Apponyi directly. It was the Germans' turn to decline politely.[42] Yet the message was loud and clear: Hungary hoped for eventual collaboration despite her current diplomatic involvement with the West.

As Germany's reconstruction proceeded apace in the mid-twenties, and her potential as a consumer of Hungarian agricultural products intensified, the Magyars became more and more interested in reaching an accommodation. Bethlen wished to support Hungary's large landowners, whose economic survival hinged on securing stable markets for their produce. Revisionism also loomed large in Bethlen's desire for an agreement; but in February 1925 Germany began negotiating with France and her Eastern European allies to settle boundary problems arising from the Great War.

The shoe was now on the other foot. The Magyars fretted lest the Germans settle with their former enemies, leaving Hungary isolated and abandoned. Hungary's diplomatic endeavours in the mid-twenties must be examined in this light.

In March 1925 Bethlen summoned Welczek and ventured that

> ...mutatis mutandis, Germany and Hungary are united in an indissoluble bond of destiny, thanks to the similarities of the Versailles Treaties and their effect with respect to the Great and Little Entente. Every Magyar is convinced that Hungary's recovery could be achieved only by Germany's side. Even though the two nations are forbidden to enter into formal treaties, the old war comradeship is close to every Magyar's heart.[43]

Welczek reported home that his two-year stay in Hungary had convinced him that Bethlen indeed spoke for all Magyars in this respect. Any Eastern agreement was of epochal importance to Hungary, providing that dreadfully mutilated nation with the last opportunity to rectify her own borders. Understandably, Bethlen begged Welczek to inform him with detailed information about Germany's negotiations with France and its intentions in this respect. Welczek seemed to trust Bethlen, for he advised the Foreign Ministry to keep him fully informed.

Germany's negotiations with the Entente reconciled even bitter enemies of the Reich in Hungary to the need for a German orientation. *Szózat* declared that Hungary must reestablish the old, intimate ties with rising Germany, which would become a giant power very soon. The sheer demands of *Realpolitik* demanded Hungary's adjustment to this fact of life. *Szózat,* which had hitherto pilloried the Swabians, complained that Bethlen's current drab German policy must surely offend them. Hungary ought to enlist Swabians to aid German-Hungarian rapprochement, and thus Hungary's national aims. *Sonntagsblatt* noted gleefully the change in tune of the Swabians' erstwhile detractors. Once more, Swabians had every reason to believe that at long last Bethlen would be pressured into adopting a pro-German policy. In due course, Swabian aspirations would have to be met as the price for Germany's Hungarian revisionist endeavours. Pursuing the same theme, Karl Czerny, a former Member of Hungarian Parliament, wrote a prominently featured article in *Pester Lloyd.* Czerny rejoiced in the diplomatic triumph of the Stresemann-Luther regime, which stabilized Germany's western frontier, but left the East open to peaceful change. He saw Hungary literally riding Germany's coat tail, both endeavouring in tandem to alter their respective eastern frontiers in the spirit of the League of Nations Article 19, which promised territorial adjustments if current agreements became impracticable or dangerous to world peace.[44]

Of course, Germany was not enchanted with Hungary's sudden enthusiasm for an entente, for the Magyars were considered opportunists who would not shrink from dragging Germany into armed conflict in order to realize their own revisionist ambitions. The Wilhelmstrasse feared expressions by German citizens which might convey the impression that covert, bellicose German-Hungarian plans existed. The Magyars, on the other hand, welcomed declarations that tended to link German-Hungarian destiny in a common cause. One such embarrassing incident which mortified Welczek occurred in connection with the visit of a German official in Hungary. Henrich, the Hessian minister of finance, headed a delegation of agricultural experts to inspect Hungary's farming facilities. He visited many localities and delivered numerous speeches. These, Welczek thought, were far too servile and flattering. Henrich praised the high niveau of Hungarian wine culture and gushed over excellent Swabian treatment. What really annoyed the Minister was Henrich's remarks in *Pesti Hirlap:* Hungary and Germany could not continue to live under the present circumstances—they would be justified in altering these conditions "at all cost."

> We are determined. . .to shrink from nothing. I wish with all my heart that Magyar shrewdness, and if necessary, Magyar bravery, should achieve this goal as soon as possible.[45]

Welczek thought it would have been far wiser had Henrich checked with the German legation before delivering such embarrassing and incendiary statements.[46]

Enthusiasm was difficult to contain, however. Without even knowing the specific provisions of the Locarno Treaty, Bleyer rejoiced. By guaranteeing the inviolability of France's western frontier Germany, and by association Hungary, now had gained an open hand in the East.

> We know that Hungary will also experience its own Locarno soon. . . .The axis of world events has extended to Berlin without any doubt, and we must, as even Prime Minister Bethlen has declared, seek new avenues for our foreign policy. We wish to traverse the same path as Germany. . .in trusting harmony.[47]

Bethlen was far more cautious. In a dinner speech, he engaged in generalities, pleading ignorance about the proceedings and details of the Locarno Conference. He would not go beyond hoping that Locarno would establish the equality of all nations—victors and vanquished alike—and one would have to go on from there.[48]

Nonetheless, there was definitely something new in the wind. Only a few days later, Bethlen defied continual League harassment on the minorities issue. The League was in no position to judge these matters, thanks to its subjectivity. Under certain conditions Hungary might withdraw from the League, but cling to her traditional German relationship. Soon Germany would join the League, and Hungary expected major world changes. Hungary would therefore remain in the League and, in tandem with Germany, settle Europe's minority problems. For the first time, remarked Welczek, Bethlen announced publicly and energetically German-Hungarian community of interests. In fact, Bethlen even designated Germany as the only power able to achieve Hungary's foreign policy aims. Count Khun-Héderváry, Hungary's deputy foreign minister, confirmed Welczek's impression that German-Hungarian relations had entered a brand new course, one that acknowledged Germany's newly-won status as a fully-fledged world power. Far from being elated, Welczek cautioned that "Hungary's friendship and their expectations from us, could undoubtedly present a considerable burden for our diplomacy."[49]

Political expediency and lust for revisionism, now clearly in sight, impelled Bethlen toward a pro-German orientation. Count Klebelsberg, an alumnus of Berlin University, delivered a long speech in the very hall where he had graduated thirty years earlier. He sought closer German-Hungarian cultural relations. In particular, he favoured the projected Collegium Hungaricum in Dahlem, an institute designed to train young Hungarian scholars in the German tongue. In his interview with the German press, Klebelsberg touched upon a number of problems, the most important of which was Swabian education. The recently released school ordinance had solved most, though not all, the difficulties. Parents' conferences could be intimidated no longer because school inspectors determined which of the three school types should be introduced in any given community. Already, about one hundred German schools functioned. German courses in teachers' academies would expedite this process. The confessional schools posed the only difficulty. The German press hailed Klebelsberg's presentation. The *Berliner Lokalanzeiger* wrote, for example, that at last, Germans could contemplate expatriate Germans without any worry or concern. They had the feeling that the Swabians' cultural welfare lay in the sympathetic and capable hands of Bethlen and Klebelsberg. Other German newspapers also abandoned their anti-Magyarism. The *Hamburger Fremdenblatt* wrote favourable reports about Bethlen (10 July 1925); so did the *Frankfurter Zeitung* (9 October 1925). On 15 July 1925 *Hamburger Nachrichten* published an article written by Guido Gündisch. In a rare display of solidarity with the Magyars, Gündisch stressed that Swabians and Magyars were not embroiled in any conflict, and begged Germans to sympathize with Hungary.[50]

Until 1926, Hungary's diplomatic, economic, and financial freedoms were so severely curtailed by the limitations imposed by the League of Nations, that it is perhaps inappropriate to speak of an independent and active Hungarian foreign policy. It is possible, however, to guage Hungarian inclinations during these formative years, which was to regain Hungary's lost territories and populations, whether by peace or through war. Hungary's aims were selfish. Her statesmen exploited any crack in the armour of their enemies, and utilized the friendship of former or potential allies. Thus, by the mid-twenties, Hungary found herself in a paradoxical position. Germany was the only nation large enough and sufficiently interested in the fate of a former ally burdened with similar problems to be of any help. At the same time, Germany posed a threat due to her size and potential influence. The presence of over ½ million Swabians, their national consciousness thoroughly aroused by exposure to fellow Germans in the late war, filled the Magyars with dread. Suspended between two fires, they manoeuvred the Swabians as pawns in their diplomatic gambits with Germany. The Magyars feigned interest in the Swabians to arouse Reich sympathy for Hungary, but offered only mock concessions to the Swabians as recompense for their services. However valuable Reich support might be, a vigorous and *volksbewusst* Swabian presence in Hungary was clearly deemed to be a Magyar national disaster. Hungary's sudden pro-German enthusiasm, and Klebelsberg's new, "improved" Swabian school regulations, were merely symptomatic of Hungarian opportunism.

CHAPTER VI
HUNGARIAN TRADE AND FOREIGN POLICY: THE YEARS OF DISENCHANTMENT (1926-1931)

Hungary's economic and political problems became aggravated in the mid-twenties. The Magyars still had to reckon with the uncomfortable presence of some half million Swabian Germans, whose past patriotic record was good, but they began slowly to gravitate towards Germany because of an ethnic consciousness aroused by the war. Eliminating the Swabian threat thus became Hungary's principal domestic task, an undertaking enmeshed in international complications. The Magyars aimed to prevent the Swabians from becoming an irredenta that would open the gates to German influence, and Germany from becoming an overwhelming power in the Danube Basin. Given these opportunities, the Magyars hoped to turn Hungary's good strategic position to their own advantage. Hungary would become the commercial hub of Southeastern Europe under Magyar guidance. Germany would then perforce accept the Magyars in their new role as "middle men" as the Second Reich had done with the Austro-Hungarians. In the Magyar scenario, the Germans would have to recognize the Magyars as the dominant people in the East and abandon the Swabians to unconditional Magyarization.

With this in mind, Bethlen planned his postwar strategy. He meant to reduce Hungary's pressing fiscal and economic problems by means of trade agreements with friends and foes alike and convince the world that Hungary was peaceful, industrious, and dependable, a nation that honoured its international obligations. Although the slogan "nem, nem, soha!" (No, no, never!) was retained, Bethlen prudently avoided armed conflict. In Bethlen's words, clever diplomacy, consolidation, and gathering of strength would be the first tasks of his regime.[1] Only thus could Hungary be restored to its past grandeur. Before 1925, this programme encountered great difficulties because Hungary was forbidden by the Victors to pursue an independent economic or diplomatic course. The League not only regulated Hungary's treaty-making powers, it even claimed her agricultural output as reparation payment. But by submitting to the League's rigorous two-year economic control and financial reorganization, Hungary became master of her own economic destiny. On New Year's Day 1925, when the Magyars assumed sovereign control of their tariff system, the first major step towards economic independence had been achieved.[2]

In the five-year interval following Hungary's economic liberation, until the Great Depression dashed all hopes for stability, Bethlen earned limited but significant economic laurels by gaining most important nations as Hungary's trade partners. The volume, unfortunately, never reached major proportions. The four neighbouring countries remained Hungary's most active clients during the prosperous years, mutual animosities notwithstanding. Germany, Hungary's greatest hope as major trade partner, failed to fulfill Magyar expectations. The Weimar Republic lagged in imports, forged ahead in exports, and refused to conclude formal trade agreements. By 1925, the commercial pact of 1920 was dead. For the next six years the two nations transacted business on a flimsy, provisional, most-favoured-nation formula. This arrangement caused an unhealthy Hungarian trade balance, a situation highly detrimental to the interests of a small, predominantly agricultural nation. This difficulty served as still another barrier to German-Hungarian friendship, at a time when Magyar resentments born of Germany's refusal to favour Hungary in the Burgenland dispute had begun to subside.

The Magyars were partially to blame for Germany's intransigence, for they celebrated Hungary's rebirth as a sovereign economic power with a major blunder. In January 1925, they imprudently repudiated the 1920 German-Hungarian commercial agreement by imposing harsh tariffs on most manufactured items, largely from the Reich. This unilateral action, spawned by a desire for greater autarchy, was interpreted by one German diplomat as a handwriting on the wall. He believed that the Hungarians were retaliating against Germany's shabby performance under the late treaty. Hungary's conduct drew bitter complaints from German manufacturers, and shortly the Weimar Republic retaliated. On 1 September 1925, Bulow's 33% prewar tariff on a host of agricultural imports was restored. The following year it was raised to 100%, and the government also reimposed the very stringent hygienic inspection standards, the so-called Veterinary Code, on all meat and livestock imports from Hungary. In the face of shrinking world markets, Hungary could not afford to lose even a relatively minor client such as Germany. As a result, by the middle of 1925, Hungarian officials began to seek new commercial talks, which Germany constantly postponed on one pretext or another. While making vague promises, the Germans refused even to consider discussing the terms of a new trade agreement, in the interim refusing to lower the tariff, or relax any of the other regulations so prejudicial to the Hungarian export trade. Consequently, Bethlen faced a difficult situation at home. The industrialists demanded immediate rupture with Germany, whereas the powerful landowners and the Swabians pressed for immediate agreement, whatever the cost.[3]

The risk of losing Hungary beyond recall prompted the Germans to act at last and they agreed to hold preliminary talks. Bethlen and Stresemann met in Geneva on 6 December 1927, but the results were nugatory and led to continuing frustration for Hungary. Germany's tactics evoked a two-pronged Hungarian response. Flattery, laced with a veiled threat, was one. On his way home from Geneva, Bethlen visited Venice. There he engaged in talks with high Italian officials, who allegedly proposed a military alliance, to augment the existing treaty of friendship. According to a German diplomat, Bethlen was said to have refused this blandishment because Hungary would never establish close ties with Italy until it stopped persecuting South Tyrol's German minority. Furthermore, Hungary favoured Germany, hence any alliance imperiling friendly German-Hungarian relations was out of the question. Clearly, Bethlen leaked this information to prod Germany.

Another Hungarian response appealed to Germany's sense of honour and justice. A verbal note excoriated Germany for callously disregarding the dire economic straits of an old and trusted ally. Hungary expected her friends to import livestock. Before the war, Germany had averaged nearly half a million head of live Hungarian cattle annually; during the past twenty-one months Germany had used only seventy-two heads of sheep. This was ruinous, since Hungarian livestock breeding catered to German needs and because Austria enjoyed immunity from import restrictions. Germany's preferential policy thus enabled Austria to reap profits at Hungary's expense. Since the embargo, cattle from various Balkan nations reached Germany through Austria, while the Hungarian producer found himself completely eliminated from competition. The Magyar public deemed the Weimar Republic's behaviour unfounded and unjust, and consequently Hungarian Parliament would never ratify any agreement with Germany, unless this intolerable situation was redressed.

There was a great deal of truth in the allegation that Germany favoured Hungary's Balkan neighbours. At a cabinet meeting, held in Berlin in March 1928, it was agreed to postpone trade negotiations with Hungary until accommodations with other East European nations had been secured. In plain language, Hungary was to be given no opportunity to seek an arrangement suitable for her own needs. To add insult to injury, the

Germans decided to hide their real intentions. Delays would be ascribed to lengthy preparations, and to the impending parliamentary elections in Germany. At the same time, Hungary was to be soothed that negotiations would eventually materialize. Stresemann had promised the same thing as far back as January 1928.[4]

Germany's reluctance triggered angry outbursts in Hungary, even among Swabians. In Parliament, Germany's behaviour was roundly criticized by László Pintér, a *Magyarone* Swabian. Pintér ascribed Germany's hesitancy to deal fairly with Hungary to sheer jealousy. Germany resented blossoming Italian-Hungarian friendship. The Germans must beware lest the Magyars lose their traditional feelings of affection for them.[5] Others in Hungary were far more strident, although the Swabians and the landowners maintained their pro-German outlook. By the fall of that year, Hungary's industrialists were so disgusted with German delays that they demanded a break with the Weimar Republic.[6] As domestic criticism of government policy mounted, a German trade delegation finally arrived in Budapest, and negotiations resumed once more in October 1928. Discussions soon bogged down, however, since neither side wished to yield. The Magyars demanded the unconditional lifting of Germany's Veterinary Code, whereas the Germans insisted with equal heat on total exclusion.[7] Although only they knew it, the Germans were not really interested in reaching an agreement with the Magyars at that moment.

Naturally, Hungary resented the endless delays and demanded an explanation. On 1 December 1928, Schön, having just returned from a briefing session in Berlin, met with Hungarian officials. German-Hungarian relations suffered badly, he was told, thanks to Germany's cavalier handling of negotiations and its attitude in general. The Hungarian press no longer favoured Germany, and Hungary's overwhelmingly agriculturalist population had already concluded that Germany's uncooperativeness caused their growing economic distress. Schön's partly insolent, partly evasive response was disconcerting. He urged Hungarian producers to compete in the free market, in categories not covered by the German import ban, just like other foreign producers. With respect to the banned items so vital to Hungarian economic recovery, Magyars were to stop harassing Germany publicly about removing the restrictions as a precondition for an agreement, because they knew quite well that for the Reich this was impossible, and only caused unnecessary turmoil. He discouraged the Magyars even more by asserting that in the next fiscal year German imports would be reduced by 25%, or from four to three billion marks. All in all, the Schön interview was a low point in German-Hungarian relations. The episode gave Magyar planners something to think about. Apparently, Germany preferred to deal with

Hungary's enemies, thus outflanking and outmanoeuvring the overconfident Magyars.

The Magyar response was swift and acrimonious. Two weeks later, Bethlen reiterated his well-known opposition to the export ban. Schön's suggestions were worthless; Germany's image in Hungary was not good. We Magyars are justified in being angry, lectured Bethlen. Denmark, a nation that had obtained territories at Germany's expense at war's end merited greater consideration than Hungary, a trusted ally. Why should Danish agricultural products enter Germany unencumbered, while Hungary had to endure humiliating and galling restrictions? Bethlen threatened Schön that Hungarian legitimists were trying to reestablish connections between Hungary, Austria, and Czechoslovakia. Bethlen thus raised the spectre of a Habsburg restoration in order to intimidate Germany. As before, threats failed. The Germans countered that their own agriculture was in a precarious position, to explain the delay. Bethlen's threats were curtly dismissed, for everybody knew that no Hungarian politician would survive a proposed Hungarian *Anschluss* with Austria and Czechoslovakia under Habsburg auspices. In view of all this rancour, negotiations reached a total impasse shortly after the new year and the conference was prorogued.

Convinced now that Germany would not yield to threats, Bethlen resorted to more gentle forms of persuasion. During his customary Easter press conference, he emphasized Hungary's moderation and hinted at a compromise. German-Hungarian relations were good and friendly, despite German newspaper attacks. The Germans ought to emulate the friendly Hungarian press. He hoped that trade negotiations would soon resume in a spirit of friendship. An agreement would hasten amity in the political arena. In another interview Bethlen ventured that an impending trade pact would satisfy both parties. Germany's agricultural crisis was regrettable, yet Hungary's export was too niggling to endanger German agriculture. He would relax high tariffs if Germany abandoned its import ban on Hungarian livestock.[8]

Shortly after, Hungary's envoy continued the commercial offensive in Berlin. But the Wilhelmstrasse wanted the Magyars to be patient until Germany concluded an agreement with Poland. The envoy hoped it would be soon, stating ingenuously that he knew the Germans always obliged smaller nations in distress, especially Hungary. Besides, a German note in 1920 had pledged that negotiations would resume at an opportune moment, hence Germany was morally bound. Further, Germany had already concluded the types of agreement Hungary also desired with Austria, Lithuania, and Russia—why not with Hungary as well?

One week later, the Magyars foisted another familiar figure on the

Germans. In Berlin, Klebelsberg reiterated Hungary's position still one more time. Other problems could wait, but Hungary's agricultural crisis could not—it demanded instant remedy. Klebelsberg tried to be delicate, but his message could not be phrased gently: Germany's laggardness had created feelings of alarm and a certain bitterness against Germany among the Magyar public. The German response was discouraging. Foreign Ministry functionaries duly recited the litany of Germany's difficulties; they could not even hazard a guess about forthcoming discussions. Hoping to arouse republican sympathy for his ultra-conservative country, Klebelsberg ventured that Bethlen's ultimate aim was a political democracy in Hungary. The recently introduced "cultural democracy" pointed in that direction. This shows to what lengths the Magyars were willing to go to attain their objectives. For the aristocratic and a socially conservative Klebelsberg this must have been a humiliating experience.

The German Foreign Ministry's annual report for the year 1929 considered the trade impasse the most divisive issue separating Hungary and Germany, transcending in importance even the Swabian question and Hungary's unremitting efforts to undermine Germany in Eastern Europe. Clearly, the Magyars did not wait idly for the Germans to make up their minds. Once again, they resorted to veiled threats. This emerged at a meeting between Bethlen and Foreign Minister Curtius at the second Hague Conference. Fresh from his discussion with French Foreign Minister Tardieu, Bethlen informed Curtius that France desired an understanding with Hungary. From this, the German diplomat deduced that France was courting Hungary and had made unmistakable offers of a political accommodation. Curtius reported that, although Bethlen claimed to have been noncommittal, he admitted being greatly moved by the offer.[9]

On this occasion the Wilhelmstrasse was duly alarmed. Reluctantly and without enthusiasm, the idea surfaced for the first time that Bethlen ought to visit Germany to discuss trade and all other outstanding controversies. The Foreign Ministry conceded Hungary's contention about German promises for an early trade conference. Germany had indeed committed itself back in 1920 to negotiate an import agreement on livestock. A subsequent position paper outlined options and alternatives, and recommended nonetheless that, in order to protect domestic producers, Germany should under no circumstances import Hungarian meat products, especially cattle and hogs. These happened to be the two most important items to Hungary. Further, since the German-Polish commercial accord had yet to be ratified by either party, it would be futile to promise the Magyars anything.

Under the pall of this discouraging report, the Foreign Ministry initiated preliminary negotiations the following day with János Bud, Hungary's Minister of Agriculture. The negotiators could only agree that formal talks ought to begin as soon as possible. Bud was alerted that the German-Polish accord would take a long time to ratify, perhaps until July, and the Magyars ought to realize that since Spring 1930, Germany had a higher agricultural duty, the so-called Schiele Tariff. In the end it was decided that Bethlen ought to visit Germany. Even here, difficulties arose. Bud complained because the scurrilous Social Democratic press poisoned the atmosphere, a charge his hosts found difficult to deny. Curtius promised to "prepare the ground" for the journey.[10]

Bethlen's visit, slated for November, prompted the Wilhelmstrasse to assemble an exhaustive dossier on German-Hungarian relations. The rapporteur stressed that the visit had no particular political significance, except to testify to existing friendly relations. This was confirmed by the Magyars, since they had few illusions about results. The report optimistically claimed that points of political friction between Germany and Hungary were negligible, and that even the temporary discords of recent years could not shake this firm foundation. However, friendly relations could easily deteriorate if the unsatisfactory situation in trade continued. Nonetheless, Germany must not yield on substantive issues, and should only express sympathy and good will. Another memorandum, dated five days later, was more hostile. It lumped Hungary indiscriminately with the other anthrax-ridden East and South European states. Only Austria, for special reasons, should be exempted from Germany's stringent veterinary regulations. Only in grain should the Reich desire substantive trade. Even here, the Magyars were to be treated no differently than other Eastern agricultural producers. The reason for German hostility was clear. At the recent Bucharest economic conference the Hungarian delegation supported a resolution that would permit retaliation on an industrial country that discriminated against an agricultural state. The Germans considered this Hungarian action as coming very close to a declaration of a trade war.

Under such circumstances the conference was doomed from the start. The Germans were willing to establish a preferential wheat tariff for Hungary, but the Magyars merely saw this offer as a trick. Even Ritter, Germany's chief negotiator, admitted that such a tariff would enable all other wheat producers to become more competitive in the German market, to Hungary's eventual detriment. Indeed, Ritter stressed that Germany preferred dealing with the Balkan states, Hungary included, as a bloc. This would throw Hungary to the mercy of the Little Entente states with their greater productive capacities, and their ally France. The Magyars found the offer distasteful and dangerous to their sovereignty. It might be an excellent long-range plan, Bethlen ventured, but Hungary required instant remedies. Besides, cattle and hogs were more important at the moment than wheat. He then accused Germany of playing favourites. Austria was a privileged middle man, gleaning all the profits from Hungarian livestock transshipments, while Hungarian peasants starved. Germany's veterinary code was thus a sham. Ritter was indignant and denied that Hungarian cattle reached Germany through Austria in any appreciable numbers. He offered to buy corn instead of hogs, a suggestion rejected as impracticable. Greatly distressed, Bethlen inquired whether and when the stalled trade discussions would resume. Ritter promised soon, possibly at the end of February or early in March 1931. Except for their vague promise to reestablish trade negotiations in the foreseeable future, and to accept a stipulated small amount of livestock from Hungary, the Germans permitted Bethlen to depart emptyhanded.[11] Bethlen obscured the difficulties and overstated Hungary's achievements to the domestic press. He stated, for example, that German-Hungarian relations must be restored to the old, friendly level. This was the first public admission by Hungary that all was not well. Bethlen stretched the point, however, by maintaining that Germany had not only agreed on a firm date for negotiations, it had promised that an eventual agreement would not hinge on Germany's success with any third parties. For the rest, he limited himself to generalities.[12]

Bethlen's trip transpired in an atmosphere of deepening economic gloom. The Great Depression began to cast its shadow over Central Europe, a catastrophe presaged at least two years earlier by declining grain prices. Agricultural nations were hardest hit, since they could not place their produce in the shrinking markets of the industrial states. Hungary was no exception. Caught in the midst of a modest industrial development programme, Hungary was trapped in a vice. On one hand, her infant industries could not meet the demands of even a relatively modest buying public, on the other hand, her exclusionist tariffs discouraged industrial nations from purchasing Hungarian agricultural products. no wonder that Germany preferred dealing with Hungary's chief competitors—they did not pretend to seek autarchy. As a result, after arriving at home, Bethlen faced a catastrophic economic crisis. Two of Hungary's best customers, first Czechoslovakia, then Austria, terminated their commerical agreements. to appreciate the enormity of this disaster one must consider that in 1931 Hungarian exports to Czechoslovakia declined to 15% of their 1930 volume, whereas trade with Austria diminished by 45%. Under these circumstances Hungary had to solicit Germany's bounty more than ever before.

Paradoxically, Czechoslovakia's trade renunciation finally gave Germany the incentive to renew negotiations with Hungary more seriously.

Hitherto, Czechoslovakia had been Hungary's major trade partner, supplying relatively inexpensive industrial commodities. Now, German industry had an excellent opportunity to fill this gap. For the first time since the war, it became important for the Germans to negotiate a preferential tariff agreement with Hungary, in order to expedite the expected heavy outflow of German industrial productivity into Hungary. France's determined efforts to foil a successful rapprochement lent urgency to Germany's changed priorities. In view of these exigencies Germany kept its word. By the end of January 1931, the Germans were eager to meet the Hungarians within only four weeks. Preliminary negotiations began in Vienna in March, and full-fledged talks resumed in Berlin by May. The agreement, signed on 18 July, had to be ratified by both parliaments, although certain provisions went into effect at once.[13]

Far from soothing troubled relations, the trade agreement exacerbated them. According to one provision, Germany was to reduce the existing wheat tariff of 25% to only 18.75%, exclusively for the benefit of Hungary. It emerged, however, that Germany's pledge to import one million tons of Hungarian wheat under these conditions was a hoax. The wheat tariff was raised from 6.5% in 1930 to 25% just before the negotiations began; hence the special "reduction" for Hungary's benefit was hardly a benefit at all. While in previous years Hungarian wheat shipments were frequently stalled, Germany purchased large quantities of overseas grain, as well as the harvests of Yugoslavia and Rumania, Hungary's biggest competitors and bitterest enemies. The insult heaped upon injury was when Hungary began to deliver its wheat. The grain was not used for human consumption, as specified, but as chickenfeed. There never were quotas or tariffs on animal fodder imports. In fact, Germany had been purchasing Hungarian wheat fodder in large quantities for some time.

Another provision of the treaty established an annual Hungarian export quota of 6,000 live cattle and 80,000 slaughtered hogs at prevailing market prices. Although numerically the quotas were adequate, the Magyars were unable to take advantage of them. The cattle had to be shipped circuitously across Czechoslovakia instead of Austria, inspected painstakingly at only one specifically designated border checkpoint, delivered to the Dresden stockyards, and sold at auction. Since Czechoslovakia abrogated its own treaty with Hungary, it forbade Hungarian livestock shipments to go through. By the time Germany provided transit guarantees to Czech authorities, much valuable time was lost. Yet Germany refused to open up the far more accessible and prestigious Munich stockyards, despite firm assurances that they would do so in case of a snag. As a result of these obstructions, only seven head of cattle reached Dresden over a six-month period and fetched miserable prices. Respecting the slaughtered hog quota, even the Hungarian government's spokesman in Parliament admitted that the agreement was mere legal fiction. At the prevailing high tariff rates Hungary could not compete successfully with other exporters. Yet, in return for these "concessions," Hungary had to admit freely a host of German industrial products, principally chemicals, toys, machines, textiles, and ironware. Germany certainly struck an excellent bargain. It was detrimental to Hungary's infant industries and of negligible value to Hungarian agriculture.[14]

But agricultural circles in the Reich resented the law. German farmers were unconcerned with the fine points of commercial diplomacy, and they were uninterested in the welfare of the Magyars. When details of the trade negotiations trickled out, the *Deutsche Getreidezeitung,* the German grain producers' paper, attacked the government for abandoning protectionism and excoriated Hungary for extorting preferential treatment "through the back door." This was allegedly only the beginning of a Hungarian grain monopoly, to the detriment of hard-pressed German producers. The article epitomized German rural public opinion and became the subject of cabinet discussion in Germany.[15] In a way, the German government had little choice. It had to satisfy the contradictory requirements of two disgruntled parties, of whom the Magyars were more expendable.

Germany's problems surrounding the ill-starred treaty had only begun. In rapid succession, several events occurred, each extremely detrimental to Germany's interests, each linked to the late treaty. On 15 August France granted Hungary a large loan. Although there were no visible strings, it was an open secret that France wished to sabotage the recent Hungarian-German agreement. France also wanted to detach Hungary from what appeared to be a developing counter-block to French interests composed of Hungary and Germany, the two principal revisionist nations in Europe. On 18 August, a French trade delegation arrived at the Hungarian resort town of Lilafüred, joined the same day by a contingent from Czechoslovakia. Curtius noted sadly that the Hungarians evidently considered the recent treaty a fiasco, a circumstance also known to the French, and a situation they wished to exploit. Curtius knew that the French had approached the Magyars as far back as June 1931. The gist of the French proposal was to offer Hungary essentially the same wheat deal as Germany had. Curtius concluded that the Magyars had no confidence that Germany would honour its agreement. Another blow to German hopes came the following day. Unexpectedly, Bethlen resigned, almost exactly ten years after becoming Prime Minister. Curtius ventured that a combination of factors—Hungary's disappointment with the trade treaty, Bethlen's reputed Germanophil orientation, and the Prime Minister-designate Julius (Gyula) Károlyi's pro-French sympathies, had hastened Bethlen's sudden political demise.[16] Bethlen's departure was indeed a bad omen for Germany, not because he loved the Germans, but because his connections with Hungary's large landed interests predisposed him to pursue pro-German policies.

This was truly Germany's black week in Central Europe. Bethlen had been a wily opportunist, but at least he pursued a basically pro-German course. With Károlyi in office, Hungary—and possibly all of the Balkans—might be swept into the French orbit. As matters stood, Germany's plans in the East might have to be scrapped. Curtius recommended salvaging the wrecked Hungarian-German agreement. "Let us at least activate the livestock import provision of the treaty, and let us also explain to the Magyars that due to our own unfortunate economic position we were simply unable to meet their demands, and that we hoped for better times and a more favourable German economy that would benefit both of us."[17] Germany's economic ambitions in Eastern Europe were already a shambles when on 3 September France administered the final blow. France, and two days later the World Court, forbade the greatly touted creation of a German-Austrian customs union. Overnight, the Balkan nations, which had more or less resigned themselves to eventual German economic hegemony, now turned to France. Hungary was no exception. Essentially, this is what envoy Koloman (Kálmán) Kánya told the Germans bluntly in November of that year. Curtius had not erred three months earlier. The Magyars were disgruntled and felt no obligation to a nation that had tricked them into signing what appeared to be a spurious treaty. In Kánya's words,

> . . .for years, Germany had been seeking to gain the good will of France; this has not prevented the Hungarian government from doing all it could to deepen Hungarian-German friendship. Unfortunately, these efforts of ours have found no understanding here [in Berlin]—neither politically nor economically. Magyar-German friendship depends not only on Hungary but on Germany's behaviour.[18]

Magyar bitterness welled in the Hungarian press. Schön bombarded the Wilhelmstrasse with abstracts from Budapest. They pilloried Germany for permitting the publication of books insulting to the Hungarian nation, for trying to impose economic vassalage on Hungary, and for deceiving her in favour of enemy states since war's end. In May 1932, the beleaguered Schön held a press conference. He wished to explain Germany's extraordinary economic position and to prove that she nonetheless did everything in her power to help Hungary. Schön's efforts were futile. He could not arrest the wave of disaffection sweeping the Magyar press and the new government. Schön warned that according to Count István Csáky, Hungary's Foreign Ministry press attaché, "it is quite possible that the anti-German polemic will now spill over into the realm of minority [i.e., Swabian] politics."[19]

After the League's supervision of Hungary's economy ceased, the Magyars vigorously restored control over their foreign trade. When, about the same time, the League's political restrictions also ended, Bethlen plunged into feverish diplomatic activity. Hungary's strategic veographic position was a great asset. Bethlen thus felt confident that Hungary's diminished size and small population would not impede her reemergence from isolation. Slowly but surely, Hungary must recoup her fortunes, redress the injustice of Trianon, and restore her prewar frontiers and population.

In order to achieve these goals, Bethlen unblushingly concluded temporary deals with former enemies. A typical example of this opportunistic policy was Hungary's relationship with France, a nation dedicated since the war to maintaining the *status quo* in East-Central Europe. This would benefit not Hungary but the three Successor States, which had grouped themselves into a defensive-offensive alliance. The Little Entente was expressly designed to counter Hungary, and encouraged, supported, and even manipulated, by France, its creator. The Magyars tried to convince the French that Hungary's demise was both undesirable and impractical, and certainly not by means of the Little Entente. It would not only stretch French power to the breaking point, but would expose the region to German penetration some day. Hungary endeavoured therefore to weaken the Little Entente as a demonstration to France that its support of Hungary's hostile neighbours was impracticable from the strategic point of view.

Hungary had enjoyed a special relationship with Italy ever since the end of the War. Italy had provided moral and practical support in the Burgenland dispute, an action that led to the plebiscite and a partial Hungarian victory at the polls. The Magyars were grateful. Italy was one of the disgruntled victors in the Great War and the Magyars intended to turn this situation to their own advantage. They solicited Italian support ever after the Burgenland episode, a strategy they hoped might pay future dividends. Italy might use its influence with the other victors to mitigate the wrongs of Trianon. Italy was also a sworn enemy of Yugoslavia, one of the Successor States and member of the Little Entente. Hungary might use Italy as a wedge to weaken, or even bring to heel, this important and strategic link in the Little Entente. Italy might also become an important client for Hungary's swollen agricultural larder. Of course, Italy also had much to gain from an alliance with Hungary. She looked northward, to the Balkans and beyond. An Italian-Hungarian combination would encircle Yugoslavia and discourage a German drive into Austria. But even if Austria were to fall, Hungary, with Italy as a deterrent, would stand in the way of any farther German eastward expansion. Hungary constituted an indispensable strategic link in Italy's scheme to dominate Eastern Europe from the shores of the Adriatic to the Baltic Sea and would be an effective instrument not only against a German *Drang nach Osten,* and French attempts to dominate the same area, but it would also be an important instrument against the Pan-Slav menace.[20] In all, cooperation appeared to be a perfect arrangement. On 5 April 1927, a treaty of friendship inaugurated a decade of intimate cooperation between the two nations, a relationship disturbed only by mistrust, frustration, and anger on the part of the Germans.

The main deterrent in German-Hungarian relations was that effective German help lay far in the future. Although officially Germany and Hungary were friendly, even the Wilhelmstrasse admitted that Germany's interests did not always correspond with Hungary's. Consequently, generally speaking, Germany could not help Hungary in the pursuit of her foreign policy effectively. Germany's refusal to negotiate an effective trade treaty with Hungary was only one typical example. Beyond providing limited economic aid, and lending occasional diplomatic support in the League and elsewhere, the Germans were of little use in the short run. Whether Germany would ever satisfy Hungary's aspirations as an active revisionist partner remained an open question in the mid-1920s. On the basis of past performance, the chances of a vigorous German involvement on Hungary's behalf seemed remote. Germany's indifference to the Burgenland episode and its more recent sequel in 1927 left a great deal to be desired from Hungary's viewpoint. Germany's pro-French orientation, manifested by Stresemann's Locarno diplomacy, left the Magyars with few illusions about German fidelity. The recent fiasco in trade discussions, and the revelation that Germany favoured Hungary's eastern adversaries, convinced Hungarian policy makers that for the time being their opportunities must lie elsewhere.

On 25 January 1927, Germany had its first inkling that important events were afoot involving Italy and Hungary. On that day, Hungary's chargé in Rome informed Germany's ambassador von Neurath, that Bethlen was invited to Rome for political discussions. Although a formal political agreement was not on the agenda, Neurath's suspicions were aroused by the charge's hint that the two nations shared many common political interests. Moreover, the meeting had England's blessings. Should all these plans materialize, Germany's *Ostpolitik* must suffer. German concern was accentuated by rumours that Bethlen's trip had some connection with a possible Habsburg restoration in Hungary.

When the Hungarian-Italian treaty of friendship materialized in April 1927, it evoked only a timid German response. The Weimar Republic retaliated with a half-hearted offensive aimed at Rumania and Yugoslavia and became a topic of conversation between Schön and Bethlen about five weeks later. Unimpressed with Germany's clumsy Balkan diplomacy, Bethlen claimed to be strictly neutral and hoped the German press would not make too much of it. Bethlen also ignored hints that Krupp planned to establish a weapons plant in Brod, Yugoslavia, near the Hungarian frontier. Reports of a projected Franco-German-Russian alliance, with Yugoslavia and Czechoslovakia in tow, left him cold. Nor would he comment on gossip that German-Hungarian relations were crumbling, thanks to Germany's support of Austria in the renewed Burgenland controversy. In his report Schön ventured that it might be advisable to allay Magyar apprehensions by assuring them that rumours implicating Germany in various anti-Hungarian plots were without foundation. The Wilhelmstrasse agreed and notified the German press to drop the subject of German-Yugoslav political rapprochement until further notice. Bethlen had successfully weathered Germany's clumsy bluff.

Events later that year lent credence to the impression that Germany and Hungary were drifting apart. The Hungarian press condemned Germany's pro-Soviet tendencies and its support of Austria in the Burgenland controversy. Germany's Locarno diplomacy was seen as a prelude to a diplomatic revolution favouring the Little Entente. Languishing trade talks were cited as only one notable example, deteriorating relations. German officers on manoeuvres in Hungary complained of encountering suspicion wherever they went. Klebelsberg hesitated to accept a German invitation in view of Germany's pro-French sentiments. Tibor Eckhardt, an influential anti-German politician, wrote in *Magyarság* that Hungary must rid herself of the stigma German satellite. Hungary's future, and the future of world peace, rested with England, France and Italy, not with Germany. He cited Tisza's letter to the effect that should the Central Powers prevail, Hungary had better ensure that a good portion of France remained intact behind Germany. By the same token, it would be in French interests to preserve a considerable portion of Hungary in the event of a German *Drang nach Osten*.

Despite Hungary's drift from Germany to Italy, it still remained important to cultivate the support of both nations. In the long run, Italy would never be able to match Germany's capacity to absorb Hungary's excess harvests, nor to muster the requisite strength to recover Hungary's lost territories. It was in Hungary's interest, therefore, to keep her options open and try to reconcile the conflicting interests of Italy and Germany as a third party. In November 1927, the first trial balloon on behalf of German-Italian rapprochement under Hungarian mediation floated aloft. In the presence of Stresemann and the Foreign Ministry's Schubert in Berlin, Hungary's Minister Walko unveiled a plan for a new alliance consisting of Italy, Germany, Austria, and Hungary.[21] Unfortunately, Stresemann disparaged the idea, as it would imperil Germany's hard-won understanding with France and Yugoslavia. He believed, moreover, that the offer was a smokescreen concealing a stronger Italian presence in Austria. Deeply distrustful of the Magyars, he charged his staff to exercise extreme caution in the event the subject should be broached again, and to be as evasive as possible. He particularly wished to be kept informed in great detail about Italian plans against Austria. Clearly, Stresemann considered Hungary to be securely within the Italian orbit and hence opposed to Germany. Hungary had to find a way to assuage German fears. This may partially explain the reason why, several weeks later, Bethlen allowed the gist of a conversation with Grandi to leak to the Germans. Bethlen claimed, on that occasion, to have refused an Italian offer of a military alliance because Hungary followed a pro-German course.[22]

In the new year, Walko resumed his attempts to reconcile Germany and Italy. In his discussions with Schubert, Walko analyzed the reasons for Germany's poor relations with Italy. He drew an analogy which greatly embarrassed Schubert. Walko said that Germany paid too much attention to Italy's German (South Tyrolean) minority, at the expense of Italy as a whole. This paralleled German-Hungarian relations. Germany focussed on the Swabians, but treated Hungary indifferently. Schubert tried at first to deny these allegations, but had to admit at last that Walko's analysis was 50% correct. The Wilhelmstrasse was so caught up with its Locarno policy and with Poland that Germany's foreign policy had grown decidedly one-sided. He begged for understanding and pleaded for an opportunity to demonstrate Germany's concern. Walko obliged him on the spot by requesting German intercession with Rumania. When later Walko repeated his request, Schubert demurred. He finally asked to consult the other great powers, but promised to intervene only if France also exerted pressure on Hungary's behalf. It was Walko's turn to ponder whether Germany had ceased to have an independent foreign policy and become France's satellite. A few days after these meetings Schön announced in Budapest that trade negotiations would soon take place. Thereupon relations improved somewhat, while the Magyars waited impatiently for Schön's promise to materialize.

The slight thaw, reflected by improved Magyar attitudes towards the

Swabians, also occasioned pro-German pronouncements by Magyar diplomats. Once more, Kánya assured German representatives that Hungary fervently desired to mediate between Germany and Italy. He gushed to Schubert that Hungarians had an ineradicable love for Germany. He even quoted an allegedly confidential remark uttered by Horthy at the time of the signing of the Locarno Treaties, in which the Regent gave vent to the sentiment that "even though Germany has no need for us now, whenever Germany should require the services of Hungary at any future date, we will come."[23] Schubert obeyed Stresemann's injunctions and remained noncommittal. If Kánya hoped to look for straws in the wind, he was totally disappointed.

Without committing themselves to any definite course of action, the Germans benefited by mere promise to resume trade discussions. Schon Hungarian Parliament had suddenly begun to discuss German-Hungarian relations in a friendly fashion after a long lapse. One committee member praised Stresemann for promising to intercede with Rumania on Hungary's behalf in the complex Optants' question. Both Bethlen and Walko hailed Hungary's excellent relations with Germany, especially after the League's support of Hungary in the Rumanian dispute. They thanked Schön assiduously for Stresemann's timely intervention. But Magyar enthusiasm hinged more on trade than any other factor, as Schön commented in his dispatch. At the same time, he deplored Gratz's discordant note. Gratz was dissatisfied with German official attitudes toward Hungary, which left a great deal to be desired. Gratz evidently wished to be objective towards Germany, unlike his fellow-Swabians, who had a blind spot where Germany was concerned.

In the meantime, Hungary continued to cultivate a tripartite alliance that would equalize the pressure on Hungary from the two super-powers. In various guises, these notions surfaced time and time again, including during the Hungarian parliamentary debates of 18 April 1928. Malasits evoked opprobrium by condemning the Hungarian-Italian alliance because it was contemptible to associate with a fascist government that had murdered Matteotti. Walko fulminated that the deputy deserved the nation's contempt. Pintér urged the speedy creation of a triple alliance, composed of Italy, Germany, and Hungary. This was a primary task. Indeed, it was the basic plank of Hungarian foreign policy, which prompted the rejection of recurring French suggestions for a Danubian Federation under French auspices. But Germany rejected Hungarian proposals for a tripartite alliance, politely but firmly.[24]

Meanwhile, Italian-Hungarian friendship blossomed. In a speech to the Italian Senate, Mussolini boasted that Italy was the first nation to have championed the cause of heroic, millenial Hungary and had made major contributions to her economic recovery. Italian-German relations Mussolini labeled as cordial. Only the interference of certain irresponsible quarters, which want to interfere in Italy's internal policy—a clear reference to South Tyrol—blocked a full understanding. Regarding Hungarian efforts to mediate the German-Italian dispute, Mussolini stated that relations between Italy and Germany had improved in the past few months.[25]

There were certain harbingers that the Germans favoured, if not a tripartite treaty, then at least improved relations with Italy and Hungary. They realized, of course, that their aggressive intentions in East-Central Europe, as in Austria, and farther north, in the Polish Corridor, and with the Little Entente, obstructed an accommodation between themselves and the Italian-Hungarian camp. Germany wished to lull these fears during a conversation in Berlin between Köpke and Bessenyei, Hungary's charge *pro tem.* Köpke stated that for the time being Germany was not interested in *Anschluss.* It could be deferred indefinitely. Nor did Germany wish to encroach on the Little Entente except economically.[26] Köpke's assurances only partially soothed Magyar fears of *Anschluss.* Still, Köpke's pledge of restraint was welcomed. But news on Germany's peaceful intentions toward the Little Entente struck a sour chord. In this region, the Magyars expected eventual German aid that would restore their former possessions. Germany's "assurances" thus missed their mark. Bessenyei was annoyed and made Köpke feel his chagrin by pointing out the fallacies in Germany's foreign policy. There was a "natural antithesis" cleaving Germany and the Little Entente. As long as Germany ignored Eastern Europe, the Successor States would overlook this antithesis. But the moment Germany became even slightly aggressive—as it shall and must—the Little Entente's combined fury would descend. Then, prophesied Bessenyei, the mutuality of German-Hungarian interests would emerge at last. Köpke conceded Bessenyei's point. He, in turn, assailed an anomaly in Hungarian foreign policy. Hungary's Italian friendship also made little sense. Italy had not helped Hungary substantially as Germany had, either in the Optants' question, or in the St. Gotthardt affair. Once more, and not for the last time, he declined Hungary's offer of German-Italian mediation. Kánya later confirmed that German diplomats consistently deprecated Italy as unreliable.[27] This conversation indicates Germany's growing concern that her peaceful Locarno diplomacy might long delay redressing the wrongs of Versailles and leave the Reich empty-handed among the more aggressive European states such as Hungary and Italy.

At year's end, when German-Hungarian trade discussions were still in progress, Bethlen tendered an enthusiastic and optimistic interview to the Viennese *Neue Freie Presse,* in which Hungary's relations with Germany loomed large. If only we could conclude a mutually beneficial trade agreement, all other problems would vanish. Bethlen anticipated close future collaboration with Germany on disarmament, reparations, and minority questions, but he omitted mention of Italy, perhaps in deference to the Austrian readers for whose consumption the interview was intended.[28]

While Germany meditated about resuming trade talks which ruptured towards the end of 1928, Hungary was not idle. The year 1929 witnessed the most vigorous, complex, and aggressive Hungarian diplomacy since the war. Hungary's convoluted international relations tended to confound even experienced observers. A Wilhelmstrasse memorandum conveys this confusion. Hungary was seen closely linked with Italy, and was principally engaged against the Little Entente; at the same time, however, Hungary also sought friendlier relations with France, which contradicted Italian interests. In due time, the Magyars cleared up some of these inconsistencies. In the *Neue Preussische Kreuz-Zeitung,* Walko explained that Hungary's French diplomacy had the blessings of Italy, whereas France understood that Hungary would never waive her right to Treaty revision. Walko observed also that no nation in the world could do as much for Hungary financially as France. This was no idle boast, as France was keenly interested in Hungary. Schön ventured that the Magyars preferred a pro-French orientation, because only France had the power to revise the Treaty in Hungary's favour. In a subsequent dispatch Schön observed that the French had ulterior motives. They did everything possible to detach Hungary from Germany, a prospect Schön viewed with alarm. But Hungary, too, had ulterior motives. The Magyars were getting nettled with Germany's snail's pace diplomacy and they wished to alarm the Reich into paying more attention to Hungary's needs. As a stop-gap remedy Schön recommended an immediate cessation of German press attacks against Hungary. His advice was heeded.[29]

Nor was this the whole extent of Hungarian diplomatic activity. The Magyars extended more or less effective feelers to Austria, Poland, Yugoslavia, and even Rumania, a nation that had not yet settled the Optants' question to Hungary's satisfaction. The alarming thing about all this was, from the German point of view, that Hungary, in tandem with Italy, was slowly forging a cordon sanitaire from the Adriatic to the Baltic, and from east of Bavaria to the Black Sea. This was a vast region, from which German economic interests might in future be excluded. Having momentarily cut the Gordian knot of conflicting Franco-Italian claims in the area, Hungary seemed to be emerging as the hub of a vast axis, in which the Magyars would enjoy a privileged and strategic position. Italy's growing support of Hungary, and France's apparent change of policy in Central Europe, played straight into Bethlen's hands. As Horthy was wont to say, whoever controls

Budapest controls the Balkans.[30]

Bethlen's current Italian diplomacy did not terminate Hungary's dependency on Germany. Germany's importance as the only nation able to absorb a good portion of Hungary's agricultural output remained constant. Consequently, Hungary continued to cultivate Germany's friendship, even while she concluded agreements with Germany's adversaries and rivals, even enemies. Bethlen used every opportunity to say something flattering about Germany. In his interview of 16 January 1929, for example, he singled out Germany as the only great power whose representative in the past year had stood up on Hungary's behalf, an allusion to Stresemann's efforts in the Optants' problem.[31] In his interview with *8-Órai Újsdg*, Bethlen promised good political relations with Germany as soon as a mutually beneficial trade agreement had been reached. He also praised Germany's contribution in the League in connection with the minority problem, in which Hungary had a crucial stake. As revealed by Schon, the Magyars generally shamed Germans by adopting the air of one betrayed; they complained ceaselessly that Germany and the German public neglected Hungary, not the other way around. The Magyars gave German guests warm welcomes and lots of *"éljen"* (hurrahs) while in Hungary. Such was the experience of General Blomberg, who was dined, wined, and feted during his stay. If the Hungarian press gave little coverage to his visit, Schön consoled himself that Blomberg received at least as loud an acclamation as he entrained for home as the Italian military delegation just arriving. The Wilhelmstrasse was pleased with the results of Blomberg's visit from the point of view of German-Hungarian friendship. The Hungarian Foreign Ministry also crowed about the apparent thaw, although it doubted whether Germany's financial crisis would permit more active German economic and political involvement in Hungary.[32]

The grand old man of Hungarian politics, Count Apponyi, also stressed Hungary's natural association with Germany in numerous areas of common concern, although he had never found Germany's tempo breathtaking; he considered Italy more and more the foundation pillar of Hungary's foreign diplomacy.[33] The Germans had to admit, as indeed they did, that Hungary had no choice but to follow Bethlen's course. A Wilhelmstrasse summary of the year 1929 struck the following pessimistic note: "Germany, to be sure, can offer Hungary no aid in the pursuit of her foreign diplomacy. Germany's interests simply do not agree with Hungary's"[34]

One other reason why Hungary followed only a cautiously pro-German course deserves scrutiny. The Magyars grew increasingly suspicious when Germany showed a growing interest in Germans living beyond the homeland. Two episodes in 1929 served to alarm the Magyars. In February,

Schubert was informed concerning a rumour that Germany planned to create a unified German cultural nation. Its gist was that, culturally speaking, political boundaries would cease to exist, as far as Germany was concerned. The directory of this cultural condominium would be located in a Berlin Center where delegates representing all the expatriate German minorities would sit in permanent session. Dr. Karl von Loesch of the *Deutscher Schutzbund,* considered a notorious ultra-nationalist agitator by the Magyars, was to be affiliated with this venture. Schubert replied ambiguously that "in this precise form the idea is entirely new to me, and I have never heard of such an idea before." Schubert claimed to be completely baffled as to what a "German cultural nation" meant. Perhaps, he ventured ingenuously, it pertained to the very natural, even needful, cultural exchange programmes already existing between Reich Germans and expatriates.[35] Schubert's response was neither reassuring nor truthful. It merely intensified Magyar concerns that a German cultural wave would soon be sweeping over Hungary's Swabians.

Under the circumstances, Schön did not exaggerate when he reported from Budapest six months later that the Magyars greatly resented evidences of interest by Reich Germans in their Swabian brethren. The Magyars tended to label such an interest as a Pan-German menace, as recent debates in the Hungarian Parliament indicated. What the speakers had referred to was that Pan-German agitators from the Reich swarmed all over the Hungarian countryside. In Schön's view certain German circles had given the Magyars ample reason for their suspicions. Only the French benefited from the poor opinion Magyars developed of the Germans, who heedlessly and tactlessly lionized the Swabians. Two examples of German bungling were offered. One concerned a map issued by the *Österreichisch-Deutscher Völksbund,* with the provocative title "Das ganze Deutschland soll es sein" (All this should be Germany). The map showed an expanded Reich, including not only all of Austria and Hungary's share of Burgenland, but even Magyar-inhabited portions of Southern Slovakia, as well as purely Magyar regions in Hungary itself, as far east as Győr. Another example of German thoughtlessness was the plan by a German scout organization *(Bund des Reichspfadfinders)* to loose some one-hundred fifty German young men on Hungary's Swabian settlements as summer visitors. Schön considered the undertaking as bizarre, and highly prejudicial both to German and Swabian interests. He urged that the excursion be cancelled both in Hungary and in neighbouring Austrian Burgenland.[36]

Magyar fears were justified.

The Germans have become intensely conscious of the solidarity of the worldwide German cultural community, a feeling never felt so strongly before as since the lost war. . . .Germans living abroad should have no [separate] parties only Germany. . . .More important by far is the common struggle for the German people and the German future.[37]

These were the words not of a Pan-German agitator but of the eminently respectable Stresemann, at the annual convention of the *Deutsches Ausland-Institut* in May 1927. Since the war, the *DAI*, the pioneer of this new thinking, had become a dynamic central bureau, which sifted news from the German diaspora and from worldwide German cultural organizations, and planned global strategy in conjunction with the German Foreign Ministry, whose financial aid and moral support it enjoyed. By 1927, the *DAI* had overcome the financial constraints of the immediate postwar and inflationary years, and embarked on an ambitious two-pronged programme. It established course offerings in German universities on all aspects of *Auslanddeutschtum*; and it published a monograph series written by experts on aspects of expatriate German life, and its contribution to the German *Kulturgemeinschaft*. One such work investigated the significance of German commercial policies abroad; another discussed the fundamentals of German foreign policy. An atlas and a bibliography of *Auslanddeutschtum* topped the agenda of such literature. All proceedings were conducted with great panoply and reported enthusiastically by the German press. The *Schwäbischer Deutscher Merkur,* for example exulted about

> the development of a new German idea, which transcends both space and frontiers, and [subscribes to] a new, never-before-experienced expression of all people whose mother tongue is German, in a feeling of common destiny. . . . The concept of Nation has today yielded to the idea of the German Volk, whose 90 million members form an inseparable whole.[38]

In other words, an expatriate was an integral part of the German nation, regardless of location, citizenship, political affiliation, or any other loyalties. It was a frightening prospect for the numerically inferior Magyars in their vitally strategic position guarding the Balkans.

The Magyars particularly feared the steadily rising influx of Reich German academic personnel into Hungary, supposedly bent on harmless research expeditions. Their reports generally found their way to *DAI* headquarters. Frequently, these individuals represented subsidiary organizations devoted to German minority affairs abroad, with chapters scattered throughout Germany. The *Verein für das Deutschtum im Ausland,* for example, functioned even during the difficult years shortly after the war. One report is worth mentioning, especially since it was written by a Dr. Maurer, who later, under National Socialism, became a leading official of the *Forschungsstelle Schwaben im Ausland* (Research Group for Swabians Abroad), a subsidiary of the *DAI*. It was the task of the *FSA* to gather information and disseminate news about Swabians living abroad.

During the summer of 1924, Dr. Maurer undertook a lengthy "study trip" to various Swabian regions throughout Hungary, ostensibly to collect historical mementoes and artifacts from the Swabian past. He kept in close touch with Hungarian officials, who were aware of his purpose. Maurer described his relations with them as excellent, their attitudes as cooperative. On the treatment of Swabians his opinion was poor. His report betrayed a great deal of mistrust, if not contempt, of Magyar functionaries and of Magyar official policy. His impressions were gathered from first-hand experience in the field, and from discussions with Swabian leaders, including Gündisch and Bleyer. According to Maurer, the two Swabian leaders were happy, because the *UDV* had just been established, but they were by no means keenly optimistic. Maurer thought the Magyars still pursued their old delaying politics, the same old insincere tactics, that would lead to a dead end, and through a policy of gradual denial destroy the Swabian people and rob them of their confidence in their leaders. Maurer was displeased with the intellectual niveau of Swabians, and to remedy this plight he arranged to have six worthy Swabian students provided with higher education in Germany during the coming year.[39] This document shows that German agents enjoyed the confidence of Hungarian-Swabian leaders, whose complimentary public utterances about conditions in Hungary differed substantially from what they revealed to kinsmen from the Reich. It also suggests that even by the mid-1920s, Reich Germans took a keen interest in their brethren in Hungary, and chafed at the alleged injustices under which they laboured.

What began as a trickle in the mid-1920s became a torrent by 1930. A plethora of Reich organizations, devoted to the most extensive array of interests concerning the state of Germandom abroad, began to bombard the Wilhelmstrasse for moral and financial support. In connection with a conference of German minority leaders in Berlin (30 April - 1 May 1930), a gathering also attended by Bleyer, a preliminary secret meeting took place in order to discuss the matter of German international undertakings. C. G. Bruns, a self-styled legal advisor to German minority groups abroad, requested that Schubert also attend. According to Bruns, Schubert was quite familiar with the topic, having been briefed previously. Undoubtedly, the group desired and received Foreign Ministry blessings of its endeavours, as well as aid of every kind.

Another extant letter, dated 26 April 1930, addressed by F. O. Rödiger, a minority expert of the Foreign Ministry to Curtius, verified the payment of 25,000 RM by the Wilhelmstrasse to the *Verband deutscher Volksgruppen,* and cautiously requested an increase in its annual stipend. The *VdV* was still another minority organization whose aim was to draw together the various German minorities, partly through travel, and partly through publications. Although Rödiger recommended the requested increase, he complained that the *VdV* frequently sought to escape government control and desired to function independently, at times to the government's detriment and embarrassment. Roediger suggested that the *VdV*'s allocation be curtailed temporarily to teach it to refrain from pursuing a foreign policy of its own. The usefulness of the *VdV* was recognized, however, as for example in Paris, and its agent there was to be made foreign correspondent of a German newspaper chain as a decoy. The Foreign Ministry was also asked to underwrite the expense of other, similar, agents elsewhere, whenever their tasks coincided with the aims and purposes of the Foreign Ministry. A separate note on the same date revealed that Bruns' bureau enjoyed considerable financial support in the Wilhelmstrasse and that Bruns had applied for additional funds to enable him to pursue an ambitious array of new tasks.

Through 1930, the Wilhelmstrasse assembled an impressive and exhaustive dossier of all organizations and publications devoted to the nurture of *Auslanddeutschtum.* Three of these deserve special mention. *Die Akademie zur wissenschaftlichen Erforschung und zur Pflege des Deutschtums—Deutsche Akademie* for short—was founded in Munich by the noted Bavarian Professor Friedrich von Müller shortly after the war. This sophisticated scholarly organization, which initially ran afoul of other, similar associations, had many facets. It published ethnographic studies connecting Germans abroad with the mother country; it provided stipends for those wishing to study in the Reich or interested in publishing. The dissemination of German culture and German language in the schools abroad was one of the central aims of the *DA,* and it established courses at German universities, designed especially for German teachers abroad. In the opinion of the Foreign Ministry rapporteur, the *DA* did its work quietly and effectively. The *DA* even enjoyed the financial support of the Bavarian government, and the Premier of Bavaria participated in its endeavours.

The *Arbeitsgemeinschaft Deutschen Zeitschriften für die Interessen des Grenz- und Auslanddeutschtums,* founded in 1920, was another organization devoted to minority affairs. Its aim was to provide information and arouse the interest of German periodical publishers in the fate of Germans abroad. It arranged conferences in Germany, at which experts in various fields pertinent to

German ethnic groups living abroad held forth. The group conducted propaganda on behalf of expatriate Germans. Under the impetus of constant publicity, the Reich public was taught to cherish the fate of their distant compatriots. A special bureau devoted its efforts to proliferating Reich periodical propaganda literature in the German diaspora, especially among the leaders. Frequent meetings in Germany linked *Auslanddeutsche* and Reich colleagues, with expenses defrayed by the *Arbeitsgemeinschaft*.

Perhaps the most ambitious organization was the *Das Institut für Grenz- und Auslanddeutschtum*. This society, located in the Berlin academic area, provided not only stipends and subsidies for visiting scholars and students from the diaspora, it offered guest rooms, study halls, archive and library facilities, each dedicated to research into the German presence in other lands. A graduate student might satisfy the partial requirements of his dissertation or seminar work at the Institute. It also published the results of its own research endeavours, with emphasis on the works of young members. Facilities were not limited to Germans; the Institute greatly prized alien scholars, as a means of raising its international prestige.[40]

Clearly, Germany endeavoured to achieve a new type of bond, based on cultural and ethnic community, among Germans scattered throughout the globe. This programme assumed ominous proportions by 1930, arousing particular concern in Hungary, where the official ideology of Magyar racial supremacy clashed head-on with this dangerous rival doctrine. By 1930 it was futile to argue that in Germany the promotion of *völkisch* strivings was limited to a small lunatic fringe of ultra-nationalists. The idea of a German *Kulturgemeinschaft* had been given the aura of respectability by the universally esteemed "moderate" Stresemann, and even more recently, after the latter's death in September 1929, by his successor, the eminently respectable Curtius. Lest anyone harboured any doubt about the intentions of Germany's government, Curtius, in a speech delivered on the occasion of the annual meeting of the *DAI*, reaffirmed Stresemann's position on Germany's cultural revolution. Curtius embraced Stresemann's programme on behalf of German *Volkstum* and *Kultur*, and promised to continue and nurture the government's relationship with the *DAI* and with other circles connected with it. He pledged to provide ever greater funds for this purpose among Germans abroad, despite Germany's deteriorating financial situation. Although denying that Germany had ulterior political motives, and paying tribute to the ethos of other nationalities, he proudly declared that the German ethnic idea was the wave of the future.[41] German elections in the fall of that year for the first time returned a large Nationalist and National Socialist contingent in the German Reichstag. This exacerbated the fears of peoples such as the Magyars, whose interests were diametrically opposed to the nurturing of German *völkisch* concepts.

The Hungarian government knew of these activities, and feared their consequences for Hungary's Germans. In November 1930 the Foreign Ministry submitted an exhaustive report to Bethlen on the eve of his Berlin trip. It was based on thorough investigation devoted not only to Germany's intentions in Hungary, but in the entire Danube Basin.[42] By then, much of the information was neither new nor startling. The *DAI* was said to be masterminding a virtual conspiracy, incorporating all Danubian Germans, the Swabians included, into a Great-German politico-economic-cultural *Gemeinschaft*. The essence of the plan was that Germans constituted a distinct racial group. In Hungary, the Magyars would be forced to abandon Magyarization. Swabians in process of being assimilated, as well as German-Hungarians already thoroughly Magyarized, would be re-Germanized and reattached to the German cultural community. German industry and commerce would play an important role in bringing this about. German business and banking would finance the Swabian press and cultural and religious organizations along *völkisch* lines. Another important disseminator of *Kultur,* the German agent, would be disguised as student or researcher, and would submit detailed reports and issue recommendations to the *DAI* or the Foreign Ministry.

The Ministry rapporteur painted an apocalyptic picture of wholesale subversion in progress. Already, the pictorial supplements of *Sonntagsblatt* carried the same Pan-German propaganda published in German newspapers throughout the other Danubian countries. Already, German agents were mingling with innocent German students. Sooner or later, these centrifugal forces would be used against Hungary. The Swabians would become an ethnic bridge connecting Austro-Germans with Germans residing east of Hungary, and ultimately Germany might dominate the Danube Valley.

In the meantime, the Hungarian Foreign Ministry also prepared a suggested agenda for Bethlen's Berlin visit. The question of German subversion ought to be strongly broached. The Wilhelmstrasse must be told that it harmed the German minorities in the Successor States not to cooperate with the Magyars residing there. Indeed, currently, the Germans were disseminating propaganda detrimental to both the Magyar minority and to Hungary. Germany must be persuaded that any subversion in the Danube Basin must be aimed exclusively against the Successor States; Hungary's Swabians, on the contrary, must be permitted to enjoy their current status of a non-persecuted minority enjoying full civil rights. They must be loyal to the Hungarian, not to the German national idea. International politics, as well as trade, were to be the other important items on the agenda.

In preparation for the conference, the Wilhelmstrasse also accumulated reams of information on all aspects of Hungarian life and German-Hungarian problems. The rapporteur systematically divided the balance sheet into two categories: "burdens" and "favourable aspects." The Swabian minority issue he deemed to be one of the two weightiest problems, but not because of Swabian ill treatment. On the contrary, Bethlen significantly improved many facets of German minority life. The problem rested with the German press for labeling Swabian treatment the worst among all the Successor States. Further, the Magyars considered Reich agitation to be a very serious matter. Bethlen, for example, vehemently resented the recent German practice of bestowing stipends on Swabian students tenable in German universities. Returnees allegedly became fullfledged *völkisch* agitators. Burgenland had become once more a source of friction. Germany's excessive preoccupation with Burgenland, coupled with attacks in the German press against Hungary's alleged mistreatment of Burgenlanders, had intensified Magyar resentments. Incidents, such as Lobe's anti-Magyar tirade in Vienna, various speeches delivered and articles published under the auspices of the *VdV,* and a provocative map of Greater Germany recently distributed by the *Deutsch-Österreichischer Volksbildungsverein,* exacerbated existing bad feelings. The rapporteur also criticized the German press for its indifference to Hungarian revisionist aspirations and for its downright hostility. Recent improvements were belated. In retaliation, the Hungarian press had turned Magyars against Germany. But the most deeply rooted Magyar hostilities arose from Germany's refusal to conclude a trade agreement that would respect Hungary's economic requirements.

On the credit side, even the limited German-Hungarian cultural cooperation in Geneva was a hopeful sign. The referent listed a number of examples and noted that since Hungary strove to establish similar links with Italy and France, the significance of the connections should not be underestimated. A German-Hungarian rapprochement was supremely important, mainly to prevent Hungary from going over to the camp of Germany's opponents, and also because it would make it easier for Germany to achieve certain major objectives, as an Austrian *Anschluss,* seizure of the Polish Corridor, and prevention of annoying problems, such as Restoration in Hungary, and French plans for a Danube Federation. On the whole, however, chances for an early accommodation or agreement with Hungary were deemed minimal.

When the talks finally began, the vast gaps separating the German and the Hungarian viewpoints became apparent. Curtius hoped the two nations might discover some areas of common action, since he saw no fundamental differences in their foreign policy aims. He particularly had in mind two areas: revisionism and disarmament. The Magyars thought the Germans wished to create a block of the losers but they were disappointed. Curtius soon declared that Germany had no intentions of creating new power blocks or of concluding alliances. German foreign policy would proceed, as before, in an *ad hoc* fashion, reaping windfalls, reaching agreements with individual states on particular issues. Curtius meant to deal thus with Hungary and Italy. Bethlen rejected Curtius' political strategy. His own aim was to divide Europe into two distinct camps: revisionists and anti-revisionists. First Hungary must destroy the Little Entente, and prevent the formation of an impending Slavic barrier in the guise of a Yugoslav-Bulgarian alliance. Hungary and Italy admittedly conspired to encircle and fragment Yugoslavia, albeit peacefully. Simultaneously, Hungary was tendering economic approaches to Rumania and Yugoslavia, in order to detach these states from the Little Entente and thereby isolate Czechoslovakia. Bethlen ventured that the French would not object to the confounding of its favourite Central European state, as they wearied of Beneš's eternal machinations. Respecting Poland, both Curtius and Chancellor Brüning expressed concern about developing Hungarian-Polish friendship. Bethlen replied evasively. When Italy and France emerged for discussion again, both Germany and Hungary kept their intentions to themselves. On the whole, it was an unsatisfactory interview for both parties. It obscured more than it illuminated. The Germans worried about Hungary's ulterior motives in Poland, and about the possibility that she might participate in a vast East European alliance under Franco-Italian auspices. This would leave Germany completely in the lurch. Hungary was kept guessing about Germany's intentions in Austria, and Poland loomed as an early target in Germany's *Drang nach Osten*. The demise of both these nations would destroy Hungary's favourable strategic position, and cashier Magyar dreams of creating an East European imperium with Hungary as its privileged hub.

The conferees fared no better with the Swabian question. Bethlen assured his hosts that the situation of the Germans in Hungary was particularly close to his heart, and that he was determined to fulfill the wishes of the German minority in matters of education and religious instruction. However, agitation in Hungary by German-based organizations had made implementation impossible thus far. These agitators successfully alienated Swabians and Magyars. The Swabians' loyalty to Hungary had begun to falter. Even in the Successor States, Reich agents systematically indoctrinated Germans against Magyars. Curtius was indignant but evasive. Bethlen's charges were news to him. Reich agencies were limited to cultural matters. The two governments ought to resolve this serious problem without delay. Bethlen agreed, and reiterated that as soon as agitation ceased, the Swabians' cultural demands would be granted. Curtius and Brüning requested an itemized white paper, whereupon a mixed commission would be established. Bethlen agreed.

The last political topic on the agenda concerned a matter of great importance to the Magyars. Since war's end, they had been campaigning for joint Magyar-German action in the Successor States. To date, Hungary had failed to achieve cooperation. The fault lay both with the German minorities, who disliked the Magyars, and with the German government, which for reasons of its own discouraged collaboration. This had emerged in a position paper prepared by the Wilhelmstrasse prior to Bethlen's visit. Hitherto, German officials had alternately reassured the Magyars or evaded the issue. Now, the Germans decided to try a ruse and persuade the Magyars that the cooperation they so avidly sought would be forthcoming. They had no intention whatever to accommodate the Magyars, however, because collaboration might injure the German minorities. Diaspora Magyars lived in compact enclaves contiguous with Hungary, and hence their battle cry was annexation. The Germans resided in small, scattered ethnic groupings, none of them contiguous with Germany, with the exception of Sudetenland. Consequently, they only sought autonomy, not annexation. The Germans felt that the extremist Magyar irredenta could only harm their cause, and rather than cooperate with the Magyars, they wished to be disassociated from them. Both diaspora Germans and the Reich felt, moreover, that Hungary treated the Swabians miserably and deserved neither German aid nor cooperation. All this was to be kept secret from the Hungarians in Berlin. Bethlen would be apprised that Curtius had indeed discussed with expatriate German leaders the question of collaboration and that they had not categorically rejected it. The Magyars would also be told to rely more on the League and the various minority congresses to ameliorate the minority problem. Finally, any meaningful German-Hungarian cooperation would have to await improved treatment of the Swabians.

At the meeting, the Germans implemented this plan by offering the Magyars vague generalities on cooperation. Apropos his talk with Yugoslav-German minority leaders, Curtius declared ambiguously that they were fundamentally prepared to pursue a more intimate exploration of the possibilities of cooperation with their Magyar counterparts. Of course, there were differing political goals to be pursued by either side, so that there would have to be a great deal of tactical procedural nuances in the respective approaches. The Yugoslav Germans also demanded to see how the position of German-Hungarians progressed from time to time. Having delivered this obscure message, Curtius turned to the Czechoslovak German minority.

There, the Germans were divided, and he refused to interfere. Nor did he wish to get mixed up in the minorities' political affairs. Germany's aim was to limit involvement to strictly cultural matters. Curtius ignored the Rumanian Germans. With them, the Magyars had bitter memories.[43] Bethlen left the conference with empty hands. Subsequent discussions on trade brought nugatory results. Fortunately, the Magyars expected very few concrete accomplishments, hence they were not disappointed.

About the only agreeable consequence of Bethlen's journey was that it made greater waves than it was foreseen.[44] The French and the Poles were especially nervous, and feared the creation of a German-Hungarian revisionist block. The Germans encouraged these tales by praising the superb behaviour of their Magyar guests. For reasons of their own, they boasted that the visit had brought Magyar-German commercial rapprochement much closer to fruition.[45] The Magyars had some consolation, as they wove their intricate diplomatic nets under the faint aura of success for a little while longer.

Until Germany reappeared in the Danubian area as a political and economic superpower, Hungary paid only lip service to the Swabian problem. It was sufficient if Swabian and German public opinion did not exceed the point of indignation. That danger was remote. Hungarian minority policy was frequently callous but seldom brutal. After 1925, however, Bethlen's Swabian policy grew more circumspect, since Hungary could no longer risk to offend the *volksbewusst* Germans and their Swabian clients. Nor could Bethlen ignore a growing anti-Swabian groundswell in Hungary, especially in provincial official and intellectual circles. This irreconcilable conflict of interests resulted in a contradictory government policy. It became common practice to attract Germany's support by making elaborate promises to the Swabians, while leaving the execution of the minority laws to the tender mercies of hostile lay and ecclesiastic provincial administrators. A nimble politician, Bethlen preserved his image as a well-meaning Swabian patron, a tactic that shifted the government's responsibilities and blame onto the shoulders of thousands of elusive provincial officials. The equivocal treatment of the *UDV,* and the cavalier manner in which minority education policy was executed, were typical manifestations of this approach. For all his boasts and promises, Bethlen failed to improve the Swabian elementary school system; he procrastinated publishing and distributing German texts; and he neglected to train and allocate suitable minority teachers. After the mid-1920's, Swabian minority life thus became linked with Hungary's political and economic relations with the German Reich. Swabian minority policy became an integral part of foreign diplomacy.

Internal Problems—The UDV

After 1926, businesslike relations between the *UDV* and the Hungarian government barely veneered mutual dislikes and suspicions. Bethlen prided himself on having permitted the Swabians to organize nationwide along ethnic lines. It was an unprecedented gesture in postwar Hungary, and Bethlen believed the Swabians ought to be content. But they were not satisfied, and deemed Bethlen's concession meagre, a basic birthright, and an initial gain to be greatly augmented. Swabians and Magyars began rubbing each other the wrong way, and the government steadily tightened its control over the *UDV*, an organization it did not quite trust. Simultaneously, harassment by local officials intensified Swabian resentments, and cast the government's sincerity into doubt. The regime, though taken aback by the vehemence of provincial opposition to the *UDV*, paid only token attention to remedying the abuses.

The contemporary literature captured the essence and intensity of the alleged violations. At the 1926 *UDV* General Assembly, most speakers complained about and deplored what they considered to be unprovoked and unjust harassments by Magyar and Magyarone administrators.[1] In his opening speech Gratz stressed that the *UDV* had enjoyed modest progress despite misguided obstructionism by certain local officials. He counselled perpetual patience. Neuberger and Huber each assailed the intensity and unfairness of violations. In his closing speech, Bleyer alluded only indirectly to the perils of de-ethnitization by stressing the need for a "Swabian spiritual and moral renaissance through [our] inclusion into the greater German spiritual community [*Kulturgemeinschaft*] and through a faithful nurturing of [our] German national character."[2]

Although Bleyer's statement had only cultural connotations, to the Magyars it sounded like Pan-German agitation. Bleyer's outburst was probably triggered by his suppressed rage against the government's high-handed methods prior to the Assembly. Bethlen had "persuaded" the *UDV* to "admit" certain trusted government nominees into the executive council as this would silence the opposition. But the executive already burst with government appointees. It was bizarre, therefore, when Bethlen pressured three of these Members, including the noted author Ferenc Herceg, a thoroughly Magyarized Swabian, to resign and clear the way for the new appointees. In exchange for this favour, the *UDV* would be allowed to operate in currently forbidden counties. This compromise, foisted on the unsuspecting rank and file membership at the general assembly, was received with universal indignation by the normally disciplined Swabians, and physical violence was only narrowly averted. Publicly, Bleyer had to bend to prevent being broken by Bethlen. Privately, he was furious. The government might prevent further outrages against the *UDV*, but its prestige among Swabians and particularly in the Reich, not to mention his own, might become irretrievably tarnished. Of the three Magyarones foisted on the *UDV*, Bleyer and his entourage might have tolerated two—the Roman Catholic Reverend Heckenberger of Baranya and Chief Justice Sieb of Tolna; but Bethlen's third choice, Deputy Perlaki, was another matter. Perlaki was not only a personal enemy and relentless adversary of Bleyer, he opposed German associations in principle, and—with quiet government encouragement—had been successfully throttling *UDV* activities in Baranya with his own *Faluszövetség*, a rival Magyar village association. At the same time, Bleyer knew that the Prime Minister had the legal right to demand government representation in the *UDV*. It had been the precondition for permitting the establishment of the organization in the first place.

In contrast to the indignation among the Swabians, German observers surprisingly saw nothing wrong in this meddling with the *UDV*'s autonomy. The German Minister hailed the Assembly, its achievements, and *UDV* prospects for the future, and even ventured that the Swabian leaders were generally satisfied with the situation.[3] This incident dramatized how successful Bethlen's *Realpolitik* was. The Germans apparently appreciated his political genius, while the Swabians had really nothing tangible to complain about. After all, had not Bethlen promised to solve the *UDV*'s most serious problem—prohibitions by local authorities, especially in Baranya?

If Bethlen had kept his word, indeed, had he been able to, given the growing chauvinism of his countrymen, all might have been well. Unfortunately, however, the controversial Baranya County remained a sore spot in Bethlen's time, and Magyar-Swabian tensions increased. Certain limited improvements in other areas of minority life notwithstanding, notably in the schools and in Swabian representation in parliament, the Baranya issue continued to rankle. In a speech later in 1926, Bethlen promised once more that "the government will under no circumstances tolerate obstructionism by officials who labour under antiquated beliefs."[4] Nonetheless, violations continued. His personal offer to redress Swabian grievances passed as mere rhetoric.

In the meantime, the government began to fear the *UDV*'s growing power and organizing zeal. In October 1926, the *UDV* proposed to conduct giant publicity rallies in some eighty-six localities, principally in strategic Pest, Tolna, and Baranya Counties. The Hungarian Praesidium balked at this ambitious programme, and in the end the *UDV* was forced to suspend recruiting operations altogether in the three counties. The Praesidium, in its decision, was guided not only by what it considered creeping Germanism rampant among the Swabians; some of the Swabian leaders had overstepped the boundaries of common sense. There was the leakage of unfavourable reports to the Reich press about Swabian treatment. The culprits were believed to be Swabians. In Parliament Bleyer admitted the accuracy of these charges. Goaded by a heckler, Bleyer stated defiantly that as long as the Magyars mistreated the Swabians, he would feel justified in alerting the foreign press. It stretched the credulity of many Magyars when, in the same breath, Bleyer also claimed to be a Magyar patriot.[5]

At a time when Hungary wished to create a good impression in Berlin, sparks flew between Magyar and Swabian. Bethlen wished to rid himself of the most nagging problem, Baranya. Accordingly, in the fall of 1926, he ordered Baranya County Lord Lieutenant (főispán) Ferenc Fischer and the UDV to settle their differences once and for all. Next March Fischer convened a conference, attended by local and government officials, Baranya teachers and clergymen, and UDV leaders. What was to have been a session to soothe the lingering conflict, turned into a phillipic against the UDV. Its leaders drew charges of Pan-Germanism and treason by indignant Magyar super-patriots, so that Fischer had to terminate the session abruptly lest more harm be done. Bleyer had tried to justify the UDV's existence in Hungarian life on patriotic grounds. He told the conference that far more was at stake than survival of the organization. The UDV might help achieve revision of the Treaty of Trianon. He meant that the Swabians might act as intermediaries to enlist Germany's support for Hungary's claims against the Little Entente nations when the time came. Unless Hungary demonstrated that she honoured the rights of her own minorities, the Magyars in the Successor States were bound to be persecuted. Gratz and Bleyer then reassured the antagonistic assembly that the UDV's philosophy and pro-gramme were preeminently patriotic. In Gratz's view, the organization had no right even to exist unless it functioned unflinchingly in the Magyar spirit. Finally, the UDV, after all, was a sanctioned organization, both founded and personally endorsed by the Prime Minister. Through the mediation efforts of the influential Bishop Virág of Pécs an agreement was reached that looked good on paper. The UDV would be permitted to commence preliminary studies in preparation for the creation of new local chapters. To sweeten his vague promise, Fischer granted the UDV permission to begin organizing sixteen local chapters prior to the convention in August next year.[6] The Magyars had demonstrated their negotiating skill once again. The Swabians were thrust on the defensive and settled for a pittance at a steep price.

The Swabians' poor bargain emerged only later. Gratz's speech on 20 August at the 1927 UDV Assembly was still couched in optimistic clichés. He spoke about Baranya at one point, exulting that the seemingly insur-mountable problems of yesteryear had yielded before the "energetic support of the government." The UDV had achieved a compromise solution with the Baranya authorities, so that henceforward the County would become a fruitful recruitment area and a model for other regions, such as Pest County, another trouble spot. Spurred by Bethlen's 17 June posture as a Swabian champion, the gullible Gratz became overconfident and failed to acquaint the Assembly with the nature of the agreement in Baranya. It was a compromise only as to method, but not as to essence, was all he revealed. Gratz's euphemisms barely concealed the trap into which the UDV had blundered. The supposed "compromise" in Baranya entailed sundering the central government's control over UDV operations in that county. This meant that henceforth Magyar officials, nominated by the chief executive of Baranya County, would join Swabians as leaders, and all activities would have to be approved by both county and church officials. The agreement had come about with the blessings (and no doubt relief) of Bethlen. In other words, the UDV had bartered away its only strong asset, the government's support, in exchange for elusive advantages.[7]

On the surface, the era of good feelings continued between government and Swabians. Bethlen eagerly courted Germany, and consequently sought the Swabian community's approval for his minority policies. By 1926, Germany had joined the League of Nations and almost overnight became a great power once again. The German government let it be known that German-Hungarian friendship related largely to the treatment accorded to the Swabians. Although government-UDV conferences generated few substantive benefits, the Bethlen regime insured that the Swabians always left the conference table in an optimistic mood. It was also no accident that beginning in 1928, Bethlen gave the UDV permission to accept sizable annual subsidies from the UDA for cultural purposes, at a time when the government's own yearly contribution remained a trifle. While keeping an iron grip on the UDV, Hungary succeeded in shunting the expenses of its maintenance onto a foreign power, that was only too eager to establish a cultural beachhead. Bethlen blundered by opening a wedge to German influence.

The large German subsidies emboldened the Swabians and caused a gradual reaction in government circles. For nearly one year, Bethlen stuck by his June 1927 agreement with the UDV but would not improve it. Bleyer's attempts in October 1927 and January 1928 to penetrate this invisible wall failed. In March 1928, he became far more aggressive and finally wrung further concessions for the UDV from the beleaguered and reluctant Bethlen—more concessions in the schools and no further harassments of the UDV. To underscore the importance of the UDV, Klebelsberg urged the organization to form a school committee and proffer recommendations. He also pledged that owing to Swabian importance, a special

German division would be created in the Ministry of Education. It was no coincidence that Bethlen capitulated to Bleyer. Trade negotiations with Germany had entered a critical phase and Bleyer had laced his latest requests with an overt—and prophetic—threat: Should Bethlen fail to heed his demands, the matter would no longer rest there. "Not because of us or through us—on the contrary! After us, or in our place, the extremists must follow.[8]

The Magyars had always over-reacted to external danger. When the German menace from without threatened to fuse with the one from within, Bethlen predictably resorted to evasions, promises, and excuses. The year 1928 can justly claim to revealing the widest gap between promises and achievements. After, emboldened by Gemany's growing might and Hungary's economic dependence on that nation, the Swabians confronted Bethlen with increasingly more militant demands. At the beginning of 1929, Bleyer showered Bethlen with a cascade of grievances arising from the UDV's recruiting and organizing activities, especially in Veszprém and Baranya Counties. The Prime Minster merely promised to take the matter under advisement and have the grievances remedied.[9]

The Swabians' March 1927 agreement with Fischer of Baranya had also miscarried. Only the most immediate results of the pact had justified Gratz's optimism. By 1929, there were 38 UDV chapters functioning in the county, but in 1930, Faul-Farkas reported at the annual Assembly that the authorities in Baranya had suspended association operation once again. Sonntagsblatt's complacent boast that this year, representatives from all regions of Hungary were present, was premature. In an unusually militant speech, Gratz blamed this new crisis on influential members of Hungarian society and various subordinate administrative organs who had thwarted the good intentions of the government, which wished to pursue a new minority policy. The obstructionists succeeded all too frequently, Gratz complained. He referred not only to Baranya, although it was the most flagrant example, but several other counties as well, notably Tolna and Pest. Gratz raised the spectre that the Swabians might someday become radicalized, although he foresaw no such immediate danger. But he did warn Magyarizers that pressure evoked counterpressure, and assimilation efforts had always been the best method to prevent assimilation. Nothing could stop the Swabians' search for ethnic identity, even if it took thirty years. While dismissing certain hotheads in Germany who wished to agitate among the Swabians against the Magyars as inconsequential, Gratz served notice that certain organizations in the Reich were keenly interested in the Swabian fate, and henceforth Germany would not permit the Magyars to abuse them.[10] It is interesting to note that Gratz's speech coincided more or less with the great renascence of *volksbewusst* organizations in the Reich, generously subsidized by the increasingly militant Weimar Republic.

Baranya authorities relented somewhat the following year, but the UDV's victory was shortlived. The moment Fischer released his decree empowering the UDV to resume recruiting operations, members were tendered writs of resignation by local notaries. Consequently, the ban merely continued in a roundabout way. By the year 1931, obstructionism of this type was rampant. Bleyer painted a discouraging picture both of overt and covert persecutions. As far as the central government was concerned, the minority problem had been solved by various administrative and statistical devices, but neither the Swabians nor the Magyar public shared in the regime's enthusiasm. The latter bitterly opposed every shred of culture that was not Magyar, and as a result, the UDV was forbidden to function in many areas in which it had a legal existence. Anyone had the right to join the UDV, for example, yet many Swabians were dissuaded by the local authorities on flimsy pretexts. In many places, the UDV was forbidden to collect dues, and funds were impounded. Meetings were frequently harassed by the police, and attendance at certain party functions was forbidden to minors, women, and visitors. Village notaries took great pleasure in taunting UDV officials, and prospective members prominent in public life risked public humiliation, house searches, and other persecutions. The Magyar public obviously made its choice; according to Bleyer, it demanded the unconditional Magyarization of all Swabians and hated the UDV.[11]

The UDV General Assembly in August 1931 publicly ignored the growing crisis in the countryside. There were strong indications, however, that the Swabian movement came under mounting internal pressure to radicalize. Gratz devoted a good portion of his long speech to this topic. He carefully analyzed the prevailing political climate and concluded that it would be a grave error if the Swabians were to field a political party of their own. It would be poor strategy to pursue purely cultural concerns one second, and political aspirations the next, depending on the vagaries of the moment. He pleaded for the continuance of the Swabians' traditional policy of compromise.[12]

Bethlen's departure from the political scene in the fall of 1931 exacerbated the UDV's status. Whatever restraint the former Prime Minister might have exercised was now gone. Károlyi was considered to be at best indifferent to the Swabian cause. Local officials were subtly encouraged to take unilateral action against the UDV, for lack of restraint by the central government. The trend of persecutions, begun in earnest one or two years earlier, now intensified. Press attacks against the Swabians shifted from the relative obscurity of the provinces to the pages of the larger Budapest newspapers, in which *UDV* members were characterized as Pan-Germans, traitors, and demagogues, their leaders accused of the most outrageous intentions. This, and Károlyi's failure to intervene, emboldened provincial officials still further. In ever more counties *UDV* activities were curtailed. In Moson, for example, the *főispán* charged the *UDV* with politicizing and suspended recruiting operations. In Szár the authorities cancelled a musical contest sponsored by the *UDV*. In Pest, the *UDV* was forbidden to establish new chapters, and existing ones were denied permits to hold meetings. *Der Auslandsdeutsche* deplored these conditions and observed that a positive solution was even more important for the Magyars than for the Swabians. The publication referred to Hungary's economic dependence on Germany, especially in view of the current economic crisis.[13]

Árpád Török, a Bleyer collaborator, saw the situation in a more correct light. He noted that the Magyars cared not one whit about the Swabians or about German public opinion, inasmuch as the new Prime Minister pursued a pro-French policy. Török cried havoc, foreseeing a new, more terrible Trianon looming where Hungary's economic independence would be sacrificed to the grasping French. He also cautioned that the torch of national hatred was being lit in Hungary by chauvinistic Magyars, in the guise of a hate campaign against the Swabians. Yet Török was confident:

> Only narrowminded and naive people can possibly believe that the unity of Hungary's Germans could be destroyed by forceful measures. This feeling of unity is so strong now that it is indestructible. What a policy of needling and intolerance will reap is not the destruction of the German movement but dissatisfaction. . . .Whosoever. . .shall disturb [the situation of the Swabians] will have lit the torch, he will have begun the war. . .of nationality strife in our misery-laden land.[14]

Gratz's speech at the Ninth General Assembly in August 1932 was couched in somewhat more diplomatic language, yet it echoed Török's sentiments. It had come to Gratz's attention in early summer that Karolyi's decision to adopt a hard-line strategy against what he considered the *UDV*'s policy of agitations was final. According to Gratz, Károlyi was convinced that creating the *UDV* had been a grave error to begin with, a mistake that could never be fully redressed. Károlyi apparently believed that if only the Swabians were left alone, they would stop agitating and become "loyal, correct and satisfied citizens" just like their fathers and grandfathers before them.

Confronted with growing evidences of intransigence on both sides, Gratz tried from time to time to pose as the perennial disinterested mediator, a cosmopolitan figure who attacked extremists on both sides. He criticized certain hotheads in Germany who wished to influence the thinking of Swabians. Not for the first time, Gratz repudiated

> short-sighted and colour-blind leaders who...without knowing our situation, would involve German-Hungarians in a conflict with the Magyars; who would dictate to the Swabian leaders what they might or might not do....One has to reject decisively such rude and senseless intervention in the internal affairs of the Swabians.

But Gratz also pilloried Magyars who ignored the legitimate cultural aspirations of the Swabians, as they demanded justice for their own brethren in the Successor States. He labelled their behaviour as suicidal, and begged the government not to abandon Bethlen's minority policy:

> Every deviation from [his] principles will, in my opinion evoke bitter revenge and will seriously endanger [Hungary's] great interests of state.[15]

Following these prophetic words, Gratz resigned the presidency of the UDV, which he had held for the past eight years.

Gratz's sudden resignation had deep roots. Less than two weeks before the UDV Assembly he had received a letter in which Bleyer expressed total disillusionment with the Magyars and the government. For fifteen years, wrote Bleyer, he had been labouring under the illusion that Hungary would solve the German question on her own accord:

> I had counted too much on right and righteousness, on consideration, and on sober appreciation of self-interest....I have completely abandoned this belief. Hungary will never solve the German question, certainly not of her own accord. Magyarization has never been pursued so inconsiderately, so purposefully, and so thoroughly, as today.

Bleyer dismissed suggestions that the League of Nations or some other international agency might serve as a possible forum for the Swabians. For the first time in his life, Bleyer also turned his face resolutely from his homeland:

> Since Germany and Germandom all over the world wish to rescue each individual German group (*Volksgruppe*), they will now have to exert all the strength at their disposal against Hungary. Then we shall see whether Hungary's power of resistance is greater than the combined might of

worldwide Germandom. If it is, then the Germans of Hungary are doomed.[16]

For, declared Bleyer, while right and righteousness might be on our side, the Magyars exercized all the power, and superior, as well as unscrupulous tactics. Consequently, it was useless even talking to Károlyi (Bleyer and Gratz were scheduled to hold discussions with the Prime Minister on 27 August), since nothing would come of it. Only a discussion between Budapest and Berlin would be of any significance. After this, Bleyer sank into the deepest gloom.

Several days later, Gratz sought to persuade the distraught Bleyer to foresake policies that might imperil long-run Swabian survival. Gratz seemed to be living in a different world than Bleyer. He saw the flagrant Magyarization measures that so disturbed most Swabians as only a transitory phenomenon. Gratz was upset because Bleyer no longer wished to negotiate with the government. He granted that Károlyi was no friend, and he no doubt wished to ignore Swabian wishes if he could help it. He had nonetheless steadily reiterated his willingness to settle all outstanding issues through negotiations. Gratz saw no reason for despair as long as the Magyars were willing to talk. The government moved slowly and circumspectly, and the Swabian cause could stand further setbacks. In other words, what Bleyer considered to be the final straw, Gratz saw as nothing of the sort. The government merely feared adverse Magyar public opinion and moved slowly. Gratz warned that it would be a fatal error to permit the Swabian problem to be solved in Berlin rather than in Budapest. The suggestion not only violated Gratz's patriotic sentiments, it was counterproductive, since it would merely strengthen the government's resolve not to negotiate under duress. Further, such strategy would impair relations between Hungary and Germany and would not benefit the Swabians in the least.

The year 1932 was a fateful watershed in the affairs of the UDV and the entire Swabian community. *Volksbewusst* radicalism in Germany, and the concomitant counterpressure of integral Magyar nationalism clashed head-on and placed the UDV into a difficult position. Dedication to German cultural and ethnic values had been hitherto consistent with both the aims and purposes of Bleyer's and St. Stephen's concepts of the Hungarian polyethnic idea. Both had left a great deal of room for manoeuvre and compromise. But soon, every Hungarian citizen of Swabian descent would have to make an agonizing choice between two extremes. It was a matter either of submitting to a Magyar-dominated Hungary, in which Swabians would play a subordinate role; or of championing a separatist Swabian irredenta dedicated to the principle of parity, or even dominance. Bleyer, who could no longer tolerate what he considered to be actions by Hungary bordering on cultural genocide, decided that in his hierarchy of values Germanism would have to transcend Magyarism in importance, and hence he could no longer support the government. On the basis of the same evidence, Gratz concluded that on the contrary, a person's first loyalty was to his nation. Gratz was to lament six years later—quite erroneously—that Károlyi's insensitivity had engendered the crisis of deep hopelessness in Bleyer and most Swabians, a sentiment that finally grew into a spiritual depression. In his view, the subsequent splintering of the UDV was simply the natural outgrowth of these conditions.[17]

Bleyer's disillusionment was neither a sudden nor passing fancy. It manifested itself with increasing intensity after 1931 and prompted a radicalization of the moderate Swabian viewpoint. The UDV was hemmed in on all sides at the time, partly through local interference, and partly through the central government's non-concern. The organization was so overrun by government appointees that it could no longer rightfully claim to be the voice of the Swabian minority. As the UDV continued to impose itself on a resentful Magyar public, Bleyer unobtrusively shifted the focus of effective Swabian leadership. Since 31 August 1931, the editorial board of the Sonntagsblatt, led by Bleyer, had been functioning as an informal, amorphous forum, the Deutsche Arbeitsgemeinschaft um das Sonntagsblatt (DA), which extended beyond the purview of the weekly paper. Besides Bleyer, the most important members were Faulstich, Fellner, Schnitzer, Leber, Hufnagel, Faul-Farkas, Jekel, König, Teutsch, Basch, and Kussbach. Gratz was conspicuously missing. At a secret two-day session on 20 and 21 August, Bleyer disclosed the gist of his conversation with Károlyi on 18 August. Bleyer claimed to have informed the Prime Minister that the Swabians' present situation was totally untenable, especially in the minority schools, and complained that the UDV could not elect its leaders or operate freely. Bleyer had also notified—and misled—Károlyi about Gratz's resignation as President of the UDV, because he no longer believed that the new regime seriously intended to solve the Swabian minority problem.

Bleyer was exasperated, and suggested to his colleagues that all their approaches to the government thus far had been in vain. The time had come, therefore, to change strategy. No longer should Swabians support the government's unity party automatically. They should promote only groups and individuals whose programme unambiguously considered Swabian interests in a favourable light. "Our final goal," declared Bleyer, "is to create our own party." Once they had such a party, all Swabians would have to declare themselves in favour of it, or else be excluded from German Volkstum. At this meeting, an elaborate leadership system was evolved. As before, the UDV would publicly eschew political or economic activities, and limit its scope to cultural affairs. But under Bleyer's clandestine leadership, the *DA* would henceforth assume effective direction of Swabian affairs, especially in the political and economic realm. Franz Rothen and Franz Kussbach, Bleyer's son-in-law, spoke about the *modus operandi* of the *DA* as a political action group. It would endeavour to plant one *volksbewusst* leader in every Swabian community. There would be a search for reliable Swabians to fill these posts, and the *DA* would educate them in their duties. By means of informal political discussions, the various Swabian communities would be brought into contact with *völkisch* ideals. This primitive cell system would slowly, gradually evolve into sophisticated leadership cadres, comprising the entire Swabian intelligentsia. This would take a long time, however, thanks to the current dearth of a Swabian intelligentsia.[18]

From the day of its founding until the end of 1932, the plight of the *UDV* remained nearly constant. Neither Bethlen nor Károlyi really took the Swabians seriously. Bethlen might have exercised greater skill in avoiding Swabian wrath than the blunt Károlyi, upon whose hapless shoulders the disappointed Swabians heaped all their indignation. To the detriment of Hungary's interests, both men miscalculated the extent of the Swabians' devotion to *völkisch* principles and their simultaneous devotion to the *natio Hungarica*. Among the Swabians, elements of medieval and modern loyalties were strangely blended. The Magyars, who were gripped by an intense nationalistic reaction, neither would, nor could, comprehend their German minority's thinking. After 1932, it was too late; the Swabians, emulating their brethren in Germany, began to tread the radical ideological path with the same intensity as they and the Magyars.

School Problems

In Hungary, the prospects of closer relations with Germany created much controversy. Most Magyars, despite their anti-German sentiments, realized that Germany was the only powerful nation able to support Hungary's revisionist claims in the League of Nations. It also appeared that if commercial negotiations could be driven into favourable channels, Germany might some day become a more reliable export market and relieve Hungary's economic dependence on the Successor States. Yet in spite of these advantages, both the public and the government had serious reservations about committing Hungary entirely to a course which might lead to German domination. They feared that a strong and militant Germany might some day overwhelm Hungary culturally and economically—perhaps even militarily.[19]

Bethlen's public pledges to assist the Swabians' cultural and educational efforts had even greater repercussions than his foreign policy that heralded closer German-Hungarian economic and political collaboration. Most Magyars believed the government's pro-Swabian declarations portended a change in official policy. They were unaware that the government shared their fears and had no intentions of ignoring its traditional policy, which was opposed to the nurturing of any non-Magyar ethnic ethos in Hungary. As a result of the government's need to preserve the secrecy of its real intentions, the public failed to grasp that the regime shared its apprehension of the alleged German peril. In fact, both feared that the Swabians' latent Pan-Germanism might manifest itself in action and assist Germany in the achievement of its ambitions in the Danubian region, including Hungary. It was impossible, however, for the government to ignore completely the needs of the Swabians and to risk offending Germany during the prolonged trade negotiations. In attempting to steer between its exaggerated pledges to the Swabians and resentful domestic public opinion, the Bethlen regime adopted a policy of opportunism in both foreign and domestic affairs.[20] All subsequent government action with respect to the Swabian problem must be viewed within this context.

Due to Bethlen's promises and strategic delays, the government came under mounting pressure from the minority press, Swabian leaders, and the Parliament. Surveying the achievements of the 1925-1926 school year, *Sonntagsblatt* concluded they were meagre: the government had yet to solve the school problem; the vulnerable parents' conferences still existed; and most C schools taught German only from the third grade on. During the same year, a typical grievance came to light, involving the government's half-hearted and ineffectual intervention in a school dispute. In Kőszeg, where three-eighths of the population of about 8,500 were Swabians, Klebelsberg personally instructed the diocese to introduce limited (probably B) German instruction. *Vasvármegye,* a provincial newspaper, campaigned to overturn the government's decision. The local clergy, encouraged by their bishop, joined the chorus of dissent, whereupon the school board refused to put Klebelsberg's order into effect. Without the benefit of further investigation, and without consulting the wishes of the parents' conference, Klebelsberg capitulated to the clergy. One of the strongest condemnations of Hungary's German school establishment came from a Swabian writing under the auspices of the *VDA.* Franz Anton Basch denounced the system as a non-functioning paper plan:

> With what incredible skill and systematic tenacity the provincial functionaries evade the successful execution of the government's rather tame regulations is proven by the fact that as of 1926 we have no German schools.[21]

Basch conceded that Burgenland boasted a few German village schools, but these had not evolved out of the recently developed Swabian cultural struggle, they were there thanks to the proximity of Austria.

By mid-1927 the tantalized Swabians' patience was wearing thin. *Sonntagsblatt,* reporting from the fourth General Assembly of the *UDV,* declared:

> Every time a speaker mentioned 'school' or 'instruction in the mother tongue,' many hundreds stirred, as if touched by electric currents, and with frenetic interruptions gave vent to their wishes and expectations. . . .Clear proof that our people consider the school question to be the most essential question. . . .[22]

In his opening speech, Gratz had insisted with equal vigour that the school issue indeed transcended all others in importance.

In May, the minority school issue received a major airing in Parliament. In the course of comprehensive debates on minority problems, Malasits denounced the government for failing to alleviate a wide range of Swabian grievances, including the need for genuine reform in the school system. Malasits claimed that due to poor pedagogical methods, illiteracy had increased among the Swabians by an average of 20% since 1910. It was especially on the rise in the Budapest region, for even in the capital itself, local officials flouted the school laws. In support of his allegations he cited the folllowing illiteracy rates in the vicinity of Budapest:

Locality	% of Illiterates in 1910	% of Illiterates in 1920
Szár	7.6	9.6
Zebegény	14.0	16.3
Parbál	14.5	18.0
Vörösvár	9.3	11.0
Pesthidegkút	29.0	41.0
Békásmegyer	unknown	8% increase since 1910

Malasits continued with the accusation that because of the neglect in the minority schools, Swabian pupils learned neither their own language nor Magyar properly. Malasits next condemned the government's failure to establish minority schools in which students enjoyed instruction in their own mother tongue. He also wished to see an end to the current system of ineffectual parents' conferences being dominated by aggressive school boards, in favour of a compulsory system of minority education based on the 1920 census.

Malasits' skillful speech drove Bethlen on the defensive. The Prime Minister maintained his government against Malasits' charge that Hungary lacked even one *bona fide* German minority school. Admittedly, progress had been slow, yet communities with the requisite population of at least 40 Swabian school age children had 48 A schools, 63 had B schools, and 252 possessed C facilities. Bethlen also conceded that further progress encountered great obstacles that could be overcome only gradually. Moreover, most schools were confessional institutions, and hence the government was unable to exert legal pressure on autonomous ecclesiastic authorities. Certain delays in this area would be unavoidable. Another problem was the one-teacher, one-room elementary school, a predominant feature in Swabian regions. In these localities, instructors were seldom sufficiently proficient to teach both Magyar and German effectively. He hoped that the government's current programme of establishing special German courses in teachers' academies, designed specifically for minority school teachers, would eventually rectify this problem, as all others. As a matter of principle, Bethlen rejected the suggestion that minority education become compulsory. At the same time he pledged to see to it that his orders were taken seriously and carried out word for word.[23]

The following week, Bleyer joined the debate. He conceded Bethlen's good intentions but nonetheless sharply condemned both the spirit and the substance of the minority school laws. Decisions concerning school types should not be entrusted to the vagaries of impressionable school boards and parents' conferences. This system set extremists at each others' throats and poisoned the atmosphere. School types should be selected on the basis of recent official census figures, and the central government should bear the responsibility for their maintenance. A schools were too predominantly German, Bleyer thought, and hence evoked Magyar hostility. On the other hand, C schools were so emasculated that they were not minority schools at all and thus misled the public. Only the B schools were properly balanced but pedagogically unsound. Children, who generally knew only German, received their initial instruction in Magyar only and consequently became disoriented and discouraged. For the best results, first graders ought to be taught exclusively in their native tongue, and Magyar should be introduced gradually thereafter. The Minister of Education, in whom he had great confidence, should exert his authority effectively on behalf of the existing school laws, such as they were. Bleyer's speech was assailed, his pedagogical theses refuted as patriotically unsound, especially by Miklós Weicher, during subsequent debates about two weeks later.[24]

As the result of the publicity given to the debates, and while the Swabian leaders were optimistic after the limited *UDV* gains in the spring, the government summoned them to a meeting with the Minister of Education to discuss the minority school problem. An understanding reached on 17 June 1927 was described by Jakob Bleyer as a step forward in the quest for reestablishing the educational grounds lost in the last two generations. According to the agreement, most elementary schools in which German was taught merely as a subject would be converted into mixed-language Magyar-German institutions within the next four to five years. This seemed to be a vague promise to transform some of the C schools into B institutions. If carried out, it would at least have compensated for some of the losses suffered after 1923-1924, when German minority education had reached its low ebb. However, the time table for carrying out the provision was too vague, and in the end very little was done in fact. The government also decided to maintain the pure German schools in their present diminished numbers. This merely preserved the status quo of the A schools located mainly in Burgenland, whose original number, most Swabians hoped, would be restored some day. In the 400-odd mixed village communities where the number of Swabian school children was below forty, and where German was taught only as a subject, the administration planned to establish parallel Magyar-German classes on a trial basis. If the experiment proved practical, it was to be retained permanently. This promise was hazy and the government could easily ignore the entire project on any flimsy pretext.

Additionally, in mixed-language Swabian schools, where currently all subjects were introduced in Magyar and repeated in German the following year, the Ministry decided to reverse the procedure by initiating subjects in German and repeating them in Magyar. This appeared to be not only a minor concession but a questionable one pedagogically; yet it pleased Bleyer, who had suggested it. Finally, in response of charges of pressures on parents' conferences, the government resolved to relieve them of some of their responsibilities. In case of disagreements between parents and local school boards the 1920 census and other statistical indicators would be consulted. This provision was not only vague, it also provided hostile local administrators with ample legal pretexts to overrule intransigent parents' conferences, or to interpret statistical information to their own liking. The entire agreement portended a decline, instead of an improvement, in Swabian school affairs.[25]

The school agreement and the parliamentary debates that preceded it evoked a mixed reception in the German-speaking world. The *VDA* was unimpressed with the results. It treated Bethlen's claim that the Swabians had 363 German schools with skepticism. His statement contradicted every known fact concerning the Swabian minority school system. Even so, accurate information was admittedly difficult to come by, since even Bleyer had to choose his words carefully for tactical reasons. It was considered an ominous sign that Klebelsberg, who had paid a great deal of attention to Bleyer's parliamentary speech, and who had analyzed many aspects of it, completely ignored that portion which dealt with minority education.[26]

When the terms of the school agreement were released to the public, Bleyer ventured that the Swabians ought to be content. At least, their children would henceforth learn the most essential elements of German speech. Admittedly, the agreement was a compromise solution, an attempt to terminate the squabble between pro and anti-minority factions. Bleyer urged his followers to have full confidence in the Hungarian government. Gundisch was more skeptical. The agreement represented a modest gain, a mere compromise that would have been far more effective had the government granted the UDV supervisory powers within the broader framework of cultural autonomy. Unfortunately, it was difficult to resolve the Swabians' difficulties and grievances because it was not merely a matter of defending old, neglected positions but of regaining old positions already lost.[27]

At the fourth UDV General Assembly, Gratz spoke far more optimistically about the agreement than either Bleyer or Gündisch. He characterized the compact as substantial progress. The government now believed it would be desirable if children in German-speaking areas were to acquire all the necessary skills to speak and write German fluently. Gratz rhapsodized about the government's projected German teacher training programme, and spoke approvingly about "a whole number of German communities, in which school types would be changed, in agreement with parents' groups. As a result, German instruction in many communities with German populations would be considerably expanded."[28]

Gratz was not alone in praising the agreement. A Budapest correspondent of Der Auslandsdeutsche, undoubtedly a Swabian who preferred to remain anonymous, wrote that the agreement was important because it gave the Swabians certain definite advantages. No longer would the government introduce C schools into purely German-speaking communities. Nor would the establishment of B schools depend on the vagaries of parents' conferences, and thus indirectly hinge on the tender mercies of local authorities; within five years maximum, B institutions would become mandatory in all German communities. Nonetheless, in Hungary achievements of this sort could not be measured by written agreements, only by actual implementation. This would mean overcoming many technical and psychological obstacles.[29]

The editors of the same publication were considerably less impressed with the agreement than their correspondent. The pact was a clear admission by the regime that the present situation, especially respecting the school types, was intolerable. But why had the negotiations been shrouded in so much secrecy? What guarantees did these concessions embody? Why was the Magyar public kept in total ignorance about the agreement? How come that Bleyer alone was permitted to announce it in his own newspaper, a report so brief and stilted that it read like a *Diktat*? Obviously, the agreement was transitory, since its authors feared the displeasure of the only group that might conceivably assure the success of the Swabian minority school system—the rural administrators.[30] Stresemann's newspaper, the *Tägliche Rundschau,* shared the concern of some of the Swabian and German observers. Although it hailed the government's decision to transform C schools into B institutions, grave doubts were expressed whether the law would ever be introduced, let alone be observed. The widespread resistance of the Swabian (Magyarone) intelligentsia to any manner of German cultural accommodation foredoomed it.[31]

Amid all these speculations, the government's pseudo-liberality continued. In September 1927, the Ministry of Education released an authoritative hourly study plan for partially and fully divided German minority schools. This was a good omen, because in the past, most school regulations had ignored partially divided schools; yet these constituted a respectable share of the Swabian school system. Gündisch rejoiced because the new regulation exceeded the promises embodied at the June conference. Henceforth, teachers in mixed-language schools would have to satisfy the school inspector that pupils were equally proficient in both Magyar and German, even if a particular subject was taught only in the Magyar language. Minority school teachers were also ordered to use the pupils' mother tongue generously during school activities designated as quiet studies, such as drawing and handicrafts. Gündisch considered this a very significant gain because Swabians stressed the importance of such activities. Gündisch eagerly awaited the official roster containing the list of C schools that had been transformed into B institutions. The government had promised to produce such a list. Rumour had it that there were to be 45 such conversions that year.[32] Since the new ordinance appeared to be compulsory, the Swabians had every reason to believe that the long period of darkness had finally yielded to the light of reason. In fact, the motivations behind the new attitude had to be sought in Hungary's commercial policy with Germany rather than in an upsurge of enlightened interest in Swabian affairs.

All but the most astute observers believed that Swabian-Magyar relations progressed satisfactorily toward total rapprochement. Huber was one of the few who disagreed vehemently. In a vitriolic article, he rent the precarious peace. The Swabians' school demands languished unfulfilled still; they really had no German schools; promises, made year in, year out, were ignored; regulations came and went, but nobody paid the least attention to them; the solemn promises of the previous year to transform C schools into B institutions were a sham; in fact, the trend was headed in the opposite direction: in many B schools German instruction had been reduced to only two hours each week. Huber expostulated:

> We can keep silent about this no longer; no longer do we ask or beg, we demand; we demand in the name of justice; we demand performance and fulfillment. Divine and human right are on our side; this must penetrate....[33]

Huber's outburst was precipitated by a bitter polemic in Parliament involving Bleyer and a Jewish deputy. In the course of the exchange, the Swabians were repeatedly insulted and called Pan-Germans. Nonetheless, this was the only nettle in Magyar-Swabian relations for the moment. The offending newspaper copy was confiscated, and Huber found himself at the centre of a penal process by the public prosecutor on charges of insult to the nation. Formerly, an incident such as this would have rallied Bleyer to his friend's side. Now all was silence. Bleyer believed the Swabians neared a total detente with the Magyars and he refused to endanger it by championing Huber. Bleyer declared in Parliament that, although the Swabians still had certain improvements in mind—school matters, use of the mother tongue, cultural organization, and the status of the Swabian intelligentsia—the laws were good. In fact, in some respects they were too good, as with the A schools, which taught too much German. In some respects the laws were not too good, as with the C schools, which were pedagogically absurd. Bleyer hoped that the Magyar public and officialdom would learn to trust the Swabians, and all would be well.[34]

Three weeks later, Bethlen continued the honeymoon in Parliament. First, he defended Bleyer against parliamentary and press attacks arising from his disastrous February debate. Next, Bethlen turned his attention to the school problem. In a cleverly constructed speech, he made the most of recently achieved modest improvements in the minority schools and forestalled future criticism by warning the Swabians of troubles ahead. Bethlen told Bleyer to be patient, since the government had "great technical difficulties" to overcome in the schools, and these defied solution from one day to the next. "Technical difficulties" was a euphemism for the solid wall of opposition gathering throughout Hungary against Bethlen's modest minority policy. The Prime Minister stressed that some 3,000 of Hungary's

6,300 elementary schools were undivided one-room institutions, in which it was exceedingly difficult to organize units effectively for both Magyar and german instruction. Bethlen also claimed significant gains. The Swabians now had 35 additional B schools and 14 fewer C institutions; although these schools admittedly had a difficult time because frequently local authorities failed to cooperate with the government. In confessional schools the government could not intervene and church authorities often ignored even suggestions. Bethlen believed that this, as well as all the other problems, could be solved through diplomacy, not force. Bethlen expressed some annoyance with Bleyer. Whether Bleyer liked them or not, the government had to maintain C institutions because in many communities Germans were only a scattered minority and required a good expertise in the Magyar language. Moreover, C schools were specifically designed for Swabian children who already knew Magyar and had most likely spent up to three years in Magyar kindergartens. Bethlen urged Bleyer to abandon some of his experimental demands and work hand-in-hand with the government to solve educational problems within the framework of existing minority school laws.[35]

Bethlen's speech betrayed how important the Swabian issue was at the time. In the League of Nations, Hungary desperately needed German support in the Transylvanian Optants' case; in the Successor States, a good word from Berlin might induce the German minorities to join their Magyar fellow-sufferers in a revisionist crusade. Most importantly, Hungary hoped for an early resumption of the languishing trade talks with Germany. Recognizing that for once they held most of the trump cards, the Swabians failed to be fully ignited by Bethlen's tired rhetoric. In *Sonntagsblatt*, Anton König merely acknowledged Bethlen's pledges as satisfactory, and promised that in turn the Swabians would be patient, but nonetheless would continue to clamour for a quicker tempo in the schools, as in the past.[36]

Hungary's English-style parliamentary system, in which some of the minority drama was enacted, barely concealed the eastern despotism that lay just beneath the surface. It was risky business in Hungary to criticize the government, as Alfred von Schwartz and, more recently, Huber had discovered to their discomfort. Domestically, the Swabians lacked a safe or effective way to express their views, though officially they functioned through the government's unity party. Numerous unresolved issues cried out for solution by 1928. Only the school problem had even a semblance of heading toward a satisfactory solution. The *UDV*'s situation rankled, while the teacher and textbook shortage undermined the efficacy of any planned school reforms. Under the circumstances, it is difficult to discern how the Swabians really felt about Bethlen on the basis of their domestic press. The

German press, with its reports provided by anonymous Swabian correspondents, provided a clearer picture.

In this clandestine press, a writer characterized Bethlen as a controversial, Machiavellian figure, his seven-year tenure not without accomplishments. Having promised to fulfill the needs of the Swabian community,
Bethlen had kept his promise, but only to a degree. The *UDV* had reached a
certain stature, and the minority schools showed certain gains. At this point,
the writer believed, Bethlen stopped. Forgetting statesmanship and justice,
he had allowed the Magyar anti-Swabian middle classes to influence him, to
the detriment of the Swabians at home and Magyar interests abroad. Thanks
to their intervention, Bethlen now refused to exceed the first few halting
steps on the road to Swabian reform. After surveying the lamentable state of
swabian education and decrying the hopelessness of ever achieving the
blessings of cultural autonomy for his people, the writer asserted that
although Bethlen's intentions were good, the Swabians considered his
tempo as "too dragging" and could no longer accept his friendly intentions
completely at their face value.[37]

Even if the criticisms were somewhat muted, Bethlen could not ignore
the danger signals that all was not well in Swabian affairs. Throughout late
spring and early summer in 1928, he and the Minister of Education held
marathon talks with *UDV* leaders. In the end, the Swabians succeeded in
achieving a most comprehensive paper victory. The omnibus agreement
sought to solve the entire constellation of Swabian cultural problems, from
teacher education to the use of German in official intercourse, a step-by-
step organic solution, to be unaffected by economic conditions or chance,
the way Bleyer put it. In education, the most important provision was the
one which empowered the *UDV* to establish an advisory board on school
problems. It would maintain close liaison with the Ministry of Education
and act as an institutionalized channel for transmitting suggestions and
grievances. The Ministry promised to establish a special German section and
pledged to cooperate with the *UDV* on all matters affecting Swabian
education. C schools would be transformed into B institutions at the rate of
about forty to fifty each year, until C facilities would remain only in mixed,
one-teacher, single-room institutions. An official list soon to be released
would specify school types in each community. Expanded teacher training
programmes and government-subsidized German texts were also announced. Bleyer confidently believed that Bethlen really meant to solve the
Swabians' essential grievances once and for all, cautiously and farsighted-
ly.[38] *Gotthold* greeted the new agreement enthusiastically and hoped that all
the fine words might be translated into deeds. It pointed out, moreover, that
the new regulation on transforming minority schools was not at all new, but

a mere rehashing of last year's promise.[39]

Later that year, Bleyer issued his most optimistic report since becoming Swabian leader. For the first time in a decade, he believed that the Magyars were really serious about their new nationality policy. Bleyer released a wealth of statistical data to support his view that German minority education was well on its way to a solution. Since Bethlen's announcement in April, one A school and 27 additional C institutions were established. Bleyer rejoiced because the government had kept its word and released a community-by-community school type list. But the statistics revealed the patchiness of the Swabian school complex. To begin, A and B schools were not distributed nationwide. Burgenland had nearly all the A institutions, whereas Baranya and Tolna Counties shared most of the B schools. The government's steady plaint that ecclesiastic authorities were mainly at fault for the preponderance of C schools was true only in the sense that nearly all minority schools—whether, A, B or C—were confessional institutions. But the government had only one A and B school each; the rest (42 schools) were C establishments. The statistics thus revealed who was and who was not interested in German education: the Protestants had the largest percentage of both A and B schools (16.9% and 48% resp.), the government the least (2.0% each). This explains Edmond Scholtz's boast that German education, having aroused no interest at all among Swabian Protestants before the War now experienced a great renaissance.[40]

Throughout 1928, the connection between Bethlen's pro-Swabian offensive and the exigencies of his German orientation became more and more manifest. Hungary tried to steer German-Hungarian trade talks into productive channels. If Bethlen improved Swabian school conditions, the gesture was both a bribe and an earnest. For the remainder of that year, German-Hungarian trade relations and Swabian school policy became inextricably linked. As trade talks materialized in the fall, Bethlen made a highly publicized foray into Burgenland. There, he shrewdly appealed both to his listeners' nationalism and their economic interests. In mid-October, Bethlen flattered an all-Swabian audience in their own language in the border village of Wolfs (Balf): "According to Hungarian law, all communities with a non-Magyar population of at least 20% are entitled to transact their official business in their own language. By addressing you in German, however, I am not only obeying the law, I am following my heart's desire." The government had no wish to eradicate the mother tongue of foreign elements in Hungary; it merely required their loyalty and patriotism. It was in the interest of the minorities themselves, however, to be fully conversant in the official language for economic reasons. But elementary schools were obliged to produce students well versed in their native tongue. He would not be content with mere language schools; children had the right to learn every useful skill also in their own native tongue. "This is our cultural policy," intoned Bethlen. "Nobody has the right to doubt us." Whatever problems might arise, they would have to be settled between the government and the lawful Swabian representatives, never by outsiders. "These are golden words," mused *Der Auslandsdeutsche*. "We can only hope that they will be heeded not only throughout Hungary, but in every place inhabited by German minorities."[41]

Indeed, a clever Hungarian publicity campaign to win the Swabians and the Germans was in full swing. Although eminent Magyar spokesmen failed to advocate German minority schools *per se*, their studied pro-German sentiments indirectly implied that and more. In Gyönk, Admiral Horthy delivered a flattering speech in the German language, in which he held forth about German fidelity. Other Magyar public figures followed suit. Apponyi produced a foreign policy speech at the meeting of the Hungarian Foreign Society at Kaposvár. He declared:

> One of the most important aims of Hungarian foreign policy is the minority problem, which includes revisionism. . . .The revival of Germany as a power whose opinions even the victors respect, is an important development for Hungary. It might be true that Germany does not deliberately espouse Hungary's cause, but by coincidence their respective motives happen to be the same.[42]

The gist of Apponyi's speech was that Hungary must solve the Swabian problem in order to serve the higher aims of her external policy. Emil Nagy, Hungary's Minister of Justice, also advocated a policy of tolerance for the Swabians' language demands, while Count Ferenc Hunyadi, an Opposition deputy in Parliament, urged closer German-Hungarian cooperation. The noted Hungarian historian Julius (Gyula) Szekfü admitted that Hungary had erred in her past mistreatment of the Swabians, but that a new era was dawning. In an interview with a German newspaper, Bleyer praised recent developments in Magyar-Swabian relations. The paper had no doubt that German-Hungarian relations would become more and more intimate as the Magyars relaxed their oppressive practices.[43]

It was disconcerting, therefore, when on 16 December, Gündisch's pessimistic report prepared the Swabian public for the imminent collapse of German-Hungarian trade talks. Afraid what this might mean in terms of Hungary's recently relaxed attitude towards the Swabians, Gündisch carefully refrained from blaming Hungary for the impasse. Both sides must fundamentally change their attitudes. Swabians sighed with relief when Bethlen, having met in turn Aristide Briand, Austen Chamberlain, and

Stresemann, evinced no sign of anxiety about the newest strains in German-Hungarian relations. His talks with Stresemann had been the most valuable one among his recent discussions with foreign statesmen, for it had given him the opportunity to convey the friendly feelings of the Magyar people, and to reaffirm the commonality of German-Hungarian aims. He had assured Stresemann that Hungary meant to implement each and every provision of her minority programme, and hoped that this would expedite the difficult trade talks then in progress. In fact, the talks were on the verge of collapse.[44] Several days later, they were indeed suspended indefinitely.

The Swabians had cause for concern, but they need not have worried that the collapse in negotiations might presage a turn for the worse in their recent gains. It would have been contrary to Hungary's long-range interests to retaliate overtly either against Germany, or to take excessive measures against the Swabians. Temporarily, the Swabians escaped the Magyars' wrath, because the latter hoped that negotiations with Germany might soon resume. Throughout 1929, Magyar-Swabian relations remained superficially cordial and the Swabian schools remained undisturbed. Officially, Hungary exuded good will, whereas the Swabians stressed their attachment to Hungary, their gratitude to Bethlen, and their dedication to the rule of reason. Both parties knew that Germany would not resume negotiations if the Swabians suffered further indignities; yet at the same time, Bethlen refused to exceed the improvements embodied in the school agreement of 1928, unless Germany came to an understanding on Hungarian terms. It was an impasse, since the Swabians feared upsetting delicate Magyar-German relations and, for the moment, they showed good political acumen by supporting Hungary's aspirations, even against Germany.

Bleyer even became, to a certain extent, the government's apologist. At a *UDV* meeting, on the heels of discussions with Bethlen and Ministry of Education officials in Budapest, Bleyer declared:

> The German school programme is on its way to a solution, especially since the Bethlen government is pursuing a sympathetic policy. True, the solution is neither complete nor final; the public in Hungary, especially the nationalistic middle class, is very reluctant to relinquish its unyielding position. Besides, most elementary schools in Hungary are under church auspices, and these are able to resist even government policy. Even so, progress with the government itself is slow. Yet it may be said, that unlike in the past, almost all Swabian children are now receiving German religious instruction, and are able to write in their mother tongue.[45]

In Parliament, Bethlen vigorously defended his floundering minority school programme. He promised to carry out the minority laws, and appealed to church officials to do likewise. In effect, this became the battle cry of the government; namely, that it valiantly sought to enforce the minority laws in the face of unreasonable and stubborn local authorities. Bleyer steadfastly reaffirmed his faith in Bethlen, while bitterly condemning secular and church authorities for sabotaging the German school programme. Ferenc Hunyadi also blamed not the government but local authorities which ignored the laws, and against whom Swabians and Reich Germans were indignant. These officials had to be told that Hungary suffered if Swabian children failed to learn the German language. *Pester Lloyd,* which frequently reflected government policy, declared that Hungary must make non-Magyars feel at home. Most Magyar-language newspapers, the right-wing radical press excepted, also applauded Bethlen's pro-minority speech in Parliament.[46]

Gratz chimed in to reassure nervous Magyar nationalists that they had nothing to fear either from the Swabians or their big brother Germany. Instead, he succeeded in thoroughly alarming them. The Swabians had no desire to eliminate the Magyar language, Gratz maintained. In the Swabian schools the entire discussion revolved only around the relative merits of devoting more or less time to the study of German. Those advocating complete Magyarization in the schools should remember that such methods never achieve their desired effects. They might be feasible in the assimilationist milieu of the larger cities, but not in the small village environment where most Swabians resided. Furthermore,

> Hungary cannot effectively pursue a policy for the improvement of the lot of her nationals abroad, if she in principle denies these same rights to her own minorities.[47]

Gratz then turned his attention to Hungarian foreign policy: Hungary should by no means exclude the possibility of using Germany as a means to attain her own ends, since Germany was one of the few large powers uncommitted to the irrevocable nature of the Treaty of Trianon. Hungary must beware, however, of the danger such a partnership generally entailed for a smaller nation. Yet the foreseeable future as regards Germany, he "assured" the Magyars, did not seem to portend such a peril for Hungary.

Gratz's inept "reassurance" intensified the fears of many Magyar super-patriots, who suspected Pan-Germans under every bed, and who wished to have nothing to do with even a perfunctory German school system. These outbursts prompted Gratz to observe more prudent caution. Later that year he warned the *UDV*'s General Assembly to remember to ask when planning their programme whether the activities of the *UDV* benefited Hungary's aims and purposes. Similarly, Bleyer publicly pilloried Pan-Germans for menacing the territorial integrity of Hungary. The *Österreichisch-Deutscher Volksbund* had recently published a controversial map which incorporated all German-speaking areas of Hungary into Greater Germany, and Bleyer was incensed. He bluntly ordered German extremists to keep their hands off Hungary.[48]

German extremists and Magyar chauvinists were not the only ones to spoil the Magyar–Swabian detente. To the embarrassment of the conservative Swabian leadership, the Social Democrats roundly condemned the government's handling of the minority school programme. In Parliament, Malasits charged that in many kindergartens and elementary schools attended by minority children pupils were forbidden to speak German, and in some instances were beaten if they did. As a result, Swabians were gradually sinking into illiteracy. Malasits cited three German-inhabited mining communities as examples.[49] He conceded that Bethlen was not personally responsible for some of the outrages perpetrated by brutal schoolmasters, but condemned him nonetheless for encouraging the growth of an unwholesome variety of Magyar nationalism. It was certainly true that the government did nothing to encourage the proper development of German education. Fewer than one out of twelve German minority schools were A types, and even these were unable to function properly owing to a chronic shortage of German teachers and German texts. In B schools, which comprised only 12.5% of the total number of German institutions, the school inspectors and the school boards failed to live up to their responsibilities. The school boards did not dare to complain, whereas the inspectors did not care to get involved. Consequently, most of these schools were German in name only. A few weeks later, Malasits reiterated his allegations and charged that both the Prime Minister and the Minister of Education failed to exercise sufficient authority to ensure adequate minority education in the face of determined nationalist opposition.[50]

Bethlen's platitudes, and Bleyer's defense of the Prime Minister's school programme, could not hide for long the basic truth of Malasits' allegations. While the government busied itself for the next two years bandying empty promises, in order to induce Germany to negotiate a favourable trade treaty, the Swabian school programme stood still. The Swabians obligingly forebore criticizing the regime for fear of upsetting the delicate Magyar–Swabian detente and Hungarian–German contacts. In the last year of Bethlen's Ministry, the government's subterfuge slowly began to filter through the veil of Swabian optimism. On the eve of Bethlen's resignation, Gratz had announced joyfully, on the basis of the Prime Minister's latest assurances, that the forward march of the Swabian schools would soon be resumed with the greatest energy. Five years earlier, Bethlen had promised to transform between forty and fifty C schools annually into B institutions, a pledge reiterated the following year. Since 1928, when thirty-odd schools were converted, there had been no further change. Now, said Gratz, with Horthy's recent friendly message and Bethlen's latest promises ringing in his ears, we would once again see the slow but steady transformation of our C schools into B institutions. It might take time, but what did a few years matter in the life-cycle of a people?[51]

As the chances of an immediate German-Hungarian trade agreement became more and more remote, in view of the worldwide economic crisis, conditions in the minority schools deteriorated. This change, in turn, was reflected in complaints by pro-Swabian church authorities. Bishop Béla Kapi voiced the concern of Hungary's Protestant Swabians. In addition to the alarming shortage of German teachers and German texts, there was also a dearth of German-speaking clerics. Should the Swabians prove unable to solve these problems, then Bethlen's grandiose plans for transforming C into B institutions would have to fail.

At the heart and core of the matter was the nature and organization of the churches. One out of every five Hungarian Protestants was a Swabian, and together with the Slovaks comprised nearly half (44%) of Hungary's Protestant congregations. Nonetheless, they enjoyed no ethnic autonomy. Paragraph #31 of the Protestant church constitution expressly forbade designating church communities according to language, although each congregation could determine the language of divine service. This partial concession was insufficient to engender a strong movement in the churches in favour of German instruction. The only exceptions were Burgenland and Baranya, where a strong pro-German consciousness assured the presence of most A and B schools to be found in Hungary. But in most other communities, especially in the urban centres, Germans fought hard for their very ethnic existence. Magyarization was seldom brutal, but it was inexorable. The Protestant clergy, with the exception of a few stalwarts, considered the use of the German language unpatriotic; yet few of them forced the Magyar language on their parishioners overtly. Since German was compulsory in Hungary's middle schools, but poorly taught, teaching positions in German elementary schools had to go unfilled; applicants simply could not speak German properly.

Occasionally, however, even the Protestant church organizations resorted to strong measures against minority education. At an Evangelical district convention, the secular inspector D. Stranyavszky ordered church authorities to transform all A schools into B institutions. At the Montan District

Convention, Bishop Raffay delivered a vicious attack on the *Sonntagsblatt* and *Gotthold* for championing the right of Germans in Csepel and Hárta. At the Evangelical Convention of the Trans-Danubian region, a resolution of censure was passed against the existence of A schools in the diocese.

Government control of the minority church organization proved to be an indirect although most effective method for converting minority schools into Magyar institutions. The government sought to eliminate non-Magyar influence of all kinds from amongst their clergy quietly, hoping that such a policy would once and for all remove the danger that Swabian clergymen might some day exercise their prerogative in choosing German schools for their parishioners. The administration firmly believed that once Magyarized, the churches would automatically transform their minority schools into Magyar institutions. According to one observer, an insidious danger was the tendency of Magyars to infiltrate the German churches instead of founding their own, and eventually to appropriate them. The obliging government transferred the autonomous rights of the German churches unto the new groups, including that of school language, and even flouted or changed existing laws to expedite the transaction. These encroachments were also reported by Theodor Grentrup, a German Catholic writer, who expressed his amazement at the rationalizations by which some Hungarian authorities opposed the crystal-clear meaning of the laws. The minority clergy had for all intents and purposes become so Magyarized that it strove only for the joint evangelical awakening of both Magyars and Swabians rather than for the cultural aspirations of the latter. All of this was the result of the assimilatory educational system in Hungary, Grentrup concluded.[52]

As the depression deepened and the chances of a German-Hungarian commercial treaty that would favour the Magyars receded, the Swabians' treatment deteriorated from neglect to abuse. Liberated from the relative restraints of the Bethlen era, Magyar officials began to persecute the Swabians more overtly. The once occasional insults became universal outrages. The list was long. In the minority institutions controlled by the Roman Catholic Church and the State, only 80-90 communities had ever overcome official hostility sufficiently to convene parents' conferences. Those who met, were frequently forced into accepting C schools or Magyar institutions on pain of threats and adverse press publicity. Contemplating the disaster of the German school system of the past decade, a German publication complained that Hungary's minority policy was a total shambles: "We stand exactly where we stood five, ten years ago." Atrocities were commonplace. In the supposedly German school in Dunabogdány a sign read: "Only Magyar is permitted on the premises." In Hárta, school children were punished for speaking German during recess, while their parents were told they would be considered enemies should they vote for German schools. In Högyész, German conversation was considered a punishable offense. In Bácsalmás, Swabian parents were threatened with tax action unless they abandoned their B schools. Even the official gazette published by the Ministry of Education declaimed against the *UDV*. The situation might never improve. For all their good will, Horthy's, and the now departed Bethlen's promises remained only words: the school authorities ignored them.[53] Gratz, writing in 1934, generally shared this view. Bethlen had loyally wished to introduce the Swabian school programme but was thwarted by chauvinistic officials. Bethlen explained that he had always honoured the minority statutes, but "certain circles did everything in their power to prevent the success of German instruction in the minority schools."[54]

There is much evidence to support the assertion that Hungary's minority school programme during the Bethlen years was a sham. Throughout, the government resorted to statistical manipulation to show gains where few or none were made. Minority schools were located chiefly in villages, where pupils were sparse. In the early postwar years many such institutions were established, serving few and enabling the government to emphasize the number of schools provided for the Swabians. In 1922-1923, for example, sixteen German-Magyar mixed schools provided instruction for some 5,300 pupils. The following year the number of schools rose to forty-six, but the student body diminished to 4,458. A few years later, when Germany emerged as a factor in Swabian relations, the method of deception became more sophisticated. Literally true to its promise, the Ministry of Education increased the number of B schools from 63 in 1927-1928 to 98 the following year, and during the same period the number of C institutions increased from 308 to 316. In listing the number of pupils in attendance, however, the government combined B and C registration figures in order to make it more difficult to assess the real gains. But even if the entire increase was in fact confined to B institutions, the improvement was meager, since the number of attending pupils increased from 46,088 to only 53,602 in this period.[55]

When observers realized after a time that it might be more meaningful to consider the number of pupils receiving instruction in Hungary's three types of minority institutions, the government changed its techniques by increasing the number of Swabian pupils, but mainly in C schools. Consequently, the number of pupils in both B and C schools rose from 43,419 in 1926-1927, to 60,861 in 1930-1931, but the number of schools diminished from 397 to 386. Sudden increases in the number of pupils in these institutions revealed another deception. In 1926-1927, the student body reached 43,419, representing an excess of 2,594 over the total number of pupils with German mother tongue. If the number of pupils in other types of minority schools are also added, it becomes apparent that at least 9,000 pupils in the so-called German minority schools were not Germans at all. By 1930-1931, this excess figure had risen to over 13,000. Thus, the government could demonstrate spectacular but illusory school attendance figures and annual increases among German pupils to casual observers who were unaware that the Swabian C schools were minority in name only and were also attended by many non-Germans, notably members of other minorities.

The practice of creating C institutions for Swabian children, which were attended by other minority students, resulted in overcrowding, while relieving the congestion in Magyar schools. The pupil-teacher ratio which had been set officially at 40:1 at the elementary level shortly after the war, deteriorated drastically, while in Magyar institutions the decline was less severe even during the Depression. Until 1927, German minority schools generally matched their Magyar counterparts, for the pupil-teacher ratio in both varied only between 41:1 and 43:1. After that, poor financial conditions caused a deterioration in all school facilities. Yet Magyar institutions maintained a more equitable pupil-teacher ratio, partly because the number of Magyar teachers annually increased.[56]

According to the 1923 school law, decisions concerning school types in each community were relegated to parents' conferences and local school boards. Many communities were denied the benefits of the law by the influence of local officials. Under these circumstances, the people had very little influence, and even if a few Swabian sympathizers managed to become elected to school boards, they could not assert their views, because either the local priest or the recording notary suppressed them. Local administrators indubitably enjoyed tacit government support in the undermining of parental rights. This became evident during a 1927 local election in Csepelen. The government's stratagem to eliminate parents' groups opposed to Magyarization attempts and to strengthen collaborationist elements among the Swabians was described by Malasits in his speech in Parliament. An unobtrusive typewritten election notice was posted much too late to bring it to the attention of the public in general. In consequence, of the approximately 5,000 voters in the village, only about 700, mainly government supporters, elected the council and school board. Social Democratic Deputy Peyer commented: "It seems as though the administrative authorities do everything in their power to cancel the laws through technicalities, which prompts us to believe that the government does not seriously wish to implement them.[57]

All the evidence indicates that the educational promises—modest as they were—had been designed to deceive the Swabians and hoodwink Germany.

Bethlen was never really interested in fulfilling his promises. Bleyer gradually realized this, yet he hesitated to exert pressure. Until near the end he continued to hope against hope that the Magyars would gradually ease restrictions if the Swabians but remained patient and did not unduly push their demands. He was aware of sensitive Magyar public opinion and feared a strong reaction in the face of excessive Swabian aggressiveness. He realized that the Swabians' position in Hungary was unique. Whenever they showed indications of activity, they were opposed by all Magyar parties. Justified or not, their demands always resulted in conditions contrary to their interests. For this reason, the Swabian movement hitherto had never been aggressive or over-demanding. On the contrary, the Swabians strove constantly to demonstrate to the Magyars that their own devotion to Hungary left nothing to be desired. The situation led to an impasse: the government continued to maintain that a liberal minority policy was desirable, but in fact it failed to put the promised reforms in operation, while Swabians refrained from pushing an unpopular issue to the point of public indignation.[58] This viewpoint was exemplified by Gündisch:

> In Hungary there exists a peculiar situation for Germans unlike anywhere else, because the German aspirations represent not new demands, but the reinstatement of old ones lost decades ago. This makes the quest much more difficult. But the Germans of Hungary consider the Magyars natural allies, and are reluctant to use extreme means in their fight, unless driven to it.[59]

For a time, Bethlen was able to benefit by his various school agreements with the Swabians. But while the government's lacklustre performance pacified the moderates such as Bleyer and Gratz, it caused an irrevocable rift between them and the more militant members of the *UDV*. The Bethlen regime exploited the reduced strain caused by Bleyer's good will and moderating influence to improve its sluggish commercial relations with Germany. For the first time, in 1928, Germany allowed the rate of Hungarian imports to exceed the rate of German exports to Hungary, and this trend continued right into 1929. Although the balance of payment was still in Germany's favour, this dramatic change contributed greatly to the eradication of Hungary's great trade deficit of 1928, and rescued her economy from impending disaster. Trade relations with Germany appeared to be improving, while the era of good feelings between government and Swabians continued for most of the remainder of the 1920's. This was not surprising. the vagaries of political, economic, and cultural necessity had accidentally made strange bedfellows of Hungary's government and its Swabian citizens. For a time, both parties had desired exactly the same thing—German help—although for different reasons and different purposes.

The Swabian school problem was compounded by many closely related difficulties. Along with the three school types, the government created a cumbersome administration, and cited the ensuing difficulties as plausible pretexts for ignoring the provisions of the minority school laws. One of these obstructions arose out of the controversy concerning the use of German textbooks. By 1927, Bethlen had to concede that local officials were unable to enforce the school laws because the lack of German texts made it impossible for them to initiate German instruction in the various types of schools. He admitted that technical difficulties had caused a two-year delay in having Magyar textbooks translated into German. Bethlen tried to convey the impression that the government's zeal in favour of minority education was boundless, and promised to have the German texts prepared soon. But even two years later they remained unpublished.[60]

In the interim, the government engaged in clever delaying tactics. In January 1928, *Gotthold* revealed that two Swabian teachers had prepared suitable German texts for all elementary grades, and had been trying for about a year to secure the services of a publisher. Even with the aid of several influential persons they had not succeeded because allegedly the venture was not financially feasible. Thereupon Bishop Béla Kapi had promised to call the government's attention to the texts. His good offices seemed to indicate a happy resolution to the textbook issue after all. It was hoped that the texts would be available in time for the next school year.[61] Bethlen's claim of technical difficulties appeared to have nothing to do with availability of suitable manuscripts, and his pursuit of material rang hollow.

Bleyer's comprehensive discussions with Bethlen on 17 June 1928 included the school book question. Bethlen reiterated an old pledge, that outmoded texts would be withdrawn by the 1928-1929 school year, and replaced by 12-13 suitable books, to be mostly in the pupils' mother tongue. The Magyars were compelled to make a gesture, because Austria had just provided Burgenland's tiny Magyar minority with an "excellent" Magyar primer, a book designed to acquaint children with the great Magyar authors. This was a moral challenge the Hungarian government could not entirely ignore.[62] It must be granted, however, that the minuscule Magyar minority in Austria was harmless, whereas the Magyars had perhaps reason to fear that a strengthened *völkisch* German minority might eventually endanger Hungary's security.

That Bethlen's promise was empty propaganda became clear in the fall. The texts did not appear in time for the 1928-1929 school season. At the start of 1929, impatient Germans and Swabians protested. Never mind thirteen texts, wrote *Der Auslandsdeutsche*. Nobody had pledged that even one book was being published. How could teachers instruct Swabian pupils effectively under these conditions? The contents of the projected texts were also questioned. Would they be edited by Swabian educators before being released? In addition to Magyar authors in translation, would they contain German and Swabian works? Experience had taught that Magyar inspectors frequently substituted their own faulty German compositions and poor translations of Magyar authors.

Early in 1929, *Nation und Staat* revealed a new delay, but according to Bethlen, it would be solved during the current (1929-1930) school year. He promised to intercede in the Ministry of Education on its behalf. This particular difficulty was caused by the Ministry, which sensibly desired to use only one book for all institutions, regardless of school type or denomination. But most Swabian schools were Roman Catholic preserves, thus creating a need for compromise. On 5 March 1929, a Standing Committee named by the Ministry to settle the dilemma reached an agreement on the question of manifold texts in the various confessional schools. To avoid fragmentation to the point of uselessness, similar books would be employed in all A and B schools, and different ones in C institutions. Even then, the issue was not entirely resolved, for the highest church authorities of both major denominations had to approve the agreement.[63]

Several months later, the Ministry of Education prepared elaborate plans for the long-heralded publications. Before being published, the texts would have to satisfy both the minority and the State. A Standing Committee composed of twelve would act as publisher and agent. As a concession, Bleyer and two other Swabians sat on the Committee, the rest were Ministry officials and Magyar academics.[64] Two texts, an ABC-book for grade 1 and a reader for grade 2, appeared in time for part of the 1929-1930 school year. The delay was caused by Roman Catholic ecclesiastical insistence on separate editions. As a result, the Ministry was confronted suddenly with a last-minute proliferation of different editions, separate ones for Protestant, Catholic, and State schools, as well as for A and B, and C institutions respectively. Nonetheless, *Sonntagsblatt* rejoiced, because the new books were attractive. the frontispieces showed German translations of the Hungarian national anthem and credo, while inside were scenes from various German fairy tales. Swabian children would be exposed to both Hungarian and German symbols, exulted Bleyer. The narratives were also excellent, being a felicitous amalgam of famous Magyar authors and German literati.[65]

Although a far cry from the originally promised thirteen texts, the two books apparently satisfied the Swabians, for whom every minute scrap was an unexpected blessing. Germans beyond Hungary's borders conceded that the books were valuable teaching aids and conformed to pedagogic and esthetic requirements; but they thought a great deal more might have been accomplished to satisfy the needs of the Swabian community. They criticized elements of Magyar chauvinism, such as listing geographic names only in the Magyar language. Already before the war, Tisza had disdained such nationalistic ploys. In any event, Swabians were emotionally attached to their ancestral communities, their German names included. Further, the Catholic editions had omitted two Swabian folk poems. One was a paean extolling Swabian life, the other German. This was an indication that the Catholic clergy still obstructed the proliferation of German sentiments among the Swabians.[66]

The creaking tempo of the school-text programme gathered a little momentum only when Bethlen began to make preparations for his November 1930 Berlin trip. He could not face his German hosts empty-handed. Accordingly, on the first school day in September 1930, the Ministry of Education announced that three additional texts had become available for German and mixed Magyar-German elementary schools.[67] Since the two earlier texts had appeared too late in the previous school year to have made any impact, for all practical purposes the five texts constituted brand new weapons in the Prime Minister's propaganda arsenal. However, as ever before, when the new school year began, it emerged that not all five texts would be available until November. It is interesting to reflect that Bethlen's trip was planned for just that time.[68]

The new delays compounded the difficulties normally encountered by each school community to obtain required texts. Still another year appeared to be slipping away without the benefit of even the few available texts after much patient waiting. In many localities the authorities were expected to cooperate with the Swabians. In others, a nice word or two to the school and ecclesiastic authorities might suffice. Each case was considered unique, to be negotiated according to local conditions. Clearly, the Swabians stood on shifting ground after many years of disappointments. As *Gotthold* pointed out, "slowly, very slowly, yet just the same, the government has finally published the urgently needed texts for our German elementary schools." Last year's texts had been the first two swallows, but they did not herald summer. The situation currently was better, but still far from good. Only the worst abuses had been corrected. Readers were needed desperately in the fifth and sixth grades, as well as texts in all subjects in the higher grades, but especially in reading. It was a heartbreaking sight to behold Swabian children ruined for life for the lack of textbooks. It was especially galling that the manuscripts for the other German texts were available, and only the lack of adequate funds prevented production. Could not the government's printing office absorb the cost?

Grumblings came from other quarters as well. *Nation und Staat* applauded the government goal to deliver the newly issued textbooks. But would they actually be used in the schools, and if so, used properly? Skepticism was justified. The next issue declared that the joy over the new school books issued in November 1930 was dampened because they were not compulsory; the school authorities made the final decision on their use. Consequently, many German schools would undoubtedly continue without them.[69] These fears were justified by subsequent developments. Even as the government announced two more German texts,[70] Peter Jekel, a Swabian spokesman, criticized the agonizingly slow progress of the already published texts.

> We were so convinced that the school authorities would be overjoyed when they saw these excellent texts that we never dreamt that it could be otherwise. Who would have believed that these texts would encounter obstacles? Who would have believed that the authorities would refuse to have anything to do with them? In 1929-30 we were told that technical difficulties held up our texts. It was a similar story in 1930-1931.[71]

Jekel hoped it would not be the same tale come next school year.

Jekel's apprehensions were borne out by subsequent developments. Although the following year two more texts appeared for the benefit of C-school pupils, difficulties continued. It was a giant step for a textbook from storage room into a Swabian village classroom, Jekel wrote dejectedly.[72] It is noteworthy that the distribution—though by no means the introduction and use—of the German texts coincided with an important milestone in Hungarian diplomacy, Bethlen's visit to Berlin for the purpose of strengthening commercial ties and friendly relations between the two countries. It had taken over seven years to produce the German textbooks, yet when they finally appeared, their ultimate use was far from being assured, and the timing of their distribution was arranged not for pedagogical purposes, but to serve the aims of Hungarian foreign policy. Had the texts been shoddy, the Swabians' disappointment might have been less keen. But domestic and impartial foreign observers alike agreed that the German texts were excellent in every way.

The dearth of minority teachers presented another serious problem, for the number of instructors in German minority schools did not keep pace with the growth of the German student body. One of the most universal and insistent Swabian complaints was the lack of their own teachers, particularly those who knew German well enough to teach it. Swabian youngsters were compelled by law to attend Magyar schools from the seventh grade upward, and even Swabian zealots were often unable to receive adequate instruction in their own language for acceptance into German teacher courses. In the urban environment the lower schools were strongly assimilationist, whereas the Swabian rural home milieu alone was unable to overcome the faultiness or absence of German instruction in the village schools. Bleyer charged in Parliament that as a result, seven out of ten graduates of German elementary schools could neither read nor write German proficiently, while nine out of ten Swabian high school matriculants could not write a letter in their mother tongue, or even compose a faultless German sentence.[73] Consequently, the few Swabian candidates in German teacher training courses fared poorly. Those who failed might still teach in German minority schools. Yet such a policy caused the superfluity of German teacher education and thrust a steady stream of incompetent German instructors into the Swabian school system. By providing indifferent German education in the lower forms, the government throttled the development of an effectual pool of German teacher candidates. By enforcing rigid standards in the higher echelons of teacher education, the regime could boast of the high academic standards maintained for German teachers, without lifting a finger to arrest the disgorgement of incompetent instructors into the minority school stream. Predictably, enrollments in German teacher courses remained low throughout, despite official promises to expand the facilities, while the number of graduates never reached significant proportions in the postwar years.[74]

The history of Hungary's German teacher training programme suggests that throughout the postwar period Swabian minority education served not pedagogical purposes but the aims of Hungarian foreign policy. In 1920, the Ministry of Nationalities promised that in order to provide minority teachers it would initiate an accelerated six-week vacation course that year in Sopron. But only eighty teachers from Hungary's eleven Trans-Danubian districts eventually enrolled, because few Swabians spoke and wrote German fluently.[95] The impending plebiscite, in which Burgenland was asked to choose between Austria and Hungary, may have contributed to the granting of even this minor concession in the disputed area.

After the loss of Burgenland to Austria, the government's interest in providing qualified German teaching personnel in Hungary's remaining Swabian schools ceased abruptly. During the next five years, Hungary saw no practical reasons why minority education of any sort should be pursued with vigour. Germany had yet to regain her former prominence in Central Europe, and in the interim Hungary's minority teacher programme languished, together with all other aspects of German minority life. Not until a revitalized Germany emerged as a noteworthy economic and political force in the mid-1920's did Bethlen "rediscover" the importance of German teacher training as an effective way to impress Germany.

The most visible immediate result of Hungary's determination to attract Germany was the revival, in 1925, of the neglected German teacher course at the Protestant teacher seminary in Sopron. According to one source, the Ministry of Education under Klebelsberg insisted on it. The ecclesiastic authorities responded languourously.[76] The Ministry urged priority for candidates proficient in the German language, but not to exclude other interested applicants. In practice, only students with excellent credentials were urged to apply, for the final examinations were to be difficult. Successful graduates obtained a certificate of proficiency and could, if they wished, become teachers in the German minority school system. Only twenty-five students participated in this modest programme in the 1925-1926 academic year; next year enrollment declined to only nineteen. Thereafter, the number of students rarely exceeded twenty-five annually. The government subsidized this modest operation entirely, and even awarded a few prizes; yet only a pittance was allocated for German texts, partly because they were exceedingly scarce. Nor was this the only disappointing feature. According to school statistics, only five candidates enrolled in 1926-1927 were Swabians by birth. Thereafter, the number of Swabian students enrolled in the whole institute seldom exceeded twenty annually. This meant that far too few Protestant Swabian teachers would enter German elementary education as a career. Even more discouraging was the fact that students in the special German course had only two hours of weekly lectures in that language. This could hardly be considered a German course, declared *Gotthold,* since every high school in the land normally provided at least two hours of weekly German instruction. *Der Auslandsdeutsche* was even more critical than *Gotthold.* The recently added theoretical course in teaching method was poor, and participants were being heckled by the other students. The courses did more harm than good.[77]

During a parliamentary debate in 1927, Malasits observed that the basic problem of the minority schools was the lack of properly trained teachers. Bethlen acknowledged the shortage of qualified minority teachers who knew Magyar and German well enough to teach both, but claimed that his government had taken decisive steps to alleviate the situation. In 1925-1926 and in 1926-1927, German courses were begun in Budapest and elsewhere. Bethlen gave the following list:[78]

Location	No. of Candidates 1925-1926	No. of Candidates 1926-1927
Budapest, District I	42	56
Budapest, District II	20	24
Győr (Raab)	33	40
Others (Prob. Kalocsa & Pécs)	32	63
Total	127	183

In 1926, the government also established German method courses for active teachers at Baja. They were initiated as a two-week course for seventy instructors, to be extended to one month, according to Bleyer, and accommodate 100 teachers. Bleyer exaggerated. In the summer of 1928, the course in Baja lasted only two weeks (6 to 18 August). Seventy-three practicing teachers from all over Hungary had six hours daily instruction in Swabian history, minority school law and study plans, and teaching problems in non-Magyar schools. A Heidelberg University professor gave lessons in proper German speech. Thereafter, the course was attended by about seventy teachers each year and lasted only two weeks.[79] Despite its limitations, the Baja summer course was probably one of the most effective means of improving the niveau of German-language teachers in Hungary. Had the course been part and parcel of an extensive nationwide German minority school programme, buttressed by other vacation courses to relieve congestion, and supported by meaningful instruction in purposeful and well-staffed teacher academies throughout the school year, the Swabians would have been soon blessed with plentiful teachers. As it was, the Baja course was only a cry in the wilderness, and could not hope to solve the fundamental problems posed by an overwhelmingly pro-Magyar educational mystique.

In the summer of 1928, Swabian leaders and the Ministry of Education considered the pressing need for minority teachers. According to Ministry officials, German courses in the teacher academies of Budapest, Győr, Kalocsa, Pécs, and Sopron would be augmented by one more course, dedicated to German literature and the history of Germans in Hungary. Summer courses would also be launched for practicing teachers, some having been established the previous year.[80] These were but vague promises and none of the existing programmes was complemented or expanded, in fact, beyond prior commitments. On 23 January 1929, another conference reverted once more to the problem of qualified teachers. Again, the government promised merely to develop further the question of teacher academies. Summer courses would be systematized and proper personnel assigned to the Ministry to handle German school problems.[81]

These promises masked inertia, and the general trend of neglect in the minority school system also enveloped the German teacher programme. Swabian parents had ample reason for concern, declared *Gotthold.* A lost teacher was irreplaceable because even those who knew German well could not learn how to teach it properly in such a short time. *Gotthold* castigated Bleyer and his associates for not pressing the government for improved teacher training facilities, if not for an academy of their own. To partially alleviate this crisis, the Sopron seminary had tried an experiment during 1928-1929. Twenty-three volunteers observed a rigorously supervised study programme. In addition to their normal German study load, students received two hours of weekly German instruction. School authorities ventured that even this was inadequate. More time, perhaps ten hours each week, was required to prepare future German teachers to discharge their responsibilities adequately. Moreover, currently students could be employed without a certificate of proficiency in German. No wonder that many future teachers disdained these courses. The government was urged to make German proficiency tests obligatory in minority regions and to give preference to holders of certificates.

Despite the achievements of the experimental German course at the Sopron seminary, which subsequently served nearly two dozen candidates annually, and despite the undoubted success of the extension course in Baja, the number of suitable German teachers did not rise appreciably the next few years. Béla Kapi complained in his annual report to the Ministry of Education,

> I most particularly stress the deplorable situation that our German elementary schools are frequently without teachers. Among the young teachers who graduate from our seminary there are not enough who possess sufficient proficiency in the German language to qualify them for a teaching position in that language.[82]

Kapi chafed because the seminary could not operate successfully under the present limitations, since two hours of German instruction failed to prepare teacher candidates properly. He also argued that only students with German mother tongue be admitted into the German teacher preparation programme. Kapi also complained because the Ministry had notified him almost too late to notify his teachers that the Baja summer extension course would be held that year.

Neither Kapi nor the Swabians seemed to realize that the Swabian teacher shortage was only part of a far greater and involved phenomenon grounded in the complexities of modern life. In Hungary, as elsewhere, the intelligentsia gathered in the towns and cities, while the countryside lacked essential services. In a country where all middle schools offered compulsory German courses, qualified teachers need not remain in tiny, backward villages, where most Swabians resided. While qualified Swabian teachers swelled the ranks of the Hungarian middle class in urban centres, less qualified instructors had to settle for the lesser positions in village schools. Naturally, they were not always the best suited pedagogues to provide effective instruction in the elementary schools. The Swabian teacher shortage thus posed a sociological as well as ethnic challenge, one that defied simplistic solutions.

In 1931, responding to mounting complaints from the minorities, the Praesidium issued a status report on minority teacher courses. The government claimed to have taken infinite pains to provide minorities with uninterrupted educational facilities despite the depression. In the 1930-1931 school year, 303 teacher candidates, of whom 241 were Swabians, attended various minority language courses, and confessional and state minority teacher training schools were augmented with a vacation class. The Germans greeted the report with skepticism. Der Auslandsdeutsche observed, having examined the 1931 roster of the seventy teachers at the Baja extension course, that judging by the participants' names, the course must either be drawing an unusually large number of Magyar teachers, or numerous German instructors must have Magyarized their names. A survey of the seventy enrollees in 1932 suggests that on the basis of their names alone, forty-three participants were not Germans.[83] Apparently, most participants in German teacher courses were non-Swabians, whose teaching careers were not bound up in the minority education system.

The government's neglect of the German teacher programme was of marginal interest to the Magyars but of crucial importance to the Swabians. In 1931, Gotthold became far more belligerent than on any previous occasion. The Protestant church's lack of properly educated German teachers and ministers was indefensible. Teachers in Swabian communities frequently lacked the common decency to learn German. Undeniably, Swabian objectives demanded far more radical measures. Unfortunately, most Swabian youngsters above the elementary school level became Magyarized. These children were the most gifted representatives of their people, yet a total loss to them. The entire elementary school system would have to be reorganized along the lines of A schools in order to create a nationally-aware Swabian intelligentsia. Needless to say, this was just what the Magyars feared most and wanted to avoid at all cost. Their minority school policy made much sense, for it aborted the development of a nationally-aware, irredentist Swabian intelligentsia.

One year later, Gotthold nearly reached the end of its tether. It urged

Protestant bishops to complain to the government because the minority schools were in terrible shape. Even the teachers were not well versed in the German language.[84] A two-week vacation course, given annually and attended by about seventy teachers, most of whom were not even Swabians, could not solve the fundamental problem of suitable German minority education. In a bitter speech in Parliament in May 1933, Bleyer furiously denounced the entire system: Hungary lacked even one middle, urban, or teacher preparation school capable of turning out teacher candidates competent to provide proper German instruction in the minority schools. Bethlen rebutted. Bleyer's allegation was totally erroneous, as proved by the existence of eight teacher academies throughout Hungary, in which German courses were being offered, and in which 447 minority students were enrolled in the past two years alone. Bethlen also cited the Baja summer course as an important contribution to German pedagogy, maintaining that since 1926, no less than 494 teachers had attended these annual vacation courses.[85]

Given the proposition that a minority is legally and morally entitled to enjoy ethnic cultural privileges, including the right to maintain its own elementary schools, the Hungarian government's treatment of the Swabian school programme leaves a great deal to be desired. According to official statistics, the number of elementary school instructors professing to be German was 101 in 1922-23, representing only 16.3% of all teachers of German in Swabian minority schools; by 1927-28, their number had declined to only 74 (6.0%). Moreover, almost half of these teachers did not teach in German minority schools. Forty-five out of 95 instructors taught in areas inhabited by only 8% of the Swabian population, while only five out of twelve German kindergarten teachers taught in Swabian regions.[86] The numerical decline of Swabian teachers cast the validity of the government's promises into doubt, especially since even the faithful execution of existing school regulations would have failed to realize Swabian aspirations for an effective school system.

Throughout the postwar period, Hungary solicited German aid in one form or another, and wished to impress Germany with attendance figures in Swabian minority schools, including teacher training facilities. The very low graduation statistics during these years were suppressed. The government instead stressed the number of teacher candidates attending academies in an effort to impress observers. It would have been far more significant to ascertain the number of graduates, or at least those who proceeded into the teaching profession as effective minority teachers. Judging by the number of graduates, the size of the teaching staff in Hungary, and the pupil-teacher ratio in German minority schools, the German teacher training programme was a failure from the Swabian perspective. Even if other jarring issues had not intruded, the Swabians' difficulties with the government over cultural and educational policy would have been serious enough to warrant concern. But other problems also rent the precarious peace.

The lack of Swabian representation in Parliament was an issue compounded by the complexities of the political system. In Hungary, election laws and established practice favoured the urban sector and the incumbent party. Excepting some forty-six urban electoral districts, where the electorate enjoyed the secret ballot, Hungary had the open ballot system. To be eligible, rural candidates had to produce a voter's list of at least 10% of the total electorate in that district. This system engendered abuse and gave government candidates a distinct advantage. They obtained the electoral rosters ahead of their rivals, and thus could entice the voters. This they did, with the aid of wining and dining, bribery, promises, cajolery, and veiled threats. Under Bethlen, government candidates enjoyed the immense material resources of the Unity Party, the government press, the police, and other administrative organs, and candidates did not hesitate to use their amenities.

The government's overwhelming power placed the Swabians in a quandary. They lacked the financial resources to establish their own political party, and even if they did, they would not be able to prevail against the odds. They consequently had no choice but to support the government and its candidates, and hope to benefit. Experience had shown, however, that once elected, government candidates failed to keep their promises. During the early Bethlen years the Swabians had little political influence and were represented in Parliament entirely by Magyars or by largely assimilated Swabians. But by 1926, the political climate had changed. Bethlen wished to please the Germans, and hence the Swabians, and gave Bleyer permission to stand for election, along with two other Swabian leaders.[87] The trio had to run as independents in rural districts, but with Bethlen's pledge of support, in exchange for adopting the government's electoral platform. The Swabians perforce accepted this compromise. They were convinced besides that fundamentally Bethlen championed their cause and had the wherewithal to marshal the Unity Party and the government organs in their support.

Bethlen appeared to support the Swabians without identifying his regime with them, but the Magyar public would not tolerate even his limited endorsement of the unpopular Swabians. In Bonyhád, the Magyar intelligentsia opposed Gündisch's candidacy. The County Lord Lieutenant painted such a black picture of Gündisch and of Swabian intrigues that Bethlen revoked his support and forced Gündisch's demission. The more dependable

Gustav Gratz stepped into the gap and won handily. The stubborn Bleyer encountered still greater difficulties. In overwhelmingly Swabian-inhabited Villány, where Joseph Wild had defeated him four years earlier, Bleyer nearly succumbed again. Magyar nationalists nominated Jenő Földes-Forster, an influential local figure, to run instead of Bleyer. Földes-Forster was not only powerful as the government's agricultural inspector in Baranya County, he also headed the county chapter of *Ébredő Magyarok* (Awakening Magyars), a bellicose Magyar racist organization. His powerful sponsors convinced Josef Wild to persuade Bethlen that Bleyer was an unsuitable candidate and to sponsor Földes-Forster instead. Bethlen gave in and begged Bleyer to step down in Villány and run elsewhere. Bethlen meant to oust Franz Neuberger, a Swabian-born government candidate, from his own district to make way for Bleyer, but the latter demurred. Bleyer asked Bethlen's permission to campaign against Földes-Forster in Villány on his own hook, a request that was reluctantly granted.

But Bleyer's travail had only just begun. His campaign had been delayed by one week, sufficient time to provide his opponent with a dangerous edge. Nonetheless, Bleyer's personal appearances in the electoral district's thirty-two communities tipped the balance. His tour assumed the appearance of a triumphal march. The large Swabian electorate repudiated his opponent as a man devoted to racist, anti-Swabian principles. Földes-Forster retaliated with terror, loosing his bully boys on Bleyer's aides, a number of whom suffered injuries. In a few communities, teachers were ordered to lead children in prayers for Földes-Forster's victory. Undaunted, Swabian adults streamed into churches to pray for Bleyer. As a last resort, Földes-Forster instigated Bleyer's and Gündisch's arrest on election eve in a last-ditch attempt to intimidate the Swabian electorate. In the dead of night, the two were hustled to Mohács, and made to appear before the County Chief Justice in the morning. Unshaken, the Swabians gave Bleyer an overwhelming mandate. The two leaders were released at once, of course. No charges had been laid, and Bethlen sent Bleyer an effusive letter of apology. Although Faul-Farkas lost in Soroksár, the Swabians had something to rejoice about. Besides Gratz and Bleyer, several other Swabian candidates and sympathizers had won victories.[88]

For the Swabians, the election of 1926 was a pyrrhic victory. The campaign demonstrated how determinedly the Magyar provincial intelligentsia wished to prevent the candidature of even government-supported Swabians, especially in sensitive border districts with sizable minorities like Baranya.[89] It also demonstrated Bethlen's opportunism and infidelity to his own given word. The Swabians would have been foolish to trust his promises thereafter, but unfortunately they had no choice. Should Bethlen resign, his successor was bound to be even less palatable from the Swabian point of view.[90]

The strengthening of the Swabian parliamentary contingent had few salutary effects on the overall position of the German minority. In some respects it grew even worse. The government's tremendous election victory reinforced Bethlen's position. It also made him more aware and sensitive to the anti-Swabian groundswell in the provinces than before. Except for the uproar caused by Bleyer's brief arrest, Reich Germans generally welcomed the election results. The Swabians had not gained the fourteen seats German nationalists thought was their due, yet the German press applauded Bethlen's minority efforts and considered the Swabians' rightful place in the Unity Party.[91] Thus strengthened, Bethlen was less inclined than before to make concessions. In part, this explains why he relinquished government control over the UDV in Baranya County and permitted county authorities to take over instead, and why he was tempted thereafter to make more and more extravagant promises while delivering less and less.

The 1931 election occurred in the midst of the most serious postwar financial crisis and the steady deterioration of the Swabian position. Bethlen's promises of the late 1920's became the Swabians' disappointments in the early 1930's, with no relief in sight. Swabian discontent could best be gauged by their recurring demands for an independent and unfettered Swabian political opposition party. It was felt by many Swabians, even moderates, Bleyer not excluded, that a minority without political power would never be taken seriously and never amount to anything. A Swabian party need not be unpatriotic; it might even support the government's foreign policy and confine its opposition exclusively to minority affairs.

The idea of a Swabian political party had been discussed and dismissed shortly after the War. But when Bleyer advocated it, those familiar with his views in the early 1920's were startled. The 1930's had ushered in a new, more radical era, and Bleyer's convictions changed literally against his own will. Currently, Germans had political parties in all the Successor States except Hungary, and German minority leaders had cabinet posts, or enjoyed other honours. The latest of these distinctions occurred in Rumania, and gave Bleyer food for thought. His old rival, Rudolf Brandsch, lately a deputy in the Rumanian Parliament, had recently been elevated to cabinet rank and put in charge of a newly created Ministry of Nationalities.[92] The contrast between Brandsch's exalted status in a country allegedly notorious for its persecution of minorities, and his own lowly position in Hungary, which prided herself on being a haven for non-Magyars, must have given Bleyer pause for bitter reflection.

In his public utterances Bleyer prudently stressed the need for Swabian solidarity with the government. Privately, however, he had for some time begun to contemplate establishing a Swabian political party of his own.[93] This plan gained momentum as the election of 1931 approached. Although ten deputies of Swabian descent sat in Parliament, only one—Bleyer—had gained official accreditation in the Unity Party. Bleyer informed Bethlen that unless the government agreed to sponsor four or five Swabian candidates, he would bolt the Unity Party and start his own. As election time approached, Bleyer used Gratz as intermediary to relay a roster of suggested candidates to the Prime Minister.[94] But Bethlen evaded Bleyer, who finally poured out his chagrin to von Loesch. For years, the Magyars had been abusing him. Bethlen might be cynical enough to deny a Swabian caucus. In that event, Bleyer feared, he would be ridiculed as a puppet, and his effectiveness as minority leader would cease. In the eleventh hour Bethlen capitulated. Even so, only two Swabians, Bleyer in Villány and Kussbach in Szent János, were government candidates. Faul-Farkas in Pilisvörösvár had only semi-official status. Bleyer grudgingly accepted this meagre accommodation, partly because he believed that Bethlen was the Swabians' only defender against the machinations of hostile administrators and narrow-minded politicians. Still, he considered the arrangement poor enough, although an improvement over 1926.[95]

Bleyer won by about the same margin as in 1926, but he was not gladdened by it. He admitted that Bethlen had kept his pre-election promises, but complained because the local authorities had gone all out to sabotage the agreement. With Faul-Farkas and Kussbach the anti-Swabians succeeded; they were both defeated under suspicious circumstances. Thus the Swabians were no better off than before. Bleyer resented the briberies, chicaneries, threats, and shameless blandishments practiced by the unscrupulous Magyar opposition. Never had they poured so much money into an electoral fight. *Sonntagsblatt* characterized Bleyer's victory in Villány as a hard fight against irresponsible demagoguery and vote hunting in which liquor played a predominant role. Bleyer also complained because his negotiations with Bethlen had forced him and his running mates to commence campaigning too late, just as in 1926. The opposition had time to do its dirty work. Utilizing the current financial crisis, they allegedly spent a small fortune bribing destitute peasants, many of whom, Bleyer admitted, were Swabians. The worst offenders were the powerful Magyar officials, who peremptorily ordered many a Swabian small-holder to vote against Swabian candidates, on pain of retaliation. Bleyer prophesied darkly that such sowing would sooner or later reap the whirlwind. When Bethlen suddenly resigned, bequeathing the Swabian problem to the unsympathetic care of Károlyi, Bleyer's political isolation and disillusionment were complete.

As an epitaph to the recent election, Gratz delivered a speech at the eighth *UDV* General Assembly. Haunted by the fear that the disenchanted Swabians would establish an opposition party, Gratz implored the Assembly to stop at the brink. A Swabian minority party was not justified by conditions prevailing in Hungary because Swabians and Magyars enjoyed approximately the same cultural level and hence had no difficulty communicating. The Swabians felt at home in Hungary, and required no separate political representation. Furthermore, neither the Magyars nor the government purposefully sought to destroy the Swabians. A Swabian party would defeat its own purpose, because the Magyars would overreact and create the very conditions the Swabians feared.[96] Gratz's moderating counsel was commendable but would soon fall on deaf ears. Even the compliant Bleyer had begun to despair that anything would ever come of the Swabians' just demands if the choice was left to the Magyars.

There were many other issues in the second half of Bethlen's Ministry that distressed the Swabians. The name-Magyarization campaign that gathered momentum in the late 1920's was one such problem. Hemmed in by vast numbers of Slavs and Germans, the Magyars naively sought to solve the difficulty by encouraging non-Magyars to adopt Magyar-sounding family names. The most intense Magyarization occurred among the intelligentsia which alarmed the Swabians no end, since it imperiled their long-range survival as a people. In the year 1931 alone, about 2,900 families Magyarized their names (twice as many as in 1930); half were Swabians, and more than one-third intellectuals. In the armed forces, the increase was tenfold between 1930 and 1931, thanks to the zeal of Gömbös, the ultranationalist Minister of War.[97] The Germans condemned Magyarization and believed that European public opinion would sour as a result. The Swabians fumed. Name-Magyarization was strictly a Magyar affair, wrote *Sonntagsblatt,* but only when Hungarians with foreign-sounding names considered themselves Magyars. But now the Magyars were pressuring avowed Swabians to change their names, and that was insupportable.[98]

Closely linked with Swabian complaints about name-Magyarization was the result of the 1930 census. Swabians were shocked to learn that they had declined in number by about 73,000 people since 1920. They ascribed this loss almost entirely to more or less forcible assimilation, of which the name-Magyarization campaign was only a small but important part. The Swabians also resented the law that enabled children to declare a different tongue than their own mother's as highly prejudicial to a fair census. The Magyars minimized the possible effects of coercion, and sought other explanations for the numerical decline of the Swabians. Bethlen pointed out, for example, that natural forces, especially in the urban centres, caused the

Swabian losses, not artificial dabblings by the government. This was a worldwide phenomenon, because minority peoples were subjected to assimilatory forces beyond anybody's control. Moreover, since 1920 the Swabians lost about 10,000 Jews, who in 1930 declared themselves as Magyars.[99] The Swabians would not be consoled by the fact that minority peoples elsewhere in Europe were also being absorbed into the mainstream of the dominant nationalities. To them, the census results were proof positive that they were victims in a Magyar plot that sought their demise as a distinct nationality. Emotion supplanted reason on both sides.

This rampant paranoia was poignantly expressed by Bleyer in *"Rahel's Klagelied,"* a withering critique of Hungarian nationality policy and a lament about the Swabians' misfortune that was wellnigh irreversible. The title stems from the Magyar poet János Arany, whose composition by the same name "Rachel siralma") of 1851 had a double meaning. Its theme was the slaughter of the innocents under Herod, and was based on the Gospel by St. Matthew: Rachel bewailed the loss of her children and would not be comforted, for all was lost. The allegorical meaning of the poem was the destruction of Hungary's freedom by Austria in 1849. In his article Bleyer applied the analogy to the Swabians "with a heavy, hesitant hand, yet I must write it." After many years of "requesting and pleading, after tireless explanations and discussions, after unrelenting struggles and sharp disagreements, after alternating hope and despair. . .always guided by honest intention and the cleanest, purest idealism, never seeking anything but truth and justice, evoking divine and human rights, swearing allegiance to the fatherland," Bleyer claimed he had arrived at the most significant question: What have we accomplished thus far with respect to the upbringing of our German children?

Bleyer pictured Hungary as an educational wasteland, where Swabian children were hopelessly trapped. The kindergartens were exclusively Magyar, even in Burgenland. Instruction in the elementary schools was almost exclusively Magyar, except for some rudimentary German reading and writing lessons here and there. Entirely Magyar were the continuation schools and the *Levente* youth organization as well. In many places, Swabian children no longer enjoyed religious services or confessional instruction in their native tongue. Bleyer likened these malpractices to a giant steamroller flattening the hopes of Swabian youth's *Volkstum*. Swabian children were forever stuck with dialect and would never learn the proper, literary German speech. This in turn meant that they would never be able to become organically linked with the great German cultural heritage focussed outside Hungary. It was true, Bleyer conceded, that the Swabians were treated as equals in every respect except as regards language and education; yet these were crucial elements not only for their survival, but for the success of Hungary's own revisionist hopes. Would the former nationalities voluntarily return to Hungary under these circumstances? Hardly, Bleyer opined. If the Swabians' fidelity to their language and culture was unpatriotic, then Hungary ought to pass racial laws, and renounce the concept of the multinational state. This would dash all hopes for regaining the lost territories with their vast blocs of non-Magyar peoples, to whom their ancestral language was as sacred as Magyar was to the Magyars. In conclusion, Bleyer cited the recently released 1930 census figures as proof positive that the Swabians were launched on the road to destruction.

The Swabian example illustrates clearly the danger small minorities face when caught in the web of international power politics. While Germany slumbered, the Swabians suffered neglect but not persecution. They were neither numerous enough nor powerful enough to warrant concern. Germany's recovery in the mid-1920's thrust the Swabian minority into the limelight. Germany hesitated to assist Hungary's revisionist schemes, and refused to commit herself as an economic partner. These irritants soured German-Hungarian relations and began to put the Swabians in a bad light. Into this impasse stepped the Swabians and began agitating for a German-Hungarian understanding. Their own reward would be unhampered cultural development, a price the Magyars considered too steep for comfort. It was a utopian scheme that completely ignored basic Magyar thinking on their own cultural and political role in the Danubian region. The Magyars disliked the Swabians, since they were a living testimony that Hungary had yet to become a homogeneous Magyar state. Nor was it likely to, so long as the Swabians retained the potential to challenge the mantle of Magyar leadership. The Swabians insisted in vain that they were patriots. Increasing German economic and political influence in the area, linked with their fanatical dedication to German *Volkstum,* induced such fear among the Magyars for their own safety, that they began to see in the Swabians vanguards of a Pan-German sweep into Eastern Europe.

Gömbös was already internationally known when he became Prime
Minister. He had been prominent in the ultra-conservative boosting of
Horthy to the Regency. In the early 1920's Gömbös maintained shadowy
contacts with Hitler and the Bavarian National Socialists. Although
partially of Swabian descent, he resisted all cultural norms at variance with
the Magyar ethos. As Bethlen's Minister of War he promoted Magyarization, aimed particularly at the influential Swabian element in the armed
forces. As Prime Minister, Gömbös wanted to purify Hungary culturally
and ethnically. He also admired Mussolini, and wished to reconcile Italy and
Germany to gain their support for economic rejuvenation and political
revision. Gömbös' programme was amorphous, riddled with vast contradictions whose execution appeared to border on the impossible. Why court
Germany when Italy staunchly opposed such a course? Why risk Italy's
proven friendship to seek tenuous German ties? Besides, given past treatment of the Swabians, Gömbös was more likely to aggravate than soothe
German sensibilities. It is remarkable that Gömbös not only weathered the
storm, but dramatically enhanced Hungary's domestic and international
standing.

At the outset, however, Gömbös found himself in difficulty. Hungary's
clamour for Treaty revision prevented a *modus vivendi* with Czechoslovakia,
Rumania, and Yugoslavia. This, and France's alienation blocked all hopes
for a peaceful territorial and economic settlement in the Danube Basin.
During the 1920's, Bethlen had relied mainly on Italian support to solve
Hungary's economic problems and revisionist aspirations. Gömbös turned
to Germany as well. But Germany's ambition pushed her eastward into
Central and Southeastern Europe, while Italy vaguely dreamt of an empire
stretching from the Adriatic to the Baltic. Gömbös planned to reconcile
them, secure their joint support in retrieving the lost territories from the
Successor States, and establish Hungary as their dominant client state in

Eastern Europe.

Although Germany's new strength under National Socialism promoted Magyar hopes that Treaty revision might soon become a reality, there were no assurances that Gömbös' self-appointed role as peacemaker would succeed. Caught between Italy and Germany, Hungary might become a battleground, and eventually a satellite of either contender. Gömbös saw not danger, but potential balance. Fearing the possible effects of German eastward expansion, Italy would offer moral and material support to Hungary, whose cooperation with Germany might otherwise open the door to German penetration into the heart of Southeastern Europe—Italy's primary sphere of influence. Conversely, German influence would be Hungary's best safeguard against any aggressive Italian intentions. Owing to Hungary's delicate strategic and political situation, Gombos oscillated between the German and Italian camps, ultimately favouring the former. His pro-German orientation, coupled as it was with Magyar anti-Swabian chauvinism, ushered in a new phase in German-Hungarian (and Swabian-Hungarian) relations—a thinly disguised assimilationist policy and attempted economic and political cooperation with Germany.

Gömbös observed the increasingly conservative course of events in Germany during the early 1930's with great interest and anticipation, convinced they augured well for Hungary's revisionist aspirations. With each regime Gömbös grew more hopeful, since each exhibited more and more of his own revisionist spirit. He besieged each new leader for assistance of every sort, persuaded that the German phoenix would soon adopt a more friendly and actively pro-Hungarian policy out of sheer self-interest. Friendly German officials raised Gömbös' expectations even before the Hitler era. Von Hassell, Germany's Italian ambassador, flattered Hory, Hungary's special envoy in Rome, into believing that Germany now regretted not having used Hungary to mediate past German differences with Italy and Austria. Germany had bungled its 1931 attempt to pull Austria into its economic orbit. In future, she would work with Hungary to make *Anschluss* attractive to Italy. Finally, the ambassador led Hory to believe that Germany no longer shunned a political accommodation and intimate economic ties with Hungary, and with Hungary's friends Italy and Austria. Bilateral trade also seemed encouraging. Negotiations between the Hungarian Foreign Ministry and German legation officials in Budapest centered on a possible joint German-Hungarian commission to investigate expanded trade relations. On 6 December Gömbös asked Chancellor Schleicher to exert his influence on behalf of improved economic relations. Schleicher promised to devote special attention to nurturing German-Hungarian relations in general, and economic matters in particular.[1]

Germany's apparent inclination to satisfy Hungarian demands for closer trade relations and common revisionist action was not motivated by enthusiasm for the Magyar cause. The Germans considered the Magyars opportunists. Schön had few illusions about Hungary's fidelity to Germany. He foresaw accurately that Gömbös would champion Austria and Italy, and demand German support for Dollfuss, in order to bolster him against France. Schön doubted that Germany's demands for better Swabian treatment would be heeded, because the Magyars had little understanding for the problem. Hungary would soon be swept irrevocably into Italy's arms, mainly because the Magyars resented the recent exclusion of Hungarian foodstuffs from the Reich. They had retaliated by terminating negotiations with the Ford Motor Company in Cologne for automobile parts, and now dickered with Fiat instead. They also threatened to introduce trade regulations that would harm Germany's economic interests. Schön feared that French influence would soon predominate throughout the Danubian region, especially as a Franco-Italian rapprochement seemed imminent. Germany must reopen her gates to Hungarian cattle and seasonal products to induce the Magyars to readmit German industrial commodities. They ought to be flattered that as a bulwark separating northern and southern Slavs, Hungary was Germany's strategic linchpin; that Germany favoured revisionism and expanded reciprocal trade; and that Germany had no wish to incite the Swabians—on the contrary; the Reich rejoiced at the prospect of having hundreds of thousands of Germans living in the Successor States reincorporated into Hungary some day.

After thorough debate, the Wilhelmstrasse recognized Hungary's role in Germany's long-range foreign policy objectives. Both nations were close on revisionism and disarmament, though their respective thrusts differed. Aims conflicted in Poland, where German attempts to force revision of the Versailles frontiers clashed with Hungary's determination to support a traditional friend. Conversely, Hungary could scarcely expect Germany to support her revisionist claims in Czechoslovakia without serious reservations. Hungary occupied a strategic position, but Germany had neither the might nor the wish, for the time being, to intrude into that part of the world. Moreover, it was not in Germany's long-range interest to create economic chaos in the Successor States, only to prevent their domination by France. Yet, military, political, and economic factors argued for a more lenient Hungarian policy. Hungary did control the gates to the East and occupied ground Germany must eventually cross to dominate the Balkans. Smoother German-Hungarian economic relations should only await the passing of Germany's current economic crisis. Even so, the Ministry of Trade must dispatch an experienced diplomat (Privy Councillor of the Ministry of

Trade, Josias Waldeck) to Budapest immediately to investigate Hungary's economic requirements. A permanent German-Hungarian trade commission must commence meaningful negotiations soon. Unlike Schön, the Ministry deemed commercial links between Hungary and the Successor States harmless, provided Germany's most-favoured-nation status was not compromised. The Ministry agreed with Schön on one important point: Swabian oppression, for which the Magyars bore the blame almost exclusively, threatened to exacerbate German-Hungarian relations.

A few days later, Schön informed Gömbös of Germany's plans. Apart from cooperation on disarmament these turned out to be meagre fare. Gömbös continually interrupted Schön's discouraging litany to stress that Germany's economic recovery promised happier days for Hungary. On balance, Germany promised only informational discussions on reciprocal trade. Even these modest negotiations hinged on Hungary's willingness to conciliate the Swabians. Gömbös received this report "with great reserve . . . just as I had expected it."[2] Any hopes that Germany's new conservatism would automatically foster fraternal relations were thus dashed. Gömbös' only hope remained that the rightward surge in Germany would eventually catapult a far more radical regime into power than any of its timid predecessors.

When Adolf Hitler assumed power in Germany, Gömbös was at the door, cap in hand. He greeted the new chancellor as a comrade-in-arms imbued with his own *völkisch* outlook, and recalled their negotiating days on the eve of the Munich beerhall putsch—a reference scarcely designed to fill Hitler with enthusiasm. Gömbös then bemoaned the decline in German-Hungarian trade relations and hoped that the promised trade commission would soon be dispatched. He also solicited Hitler's political support, particularly against the Successor States, to persuade the Germans there to cooperate with the oppressed Magyars. Since Gömbös fancied himself a mediator between Germany and Italy, Hitler decided to humour him. Nothing was closer to his heart than a reconciliation with Italy, which would also improve German-Hungarian relations. Blaming the current economic crisis and the prejudice of experts from the previous regime on poor trade relations, Hitler made vague promises. Vice-Chancellor von Papen then outlined Germany's future foreign policy course to Kánya and promised to persuade Hitler to inaugurate a more vigorous policy in Southeastern Europe, especially with Hungary, as soon as Hitler quelled Germany's internal disorders. Soon, more concrete negotiations would take place. To the Magyars' chagrin, however, only eight days after Hitler's reply to Gömbos, Germany announced new discriminatory tariffs on a variety of Hungarian agricultural commodities. This, and further restrictions on 14 July meant a virtual embargo of Hungarian exports to Germany.[3]

German Foreign Minister von Neurath cited the unresolved Swabian question as the principal source of mutual tension. Hungary's determination to link Swabian reform with German-Magyar cooperation in the Successor States was impractical and created an impasse. Indeed, conflicting priorities seriously obstructed a German-Hungarian understanding. Whereas the Magyars stressed revived trade and German-Hungarian revisionist cooperation, the Germans insisted on settling Swabian grievances first.

Diplomatic problems also confounded German-Hungarian relations. Gömbös took seriously Hitler's random statement that an Italian-German rapprochement, mediated by Hungary, was a primary aim. In fact, one of Hitler's principal objectives was to subjugate the small nations of Eastern Europe. Austria would come first, followed by Czechoslovakia, the Memel region, Poland, and finally the Balkans, to which Hungary held the key. Germany would not negotiate with Italy unless she ceased interfering in Austria. Italy refused mediation unless Germany guaranteed Austrian independence. Gömbös' first task, therefore, was to persuade Hitler that he had nothing to gain by incorporating Austria. This embarrassed Hitler, whose plans of conquest were in danger of being disturbed. Whereas the Austrian National Socialists were exhorted by Berlin to overthrow Dollfuss and annex Austria to Germany, Gömbös counseled that the Austrian National Socialists be made to cooperate with Chancellor Dollfuss instead. This would create an Austrian anti-Left coalition and pave the way for a German-Italian reconciliation. Of course, Hitler spurned a pacific solution. As the March crisis suggested, Germany's plans of conquest demanded Austria's speedy incorporation, whereas Gömbös' well-meant but ill-timed intervention dashed Hitler's hopes for a speedy surgical operation.

Despite rebuff, the Magyars intensified their diplomatic efforts with Bethlen's visit, in the midst of Germany's March offensive to bring Austria to heel. Bethlen's journey had been planned for some time, but for Gömbös it was most opportune. Without commitment, Bethlen would explain the official Hungarian position in Berlin. In his discussions with high-ranking German officials (6-8 March) Bethlen proffered all the well-known Hungarian desiderata, ranging from German-Hungarian cooperation in the Successor States to Gömbös' *idée fixe*—the creation of a quadruple alliance linking Germany, Italy, Austria, and Hungary. While the Magyars were blinded by the importance of their own diplomatic objectives, the Germans clearly had other concerns. On the day of Bethlen's arrival, a Foreign Ministry memo marked "very urgent" asked Neurath to have Bethlen influence Gömbös to remedy Swabian oppression at once. The Hungarian Section listed a cascade of broken Magyar promises, delays, and subterfuges.

German-Hungarian relations would not improve until these ceased. Bethlen's journey thus demonstrated the futility of hungary's diplomatic exertions.[4]

Hungary was still undeterred. Schön informed the Wilhelmstrasse that official circles besieged him ceaselessly with distress calls about the threatening disaster in German-Hungarian commercial relations. They begged him to find a way to reverse the deteriorating situation. In the spring, Gömbös personally complained to Hitler that recently Hungarian agricultural products had not been able to enter Germany at all, or could do so only to a very limited extent. Gömbös warned that agricultural export was to him not only an economic question but a question of political considerations, that would strengthen his political course. Hitler must take urgent measures of a fundamental nature, as an old racial-nationalist comrade holding the same *Weltanschauung*. Hitler's reply was curt and disappointing. Nothing could be done to mitigate Hungary's current economic plight, because Germany's agricultural producers were in a horrible situation. Nonetheless, Hungary's economic problem had certain political implications for Germany which could not be long ignored. But Hitler merely promised to refer the matter to the Reich Ministries.[5]

Hitler's curtness may be partly ascribed to Germany's serious economic problems, but Gömbös' continuing pro-Austrian diplomacy greatly influenced the Chancellor not to accommodate Hungary. By promoting a German-Italian rapprochement, Gömbös frustrated Hitler's annexationist designs in Austria. Had Gömbös not meddled and had he supported Hitler during the March crisis, Germany would have achieved a victory far greater than the mere acquisition of Austrian soil. Italy and Czechoslovakia would have been outflanked and outmanoeuvred, and German influence firmly ensconced on the threshold of the Balkans. Deprived of Czechoslovak support, and isolated from their French allies, neither of the two remaining Little Entente nations could have resisted German demands, and the Balkans would have been open to German penetration.[6] Instead, Hungary's diplomacy enabled Mussolini to protect Austria and prevent Hitler's coup in the Balkans. Small and defenseless though she was, Hungary held the pivotal position in Central Europe, at least for the time being.

Gömbös exploited Hungary's strategic advantages in his negotiations with Germany. These inevitably gravitated towards economic questions, for Germany's curtailment of Hungarian imports in the spring of 1933 was a telling blow. An unheralded June visit to Germany enabled Gömbös to discuss this, and a number of other urgent questions, with Hitler personally. Gömbös intended to peddle his pet scheme—the creation of an autarchic confederation fusing Italy, Germany, Austria, and Hungary. He also pleaded unsuccessfully with Hitler for normalizing German-Austrian relations. Hungary favoured eventual *Anschluss,* in deference to Italy, Germany would have to move circumspectly now. Gömbös offered to mediate the Austrian dilemma between Italy and Germany, and also pledged to keep Dollfuss from the clutches of Czechoslovakia and France. Next, Gömbös broached his revisionist plans and the active role he wished Germany to play, and finally, explained the Swabian situation, hoping that Germany would keep out of an internal problem.

Hitler had no wish to exacerbate German-Hungarian relations, and acted receptive. Germany would lend Hungary limited revisionist support, insofar as it harmonized with Germany's eastern plans. However, any joint military venture would perforce be confined to Czechoslovakia alone, because Germany needed future Rumanian and Yugoslav support against the Soviet Union. They would have to be drawn into Germany's orbit peacefully. Gömbös agreed, not because he renounced Hungary's claims against Rumania and Yugoslavia, but because he believed that eventually Italy's assistance would help settle that score. Respecting Austria, Hitler unblushingly assured Gombos that *Anschluss* was not one of his immediate objectives. For the time being, he would be content if Dollfuss ceased persecuting the National Socialists and admitted them into the government. Further, Hitler feigned gratitude in accepting Gömbös' proposal to mediate the delicate Austrian problem between Germany and Italy. He also soothed Gömbös' growing concern about Hungary's internal security. Hungarian right-wing groups, among whom the Swabians were prominent, did not enjoy Germany's material or moral support. Nor did he intend to intervene in Hungary's internal affairs, particularly since Gömbös' "new course" left little doubt in his mind that the two countries trod a common path. Finally, Hitler reaffirmed his determination to improve languishing commercial contacts—a promise broken within a month with further cutbacks in Hungarian imports.[7]

Reaction to the Gömbös visit was unanimously favourable only in the controlled German press. The National Socialist *Der Angriff* stressed common German-Hungarian aims, and favourably compared the careers of Gömbös and Hitler.[8] But Hungarian public opinion roundly condemned the visit as a rash move. In Parliament, Endre Bajcsy-Zsilinszky, an avowed foe of Germany, questioned both the Prime Minister's wisdom and his motives. He feared that Gömbös might drop Italy as an ally, and become a German stooge, all for the sake of economic advantage. Initially, Italian officials were also annoyed with the visit, particularly since they were apparently not informed until the last moment. Eventually, however, they accepted the mission as an "entirely welcome establishment of contact between the leading statesmen." Dollfuss felt betrayed, convinced that Gömbös had exchanged Austrian independence for the restitution of Burgenland to Hungary.[9] But the Hungarian press was most embarrassing. Although the Budapest dailies dutifully printed the glowing official communique, one of the most prestigious publications, Pester Lloyd, severely criticized the visit.

Gömbös ordered Kánya to apologize to the Germans for the Pester Lloyd's "blunder," and to reiterate his satisfaction over the course of his visit. Gömbös rejoiced because "urgent economic questions were being fully tackled," Kánya confided. Gömbös had disarmed Dollfuss' fears of German annexationist ambitions. At the same time he had warned the Austrians that Hungary was, and would remain, Germany's friend. Finally, Gömbös had promised to continue his efforts to prevent a Franco-Austrian rapprochement. Gömbös kept his promise by suggesting to Dollfuss a few weeks later that Hungary would not protect Austria in its struggle against National Socialism.[10]

Gömbös' Berlin visit occasioned a thorough airing between Italy and Hungary, especially since certain other developments suggested a cooling between the two allies. On 15 July 1933, one of Mussolini's favourite ideas, the creation of a Four-Power Pact comprising Italy, Germany, England, and France, materialized. It was to re-establish Great Power control in Europe, a plan that threatened Hungary's political and strategic importance, perhaps even her existence. Italy now might accommodate France and her eastern allies, thus dashing Hungary's revisionist chances and wrecking her new order in Eastern Europe. Gömbös also feared that Hitler's aggressive Austrian policy might seriously strain German-Italian relations. Either way, Gömbös saw Hungary's role as Eastern European hub and German-Italian mediator in jeopardy.

Gömbös' end-of-July Rome visit rectified some of these difficulties. Mussolini pledged to maintain good relations with Germany and to support Hungarian territorial demands against the Little Entente, whereas he recognized that Gömbös' Austro-German mediation efforts were not meant to exclude Italy from a general settlement. Expanded trade was also on the agenda, including the particularly touchy problem of Hungarian wheat imports to Italy. Thanks to this visit the Magyars took heart, and rejected as not feasible French offers of limited support of certain Hungarian demands against the Little Entente in return for accepting Beneš's offer of a prolonged political truce of God.[11]

Shortly after Gömbös' Berlin journey Masirevich, since August 1933 Hungary's Minister to Germany, paid his respects to Hitler. Having recently served in Prague, Masirevich turned the conversation to Czechoslovakia. Most German parties there had lately unified, and he hoped that this would engender mutually profitable political cooperation with the Magyar minority. Hitler countered that he favoured a coalition comprising all of Czechoslovakia's dissident ethnic groups—Germans, Magyars, and Slovaks—to gain greater freedom for all minorities. This contradicted Hungarian desires. The Magyars wanted all of eastern Czechoslovakia, including its Slovak population. Mutual complaints further jarred amity at this meeting, optimistically characterized by State Secretary von Bülow as harmonious. Whereas Masirevich complained that German agitators in Hungary attempted to re-Germanize Magyarized Swabians, Hitler charged that the hostile Hungarian press slurred his regime. However, the Germans recognized the danger of antagonizing the Magyars. About one month earlier, the Wilhelmstrasse advised Bleyer to proceed with greater caution in his activities.[12]

Hitler's evasiveness worried the Magyars, especially when they learned of a possible rapprochement between Germany and the Little Entente, as Mussolini had often predicted. Masirevich appeared at the Wilhelmstrasse to ascertain the rumours that Germany had solicited Czechoslovakia and Yugoslavia with offers of a non-aggression treaty. This would force Hungary to change her foreign policy. The Germans denied the reports but Masirevich insisted on a formal note, and he worried about deteriorating German-Austrian relations, triggered by a minor border incident. He also worried about German-Polish negotiations, indeed, about Germany's intentions in Poland and beyond. Rumour had it that the Germans demanded future concession in the Ukraine in exchange for a free hand for Poland in Lithuania. The Germans attempted in vain to placate Masirevich. He repeated his inquiry when press reports of impending non-aggression pacts between Germany and her neighbours surfaced time and again, only to be told ambiguously that Germany had offered such a pact to all nations, but not specifically to members of the Little Entente.[13]

These clumsy answers failed to satisfy Hungary. A Wilhelmstrasse memo revealed continuing Magyar fears that the Reich was indeed playing a double game. Bülow reported another visit by Masirevich where the minister attempted to force Germany to underwrite Hungary's economic and political requirements. Specifically, Masirevich desired the resumption of trade relations; the creation of a consultative pact; and a joint Little Entente policy. Hungary demanded that Germany neither desert her nor conclude detrimental agreements with the Little Entente. This was tantamount to an ultimatum, for Masirevich insisted on a reply within fourteen days. Bülow deprecated the value of formal pacts. Germany would not be stampeded but quietly wait until the current "pactomania" had run its course. Responding to these conversations, Köpke ventured that the

Magyars apparently distrusted the diplomatic activities of the Little Entente, and wished to ensure that Germany did not flirt with Hungary's enemies. Masirevich's demand for a consultative pact was unreasonable and naive, a "one-sided pleasure—and that merely on the Hungarian side." It was an outrageous request because there was no sign of a satisfactory Swabian settlement.[14]

One week later, Masirevich reappeared at the Wilhelmstrasse armed with a long sheet with questions of all kinds, claiming there were domestic pressures to change Hungary's pro-German policy. To counter these demands, Hungary had to know whether Germany would continue to support Hungarian revisionist claims. Neurath replied like Köpke: Germany would only lend "moral support." Was Germany currently negotiating a non-aggression pact with any members of the Little Entente? The answer was no. Would Germany be willing to conclude a special treaty with Hungary? Neurath professed to be no friend of "superfluous" pacts. German-Hungarian relations had always been friendly and required no special assurances. If relations were now and then troubled, it was entirely Hungary's fault for mistreating the Swabians.[15]

In their hearts the Magyars never seriously believed that Hitler would sacrifice their own willing partnership for the sake of transitory agreements with the hostile nations of the Little Entente. The main thrust of Hungarian foreign policy was to harness Germany formally to Hungary's revisionist chariot, and have it rescue Hungary from economic disaster. As far as Hitler was concerned, Germany's economic and political programme in the East had yet to mature, and there was no need to reveal his hand. Hungary's unceasing demands for an immediate commitment to action embarrassed the Reich. Thus Germany rejected Hungary, but not from peaceful motives. Insisting that Hungary remedy the condition of the Swabians as a precondition to any joint action served as an excellent pretext for inaction during the waiting period.

Nonetheless, both nations realized that each would have to vouchsafe its good intentions before the other would cooperate. As a result, by the end of 1933, certain definitive steps were taken by both governments. Only this can explain why Gömbös broke traditional protocol on the occasion of the ceremonial visit of von Mackensen, Germany's new Minister in Hungary. To Mackensen's amazement, Gömbös launched what he termed an unconstrained exchange of views particularly about ticklish questions, namely, the Swabian conundrum. Gömbös stated that the minorities question was still interfering with the development and strengthening of a truly friendly relationship with the German Reich—one of the main planks of his foreign policy. The Swabians constituted a purely Hungarian question, and never a

German-Hungarian one, but he pledged a fundamental settlement of the question, thereby eliminating it permanently from the complex of problems in German-Hungarian relations. Gömbös promised to write Hitler a detailed letter documented with statistical data, whereupon the German minorities in the Successor States would hopefully cease their anti-Hungarian agitation, as their complaints harmed Hungarian revisionism.[16]

Gömbös believed mistakenly that Swabian mollification was a key to German concessions, and he pursued vigorous paper reform. In February 1934, Gömbös dispatched his somewhat delayed long-heralded letter on the Swabian problem, to encourage formal commercial negotiations. For a letter seeking support it was remarkably arrogant, if not downright belligerent. Gömbös cited the Bismarckian concept as regards the political importance of the Hungarian state and its relations with Germany. But Hungary could not realize her historic mission and provide realistic aid unless she enjoyed total internal sovereignty, free from all types of interference. This had to include sovereignty over the Swabians. A supplicant turned remonstrant, Gömbös demanded that Germans and Magyars in the Successor States be brought into concordance at once, since both minorities must battle against a common enemy, which now ruled. In a neat syllogism, Gömbös deftly suggested that since a strong Hungary was a *sine qua non* for Germany's success in the Danube Basin, anything that strengthened Hungary was *ipso facto* a German responsibility. It followed, therefore, that Germans residing in the Successor States must support the historic aspirations of the Magyar people, the realization of which was also in the German interest. While demanding that Hitler influence Germans in the Successor States, Gömbös rejected all outside interference with the Swabians, even if directed by unofficial, German-based cultural associations. In future, the *VDA* and others must cease propagandizing and supporting Swabians. All questions must be addressed to Gömbös personally or to the accredited Minister in Berlin. German communities in the Successor States must be ordered to cooperate with local Magyars, and under no circumstances to embrace anti-revisionism. Hitler never replied to this undiplomatic letter.[17]

Gömbös centred on Germany's lack of enthusiasm concerning Hungary's revisionist aspirations, yet he was more interested in massive German aid to rescue Hungary from economic collapse. Pleas, flatteries, and Hitler's affection for an old racist comrade counted less than plain common sense, self-interest, and a Hungarian threat, in prompting Hitler to extend assistance. Encouraged by a recommendation of the League of Nations' Financial Commission, Hungary planned to denounce the German-Hungarian Clearing Agreement of 13 April 1932. This relatively obscure affair threatened to embarrass Germany. Economically it augured minor attrition in German industrial exports. Politically, and far more importantly, it threatened Germany's image as benefactor of Eastern Europe's small agricultural nations. Since Hungary was the only country professing friendly feelings for Germany, the Reich could scarcely afford to alienate even this small state.

The German government thereupon made a political decision in a matter that was overwhelmingly economic. Neurath, in his memorandum to the Reich Minister of Food and Agriculture Hugenberg, recognized that while the Hungarian step was very undesirable from the point of view of Germany's foreign policy, it was, nonetheless, justified by the dilatory treatment given by the German government to Hungarian requests for negotiations. Neurath counseled the issue be settled immediately, by taking into account, to a sufficient extent, Hungarian requests regarding agricultural imports, particularly early vegetables, fruits, and horses. Then, events began to move rapidly. On 24 May, negotiations between German and Hungarian trade representatives began, and on 2 June they signed an agreement and protocol. Hungary pledged to withdraw her denunciation of the Clearing Agreement and conclude a new retroactive compensation treaty with the Reichsbank. Germany promised to resume trade negotiations immediately. Waldeck, whose mission had been postponed intermittently since January, finally arrived in Budapest on 23 May, and talks began the very next day. Germany promised to purchase Hungarian agricultural products, mainly cereals, fruits, eggs, poultry, and fish. A new clearing agreement was also incorporated into the Budapest Protocol and signed into force on 2 June 1933.[18]

All this was only a prelude. In the fall of 1933, von Papen and Waldeck hinted to István Winchkler of the Hungarian Trade Office that Germany was now ready to negotiate. This prompted Winchkler to urge that "now is the time to beat the German iron, while it is hot, as the situation is such that we can get everything we want. . ., even things hitherto unheard of."[19] At the end of November, a mixed commission began deliberations. Two weeks later, Karl Ritter, Director of the Economic Department of the German Foreign Ministry and István Winchkler, the Hungarian representative, held confidential preliminary conversations in Berlin. On 4 January 1934, Mackensen informed Kánya that the Reich proposed to commence full-fledged negotiations in Budapest within a fortnight. Simultaneously, Neurath informed Kánya that thanks to domestic economic conditions it was possible now to negotiate over several commodities. Waldeck, selected to chair a German delegation, was ordered "to conduct the negotiations with the firm determination to reach an early, positive conclusion."[20]

There were strong reasons why Germany entered negotiations apart from various Hungarian pressures. Hitler fretted because a customs union agreement linking Italy, Austria, and Hungary appeared to be imminent. If it succeeded, German plans for Austria's annexation and her hopes of Balkan domination would be frustrated as in March 1933. Although professing to be guided by the aim of granting Hungary a position in the German market which took into account the special Hungarian needs, Reich action sprang from self-interest. On 17 January Neurath, the Reich Ministers of Finance and Economics, and other high officials, met to determine economic concessions to Hungary for reasons of foreign policy. The minutes indicate that German concessions were spurred by the fear that Italy might succeed launching an Italo-Austro-Hungarian customs union. The conferees advocated a mighty German counterpoise in Hungary in order to dash Italy's efforts, and incidentally, to create a strong political perch for future use.[21]

The unique situation caused a discarding of the usual negotiating methods on trade agreements pursued thus far. Whatever benefits Hungary might derive would be immediately claimed by others on the basis of most-favoured-nation principles. Therefore, only a unilateral tariff reduction in a veiled form was to be considered for Hungary. In practical terms, this meant that the first stage in a promising National Socialist economic policy was about to be introduced. Under it, Germany undertook economic agreements containing secret paper savings for the "beneficiary." For the sake of secrecy, funds representing these make-believe concessions would be prorated among the various Reich Ministries. This method of veiled preferential treatment was to be used sparingly, and only on special occasions, as with Hungary. The Germans hoped to gain the Magyars' confidence by making them believe that they were the recipients of extraordinary economic largesse. For this purpose, the German negotiating team was grated a maximum of 15 million RM. the first year.

Henceforth negotiations proceeded with uncanny speed and amity. German negotiators only disputed 100,000 tons of Hungarian wheat. Since the Magyars expected soon to receive a windfall from their Italian and Austrian friends, they did not object when the Germans reduced the quota by one half. In all other respects, however, Germany promised to absorb meaningful, even vast, quantities of Hungarian agricultural staples and meat products of every description. The trade agreement, signed on 21 February 1934, was perhaps less spectacular for Hungary than the later Rome Protocols with Italy and Austria, but had far greater repercussions, thanks to Germany's superior economic potential. In every instance, prices considerably exceeded world market level. In return, Hungary promised to import a multitude of German industrial commodities. Initially, the treaty was so advantageous that Hungary's trade balance with Germany showed a surplus in the first year.[22]

The agreement with Germany represented a triumphant apogee for Hungarian diplomacy, typified by Gömbös' *Realpolitik*. In the year 1934, Hungary's two "protectors" were still approximately equal in strength and influence, and hence each state offered Hungary a perfect counterfoil to its rival. Germany hoped to deter Hungary from succumbing to the still very strong political pressure of Italy. Bulow thought Hungary would not lightly risk the very considerable advantages granted her by Germany and would be mindful of this in her political attitude and also with respect to commercial policy. Indeed, the Germans had inserted a three-month abrogation clause into the agreement that could be invoked by either party for any unspecified reason. Even during negotiations the Magyars were warned that Germany would deem an Austro-Hungarian or Italian-Hungarian customs union a just cause for terminating the treaty. Thanks to Gömbös' cool head and iron nerves Hungary charted a steady course between Scylla and Charybdis in the coming months.

German demands for fidelity marred Hungary's halcyon days. Commercial agreements carried steep price-tags. One week after the signing ceremonies, Horthy summoned Mackensen. Horthy, according to Mackensen's report, assiduously and repeatedly assured him that as long as he sat in his seat the axis of Hungarian policy, namely, the friendly relationship with Germany would remain unchanged. This principle must be kept in mind in order to reduce to their proper proportions the rumours about all sorts of political alignments that circulated here continually and had arisen particularly of late owing to the Dollfuss and Suvich visits. Horthy made other points. Any idea of a political alliance with Austria was absurd. He referred mainly to rumours about a possible Austro-Hungarian scheme under Habsburg auspices. An impending agreement with Austria, as with Italy, was strictly economic. Politically, Hungary adhered to Germany, as before, even if a tripartite pact with Austria and Italy should materialize. This Hungarian reserve was clearly understood in Rome. Turning to the deteriorating Austro-German controversy, Horthy related the gist of his recent conversation with Suvich and Dollfuss. He had told both statesmen that he was a friend to them, but Germany also. He had urged both to accept *Gleichschaltung* as a natural necessity which in the end would overcome all resistance. But Mackensen should urge Hitler to pursue toward Austria a good policy, that is, one of great restraint, and based on waiting calmly with confidence in final success. He explained that Suvich feared both *Anschluss* or *Gleichschaltung* because, either way, Germany would become so powerful that she would attempt to advance toward the Adriatic (to which Neurath added in the margin with true gallows humour: "and South Tyrol.").

Horthy finally convinced Mackensen that he meant to maintain Germany as the axis of Hungarian foreign policy, even in the event of Austria's *Gleichschaltung*. Mackensen ventured that, although the Regent was not the Government, he was sufficiently influential to make his views prevail. The Wilhelmstrasse remained skeptical.[23] Indeed, Horthy double-dealt by intimating that Hungary would not oppose Austria's *Gleichschaltung*. This violated the spirit of prior pledges to both Austria and Italy. But as any observer of the European scene knew, Austria's demise was merely a matter of time, a synthetic process even the great powers could not prevent. Why, then, should Hungary not derive some benefit by supporting a development she could not in any way prevent?

The Horthy-Mackensen dialogue was followed up by Masirevich two weeks later. He conceded to the suspicious Germans that the purpose of the tripartite negotiations in Rome was both economic *and* political. But, he explained truthfully, any agreement would leave the possibility open to Germany of likewise joining at a moment that appeared suitable to her. Masirevich begged the Germans to show understanding for Hungary's friendly intentions. Köpke could not at all understand the expediency of and necessity for the tripartite pact desired by Italy. Regardless how the negotiations turned out, the world would always suspect anti-German intentions. German-Hungarian relations were bound to suffer, because even in our country it would not be easy to convince the press to the contrary and to prevent unfriendly comments in the background. Finally, Germany would never become party to the projected agreements. When informed that Masirevich wished to pursue the question of a German-Hungarian consultative pact to be effected through an oral agreement, Bulow ventured:

> I am as little pleased with this as with yesterday's statements about an agreement in Rome which we were free to join. The whole thing has the taste of a bad conscience, and a search for an alibi.[24]

Bülow advocated rejecting Hungary's offer, and proposed an excuse: We must first see clearly where the Roman journey was leading. Neurath fully agreed.

A few days later, Bülow informed Mackensen that the German government was annoyed:

> We have the impression that the Hungarian government, by repeatedly proposing a consultative pact, was chiefly intent on obtaining from us a kind

of reassurance for the negotiations going on between Rome, Vienna, and Budapest. It obviously believes that by a pact it can shield itself from German recriminations on account of excessively close ties with Italy.[25]

Bülow concluded that such a pact would serve no useful purpose and merely lead to misunderstandings and complications.

The tripartite negotiations which worried Germany so much were conceived the previous June. Mussolini had judged the time ripe to forge an alliance composed of Italy, Hungary, and Austria, to force Germany to spare Austria, and acknowledge Italy's primacy in Central Europe. Mussolini urged sound Austro-Hungarian relations as the core and point of departure for every further development of Danubian Europe. This would be the first stage of wresting hegemony in the region. The second stage would arise when Hungary and Austria, supported by Italy, would extend their influence to neighbouring nations, especially Germany and the Little Entente. All this would be accomplished without political or economic compulsion that would deliver the small states to the mercy of the larger ones. Gömbös sought to turn Mussolini's desire to dominate Central Europe to Hungary's advantage. Two weeks later he was in Vienna, attempting to persuade Dollfuss to accommodate both Italy and Germany.

At the end of July Gömbös met Mussolini in Rome, partly to report on his talks with Dollfuss, partly to ascertain Mussolini's motives in signing the Four-Power Pact. Hungary distrusted Italy's leanings to France and the Little Entente, and feared attempts to induce Hungary to adopt similar policies. But Mussolini assured Gömbös that Franco-Italian understanding would not dash Hungary's just claims. First, the Little Entente would have to consider basic Hungarian demands. Mussolini even hoped for an early Franco-German rapprochement, no doubt as still another means toward Italian domination in Central Europe, and voiced a certain disappointment with Dollfuss, who showed signs of weakness toward Paris and Prague, as well as toward Marxism. Finally, continuing Austro-German tensions worried Mussolini as well as Gömbös and Kánya.[26]

By February 1934, Mussolini was fully convinced that Hitler had no intentions to abandon his Austrian intrigues. Also, German-Hungarian negotiations caused some concern in Rome. Ambassador Cerutti cried havoc, warning Masirevich that German promises were merely a smoke screen and a play on words; actually, the Austrian National Socialists planned to seize power and achieve *Gleichschaltung*. This, of course, was tantamount to *Anschluss*. Italy vowed to prevent Austria's destruction, whether by the first or the second method. A Three Power Declaration by England, France, and Italy, sponsored by Mussolini, would hopefully deter

Germany. But if Austria fell, Czechoslovakia's fate would be sealed and Hungary's position would also suffer. Cerutti was therefore thoroughly alarmed, convinced that within six to eight years, Germany would be strong enough to dictate the peace to the rest of the world. Masirevich deprecated Cerutti's alarm. Germany might soon be strong, but the Magyars had nothing to fear. On the contrary, a strong Germany best assured the success of Hungary's foreign policy objectives.[27] Mussolini's fear of Germany gave the Magyars the perfect pretext to maximize their demands in negotiating with Italy and Austria.

The Rome Protocols were signed on 17 March 1934. The pact joined Italy, Austria, and Hungary amid rumours of Austria's imminent invasion, with Italian troops deployed on the alert. The agreement established closer tripartite economic cooperation, consultation, and common policy. It bolstered Austria against German invasion, and prevented the country from falling into the French camp. In his talk with Mussolini on 13 March, Gömbös made certain stipulations favouring Germany. Appreciate as he would Austria's independence, Gömbös nonetheless refused to offend Germany on Austria's account. Gömbös needed Italy, yet Germany's importance was manifest in Hungary's fight against Czechoslovakia, and her dependence on the recent trade accord. Mussolini cautioned Gömbös not to rely on German aid against Czechoslovakia. Sooner or later, Hitler would pacify the Little Entente. But Gömbös refused to listen. Indeed, he insisted that Germany's intentions were essentially peaceful, and once again appealed for the eventual inclusion of Germany. Gömbös laid his cards on the table. Hungary intended to pursue an opportunistic foreign policy: south of the Danube it would be Italian-based; north of the Danube it would be German-based; the central portion inbetween—the Carpathian range—would become Hungary's own sphere of influence. Gömbös repeatedly rejected as alarmist Mussolini's persistent warnings that the German colossus planned to invest Southeast Europe. Buoyed by the recently concluded commercial agreement with Germany, he told Mussolini that the solution to every problem in the Danubian area depended entirely on the price Italy was prepared to pay for Hungarian wheat. The question was a matter of life and death for Hungary, and consequently he would insist on higher wheat prices. Confronted with the reality of the German-Hungarian trade agreement, Mussolini had to agree.[28]

The Rome Pact was the most ambitious and last assertion of Italian predominance in Central Europe. To Hungary, the agreement represented a short-run windfall. The highly publicized prolonged negotiations had prodded the Germans to reach a trade agreement acceptable to the Magyars. The Rome Protocols, signed only a few weeks after the ratification of the

German-Hungarian agreement, benefited the linchpin of Hungary's econo-my, the wheat producer. Austria pledged to purchase 220,000 tons of Hungarian wheat or wheat flour; Italy's share was 100,000 tons the first year, with a similar option the following year, at twice above world market prices. In 1936, Italy and Austria jointly absorbed 400,000 tons of Hungarian wheat and wheat flour, or more than four-fifths of Hungary's total wheat export. In return, Hungary enjoyed quantities of Italian and Austrian industrial commodities until 1937, when a multitude of political and economic difficulties disqualified Italy's desirability as a trade partner.

As soon as the provisions of the Rome Protocols became known, Bülow protested that the treaty made Austria an Italian protectorate, requiring Mussolini's sanction for its foreign policy. Germany vowed to foil the Treaty by destroying Austria. Overt attacks would yield to a "new course," a long-range plan, designed to paralyze Austria's government unless it capitulated to the outlawed National Socialist Party. Hungary also felt German ire. Bülow denounced Hungary for having soothed Germany up to the very last day that no political agreements would be reached in Rome. Yet the pact had an unmistakable tendency against Germany. Hungary had hoodwinked Germany all along with her offer of a consultative pact. In an obvious allusion to the German-Hungarian commercial treaty, Bülow stated: "In spite of everything that has been discussed of late between us. . . the future development of German-Hungarian relations will be substantial-ly influenced by the practical consequences of the consultative pact of Rome." Mackensen was ordered to be "quite outspoken in your conversa-tions about this position of ours."[29]

German charges of Hungarian duplicity caused angry Magyars to attack, not cringe. Mackensen injudiciously chose a luncheon to upbraid Kánya for Hungary's behaviour. Mackensen's tirade prompted Kánya to assert that while in Rome, Gömbös never for one moment lost sight of German-Hungarian relations. On the contrary: he had almost rudely defied Mussoli-ni, especially concerning Austrian security. Gömbös would remain neutral in a German-Italian confrontation. Kánya argued unconvincingly that Hungary's consultative pact with Italy was not subservient but harmoniz-ing, since Hungary retained full exercise of her freedom. Hungary's position vis-à-vis Italy would be far stronger still had Germany responded to pleas for a German-Hungarian consultative pact. Besides, why not turn to Rome? When Germany was "flirting" with Yugoslavia, only Italy supported Hungary against the Little Entente. Hungary sought a just balance for both Italy and Germany. Mackensen substantiated this when he learned that Gömbös had clearly expressed in his Council of Ministers recently that Hungary would never treat with Italy at the cost of German-Hungarian friendship.

Magyar diplomats thereupon behaved as though sheer sincerity would exorcise German doubts. On 21 March, Masirevich confronted Neurath with the same story he had pursued ten days earlier with Bülow, asserting that Hungary was not in any way bound by the Rome Protocols, since Gömbös had reserved his freedom of action in political and economic matters. Neurath sarcastically congratulated Masirevich and Gömbös on this optimistic view, upon which "Signor Mussolini would be of a different opinion." Neurath reiterated Bülow's charge that in tendency at least the pact was anti-German. Masirevich vehemently denied this, whereupon Neurath again declined a German-Hungarian consultative pact.

German-Hungarian relations thus reached the brink of abyss. Should Germany adversely interpret the Rome Protocols, then the German-Hungarian trade pact might soon lapse. The situation demanded infinite tact and a hair-trigger sense of timing. Gömbös not only defused the issue and rescued the Rome Protocols, he also continued to generate his German-Italian rapprochement plans under Hungarian auspices. Gömbös summoned Mackensen. In view of their personal relationship of mutual trust, but with the request for the strictest discretion, he produced his own minutes of the Rome Protocols. They bore out Magyar assertions, since Gömbös had indeed told Mussolini that without German participation any large-scale solution of the Central European problem was doomed; that Hungary would not imperil German friendship by cooperating with others powers; and that the Austro-German dispute had to be settled urgently. Gömbös had disclaimed any desire to support the present Austrian regime at all cost. Both he and Mussolini believed that Dollfuss was no longer reliable. Why not resolve the Austrian controversy by a direct confrontation between Mussolini and Hitler? Mussolini had stressed practical difficulties barring such a meeting without rejecting it in principle. Yet Gombos inferred that Austria no longer obstructed a German-Hungarian accommodation. Consequently a German-Italian reconciliation was possible and would settle all outstanding Danubian issues.

Gömbös thus tried to allay German concern that Hungary's interference in Austria would once again dash Germany's annexationist plans. To reinforce this, the Magyars followed through several weeks later, stressing the need for absolute secrecy. Well they might, for it would be awkward if either the Italians or the Austrians should learn of this gambit. Kánya summoned Mackensen to a top-secret meeting with Horthy, who wished to relay a message to Neurath (who was Mackensen's father-in-law). For obvious reasons, Gömbös was the only other person privy to this interview. The Regent offered to settle the Austrian problem along German lines, because he no longer trusted Dollfuss. Dollfuss had recently promulgated a new constitution, which partially indemnified the House of Habsburg, and permitted many of its members to return. Horthy feared a Habsburg restoration, since Hungary would be swept into the maelstrom. The Regent inquired whether Hungary might somehow contribute to the solution. He suggested an Austro-German reconciliation plan along palatable lines for both Hungary and Germany.

The message, and the suggestion for joint action, were vague and insubstantial. In Mackensen's view, they provided hardly any basis for further discussion. Kánya admitted that these were, after all, merely unofficial soundings and there were weighty objections to carrying out the idea. Moreover, even if Germany agreed, he would, of course, have first to make sure in Vienna as to how far he could go in Berlin. Hungary's secret plan had a whiff of hoax similar to previous attempts. Yet it worked, if its chief aim was to assuage German fears and restore benevolence. Mackensen believed the Regent to be "by far our most reliable friend here. With him friendly relations with Berlin take a marked precedence over those with Rome." The offer also proved Gömbös' sincerity in his assurances that for Hungary the Austrian question did not belong to those questions which the Hungarians had first to discuss with Rome according to Protocol I of the Rome Pact. Despite a demurring Kánya, Mackensen thought that both Gömbös and Horthy had the best intentions. Hitler rejected the Horthy proposal, as Kánya knew he would, but Germany softened. Neurath granted that the Habsburg problem could lead to very awkward consequences, especially for Hungary. He appreciated Hungary's good intentions and would be glad to help it in averting the possible dangers of the Habsburg propaganda. Neurath commissioned Mackensen to tell Kánya, and if necessary, the Regent, that he was especially grateful for their efforts to solve the German-Austrian question.[30]

Despite his diplomatic triumphs Gömbös had to perform a balancing act lest he antagonize his hyper-sensitive Italian and German allies. In Parliament he stressed how vital the Rome Pact was for European peace and security. Italy stabilized and normalized economic and political conditions in Central and Eastern Europe. Gömbös then oozed over Germany so much that his legitimist opponents labelled him "Germanophil." Although greatly interested in Austria's fate, Magyars could scarcely ignore seventy million Germans so close to home. Since Germany wielded preeminent power in the Danube Basin, Hungary must never resist the Reich unless she was forced to adopt National Socialism.[31]

The Germans were not pleased. Mackensen criticized Gömbös for praising the Italians but not the Germans, and for ignoring the German-Hungarian trade agreement. Obviously Gömbös had to flatter Mussolini, because Hungary planned to raise wheat prices. But Germany had one consolation. Whatever his personal feelings, Gömbös was a hard-headed realist. He clearly understood what it meant to have seventy million Germans permanently ensconced near Hungary's frontiers. The ripples of Gömbös' speech washed all the way to the Wilhelmstrasse. Masirevich burst into Bülow's office in a highly agitated state, with a copy of the 24 May issue of the *Völkischer Beobachter.* Its Budapest correspondent had reacted violently to the Gömbös speech, and severely criticized Hungary's internal policies and anti-German tendencies. Bülow bagatellized the article and others like it, and tried to convince Masirevich that the correspondent had overreacted. In his report to Neurath, however, Bulow counselled caution. In view of Hungary's importance, anti-Magyar sentiments in Germany should be concealed, not broadcast among the impressionable public.[32]

In the coming months, the Germans tried to curry Magyar favour, exemplified by the Budapest visit of Bavarian Minister Esser and his entourage. They visited Hungary for propaganda purposes and to create mutual good will, under the watchful eye of a special German Foreign Ministry agent. Mackensen regaled the visitors with rosy pictures about German-Hungarian relations and smoothed over various points of friction. But Schlimpert, a brash, young legation clerk, plied Esser with the sordid "actual situation." Hungary was lost soil for Germany, a nation whose government only feigned a pro-German policy. The Italians, who treated the Magyars like low vassals, were in control. It amazed Schlimpert why the Magyars tolerated such servitude. In his view, Hungary's friendship was but a crown of thorns for Germany, who ought to propagandize more to counterant the overwhelmingly anti-German Magyar press. Esser rebuked Schlimpert, especially for not having taken the trouble to learn Magyar after three years. Publicly Esser swore that Schlimpert would be punished, but after his return, he relayed Schlimpert's views and proposals to Hitler.[33]

The Schlimpert incident caused a minor tempest. The Magyars took Schlimpert's calumnies to heart, and lodged a protest. Not content to complain about one minor matter, Masirevich appeared at the Foreign Ministry with still another offending copy of the *Völkischer Beobachter.* The Budapest correspondent had struck again, by assailing the Hungarian invitation to delegates of the French Chamber of Deputies for a brief Budapest visit. Köpke attempted to deprecate the Schlimpert incident and said jokingly: "So, that Schlimpert! It is for him that Budapest is lost territory, for he is being transferred to Montreal. He is young; he was long enough in Budapest; he should see the world a bit." Köpke implied, of course, that Schlimpert was being punished; at least this was Masirevich's impression. In fact, the Germans disparaged the matter and had no plans to curb the anti-Hungarian press. Still, the Germans gradually realized they were treading on sensitive Magyar toes. In response to numerous complaints involving mainly abuses of Magyar hospitality by German visitors, they decided to curtail organized German youth (*Wandervögel*) excursions into Hungary.[34]

These relatively minor disagreements paled, thanks partly to French machinations. During his Eastern European propaganda tour, French Foreign Minister Barthou delivered a number of inflammatory statements in Rumania. Defying historical accuracy as well as prudence, Barthou told Rumanians that Transylvania had always been theirs, and pledged that with French help it would remain theirs forever. This outraged the Magyars and rallied even Francophils to Gömbös' side. Thanks to French instigation, Hungary and Czechoslovakia collided. Trade virtually stopped. Both sides castigated each other. Italy began to vilify Yugoslavia. In Sopron, Gömbös delivered the most uncompromising speech of his career against the Little Entente. Mackensen thought that recent chaotic international events at last justified Gömbös' pet thesis. A Rome-Budapest-Vienna-Berlin axis was indeed a vital necessity for stability.[35] The problem was that events outstripped even the dynamic tempo of National Socialist objectives. At a time when France bolstered her Eastern and Central European alliances, Germany had neither wish nor capability to be swept into war. The aggressive French, no less than the impetuous Italians and Magyars, sorely tried the unprepared Germans' patience. Hungary, with the aid of Italy, or France, with the help of the Little Entente, might yet preempt Germany.

To combat these pressures, Germany acted on a variety of fronts. On 26 January 1934, Germany dented the French alliance system by concluding a ten-year non-aggression pact with Poland. In March, Germany initiated discussions with Yugoslavia. Both feared a Habsburg restoration in Austria, both resented Italian intrigues in the Balkans. Securing Yugoslavia's friendship would dash both Italian and French designs. On 14 June, Hitler and Mussolini met in Venice for the first time, but Germany failed to derive the expected benefits. On the contrary, relations deteriorated. Then, the Great Blood Purge of 30 June eliminated Hitler's sole remaining domestic opposition. Thus reinforced, on 25 July he attempted to kick the props from both the Rome Pact and the Little Entente by instigating a putsch in Austria. Thanks to Italy's timely and energetic intervention the plot failed, but it left unconcealed hatreds in its wake. The ensuing diplomatic relations between Germany and the Rome Pact nations must be viewed within this context.

Having achieved an economic accommodation with both Italy and Germany, Hungary had passed the first phase of revisionism. Next, Gömbös had to reconcile Austria and Germany before closing the rift between Italy and Germany. In the meantime, he had to exercise great care lest he offend his sensitive patrons. He also had to keep Hungary from becoming a vassal to one or the other Great Power.

German-Hungarian relations had been sorely strained by the Austrian putsch, which underscored Hungary's fragility. Her excellent strategic situation was an asset only while Austria remained independent. Fortunately, Hungary was forewarned, as the coup was not totally unexpected, but preceded by intense diplomatic activities. In April 1934, von Papen and Mussolini met twice in Rome. It was on the basis of these visits that Hitler decided to meet Mussolini face to face. At issue was not only Austria but German-Italian relations. This 14 June meeting was just as unproductive as Horthy's mediation offer. Hitler had advised Horthy two weeks earlier that Dollfuss must first establish his claim to represent the Austrian people through a plebiscite. Mussolini rejected Hitler's proposals, especially those involving a plebiscite. On its basis the Austrian National Socialists would be admitted into the Dollfuss cabinet. Mussolini also condemned Nazi terror tactics. Peace was impossible until Hitler vouchsafed Austria's inner tranquility.[36] The abortive July coup, which claimed Dollfuss' life, strengthened the Rome Pact immeasurably, but it also left Germany frustrated and resentful. For a while, Hungarian mediation efforts were next to impossible.

Gömbös thus had to soothe a ruffled Germany. A few days after Dollfuss' assassination, it came to Hassell's attention in Rome that the Magyars were reconciled to the murder. Gömbös had allegedly informed the Italian ambassador that, although Dollfuss' demise was regrettable, Germany's friendship was far too valuable to risk because of the excesses perpetrated by the Austrian National Socialists.[37] Gömbös probably had this information leaked for German consumption. He dismissed the putsch and the assassination as the work of irresponsible local elements, whom the German government had already disowned, and thus saved them the embarrassment of having to justify their complicity.

Gömbös' apparent disinterestment in the Austrian affair helped keep the lifeline to Berlin open. At Neurath's suggestion, Hitler granted a special audience to Kánya on 6 August, immediately after the funeral services for the late Reich President von Hindenburg. Kánya wasted no time on preliminaries. Thus far, Hungary had steadfastly refused to join any French-inspired Danubian federation plan. But she had become completely surrounded by a band of hostile states. The only exception was Austria, Hungary's sole link to Germany, indeed, to the outside world. Hungary desperately needed Germany's help to crack her encirclement, and therefore, Hungary had German-Italian and German-Austrian relations very much at heart. Indeed, the Danube question could not be solved either in opposition to Hungary or without her. Collaboration between Hungary and Austria, supported by Germany and Italy, was therefore desirable. This, in a nutshell, was the Gombos thesis. As usual, the Magyars flaunted it, along with their strategic importance.

Hitler parried. He would not negotiate with Austria because the new Chancellor, Schuschnigg, lacked a popular mandate, just like his predecessor. Austria might soon disappear if current conditions persisted. Yet Hitler claimed to be reasonable and did not desire *Anschluss*, which would economically burden his poor Reich. Let an honourable and neutral man become Austrian chancellor, as he had already suggested to Mussolini in Venice, and let the Austrian National Socialists enter government; and reconciliation would follow naturally. Hitler next tried to separate Austria and Hungary. He compared the martyrdom of the recently executed Nazi conspirators Planetta and Holzweber, and Austria's execution of Hungary's revolutionaries in 1849. Hitler also claimed the oppression of a large section of the German people in Austria, and appealed for sympathy, for Hungary could not keep up a friendship with a country within whose borders people of Hungarian stock were being oppressed. Hitler softened: His friendship with Mussolini did indeed matter more to him than the whole of the Austrian State. Finally, Hitler stated that Gömbös "would give him pleasure by paying him another visit."[38] Although in many ways an unsatisfactory interview, it at least gave the Magyars expectations as future matchmakers. Henceforth, Gömbös lost no opportunity to convince the Germans that reconciliation with Austria and Italy would benefit them, and that they might rely on his mediation.

Gömbös knew from experience that the Germans always distrusted Austro-Hungarian intimacies. This was doubly true when Schuschnigg appeared on the scene. Schuschnigg's tough anti-Nazi stand infuriated Hitler. A few days after the Kánya—Hitler encounter, Schuschnigg visited Hungary, where he talked with Horthy and Gömbös. In his memoirs, Schuschnigg recounts that Horthy urged compromise with the Third Reich. Schuschnigg must not rely on Hungarian help, because the quarrel with Czechoslovakia made Germany's friendship indispensable. Schuschnigg also encountered difficulties with Gömbös on the Habsburg issue. He allegedly assured Gömbös that restoration was not currently feasible, and in any event, nothing would be done without prior consultation. This was an evasion on this sensitive issue. From Hungary, Schuschnigg travelled to Florence for a meeting with Mussolini, who gave elaborate assurances of economic and military aid in the event of a German invasion. Mussolini was to have referred to Austria, Hungary, and Italy, rather optimistically, as "a bloc of 60-70 million people, who must be taken seriously.[39] Evidently, there were fundamental differences of opinion and interpretation between Rome and Budapest as to the meaning and viability of the Tripartite Pact.

After Schuschnigg's departure, Gömbös immediately summoned Mackensen in order to dispel any German suspicions and misinterpretations about the visit. If Mackensen's reportage was accurate, then Mussolini and Schuschnigg were living in a fool's paradise. Schuschnigg had created a good impression in Hungary, and Gömbös thought the new chancellor was guided by sincere German sentiments. Nonetheless, Gömbös had warned Schuschnigg that under no circumstances would Hungary get involved in Austrian intrigues. This was an euphemism for the Austro-German controversy. Schuschnigg was told to abandon Dollfuss' rigid image, slowly develop his own style, and create conditions in Austria that would promote change. This was another euphemism for Gleichschaltung. Next, Gömbös defended himself against German taunts that he was Mussolini's stooge. On the contrary, he protested. During the July crisis he had criticized Mussolini's mobilization as an offensive measure that might have invited a Yugoslav invasion of Austria. Gömbös had also taunted Mussolini that man for man, one Yugoslav soldier was the equal of four Italians. Further, he had flatly and repeatedly refused to participate in Italy's anti-German press campaigns. Finally, Gömbös deprecated as unimportant the recent Mussolini-Schuschnigg encounter in Florence, as well as circulating rumours of a Franco-German rapprochement. Mackensen detected a noticeable cooling between Italy and Hungary. Obviously, Gömbös was not kept informed about the Schuschnigg discussions. In any event, Mackensen reported, even if Italy plotted to dominate Austria with Schuschnigg's connivance, Gömbös believed that neither France nor England would tolerate it.

Hungary's diplomatic strategy with Germany was well-coordinated. On 13 September, Pesti Hirlap published a lead article commissioned by the government but authored by Bethlen. At least this is what Masirevich led the Wilhelmstrasse to believe. Bethlen clearly enunciated a refined version of Gömbös' blunt foreign policy. As Hungary's destiny rested on the principle of German-Italian balance, Hungary had to be meticulously faithful to both. The Rome Pact demanded loyalty to Italy and beleaguered Austria, but Hungary should never forget that the peace treaties had brought about the sharing of a common German-Hungarian destiny. Germany and Germandom were the chief power brokers in Eastern Europe. Magyars must also keep in mind that Hitlerite Germany had shown great concern for Hungary's economic welfare, and wished to develop favourable trade relations. The Magyars wasted little time. The very next day, Masirevich appeared at the Wilhelmstrasse expressing his government's gratitude that the German press had so rapidly and prominently commented on the Bethlen piece, which, the Minister reemphasized, had official origins. He immediately turned to German-Italian relations, reiterating that the dangerous Austrian situation would be defused immediately if only Germany joined the Rome Pact. The Germans demurred, citing their usual well-known arguments. Masirevich thereupon stated that Gömbös' impending Warsaw visit had nothing to do with Germany, and promised to keep the Wilhelmstrasse informed about further developments.[40]

That Hungary's persistent wooing of Germany bore results became manifest the following month when von Papen appeared in Budapest. Papen led András Hory (Kánya's deputy) to believe that Germany had begun seriously to consider Gömbös' pet scheme of making Rome-Berlin the axis of Hungarian foreign policy. In his conversations with Hory, and later with Papen, and in his subsequent report to the Foreign Ministry, Mackensen expressed vast surprise. He had been unaware that Germany had evolved a brand new foreign policy. But Hory refused to believe Mackensen's cautionary note because he became a victim of his own wishful thinking. Papen, too, stuck to his guns, and informed Hory that, although the matter was not acute at the moment, he had nonetheless discussed and analyzed exhaustively with Hitler the possibilities that Germany might join the Rome Pact. Whatever, Hory became convinced that Germany would soon take certain positive steps to expedite Gömbös' plans.[41]

Subsequent events strengthened both Hungary's resolve and opportunities to pursue German participation in the Rome Pact. The assassination of Barthou and King Alexander of Yugoslavia temporarily confounded the French alliance system. On the eve of Gömbös' Warsaw trip in connection with a Hungarian-Polish cultural agreement, German Minister of Education Rust arrived in Budapest for discussions with Gömbös and Horthy. Both touched upon the Austrian question and German-Italian relations in every conversation. Gömbös proposed that when in Warsaw (19-22 October), he would attempt extending the Rome Pact not only to Germany but to Poland. The idea of an alliance system composed of Italy, Austria, Hungary, Poland, and Germany, appealed to Mackensen. After his Warsaw trip, Gömbös said, he would sound out Mussolini's view on this project in person, convinced that Mussolini, who was basically friendly to Germany, would endorse the idea. If the "Gömbös plan" materialized, Germany would avert a collision with Italy in Southeastern Europe. Germany's center of gravity then could harmlessly shift northward. Gömbös apparently took his own idea very seriously, because he broached it to Papen during his next visit.[42]

In Italy, Hassell provided still another view on Hungary's mounting diplomatic offensive. Hassell reported a conversation with Kánya, who had been vacationing in San Remo and holding discussions with Mussolini and other high officials. Kánya told Hassell that Italy's leaders no longer resented Germany, but they still harboured strong suspicions because Germany flirted with the Little Entente, especially with Yugoslavia, Italy's *bête noire*. Göring's October visit and provocative assertions in Belgrade were hardly designed to soothe either Hungarian or Italian sensibilities.[43] Nor did the Italians believe that Germany had really abandoned its annexationist "Habicht policy" in Austria. Hassell countered that the idea of a conspiracy between Germany and the Little Entente was ridiculous. Connections were strictly commercial. True, Italy's anti-German press campaign, maintained ever since the Austrian putsch, might drive Germany into Yugoslavia's arms. But this merely proved that Budapest's rapport with Berlin and Rome would have to be supplemented by improved relations between Rome and Berlin. Kánya thereupon reminded Hassell of the dangers all three nations faced should reconciliation fail. He had recently asked the Italians what substitute they had to take Germany's place. The Italians had been silent. Kánya posed a somewhat similar question: What if Germany, as a result of deteriorating relations with Italy, should discard Hungary as an ally? He answered his own question. Hungary would perforce seek an accommodation with the Little Entente, distasteful though it might be. Hungarians felt great sympathy for embattled Austria, and hoped that Germany would make a *beau geste* for the sake of improved relations.[44]

Around this time, a fundamental reorganization occurred in the German Foreign Ministry section dedicated to Southeastern European affairs, an area becoming increasingly more important in Germany's plans. A position paper circulated by its new section chief on German objectives and Hungary's role in the Balkans graphically illuminated the vast gulf, but also a certain convergence in German and Hungarian foreign policies. Essentially, the plan entailed economic and political domination of the Balkans by Germany, to be achieved through the use of different sets of coordinates than those suggested by the Magyars. Hungary hoped for a four-power alliance linking Hungary, Italy, Austria, and Germany, with Poland looming as a possible fifth member; Germany would discard Rome and Vienna in favour of Warsaw and Belgrade. This was to be as effective as Bismarck's Russian strategy. Hungarian foreign policy was defective because it insisted on achieving territorial gains from three countries simultaneously. This fallacy had brought about Hungary's encirclement. Hungary's Italian connection was illusory. Italy exploited Hungary's territorial hunger, but never intended to help in any way. Germany must therefore convince the Magyars of their folly and persuade them to relinquish their Yugoslav claims entirely, their Rumanian demands temporarily. Only joint German-Hungarian action would enable the Magyars to satisfy their revisionist aspirations in Czechoslovakia, provided Yugoslavia defected from the Little Entente. Hungary's Rumanian claims would be furthered by cultivating a Polish alliance. Germany's strategy thus rested on two indispensable pillars: Hungary and Yugoslavia. Consequently Germany must reconcile those two countries. Germany must also assiduously cater to Hungary's economic needs, systematically develop domestic markets for Hungarian surpluses, and offer Hungary substantial and advantageous commercial treaties, not *ad hoc* arrangements as in the past.[45] Another important new aspect of German diplomacy was the cessation of attacks on Hungary for her abuse of the Swabians. Already in November 1933, Hitler directed Mackensen to treat the Swabian problem gently, in order not to aggravate the far more important German-Hungarian relations. This, then, became basic German policy during the Gömbös era. It explains why Göring's off-the-cuff remarks that Hungary abused the Swabians was disclaimed by all German officials. Nor was this the only incident requiring German disclaimers. Hungary's chief consul Velics in Munich assailed the noted Professor Benno Graf's public lecture on the Swabians as an unexempled outrage in the 4 March 1934 issue of *Szabadság*. The Bavarian State Chancellery thereupon rebuked Graf and promised to gag him. Even Rudolf Hess became concerned. Well he might, for Vélics detected another anti-Magyar speech delivered by Graf in Passau. Vélics also discovered that Graf was regional instructor *(Landesschulungsleiter)* of the *VDA* in Bavaria and hence closely connected with government. Thereupon the consul began to suspect German duplicity.[46]

In the new year, various complications further eroded the existing European power structure. The Franco-Italian rapprochement, modestly begun in the summer of 1934 when Barthou was still alive, gathered momentum when the Italophil Pierre Laval replaced him. This strained German-Italian relations, and imperilled the Rome Pact. On 4 January 1935, Italy's ambassador delivered to Bülow a copy of the Franco-Italian procès-verbal agreed upon in Rome. The agreement left the door open for Austria, Yugoslavia, Czechoslovakia, Hungary, and Germany. England and Rumania might also join later. Members would have to pledge noninterference in each others' internal affairs. There was also to be a Franco-Italian consultative pact, designed specifically to defend Austria. This had an anti-German ring. But the ambassador insisted that this was merely a first step to an international settlement in the East, resembling the Four Power agreement, now moribund, of which Germany was also a member. Eventually members might sponsor a disarmament or armaments convention. France and Italy even planned to heal the Yugoslav-Hungarian controversy. Bülow attacked the plan. It would dash forever Hungary's revisionist hopes, the very thing Italy had promised to support. He recalled that

> the Ambassador took this remark in bad part. He declared that Hungary had had the sense to demand only a peaceful revision based on Article 19 of the League of Nations Covenant, and Italy had recently, on the occasion of the Gömbös visit, given Hungary a binding promise, which she meant to keep, not to spoil Hungary's chances of revision, but rather to continue to further Hungarian claims.[47]

This nonetheless proved what the Germans had suspected all along: Italy wished to pay only lip service to Hungarian revisionism. Indeed, the Ambassador finally admitted under pressure that Hungary's chances for success were remote.

Only a few hours earlier, Bülow had received Masirevich. By then, both diplomats more or less knew the gist of the Franco-Italian agreement. Masirevich thought the Germans fared badly, as the pact was obviously directed against them. If only Germany pledged to respect Austria's independence unconditionally, then the Franco-Italian agreement would collapse. Bülow procrastinated. First, he would have to see the authentic text; moreover, Germany might even live with certain aspects of the pact; thus he tantalized Masirevich. Regarding Austria, nothing more could be said that had not been disclosed before. Bülow no doubt meant von Papen's statement to Bethlen in Vienna at the end of November 1934: Germany demanded gradual amnesty for the culprits of 25 July, National Socialist participation in the *Vaterländische Front,* and eventually, representation in government. Only then would Germany stop intervening in Austria's internal affairs and recognize Austrian independence. Bülow thus left the Hungarians dangling between two fires.

The following day, Bülow chipped away at the Austrian leg of the Rome Pact triangle when he divulged to the Austrian Minister the terms of the Franco-Italian pact. Evidently, there were two sets of agreements: a nonintervention pact governing the Austro-German, Hungarian-Yugoslav, and Italian-Yugoslav disputes; and a separate Franco-Italian consultative pact, "which implied a sort of protectorate by these Powers over Austria." The Austrian Minister was aghast. He thought the agreement merely guaranteed Austrian independence. Instead, Austria, while saved from the German danger, would become a Franco-Italian vassal. The two diplomats parted with mutual assurances of good will and friendly hopes for the future, sentiments the Austrian could hardly entertain in view of the bleak alternatives facing his country.[48]

Italy's diplomacy brought the Tripartite Pact into jeopardy. Hungary had tried to dissuade Mussolini from embarking on his agreement with France. In his letter of 26 December, Gömbös informed Mussolini that Hungary would assent only if Italy continued to champion Hungary's revisionist claims. Mussolini immediately agreed (on 29 December) and promised to brief Gömbös on developments. Still Gömbös fretted, and spelled out his demands in minute detail. All three Little Entente members had to agree to a territorial settlement. This was mandatory; remaining Magyars had to have cultural autonomy; and Hungary had to be granted economic political, and military equality. Mussolini thereupon briefed the Magyars on the intricacies of the agreement, whereupon Kánya wired his displeasure to Rome. It seemed to him that Italy had irrevocably repudiated Hungarian revisionism, Mussolini's promises of 29 December notwithstanding. Hungary would not join unless she obtained ironclad assurances that the Magyar minorities would be protected, and in German company. This was a blow, since Mussolini wished to pursue his African ambitions with French support. Naturally, he also wished to prevent a Franco-German rapprochement, which appeared to be in the making. Without Hungary's steadfast support in Eastern Europe, all his grandiose schemes would collapse. Shortly Gömbös complained that the Franco-Italian pact constituted an inappropriate gesture. Austrian independence ought to concern not only Italy and France but all the great Powers, including Germany. It was deplorable for France to extort a guarantee of the Little Entente's territorial integrity from Hungary under the guise of protecting Austria. Mussolini ought to revise the clause pertaining to Austria; let there be a simple statement guaranteeing her independence. Gömbös feared that the Rome Pact might not survive this crisis.

Mussolini ignored Gömbös. On 7 January he met Laval, and ratified the Franco-Italian agreement. He felt triumphant negotiating an accommodation with France over Africa, and obtaining Laval's pledge to win over Britain. To Hungary's Villani Mussolini was brutally frank; in view of the impending Ethiopian war, he needed French support desperately. As a result of these events Italian-Hungarian relations suffered. On 11 January, Baron Aloisi, Italy's League representative, castigated Kánya in Geneva for Hungary's "unfriendly posture" during Franco-Italian negotiations. Hungarian intransigence, aggravated by Gömbös' blunt letter of 4 January, had offended Mussolini. Aloisi reiterated that Hungary would benefit from a new Danubian pact under Franco-Italian auspices. Germany's place as guarantor of peace and justice in the Danube Basin would be taken by France, who would honour Hungary's territorial demands. Kánya gasped at this distortion of diplomatic realities. France would never support Hungary against the Little Entente. Hence Hungary had to obtain far-reaching minority guarantees and parity in armaments, otherwise she would sabotage the pact. Mussolini lost his credibility and his hard won strategic position in Southeastern Europe for questionable advantages in Africa. Bereft of Italy's support, and imperilled by French power, Hungary had only Germany left. Consequently Austria had to seek an accommodation with Germany as well.[49] For all practical purposes, the Rome Pact was moribund, its two junior members cast adrift on dangerous diplomatic high seas.

At the end of January, the Hungarian Foreign Ministry staff and Mackensen met to review various diplomatic options. Understandably, Germany would not participate in a proposed Danubian Pact because the meaning of "non-intervention" was unexplained and because it sought remedies for Danubian problems under the aegis of the hated League. Anti-Italian feelings mounted in Germany, especially among the military. Hitler had still not forgiven Mussolini for his extraordinarily sharp press war after Dollfuss' assassination. Hitler suspected that Franco-Italian rapprochement prompted Mussolini to sabotage the Saar settlement in Germany's favour. The Austrian problem defied solution because the German National Socialist Party treated it as a party matter rather than a foreign policy question. Thus far, said Mackensen, Hitler championed the Party's view, despite Neurath's energetic protests. German-Hungarian relations were unchanged. The news media caused much dissension in both countries. Mackensen promised to establish guidelines for the press, but conceded that little could be done. National Socialist journalists did not take orders from the Foreign Ministry, a bureau they associated with the old regime. Finally, Mackensen asked the Magyars about deteriorating Hungarian-Yugoslav relations, in which Germany had a vested interest.

Hungarian officials clarified certain moot points in the Rome Pact that still eluded the Germans and explained that current Hungarian-Yugoslav disagreements were not Hungary's fault. King Alexander's assassins had been traced to Hungary, and Yugoslavia demanded compensation. But the League had exonerated Hungary and now she wished to terminate the affair. It was regrettable that German-Italian relations had not improved. Germany's Austrian policy was correct in principle but why insist on settling foreign affairs on the merits of internal policy? This was a blunder, and the cause of France's long-standing and Italy's recent unremitting fright of the National Socialist menace. No wonder they attempted to defend themselves with every means at their disposal.[50]

This conference was important, not so much for what it accomplished in a practical sense, but for the attitudes it revealed. Mackensen's discourse indicated Hitler's growing stubbornness and paranoia, for he would not listen to Neurath's good advice and settle the Austrian question diplomatically. Nor would he curb the National Socialist Party and press, though it imperilled relations even with Hungary, a nation whose support he badly needed. Mackensen's dialogue also disclosed the growing rift in Germany between the old guard of the diplomatic corps, and the impulsive radicals of the National Socialist Party, who detested the bastion of conservatism in the Wilhelmstrasse. Paradoxically, Germany's growing might frightened Europe's Great Powers, rather than Eastern Europe's smaller, defenseless countries. The former feared the loss of their influence in the Balkans, whereas the latter hoped to derive economic benefits from a vigorous, restored German Reich. The events of the next few years must be considered in the light of this paradox.

Unreasoning fright of Germany found ineffectual expression once again in the spring of 1935. On 16 March, Germany denounced the armaments clauses of the Treaty of Versailles, and the three Great Powers—Italy, Britain and France—met in Stresa on 11-14 April to formulate common counteraction. They attempted in vain to secure assurances from Germany. Hitler refused to conclude a non-aggression treaty or air-limitation agreement, or to guarantee Austria's independence. The only tangible result toward a rapprochement, the Anglo-German naval agreement of 18 June, was a covert German victory that drove a wedge between England and France. The Ethiopian war in October alienated the Italians from England and France, and the Stresa Front disintegrated.

On 6 May, while Italy still basked in the security of the Stresa Front, the foreign ministers of the signatories of the Rome Protocols held a meeting in Venice. Suvich relayed Mussolini's message to Kánya on the question of Hungary's hoped-for participation in the Franco-Italian reorganization plan for the Danube Basin. Hungary was infinitely better off with Italy and France than with Germany. She had nothing to fear from France, because the importance of the Little Entente would henceforth diminish. But if Germany won the next war, Hungary and Austria would be incorporated into the Reich. If Germany lost the war, the victorious Western Powers would eradicate Germany's smaller confederates from the face of the map. It made eminent sense, therefore, that sticking to Germany must bring Hungary to grief. Next, Suvich sounded Hungary's reaction to the possibility of a Habsburg restoration in Austria. Momentarily, both Italy and France believed that restoration presented perhaps the only effective countervailing force to National Socialism.

Kánya completely demolished Mussolini's hopes of becoming the chief architect of a Franco-Italian Pax Danubia. He refused to extend the Rome Pact to include the Little Entente. Hungary would stick to her territorial claims, demand ironclad guarantees on minority protection, and maintain peaceful revisionist propaganda. On restoration Gömbös was antagonistic, partly to stifle considerable legitimist sentiments in Hungary, and partly to prevent a collision with Germany and Yugoslavia. Kánya even opposed strengthening the Rome Pact at this time lest the gesture offend the Little Entente. This was a virtual death blow to the agreement.

Hungary's disdain of her Italian ally had deep causes. Since January 1935, Horthy and Hitler had maintained secret personal contact. On 15 May, Field-Marshall von Mackensen, a German wartime hero, arrived in Budapest for a one-week visit bearing Hitler's personal letter for Horthy. The letter opened a new, more intimate chapter in German-Hungarian relations. Referring to an earlier Horthy letter, now lost, but no doubt soliciting Germany's revisionist aid, Hitler explained that his recent actions (withdrawal from the League and rearmament)

> belonged to the sphere of the struggle led by both our countries for their emancipation and for the reparation of the injuries suffered by them. . . .The endeavours of the two governments are, in one respect, identical: they are both striving to accomplish the restoration of their country's honour and independence, possibly without resorting to war. . . .[51]

Hitler wished to meet the Regent either in person or by proxy, in order to discuss all problems that are not suited to being dealt with in writing. He suggested dispatching Göring, who was to leave shortly on his honeymoon in Southeast Europe, to meet with Horthy. Clearly, Hitler had important developments in mind for German-Hungarian relations and Balkan affairs.

Göring arrived in Budapest on 24 May for a two-day visit. The precise nature of his discussions with Horthy must be left to conjecture. It is certain, however, that he tried to induce the Regent to detach Hungary from Italy, in order to assure an early reduction of Austria. No doubt Göring also begged that Hungary concentrate her revisionist demands on Czechoslovakia, and leave the other two countries of the Little Entente alone. A well-informed observer relates why: Germany needed Yugoslavia's military support against Italy should there be blows over Austria.[52] This appraisal makes very good sense, both in view of Hitler's and Goring's respect for the fighting ability of the Serbs, and in terms of Yugoslavia's determination to prevent the growing peril of a Habsburg restoration in Austria, now supported by Italy.

The Göring visit had immediate results in terms of Hungarian desires to please the Germans. For one thing, Masirevich was sacked on Göring's peremptory demand, allegedly for leaking confidential statements made to him which concerned Germany's relations with Yugoslavia and were obviously intended only for the Hungarian Government. Masirevich's unforgivable sin was that he gave the information to the Italians. But Masirevich was Kánya's protege. When told about his favourite's dismissal, Kánya "talked himself into a state of extreme agitation." It did him no good. Both Gömbos and Horthy had their minds made up. They decided to pursue a German-oriented policy, and consequently Masirevich had to go. In addition to this humiliation, Kánya had to submit to being badgered by Mackensen. The German Minister demanded to know Kánya's loyalties, a question the Hungarian diplomat tried to evade. "I again requested an absolutely clear reply to my very clear question. Kánya at first evaded my question," reported Mackensen. "Finally Kánya blurted out: 'Tell Berlin officially that I shall remain pro-German in spite of General Göring.'"[53] The moment the Germans believed they were in the saddle, they swaggered and threatened to undo all their patient efforts.

The consequences of the Göring visit were also felt in Hungarian Parliament. Gömbös energetically repudiated complaints by the Left about the Göring presence, then struck a decidedly martial pose, claiming Hungary's right to seek parity in armaments with the nations of the Little Entente. He went on to pay lip service to Hungary's friendship with Italy and Austria, "in order not to offend Italy," as Mackensen noted in his report. Gömbös also unveiled Germany as Hungary's most important friend. Mackensen cited one of Gömbös' provocative statements: "From a Hungarian standpoint, it is certain that a Hungarian policy that is to radiate outward from the Carpathian Basin is unthinkable without the precondition that she can evoke the aid of mighty German forces on her behalf." In conclusion, Gömbös deprecated suggestions by the legitimists to forge closer bonds with Austria by means of a customs union. Hungary had far more extensive economic space in mind.[54]

Despite Hungary's rapidly developing pro-German profile, Gömbös was far too clever to abandon the idea of German-Austrian and German-Italian rapprochement. Indeed, a new menace arose to propel him in these directions. On 2 May, the Soviet Union and France signed a mutual aid agreement, followed by Czechoslovakia on 16 May. The twin-pacts portended an ominous Soviet presence in Central Europe, a menace Gömbös both feared and execrated. Citing the looming threat to the visiting Austrian legitimist Prince Starhemberg, Gömbös delicately suggested a reshaping of Austria's German policy, another euphemism for *Gleichschaltung*. Gömbös suggested that only a rapprochement between the signatories of the Rome Pact and Germany could save European civilization. True, Italy would never accept *Anschluss,* but she might agree to some compromise solution. Gömbös offered to mediate and welcomed suggestions. Starhemberg's reply dramatized how great the gulf was that separated Austria from Hungary. Though an avid Catholic, the Prince considered not Bolshevism the great European menace but National Socialist Germany. This threatened the Christian fabric of civilization, and hence a Habsburg restoration not only in Austria but in Hungary was the only bulwark to stem the Nazi tide.

In the fall, additional world developments tended to draw Hungary closer to Germany. The looming Ethiopian conflict caused anxieties in Hungary, as war preparations tended to divert Italy's attention from Hungary and the Danube region. The Wilhelmstrasse accurately appraised Hungary's quandary. Gömbös' impending visit to Germany occasioned the following observations:

> As Hungary will in future no longer be able to depend on receiving support from Italy on the same scale as before, she evidently feels the need more than hitherto to seek support from a Germany who is becoming an increasingly important power factor. Thus Hungary is of necessity, faced with the question as to what extent the new situation in Europe demands a readjustment of her present policy.[55]

By the time these lines were written, Gömbös was already in Germany as the guest of Göring. In preparation for this visit the Wilhelmstrasse compiled a detailed analysis of Hungary's various diplomatic options. Whether Hungary would readjust to fit into the framework of Germany's overall policy could not be judged until after the Göring-Gömbös conversations. A Yugoslav-Hungarian rapprochement was indispensable for the success of Germany's Balkan diplomacy. It was equally important not to harness Germany to Hungary's bandwagon, but to maintain diplomatic elasticity. Germany shall have to proceed from the axiom that friendly relations between Germany and Hungary would chiefly and decisively depend upon Hungary's attitude. It was self-evident that Hungary could not expect Germany to take her interests into consideration if she herself did not consider German interests. Withal, Germany must avoid binding agreements with the Magyars, lest they entertain any delusions such as might later cause friendly relations to deteriorate. Neurath wrote in the margin that there was no question whatever of any commitments to Hungary.

Regarding the Danubian Pact, the rapporteur cited familiar Hungarian counter-arguments, and concluded that both we ourselves and the Hungarians must reject such pacts on principle, and he also accurately believed that Gömbös would never support a Habsburg revival in Austria as it would inevitably spread to Hungary. On the minority question, German and Hungarian experts had been meeting regularly for the past few months. The Hungarians were said to be especially concerned with two matters. They wished to sunder the Swabians from all Reich influences; and they desired closer Magyar-German cooperation in the Successor States. The Ministry must not promise the Magyars anything, but remand the matter for further talks. On economic relations, the rapporteur was exuberant, though not entirely accurate. The Italian-Hungarian trade agreement was held to be a fiasco, whereas the German-Hungarian trade arrangement worked even better than expected. The last point raised was the possibility of establishing large-scale arms deliveries to Hungary by *Rheinmetall,* a German munitions firm. The order would aid Germany's munitions industry. But the Magyars expected a handsome financial subsidy. This ought to be conditioned by "the extent Hungary is prepared to align her policy with that of Germany."[56] The memorandum revealed nothing new or startling, except for one important item. The munitions deal showed conclusively that the Magyars planned to denounce the disarmaments clause of the Peace Treaty. Indeed, an agreement in principle on the arms purchase was reached in the course of negotiations between Gömbös and Schacht a few days later.[57]

Neurath's terse jottings reveal what Gömbös had to say on the various vital issues in the course of his talks with Hitler. Gömbös first spoke about Hungarian-Yugoslav relations. He now realized that Hungary could not achieve all her territorial ambitions simultaneously. It therefore behooved him to effect a reconciliation with Yugoslavia, the nation having the smallest and therefore the most tolerable cession of Hungarian territory. A prime minister of Hungary could never renounce revision entirely, however, and the Yugoslavs would have to, at the very least, sunder their ties with the Little Entente. Gömbös was not happy about having to give up even one square inch of Hungarian soil, but he realized that without some tangible shift in Hungary's Yugoslav policy the Germans would not make concessions.

Gömbös also discussed Hungary's convoluted relations with Italy and Austria. He loyally defended Hungary's connections with both nations on the grounds that they were of political and economic benefit. Hungarian wheat sales to these countries at above world market prices were of decisive importance. He then recalled a statement uttered by Mussolini in 1934 to the effect that his differences with France would never be totally eliminated, and thus he would not permit himself to become overly dependent on that country. Gömbös ventured that once Mussolini's Ethiopian adventure was over, traditional Franco-Italian disputes would reemerge at once. All this was a preamble to Gömbös' pet scheme, cooperation between Italy, Austria,

Hungary, Germany, and possibly Poland. It would be a natural counterfoil to the Little Entente and to French influence. He recognized some of the difficulties regarding Austria, a nation Gömbös regarded as the natural bridge, both politically and economically, between Germany and Hungary. An independent Austria would be a fortunate political entity, even if *Anschluss* were regarded as a natural necessity.

This brought Gömbös to the Franco-Italian Danubian Pact question. He rejected any scheme that would include the Little Entente and France, and insisted that any political and economic combination of states must be arrived at and formulated entirely independently of previous pact projects. Discussions to this end should be held between Germany, Italy, Austria, and Hungary, and possibly Poland. Although ostentatiously omitting any mention of Yugoslavia in this connection, neither did Gömbös castigate that country, whereas he expressed deep aversion both to Czechoslovakia and Rumania's foreign minister, Titulescu. The minority question was not raised with Hitler but postponed for the following day. Gömbös came dangerously close to defying Hitler on the question of Austrian independence, where Hitler had a blind spot. Gömbös skirted the question of Germany's aversion to join an existing pact by suggesting that any new agreement complex be independent of any previous combinations.[58]

Immediately upon his return from Germany, Gömbös held a cabinet meeting (5 October). One of his Ministers divulged a detailed account of the proceedings to one of Mackensen's confidants, so that within one week, Gömbös' impressions were known to Neurath and Hitler. According to the informer, Gömbös claimed he had repeatedly assured Hitler that Hungarian-Italian relations were unencumbered by any military agreements; hence Hungary was in no way committed to rendering military assistance to Italy in the event of a European conflict. With regard to German-Italian relations, Hitler had assured Gömbös of his personal appreciation of Mussolini, and had no interest at all in the collapse of Fascism. On the contrary, Hitler hoped to preserve all right-wing European states. Gömbös also claimed that Hitler was completely disinterested in the Austrian question. Indeed, Gömbös thought he detected in leading German circles a certain conciliatory attitude towards Italy and a readiness to come to an understanding over the Austrian question. This was wishful thinking, although subsequent events vindicated his hunch. Gömbös rendered an untruthful account on the Yugoslav question. According to his cabinet report, Yugoslavia had evinced far less interest than previously, and been treated to a certain extent as a secondary matter. The Germans allegedly rejoiced that Hungarian-Yugoslav commercial negotiations proceeded favourably, but nobody in Berlin had attached decisive importance to this question. Göring contradicted Gömbös on this. On the contrary, he said, it was an essential point.

Gömbös' overall appraisal of Germany's strategy was insightful. A clash with Bolshevism was becoming the focal point of her foreign policy, and consequently the Sudeten question and favourable relations with Britain at present took precedence over everything else. Hitler was evidently startled by the Franco-Russian and Russo-Czech agreements and feared a revived Anglo-French Entente in response to Mussolini's aggressive designs in Africa. Gömbös lied that he had discussed the minorities question in almost every conversation he had in Berlin, including that with the Führer, Göring pointed out to Mackensen. The minority question was never raised. Gömbös claimed to have gained the general impression—evidently on the slenderest evidence—that the German side was beginning to lose interest in this question. What he really meant was the lack of German interest in Magyar-German cooperation in the diaspora. This was a tired Hungarian plan, and the Germans were thoroughly fed up with it. The Gömbös report concluded with a panegyric of National Socialist Germany, its leaders, and long-range prospects. A few days later, Gömbös subjected Mackensen to a similarly effusive and enthusiastic ninety-minute eulogy of his German impressions.[59]

It would be erroneous to suppose that Hungary neglected, let alone abandoned Mussolini, as some of the European press seemed to believe.[60] Despite the brevity of his visit, Gömbös had met Italian Ambassador Attolico in Berlin, mainly to reassure him that newspaper reports distorting the reasons for his visit were pure fancy. He entertained no plans for any sort of military accommodations with Germany. Aware that Mussolini feared a German-Polish understanding to which Hungary would be party, Gömbös maintained that there had been no discussions in Germany with Polish diplomats. His journey was part and parcel of Hungary's campaign to keep in Germany's good graces. He assured Attolico that Hitler held Mussolini in high esteem and regarded him with sympathy, nor did the Fuhrer overlook the considerable similarities between their respective movements. Finally, his chief aim was to bring Italy and Germany together for the sake of a new European balance.

Indeed, Gömbös strained to mollify Mussolini, and to assure him of his solidarity. Shortly before the Ethiopian invasion, Gömbös ordered his attache in Rome to convey Hungary's support and comradely greetings to Mussolini the moment Italian troops crossed into Ethiopia. This courtesy had its desired effect. According to Gömbös, Mussolini and his high officials were deeply impressed, and Mussolini responded with an encouraging, though vague promise: "Italy will never be in the position not to do everything it can for Hungary."[61]

Yet when Mussolini's ill-advised Ethiopian venture finally erupted, the Magyars were visibly nervous. In Parliament, opposition deputy Count Maurice (Móric) Eszterházy demanded a thorough review of Hungarian foreign policy in the light of recent developments. The Count believed that Italy's action would have far-reaching consequences for Hungary, and feared that her international position might deteriorate. His apprehensions were shared by the Right and Centre. Kánya tried to soothe Parliament by adroitly explaining that Hungary's best hope lay in remaining in the League and by maintaining the image of a decent, responsible, and faithful nation, especially to her friends. He meant Hungary's refusal to join the sanctions against Italy. Instead, Hungary should earn the trust of the Western Powers, especially England, by providing a reasoned countervailing force against the advocates of sanctions. Kánya's clever explanation earned great acclaim.[62]

Italy's adventures far from Central Europe left not only Hungary but Austria in a quandary. Bereft of Italian support, the Austrians sought alternative solutions to their security problems. The Germans were totally surprised when Gömbös and Kánya suddenly appeared in Vienna. Italy's defection had left Austria with two disagreeable alternatives: Germany or Czechoslovakia. Without actually denouncing the Rome Pact, Schuschnigg sought closer economic and political ties with Czechoslovakia. But first he desired to reassure Gömbös that Austria would never jeopardize Hungarian interests. Yet, Austria had no choice but to seek some sort of accommodation. Italy's support was gone, and negotiations with Germany were leading nowhere. Commenting on the meeting, Mackensen ventured that it was cloaked in mystery. The suddenness of the journey had evoked the wildest rumours in the press, and he wondered why the Magyars had failed to issue a communique to end all the speculations.[63]

Von Papen's exhaustive report to Hitler gave more accurate reasons for the Austro-Hungarian meeting. The Vatican and France were hatching a plot to buttress Austria against National Socialism. Thus they encouraged the rapprochement with France and England, as well as with the Little Entente, especially Czechoslovakia. Austria would thereupon mediate between the Little Entente and Hungary, and between Italy and England. The Vatican and France also sought to restore the economic unity of what had once been the Austro-Hungarian Empire. A Habsburg restoration was seen as a distinct possibility. France and the Vatican noted with great regret that Hungary and Poland, two predominantly Roman Catholic states, were likely to obstruct these plans. Hungary looked upon an Austro-Czech reconciliation and a Habsburg restoration with a jaundiced eye, and accused Vienna of betraying a common cause. According to Mackensen, Hungary stuck resolutely to her original plan, the creation of a bloc comprising

Germany, Poland, Hungary, and Italy, even if it meant abandoning Austria.[64] It was generally recognized, therefore, that Hungary held the key to an East-Central European settlement plan in which France would predominate, Italy play second fiddle, and Germany play no role at all.

The Franco-Vatican plan foundered on Hungarian non-cooperation and regional disparities. On 16 January Schuschnigg arrived in Prague where he held exhaustive discussions with Beneš and Foreign Minister Hodža. There were no tangible results. Austria sought closer economic and political ties among all the Danubian states, but for understandable reasons refused to terminate her existing treaty obligations. The Czechs were sympathetic. As a *quid pro quo,* Schuschnigg promised to mediate between Hungary and Czechoslovakia, and carried a concrete proposal by Hodža to the Hungarians. These were ignored. The Chancellor also convinced Beneš that Austria did not seriously entertain thoughts for a Habsburg restoration. For their part, the Czechs promised to soothe Yugoslav fears on this score.[65] The Austro-Czech conversations revealed how far apart the various Danubian states were. Each nation would have to renounce an indispensable feature of its own basic position for the sake of regional unity and collective security. Both sides would have to surrender the questionable safety of the two competing regional power blocs. No state was prepared to offer sufficient security to its neighbours that would enable the creation of a strong, anti-German, East-Central European political and economic entente.

In view of these unsettled conditions, both Germany and Italy began to consider reconciling their differences. Both worried about the rapidly developing vacuum in the Danubian area; both feared French influence at a time when Italy was occupied elsewhere, and German might had not yet evolved. As Italy's relations with France and England deteriorated, Mussolini's determination to end the squabble with Germany increased. Villani reported from Rome that Mussolini greatly valued Germany's dispatch of large quantities of goods, including war material, during the period of sanctions, and he particularly welcomed the friendly tone of the German press. Mussolini assured Hassell that the Stresa Front was dead and that Italy would never forget Germany's contribution. Villani believed that Schuschnigg's Prague journey had much to do with Mussolini's about-face. Austria would never pursue a deliberate pro-Czech policy, the Austrian ambassador had declared, but both Austria and Czechoslovakia required a counterweight against the imperialistic Reich, and obviously Italy was not there to provide it.[66]

Mussolini promised Hassell to reorient Italy's German policy. This was no idle chatter. About one week later, Villani was granted an interview, devoted almost entirely to the projected Italian-German rapprochement.

Having reiterated almost verbatim what he had told Hassell, Mussolini declared that he was through with England and France and that he now favoured Bethlen's 1927 proposal, the creation of a bloc comprising Italy, Germany, Austria, and Hungary, with the possible inclusion of Poland. Mussolini remained cautious, however. A Polish connection entailed certain difficulties; rapprochement ought to be slow and circumspect for the sake of both Germany and Italy. Should the plan materialize, however, the five member nations would constitute a powerful bloc of some 170 million inhabitants. It would ensure peace and independent political and economic development for each participant. This was indeed a momentous initiative. But for the time being, Mussolini had nothing tangible to offer that Germany might consider favourably, and Austria still remained a bone of contention. In an interview with Hassell, Mussolini suggested that Germany make peace with Austria as a precondition for a rapprochement. He feared that German intransigence would sooner or later drive her straight into the arms of the Little Entente. In late January, Italian Ambassador Preziosi assured Berger that Austria's independence ever was and always would remain the basis of Italy's Danubian policy, provided she remained faithful to the Rome Pact. But by early February von Papen detected a change in Italy's Austrian policy, which Berger tried to conceal.

At the end of January, England and France lost an excellent opportunity to pursue their own Danubian diplomacy. Statesmen from all the European nations gathered in London for George V's funeral. The joint efforts of the two Western European Powers, pursued first in London, then in Paris, suffered grievous blows. Whereas the French were overly aggressive and rigid, the British were too timid and noncommittal. Vacillating French policy now had two major objectives: to prevent a Habsburg restoration, and to induce Austria to abandon her Italian orientation in favour of one with the Little Entente. This effort foundered, as previously, on Austria's insistence to maintain her sovereignty; on Yugoslavia's indifference over Austria's fate; and on England's refusal to guarantee Austria's territorial integrity. Yugoslavia's preference for *Anschluss* to restoration was caused by German threats to terminate their lucrative trade agreement. England's reluctance to intervene in Central Europe had to do with the British public's lack of interest and with the paucity of postwar British resources.[67]

Hungary's wooing by France and Britain was even less effectual than Austria's. Both Western Powers advocated rapprochement between Hungary and the Little Entente, but would not heed Kánya's pleas for a consideration of Hungary's revisionist demands. Kánya argued in vain with Anthony Eden and Sir Robert Vansittart. An interview with Edward VIII was more fruitful but politically useless. The new king apparently sympathized with Hungary's plight. Both he and Vansittart expressed admiration for Germany and its peaceful aims, in contrast with Italy's dangerous sabre-rattling. Eden, too, refused to consider restoring good relations with Italy, and he distrusted Germany's rearmament gestures. From London, Kánya journeyed to Paris, where he avoided even paying a courtesy call on his French counterpart. France was conspiring with all the enemies of Italy and Germany, and Kánya had no wish to be compromised.[68]

Hungary's unshakable loyalty to Germany in the face of political and economic pressures by France and her allies created an excellent impression in Germany. More than ever, Germany recognized Hungary's importance and vital function as an important link in Germany's *Drang nach Osten,* and also as the only nation in Europe able to mediate German-Italian differences. Bülow remarked to Mackensen:

> . . .the attitude of the Hungarian government is naturally of particular importance from the German standpoint. This is the more so as the second partner on whose support we can rely, namely Bulgaria, lies so much on the periphery of the planned economic integration (*Zusammenschluss*) of the Danubian States that, on this ground alone, her voice is likely to carry little weight.[69]

Bülow instructed Mackensen to discuss Germany's expansionary economic plans in the Danubian region with Hungarian statesmen, to thank them for their constructive attitude that economic rehabilitation could not be accomplished without the participation of Germany, and to reassure them that the arrangements envisioned by Germany would in no way involve political sacrifice by Hungary as, in contrast, did the plans projected by others. This was a clear allusion to the French proposal, under which Hungary would have to abandon the Rome Pact in favour of the Little Entente. Bülow's instructions were also designed to lull Magyar fears lest Germany inundate the Danube region at the expense of Hungary's Italian ally. Germany clearly wished to leave the door wide ajar to any further Hungarian mediation efforts.

Germany's cautious interest in rapprochement with Italy was broached in the course of Hungarian Minister Sztójay's visit to the Wilhelmstrasse the following week. Sztójay sought confirmation of the rumour that Mussolini favoured a bloc comprising Italy, Germany, Austria, Hungary, and Poland. Bülow neither confirmed nor denied this. Sztójay next tried to arouse Bülow's curiosity by announcing the Polish Minister President's visit to Hungary in the second half of April, and Schuschnigg's and Berger's in mid-March. Still, Bülow was noncommittal. Thereupon Sztójay inquired what

Germany thought about Mussolini's pledge that Italy would never return to the Stresa Front, and continued asking questions in a similar vein. Bulow proved to be evasive. After these feelers, the two diplomats discussed an important hurdle in German-Hungarian relations—the Yugoslav question. Gömbös had authorized Sztójay to inform the Germans that a rapprochement with Yugoslavia was possible, whereas reconciliation with the rest of the Little Entente was not. A lingering Hungarian revisionist claim against Yugoslavia was conspicuously absent. Although from the standpoint of German-Italian reconciliation the Sztójay-Bülow interview was only an exploratory step, the road to mediation was now clear. But the Magyars wished to tread cautiously until they ascertained that the Germans trusted Mussolini.

The next step in Hungarian mediation occurred at the end of February. Sztójay informed Neurath that Gömbös and Schuschnigg would negotiate with Mussolini within two weeks. Did Neurath have any wishes to express? Neurath, who had already received a similar request directly from Mussolini, was grateful to Gömbös for his friendly information and kindly intentions. He had no special wishes to proffer, as all the participants knew Germany's views on all the vital issues. Although politely rejecting the perennial suggestion that Germany join the Rome Pact, Neurath left Sztójay basking in the warm glow of cameraderie by assuring him that "our having interests in common would bring us together even without the conclusion of a formal pact."[70] To the Magyars, Neurath's message had a familiar ring. Throughout, German diplomats had stressed that they would conclude formal treaties only with enemies, never with friends.

Hungarian plans for a German-Italian rapprochement moved one step closer when, on 7 March 1936, the Reich denounced the Locarno Treaty, citing France's prior violation through the conclusion of a Franco-Russian alliance. Germany prepared to send the Wehrmacht into the demilitarized Rhineland zone. Thus she sundered her ties with the Western Powers. Hungary's role both as friend and as mediator consequently assumed greater importance. Budapest was jubilant. So was Kánya, probably one of the first foreign ministers to be apprised by Germany. The Regent was also very happy. The surprise would have been even more pleasant had the denunciation been made in concert with Mussolini. But Italy would no doubt be grateful for the German action, since it would absorb the Western Powers to his benefit. Mackensen was pleased with Magyar reactions. Nearly the entire Hungarian press proved favourable.[71]

Next, Hungary tried to effect an Austro-German settlement. The time seemed auspicious, since the quarrel was the last barrier to a German-Italian understanding. During a Budapest visit by Schuschnigg and Berger on 13-16

March, the topic of an Austro-German rapprochement predominated. According to Schuschnigg, relations with Germany were not incurable, however much they left to be desired. Yet Germany had no dealings whatever with Austrian officials, and boycotted Austrian lumber from the estates of Prince Starhemberg and the Roman Catholic clergy. Schuschnigg claimed he pursued a correct policy towards Germany. In his recent negotiations with the Czechs, he had flatly refused to join any anti-German plans, nor would he now. But reconciliation would never come, unless Germany renounced interfering in Austria's affairs. Schuschnigg greatly feared that, having successfully occupied the Rhineland, Hitler would turn on Austria. He vowed that nothing would ever sway him from his allegiance to Italy and the Rome Pact.

Kánya explained Austria's predicament. Schuschnigg's recent Prague visit conjured up visions of Austria's political reorientation along French lines, and consequently Hungary's isolation from her Italian and German friends. Kánya assured Schuschnigg that Hungary's confidence in him and in Austria was unshaken. To avert misunderstandings of this type in future, he proposed that the two countries devise a common front. This was exactly what Germany desired. Further, any political rapprochement either with Russia or Czechoslovakia was to be avoided. Cooperation was possible only with Yugoslavia. A Danubian federation was impracticable since neither the Great Powers nor the smaller Danubian states could agree on any single point. Nor would Germany ever join a plan of which she was not an original participant, including even the Rome Pact. Schuschnigg observed ironically that apparently only Germany could confront the world with a *fait accompli*. Kánya, however, continued to press his point. At least until the termination of the Ethiopian war, all three Rome Pact members should approach alliance plans cautiously, and immediately inform their partners. Most particularly, anything that Germany might resent must be avoided; and all three states must jointly protest if Soviet Russia intervened in Central Europe. Kánya stressed the importance of Austro-German reconciliation. The National Socialist Party, not the Wilhelmstrasse, prevented an accommodation. The Germans had confidentially requested Kánya to draft a proposal acceptable to both Vienna and Berlin. In view of Italy's preoccupation in Ethiopia, the Austrians felt quite isolated, and were. Consequently, they offered little resistance and accepted Kánya's formulations, including his suggestion that they increase Austrian purchases of Hungarian agricultural products.[72]

After Schuschnigg's departure, Kánya immediately summoned Schnurre, Mackensen's deputy, in order to acquaint Germany with the implications of the recent talks. Kánya reassured Schnurre that the Austrians were indeed reliable, and had no intentions to leave the Rome Pact.[73] Further, the

Austrians had categorically rejected the Hodža plan, a proposal aimed at establishing economic collaboration among members of the former Austro-Hungarian Monarchy, especially Czechoslovakia, Hungary, and Austria. Hence negotiations with the Czechs had been bilateral and strictly economic, in strict conformity with recent Austro-Hungarian guidelines. Even Hungary would not hesitate to enter into bilateral trade agreements with the Little Entente states. He urged Schnurre to read his article, "Die österreichisch-ungarische Besprechungen," in the 15 April issue of *Pester Lloyd*, in which he explained the entire situation and stressed the trustworthiness of Austria. Schnurre crossexamined Kánya on Schuschnigg's good faith with Germany. Kánya made Schuschnigg appear far more pro-German than he actually was; he omitted his diatribes against Germany and he conveyed the notion that only Austria's fright of German aggression blocked a settlement. But Schuschnigg would never compromise Germany's interests. He truly cherished rapprochement; a pity that neither side quite knew how to achieve it. Kánya believed the Austrians expected to become the centre of Germany's attention again, now that Hitler had settled the Saar and Rhineland questions. Although most Austrians did not expect a German assault directly, they feared the resurging Austrian National Socialists, and expected an attack from within.[74]

At the Rome conference scheduled for 21-23 March, Mussolini hoped to strengthen the Tripartite Pact on the premise of Italian hegemony. In his view, the three allies had to intensify their mutual political, economic, and cultural commitments. A formal Entente, preceded perhaps by a customs union, was to be a distinct future possibility. Aware that the Italian leader's bruised and sensitive ego needed nursing, Gömbös agreed with Mussolini's plan, but the Austrians wished to study it in greater detail. After these preliminaries, Gömbös turned to the more substantive issues. He recapitulated the points discussed in Budapest. On the whole, Austria and Hungary travelled harmoniously on a common diplomatic path, except that Austria sought no frontier revision, and her relations with Germany were strained. Next, Schuschnigg held forth at great length, and with some passion, on the alleged hopelessness of the Austro-German fratricidal conflict. Direct negotiations were fruitless, since Austria would be unable to secure an acceptable agreement in the face of growing German aggressiveness. A solution had to be sought within the matrix of some multilateral agreement-complex. Presumably, what Schuschnigg had in mind was a Danubian pact under Italian-German auspices. The rest of the conference was spent in protocols to be released to the world.

The most hotly disputed points were embodied in Protocol #2. No member nation might negotiate with any other power without the express permission of its partners. Only commercial and bilateral agreements were permitted with the Little Entente states. In practical terms, rival proposals, such as the Tardieu or Hodža plan, were out. This was designed to please the Germans, so Kánya told Hassell. Kánya also revealed that Hungary had broached the question of extending the Rome Pact to include Germany, Poland, and possibly Yugoslavia. Austria allegedly consented, contingent on an Austro-German rapprochement. Hassell seemed pleased, and promised to notify his government immediately.[75]

But the suspicious Germans had second thoughts about the new accord. Hungarian and German diplomats tried to deal with these reservations shortly thereafter. On a visit to the Wilhelmstrasse, Sztójay stated that the new protocols would strengthen Hungary's hand in the Danubian region, especially against Rumania and Czechoslovakia. Renthe-Fink ventured that, although Germany appreciated the advantages of having a powerful friend in Eastern Europe, it was very doubtful what benefits Germany could possibly derive from them. Would it be easier or more difficult now to achieve an agreement with Austria? Had Italy imposed any secret terms on Hungary that would complicate, even imperil, her friendship with Germany? Sztójay swore that these suspicions and fears were unfounded. Refusing to be put off, Renthe-Fink deplored Italy's anti-German stance on the remilitarization of the Rhineland. The Italians, especially the Fascist Party, acted in bad faith. Indeed, the Magyars had to concede this point. Less than two weeks earlier, Count Grandi had collaborated in drafting the anti-German Locarno Protocol. At the time, Bülow had protested with the Italian ambassador in Berlin, who assured him that Italy would not participate in anti-German sanctions, and that Grandi had merely signed a preliminary draft. The incident nonetheless aroused the hypersensitive Germans. It is astonishing that the Italians committed such a *faux pas,* and that the normally efficient Magyars permitted the blunder to pass without requesting clarification. If the matter was ever discussed at the Rome meeting, there is no record of it.

A few days later, Bülow was chagrined because on 1 April, the Austrian National Assembly had introduced compulsory military service for all males between the ages of 18 and 42. Although Germany approved the action in principle and even offered Austria moral support against the opposition that threatened, Bülow chafed nonetheless because Germany had not been consulted. He grilled the Magyars. Surely, the matter was discussed in Rome. What other subjects were raised without Germany's knowledge? In the end, Bülow relented somewhat. Germany might eventually cooperate politically and economically with the Rome Protocol Powers, but would never formally join an organization that had been initially designed against her.

These examples indicate that Hungary's role as mediator was far from smooth. In addition to persistent Austro-German and German-Italian stresses and strains, German-Hungarian relations also suffered briefly. Hungary distrusted Germany's offer of bilateral non-aggression pacts both with Eastern and Western European nations, to compensate for the recently denounced Locarno Pact. Hungarian statesmen feared that bilateral agreements between Germany and individual members of the Little Entente might destroy this bulwark of French imperialism without benefiting Hungarian territorial aspirations. Mackensen had alerted his superiors earlier. When the Magyars realized that Hitler's non-aggression pact offer also applied to Czechoslovakia, they would object strenuously. Of course, the Magyars could not understand that the Germans wished to lull their enemies into a false sense of security. Germany's action reeked of betrayal. At the end of April, therefore, a very agitated Sztójay appeared at the Wilhelmstrasse.

At issue was not only Germany's offer of non-aggression pacts, but many developments that threatened to undo Hungary's carefully wrought efforts to recreate Central Europe to her own liking. Horthy, Gömbös, and Kánya were all greatly agitated about the Flandin Plan, which appeared to complement Germany's non-aggression offers perfectly, in that the former sought to arrest the European territorial *status quo* for twenty-five years. Magyar statesmen found the projected German non-aggression pact with Czechoslovakia sinister, and the Czechs' apparent intentions of forcing themselves into the Rome Pact dangerous. In Berlin, Sztójay argued. Hitherto Hungary had pursued a Germanophil policy for indirect benefits. Should the Flandin plan succeed, Hungary would suffer political shipwreck, and Kánya would have to resign. To counteract these dangers, Sztójay asked if Germany would conclude an immediate pact of friendship and consultation with Hungary as a gesture, in order to restore Hungarian prestige with the Little Entente. If this was too much, would Germany at least consider a pact of friendship, reinforced with a highly publicized visit to Budapest by Neurath?

Bülow retorted that neither Rome nor Budapest deserved consideration since neither had kept Germany properly informed at their recent conference. Sztójay spent some time justifying his government's actions and defending its honesty. He then begged Germany to join the Rome Pact, both to dash French stratagems picturing it as anti-German, and to settle the Austrian question once and for all. Sztójay was certain that Schuschnigg would treat if Germany recognized Austria's independence and concluded a short-term non-aggression pact. Bülow's response, in his own words, was provisional. Germany disdained the Flandin Plan as utopian. On a consultative pact with Hungary, Germany must reserve its attitude. On the Rome Protocols, Germany could not agree to a pact whose original thrust was anti-German. A non-interference treaty with Austria was also out of the question, as it would lead to constant complaints and interventions. Austria must first cast herself loose from Italian influences.

Sztójay had one more major request. Hungary planned to emulate Germany's example shortly by formally announcing her equality of rights. Would Germany render moral support through official statements and the press? Bülow assented in principle, but insisted that Germany be consulted to choose the right moment. Unilateral action would find Germany "hard put to it to afford her full support in the way envisaged." As Sztójay left, he hinted that the Magyars could also make life unpleasant. Improved Hungarian-Yugoslav relations might take a new turn for the worse. Austrian conscription had unleashed the ire of the Little Entente, not so much against Austria as against Hungary. How could Hungary proceed with her rapprochement with Yugoslavia under these conditions?

The Magyars were so disgruntled that Sztójay, on orders from Kánya, pulled rank on Bülow by seeking Neurath's views on the same questions. Neurath's replies were even more discouraging. A pact was momentarily completely out of the question. It would strengthen the other side rather than advance Hungary's prestige. A Neurath visit would arouse unnecessary attention. Germany eschewed the Rome Pact in view of strained Anglo-Italian relations. England would consider Germany's participation as an unfriendly act. Unsettled Austro-German relations also demanded that Germany desist. Besides, Austro-German reconciliation hinged on altered internal conditions in Austria, not on formal treaties. Neurath did promise, however, to support Hungary's justified claims arising from Article 19 of the Peace Treaty, and he reiterated Bülow's vague promise to support Hungary's claim for restoration of equality, but only after prior consultation. Finally, he attempted to allay Magyar fears that Germany's non-aggression pact offers might lead to an Eastern Pact in the french sense. A French-inspired conference was in the offing, but Germany would never join. The Germans were mystified about Sztójay's latest demarche, and requested Mackensen to ascertain why the Magyars duplicated their efforts so soon.[76]

The Magyars' best diplomatic weapon was persistence and tenacity. They proverbially believed that all things come to those who wait. The seemingly irreparable international relationships that had recently threatened to foil Hungarian plans began to sort themselves out beginning in May 1936. On 5 May, Italy's Ethiopian campaign ended victoriously. Italy might soon become reconciled with England and France, and reestablish her strength and influence in Eastern Europe. The situation merited more than a glance by Germany to safeguard her interests. Above all, the new realities not only necessitated a reconciliation with both Austria and Italy, they demanded satisfying the political needs of Germany's most aggressive and obstreperous, but useful gadfly, Hungary.[77]

At the end of April, Germany began to formulate a new policy characterized by a restraint that was unique in Austro-German relations, at least since Hitler's *Machtergreifung*. The Germans launched an operation called *Aktion Franz*, to peacefully subvert Austria. Another sign that Hitler wished to settle the Austrian crisis peacefully came during a conference between von Papen and Hitler on 11 May. Papen reported on Schuschnigg's recent rapprochement offers. In the past, Hitler would have rejected them out of hand. Unexpectedly, he ordered von Papen to accept, but "without this being permitted to result in a definite commitment to any one of the groups in Austria fighting for supremacy there." Hitler was still hedging, but he stated that "should a leading personage in Austria so desire, he would be prepared to make himself available for a personal discussion at a place to be agreed upon beforehand."[78]

The Austro-German rapprochement now had Mussolini's blessings. Mussolini had lost his faith in the Western Powers, and recognized that he could only carry out his designs in Eastern Europe with German support. Already in February 1936, the pro-German Francesco Salata replaced Gabriele Preziosi as Italy's Austrian Minister. Salata was ordered to effect an Austro-German reconciliation in conjunction with von Papen and Schuschnigg. On 13 May, Austria's two anti-German statesmen, Berger and Starhemberg, were relieved of their posts, and Schuschnigg personally assumed their portfolios. The road was clear from the Austrian side to reach a negotiated settlement with Germany.

Events flowed smoothly. In mid-May, Schuschnigg spoke with von Papen, aiming for an economic, scientific, and artistic settlement with Germany that would not jeopardize Austria's independence, and acknowledge Schuschnigg's prerogatives to maintain a one-party system, represented by the *Vaterländische Front*. In return, Schuschnigg might nominate National Socialist individuals to participate in government. Surprisingly, von Papen accepted. Early in June Schuschnigg sought reassurances from Mussolini that an impending German-Italian rapprochement would not compromise Austrian independence. Understandably, Schuschnigg suspected a German trick designed to bring Italy to the green table. Mussolini bestowed his blessings, but warned Schuschnigg against permitting known National Socialists to participate in Austrian government. Mussolini promised to visit Budapest and Vienna soon. Since this was to be his first trip abroad, its significance would be fully understood in Berlin. Thereupon Schuschnigg returned home and resumed negotiating with von Papen. A settlement was signed on 19 July, after von Papen gained Hitler's approval.

Schuschnigg seemed the total victor. Although he pledged consultation on all aspects of Austrian foreign policy that concerned Germany, the Rome Pact and Austria's unilateral agreements with Italy and Hungary still carried precedence. Although Austria was identified as a German nation, and certain National Socialists were to enter government service—despite Mussolini's warnings—the sovereignty of both countries was clearly delineated. Of course, the removal of various barriers was bound to benefit Austria in the short run, but restored commerce, renewed tourism, restoration of journalistic and artistic exchanges, and other similar measures, always carried the danger that Austria would become inundated by the products and nationals of the more powerful nation. Further, whereas Schuschnigg considered the agreement to be the final word, the Germans took it merely as the first step on the road to *Gleichschaltung*.[79] Schuschnigg hoped that Italy would turn her attention once more to Central European affairs, and out of sheer self-interest protect Austria against German encroachments. But Hitler believed more accurately that with the passage of time, the economically debilitated and overburdened Italians would be unable to stem the German tide. In the summer of 1936, Italian-German power was still precariously balanced. It was the perfect milieu for Gömbös' final goal, the Rome-Berlin axis. With the removal of the Austrian problem the last remaining obstacle towards an Italian-German accommodation was gone.

Hungarian diplomacy was henceforth dedicated to bring about the cherished goal of a new Central European order, jointly guaranteed by Italy and Germany. This meant speed, to counter the new Socialist Blum regime's current plans to conclude a Danubian pact under French auspices. After new inquiries about German-Italian relations, Sztójay was told that a progressive improvement and rapprochement in German-Italian relations was to be observed. Neurath cited a recent German overture to Mussolini where Germany would maintain a benevolent attitude in the event the question of recognition of the annexation of Ethiopia became acute. Sztójay suggested a German-Italian treaty of reciprocity, but Neurath demurred because it would unnecessarily complicate current international relations and would serve neither German nor Italian interests. Neurath thought Mussolini could expedite German-Italian relations by counseling Vienna to liquidate the Austro-German dispute. At the time, of course, the issue was being negotiated and Neurath was optimistic about the outcome.[80]

The usual summer doldrums, as well as Gömbös' fatal illness, curtailed

Hungarian diplomacy after the settlement of the Austro-German dispute. The lethargy was dramatically broken by Horthy's unexpected visit on 22 August to Obersalzberg, where he met Hitler.[81] Horthy hoped that persistent German-Italian tensions might be swiftly dispelled. He advised Hitler about his projected Italian journey in the fall and offered to act as mediator, in the absence of the ailing Gömbös. Hitler said that German-Italian cooperation was already quite intense, and would increase "as a natural necessity."[82]

Gömbös' sudden death on 6 October hastened German-Italian reconciliation. It is strange that a man so dedicated to this task should serve it best in the grave. The day after Gömbös' funeral, Goring held important discussions with Kánya. They covered the entire gamut of Eastern European diplomacy. For Göring, the conversation was mainly a fishing expedition. The Germans were quite shaken by Gömbös' death. They considered him a great friend and sincere ally. Would Hungary depart from his narrow path0 Kánya argued no. Koloman (Kálmán) Darányi might have less verve than his predecessor, but he would follow Gömbös' lead. Göring also worried about Hungary's allegiance to Italy. Count Ciano was a plucky fellow, but he had little use for Colonna, or for Italy's Hungarian policy in general. Göring feared increased Italian influence in Hungary. Kánya pointed out that Colonna in fact tried his utmost to diminish Germany's influence, yet it would be difficult to find a diplomat blessed with Colonna's virtues; he was utterly incapable of launching intrigues—but Kánya admitted that the Italians were occasionally jealous of the Germans. Two years earlier in Rome both Mussolini and Suvich had complained about Hungary's preference for Germany. Kánya had explained then that he would always cultivate both camps equally. Only if Germany spurned Hungary's friendship would he abandon his pro-German course. Mussolini had apparently understood Hungary's position and, as the current situation indicated, he now held Germany's friendship in equal esteem.[83]

Mackensen also allayed German fear. His impressions of the new Darányi government were excellent. Minister of the Interior Miklós Kozma had assured him that Darányi would follow his predecessor's path. The new Minister of War, Vilmos Röder, was pro-German, whereas József Som-kúthy, his predecessor, could barely conceal his pro-Italian predilection and his blind admiration of the Duce. Mackensen later wrote about Darányi that Germany could not wish for a more reliable heir to Gömbös' foreign policy. Anyone suspecting Darányi of lagging behind Gömbös in this respect must be in for a rude shock. Thus the Germans shed their remaining reservations about a German-Italian agreement. Gömbös missed his goal by three weeks. On 25 October, a secret protocol created the Rome-Berlin Axis. The two governments pledged to act in tandem in all matters affecting their international relations and pledged to settle their economic and political problems in the Danube Basin in the spirit of friendly collaboration.[84]

Throughout the interwar period Hungary's precarious position required great political sensitivity. Survival demanded an unoffending neutrality between the contradictory aims and demands of Germany and Italy, and Gömbös' strategy had been to exploit their mutual fear. This opportunistic policy garnered Hungary limited political but outstanding economic benefits. Gömbös' energetic diplomacy exploited Germany's fear of Italian-Hungarian collaboration and led to the resumption of German trade with Hungary. Even Hungary's mistreatment of the Swabians—a perennial deterrent to amicable German-Hungarian relations—was temporarily sacrificed to political expediency. German and Italian pliability convinced Gombos that Hungary might conciliate the two rivals and enlist their aid for the restoration of Greater Hungary. The two Powers supported Treaty revision in principle, and their joint economic weight rescued Hungary's economy from certain disaster. This was one of the triumphs of postwar Hungarian diplomacy.

Of course, Gömbös' scheme embodied certain fundamental flaws and premises. He erroneously assumed that German-Italian parity—a prerequisite for undisturbed Hungarian influence—would not change. But soon German power exceeded Italy's, and Hungary's strategic advantage and security vanished. The economic triumph also proved to be shortlived. Italy's potential was not equal to the task of permanently supporting Hungary's demands and insulating the country against German exploitation. The German-Hungarian trade agreement, hailed at the time as a major achievement, turned out to be an illusion and a snare. It was a bribe, pure and simple, designed to keep Hungary from sliding into the Austro-Italian camp at a time when the German juggernaut was not yet ready to roll in the Danube Basin. In the long-run, the Germans outwitted the Magyars, as the agreement favoured the larger, more industrialized party. Even the Swabian problem was submerged only temporarily. It surfaced later as a major bone of contention between Germany and Hungary, and was never resolved satisfactorily. Nor was revision. Even with the eventual combined aid of Germany and Italy, the Magyars never succeeded in recouping all the losses of Trianon.

In sum, the fruits of Gömbös' diplomacy were as impermanent as the shaky, kaleidoscopic world in which Hungary found herself after the war. Yet Gömbös' balance sheet is impressive. He gained the economic support of two bitter rivals; rescued Hungary's economy; temporarily saved Austria from extinction; and avoided meaningful concessions to the Swabians as recompense for German aid. Indeed, it is remarkable that Hungary, a small, unpopular, and defenseless country, surrounded by implacable foes and avaricious friends, achieved even passing success by diplomatic prowess alone. Gömbös provided an object lesson in the exercise of *Realpolitik*, although he ignored a number of variables that ultimately undermined his plans. The looming threat of the Soviet Union, and the decisive influence of the great overseas powers were mere shadows. Most important, he failed to foresee that Germany would soon overwhelm Italy completely, render a diplomacy of balance useless, and make Hungary once more a victim in the international arena.

Every postwar prime minister wanted to eradicate Swabian *völkisch* manifestations, especially Gömbös, who desired an ethnically aggrandized yet homogeneous Magyar state. He thought Hungary's strategic importance would keep Germany from supporting the Swabians. After all, they were a semi-assimilated and fragmented minority. Normally, Hungary should have had no cause for alarm, since only some 70,000 Burgenlanders might ever become Germany's neighbours. Most other Swabians lived far from potential Reich frontiers. Even so, Gömbös took no chances. As Prime Minister, his Magyar dedication knew no bounds. This and German militancy overshadowed Swabian-Magyar relations, which continued to hinge on the *UDV* and minority education.

The UDV

The *UDV* became an instant victim of the new era. Under Bethlen, businesslike relations veneered mutual dislikes and suspicions. Károlyi exacerbated all tensions, and his fall did not alleviate Swabian grievances. The *UDV* remained restricted when Gömbös became Prime Minister. German National Socialism compromised the Swabians, whose loyalty had been questioned for some time. Under Gömbös, *UDV* moderates became radicalized, activists turned more *volksbewusst,* and repressions and surveillance of the *UDV* nearly sundered Magyar-Swabian relations.

Bleyer spent the last of his life in acrid debate with Magyar chauvinists, and fruitless negotiations with the uncompromising Gömbös regime. Bleyer had no illusions about the new prime minister and had difficulty even to arrange a meeting. Both he and the Swabian movement were being slowly ground into dust.[1] The government encouraged the Social Democrats against the Swabians as the lesser of two evils. The Swabian movement was to be disrupted through preemption. At the annual Social Democratic congress, Swabian delegates demanded immediate educational and cultural improvements, and effective minority laws. In Swabian villages, Socialist membership rose by 25% in one year, and Swabian peasants elected twenty Social Democratic community leaders.[2] This allowed the Social Democrats, previously constricted, to upstage the *UDV.*

From the start, the *UDV* had been a monolithic organization with Bleyer at the helm, supported by a hierarchy of more or less trusted followers. Moderates like Gratz and activists like Gündisch were neatly balanced. After Bleyer's death on 5 December 1933, a leadership struggle developed among Gündisch, Kussbach and Huber. A Committee of Seven, Bleyer's closest intimates, was to have assumed direction of the *UDV* until the next general assembly.[3]

But the government refused to accept the Committee of Seven. At a meeting on 5 February 1934, attended by Gömbös, Kánya, other high Magyar officials, and Gratz as the sole Swabian, the government declared that the *UDV* might elect its own officials, but only if all shades of Swabian opinion were represented. This was a euphemism for "selecting" Magyarones such as Pintér and Heckenberger. Gratz's request that the *UDV* might approach the government two-three times annually with accumulated grievances was rejected out of hand. Indeed, Gratz was warned that the *UDV* was becoming radicalized and extralegal. Henceforth, only party members could attend meetings. The *UDV* might arrange occasional regional "propaganda assemblies." But nothing was said about the disposition of regions where the *UDV* was currently banned. Gombos insisted that Gratz become leader, and threatened to dissolve the *UDV* if it succumbed to National Socialist influence. When Gratz refused, Gömbös threatened to withdraw some of his contemplated concessions. Still Gratz hesitated because he doubted whether *völkisch* Reich circles or their Swabian devotees would support him. To dispel doubt, Gratz toured Germany (8-9 Feb. 1934). But German *VDA* head Hans Steinacher greeted him with open arms, promised support, and urged him to accept the government offer of this thankless job. Gratz thus became president. Gömbös greeted him with great relief. To solve the deteriorating Swabian situation now had become a patriotic duty.

Gömbös' exuberance was understandable. Gratz was a trustworthy supporter of Magyar hegemony yet widely respected by Swabians. With his aid, the *völkisch* movement might be defeated. But why did Steinacher, a staunch, *volksbewusst* German, support Gratz's candidacy? The answer lies in Swabian conditions at the time and Hitler's ethnic strategy in Eastern Europe. Bleyer's death during a sensitive transitional period, when most moderate Swabians still hoped for a fair settlement, impeded a middle-of-the-road Swabian solution. Under the circumstances the Reich could not support the inexperienced *völkisch* faction and risk losing the Hungarian government's slender trust. This also explains why the Reich failed to support the radicals unequivocally until later, when the Magyars had outlived their usefulness.

A *UDV* meeting on 6 May 1934, ratified Gratz's presidency and Franz Kussbach became Executive Vice President. Although relatively unknown in Swabian circles, he was accepted by and large as Bleyer's natural heir. It seemed like a good idea to lard the moderate centre with a Magyar-oriented plurality, and admit a token from the *volksbewusst* wing into the upper echelons. Pintér as Director predominated among the assimilants, whereas Franz Basch, the youthful new Secretary-General, championed the *völkisch* faction. From the start, Kussbach encountered opposition, especially from Gündisch and the radicals, but as the younger generation still supported him, the leadership crisis was resolved with deceptive ease. This was merely an illusion. A mighty opposition force, composed largely of academic radicals, the "electrified group," gathered, indignant against Swabian moderates and government mockery of Swabian rights.[4]

The Gömbös regime sought to curb *UDV* activities, to assuage the "invisible terror" (a phrase coined by Alfred von Schwartz) of Magyar journalism and public opinion, and because of its own policy of vigorous Magyarization. *Budapesti Hirlap,* a semi-official daily, regularly abused the Swabians—a bad omen, observers thought. *Sonntagsblatt* complained bitterly because *Magyarország* and *Esti Kurír,* two Budapest dailies, conducted an impassioned anti-Swabian campaign, lumping Swabians and Nazis into the same category. Árpád Török, leader of the Sopron chapter of the *UDV* and outspoken editor of the *völkisch Ödenburger Zeitung,* complained because *volksbewusst* Swabian leaders were being unjustly criticized by Magyars for being part and parcel of the Hitler movement, and for spreading Nazi propaganda in Hungary. Indeed, as Anton König observed, anyone daring to criticize current Magyar nationality policies was immediately branded a Pan-German.[5]

In the past, when negotiations with Germany were hopelessly deadlocked, or when Germany was weak, Hungary generally pursued a frankly anti-Swabian policy. Now, when agreements with Germany were imminent, the Gömbös regime hesitated to offer meaningful concessions, and seldom went beyond minor gestures. Ceremonial visits by German dignitaries, important trade and political relations with Germany, not even pleas for a rule of reason by Magyar statesmen, swayed the government. This policy coincided with Gombos' 14 February 1934 letter to Hitler, which defiantly and clearly enunciated the principle of Magyar hegemony. National Socialist election successes in Germany, and even among Rumania's privileged, autonomous Transylvanian Saxons, intensified fright of the Pan-German menace and made the government more intractable.[6] The Magyar public, especially the lower echelon administrators, responded to the clear echo of their own fears and prejudices reflected from the capital, and intensified their persecution of the *UDV*, the most visible evidence and focal point of German *Kultur* on Hungarian soil.[7]

Anti-*UDV* activities appeared in many ways. Withholding chapter permits was a favourite device. Summing up eight years of *UDV* functioning in Pest County, where all meetings were cancelled on short notice, *Sonntagsblatt* was depressed. Only in ten of twenty-two Swabian communities had the *UDV* been permitted to function, with varying degrees of difficulties. Some chapters had been founded long before, but had received no permits. In Veszprém County, activities had ceased entirely. Only Burgenland, Baranya, and Tolna Counties found few difficulties. Shortly, the Swabians found themselves under attack even in Burgenland. After many years, Kőszeg gained permission to establish a chapter. A few weeks before opening ceremonies, the provincial authorities decreed a "delay." Two days before the event, a "higher authority" peremptorily cancelled the permit. Simultaneously, the central government curtailed exit visas to Swabians wishing to visit Austria or Germany.

Though the ban in Kőszeg apparently originated in Budapest, the fate of chapters was usually determined by unpredictable local officials. In Mékényes, for example, the *UDV* was forbidden to offer a course for organizers, whereas in neighbouring Varsád permission was granted. As a result, officials in Varsád invited representatives from all the surrounding villages and provided instruction in survival techniques. Despite the government's pact with Gratz, persecutions persisted. The *UDV* chalked up a meaningful success only when, after five years of vain attempts, Basch and Kussbach launched a chapter in Soroksár. Eight hundred guests celebrated, but the honeymoon was soon over.

Another favourite device by local functionaries was to prohibit or stop *UDV* gatherings. These impositions were capriciously applied and demoralized the Swabians. In Kúnbaja, a policeman terminated a meeting, claiming he understood no German and hence could not monitor the proceedings. Yet according to law, all Hungarian officials had to know the minority languages in non-Magyar districts. In Nemetboly, gendarmerie with fixed bayonets greeted arrivals to a cultural soiree with orders to search everyone and to admit only local card-carrying members. Organizers cancelled the event and urged guests to depart peacefully. They were nonetheless harassed by the police. It was no coincidence that Basch and Faulstich, the two organizers, belonged to the radical wing. To underscore the message that

Basch and Faulstich were *personae non grata,* a meeting organized by Basch in Vaskút was invaded by armed police demanding identification cards. After much confusion and delay, the meeting continued. Thereupon county officials forbade the playing and singing of the Hungarian national anthem. Basch terminated the meeting, commenting that this day would remain unforgettable for us and for our children.

The most prevalent tactic was to ban haphazardly scheduled meetings and functions. In Mágócs, the chief justice cancelled the seventh annual music festival because the *UDV* was currently involved in a great political controversy. Many meetings were never held because speakers had tended to excite people. In one instance, the application was one day late; in another, public safety was imperilled. Toward the end of the year, the government also banned all recruiting assemblies, and ordered the *UDV* to seek other means to gain members. But personal contacts were thwarted through intimidations, especially in the Somogy and Bakony regions. Faulstich complained bitterly; the *UDV* became paralyzed. Even amateur performances and balls were prohibited on flimsy pretexts.

More serious still were intimidations and harassments of Swabians by Magyar officials. Árpád Török was fined twice on trumped-up charges and ordered to resign his post. Bleyer's son-in-law Kussbach, a lawyer, had his letters censored and his clients were molested. In Hárta, the *UDV* representative and five peasants were charged with unlawful assembly and fostering Pan-German propaganda because they had entertained two German editors and a youth leader. Through the *VDA,* the German Ministry of the Interior received a steady stream of complaints from disgruntled Swabians. According to one such report, Magyar authorities in Tolna County conspired to destroy the *UDV.* Leading members were harassed by fines. Then they would be hailed before the judge or notary, and informed that persecutions would cease only if they dissolved the local chapter. In many instances, frightened Swabians obeyed. These brutal methods might create a fear psychosis and force organized Swabian life to collapse.

By early 1935, police actions and violence and threats were commonplace. In Dunaharaszti, the projected site of a *UDV* Sunday matinee, vandals broke every window at the Swabian inn. The notary sneered that the innkeeper deserved what he got for playing host to Swabians. A Magyar bystander suggested that instead, Kussbach's head should have been broken. "Torn from his neck, you mean," countered the notary. "It will come to that!" Only the arrival of the County Chief Justice, who promised action, saved what might have become an ugly incident. Basch ran afoul of the authorities when he unwittingly entered Böszénfa to attend a scheduled function, which the authorities had abruptly cancelled. Detained by the gendarmerie, he was paraded through the village—no doubt to intimidate the populace—hauled before the judge, and formally expelled.

The most serious persecution of all involved Basch. On 29 November 1933, Basch had delivered a speech at Bátaapáti, in which he declared, among other things, that "anyone who belongs to us—and you all know who belongs to us—who gives up his honest German name without being forced to do so, does not deserve to have borne his honourable name up till now." At every Swabian meeting a government functionary recorded every word being said. The Swabian-born notary cried: "So you claim that anyone who Magyarizes his name is not an honest man! Since the County Judge and I are planning to Magyarize our names, I consider your remark an insult to authority and I hereby dissolve this meeting." He kept his word and sued Basch for insulting the Hungarian nation. Under normal conditions, the charges would have been dismissed for want of evidence. But at the end of 1934, the court delivered its verdict on patriotic rather than legal grounds.

> Name-Magyarization is a spontaneous outburst of the Magyar national soul and is in the interest of Hungary's national unity, which must be furthered without fail. National unification in language and names is the highest national objective. Since every honestly patriotic citizen must be driven by these feelings, any position adopted against it must be considered an affront and denigrating the Magyar national honour and an insult against the Magyar national spirit.[8]

In the court's opinion Basch was damned by association with the *UDV* because the organization encouraged the dissemination of unpatriotic sentiments. The court also refused to examine witnesses produced by the defense, and sentenced Basch to a three-month prison term with a one-year loss of his civic rights. Both sides appealed, and the case eventually reached the Praesidium, where it rested. When the hysteria diminished, the government discreetly offered amnesty but Basch refused, convinced he was innocent, and confident that a higher court would vindicate him. Thereupon the government had no choice but to permit the judicial process to unwind.

In September 1936, the Supreme Court sentenced Basch to five months in prison. The *Kameradschaft* protested to the *VDA:* "What sort of outrage has he committed to merit such disgrace?" According to the court, he had insulted the holy soul of the Magyar nation, yet the three tribunals refused even to hear the testimony of more than sixty witnesses for the defence. Nor was Basch's case unique. Dr. Rothen, Bleyer's former secretary, was sentenced to a six-month prison term and to a two-year loss of his civic rights.

Fortunately for the Swabians, a number of prominent Magyars defended them. In a prestigious Magyar newspaper, Bethlen argued that Magyars foolishly submitted to Nazi-menace hysteria. During the Weimar Republic, Germans showed no interest in Hungary lest France object. Only conservatives starting with Brüning had begun really to care about Hungary. Bethlen claimed that Germany's conservative revolution guaranteed Hungarian security and prosperity. Shortly after the Bethlen interview, István Milotay, an anti-German publicist and Member of Parliament, revised his views. He ridiculed Magyars for fearing a German attack through Burgenland, but they had to extend to the Swabians rights equal to those demanded for their brethren in the Successor States. Milotay's "conversion" had a great deal to do with the favourable turn in German-Hungarian trade relations, and with Magyar revisionist hopes raised by German leaders. The Swabians rejoiced and expected prompt and permanent improvement in their condition, but were sadly disappointed.

Persecutions contrasted sharply with the image the central government wished to project abroad. Von Papen's appearance at the Budapest headquarters of the *UDV* was a case in point. The German Vice-Chancellor visited Hungary semi-officially as Gömbös' personal guest. At *UDV* headquarters von Papen received deferential treatment. Bleyer, at the head of his entire entourage, welcomed von Papen who spent forty-five minutes in "spontaneous and cordial discussion" with the rank and file. *Nation und Staat* ventured inaccurately that the visit showed how greatly both the Magyars and Germans valued the welfare of the Swabians. At a time when Hungary sought German help to restore her economy, the Magyars were prudent to relax their oppression and permit official German visitors to mingle freely with Swabians. Favourable Reich publicity was also uppermost in the Magyars' minds when they feted a delegation of Hitler Youth in Budapest, then took the group to nearby Budaörs to inspect the large Swabian colony. According to *Angriff,* the visit made a deep impression on the delegation; whether of shock or pleasure would be difficult to say.

Early in June 1934, Basch organized a giant *UDV*-sponsored folk festival in Mágócs. A huge crowd of some 15,000 Swabian spectators from all over Hungary encountered obliging and friendly local authorities. The government had evidently changed, commented *Nation und Staat.* Gratz intoned that the central government and the nation's "best" had never planned the Swabians' discomfort. If the Swabians trod Bleyer's path, all would be well. Even Basch forgot his experiences and exhorted Swabians to be equally devoted to *Volk* and Fatherland. Kussbach regretted the unfortunate misunderstandings and difficulties of the past two years. The clouds had disappeared, and one could contemplate the future with fresh hope and expectation. This euphoria coincided with the signing of the German-Hungarian trade agreement and was not meant to last.

Soon after becoming *UDV* president, Gratz published a sombre status report. For years, Magyar-Swabian relations had been plagued by uncomfortable feelings and mutual suspicions, exacerbated by a lack of meaningful Magyar-Swabian contacts and the Depression. Now, Magyars considered all disgruntled Swabians National Socialists. But negotiations dealing with the entire range of Swabian problems had at last led to settlement. The government would support the *UDV,* but only if it toed the line. Officials had to eschew all types of political activity or conversation.

At the *UDV*'s tenth annual assembly, Gratz argued that Magyars and Swabians were both guilty. The former were intolerant, and the latter succumbed shortsightedly to outside agitation. Swabians must be and remain good "Deutsch-ungarn." At this assembly even the moderates disagreed. Whereas Gratz stressed that Swabians must be Hungarians first and foremost and only cultural Germans, Kussbach neared the radical view. He criticized claims that the Swabians spurned national self-determination, which allegedly conflicted with patriotism. The Swabian commitments to the *UDV* proved their interest in *Volkstum,* and Swabian particularism did not violate Hungarianism. On the contrary; Hungary had minority laws, but execution lagged. The radical Basch agreed and listed neglected minority regulations the Swabians ought to invoke in their daily struggle for justice and equity. Kussbach's announcement that the government had finally activated ten *UDV* chapters in Pest County was the only good news. They had existed for six years, but only on paper.

By late summer all was not well in the *UDV* and in Magyar-Swabian relations. At the annual *UDV* assembly in August 1934, Gratz argued that irrational elements jeopardized Magyar-Swabian peace. Both shared blame and Gratz appealed for moderation. Yet he plainly meant the growing radical wing. It was certainly true that Basch and his companions disdained the recent settlement, hence their political sniping. Gratz mentioned no names, but he did warn that maladroit and tactless remarks would hurt Magyar-Swabian amity. There were bound to be absurd individuals among half a million people, but a few insignificant loners would never be taken seriously as the voice of Swabiandom. The average Swabian was a genuine son of Hungary, a true patriot, who proudly venerated both his German heritage and Hungarian Fatherland. Those whose patriotism was not all it ought to be deserved the same opprobrium as Magyar traitors. Gratz cautioned Swabians that it was too early to detect improvements; but the government definitely meant to fulfill its promises.[9] Unfortunately, the Swabians were suspect because they had powerful foreign friends. Whenever in doubt, which was seldom, the Magyars lumped "bad" Swabians with the "good." In the heated Nazi-inspired nationalist milieu of the 1930's, every Swabian had become a spokesman for all.

In Hungary, government powers had limits. The Gömbös regime had to bow to public opinion, and most Magyars were acutely unhappy about harbouring Swabians in their midst. Since the Bleyer Affair, Magyars had an automatic reaction to imagined or real affronts. More than one Swabian felt the sting of public opprobrium. It heralded future conflict and eroded moderate Swabian support for the UDV and the government. Prosecuting Basch perhaps made sense, but persecuting him did not. It endangered continued cooperation between government and Swabians, who were gradually forced into the radical camp. At last, even Kussbach found himself under attack.

The first incident arose in connection with an insult involving the late Bleyer. Lajos Méhely, a well-known Germanophobe professor, denounced Bleyer's patriotism in the January 1934 issue of A Cél. Bleyer's widow sued Méhely. Representing the family, Kussbach encountered hostile demonstrations and threats of violence when overwrought nationalistic students invaded the trial. Taunting bands of "chauvinist hotspurs" followed him through the streets afterward. Later, Kussbach, a member of Saskör, a Budapest club, imprudently participated in a debate and suggested that, although name-Magyarization was not wrong per se, some of its methods and applications were questionable. This loosed a storm of protest. The press nearly unanimously pilloried Kussbach; members launched expulsion proceedings. Hoping to avert an international cause célèbre, Saskör decided not to expel Kussbach; but the disciplinary committee's public statement forced him to resign.

> Dr. Kussbach's behaviour in Saskör was merely a link in the chain of the type of political role and German-nationalistic activity for which he is well-known throughout the land, and for which he cannot be condemned strongly enough.[10]

Even the educated Magyar public had reached the limits of endurance where Swabians were concerned. Such hostility among the normally sophisticated and tolerant Pest population augured greatly magnified anti-Swabian sentiment in the countryside.

The Magyars failed to profit from their repressions, but merely aroused more and more Swabians to völkisch awareness. What might normally have been an ordinary UDV gathering in Kisdorog drew over one thousand enthusiasts from twenty surrounding villages. At a similar rally in Vaskút, leaders from all the nearby communities arrived to pledge their solidarity. Even more significant was the growing interest in *Volkstum* among the hitherto aloof young academics. Shortly before his death, Bleyer had lamented that the Swabians would perish for want of an intelligentsia, but he would have been well-pleased with recent developments. As one *UDV* functionary explained it,

> Our organizers and helpers have been exposed to so much lies, chicanery, and false accusations, that it is a wonder they have not lost their courage and patience. Yet ten years ago, we were not even a Volk—just a mass of people who happened to speak German and who knew nothing about each other.[11]

Kussbach tried desperately to stem the tide of a losing cause. As the organ dedicated to support two warring trends—the *natio Hungarica* and German cultural norms—the *UDV* drew barbs from all quarters. The assimilationists and *völkisch* radicals battered from within, the Magyar public and the government chipped away from without. The burden of necessity impelled Kussbach to castigate the Gömbös regime. When he began to issue derogatory statements and propose radical suggestions, the government disowned him, and the Swabians were unmoved. On the Germans he made no impression at all.

At the beginning of 1935, the radicals lacked a firm public forum. They spoke up at private gatherings and *UDV* functions. Once, Kussbach was alarmed to find many of the younger members tainted with radical ideas. They clamoured to stand for Parliament, and demanded vastly expanded powers and jurisdictions both for themselves and for the *UDV*. All longed for greater independence. A radical spokesman (probably Basch) criticized Kussbach for wielding too much centralized power, and failing to respect the views of others. When some of the young extremists forced a vote on a number of sensitive issues, Kussbach resigned rather than court a schism. When begged to reconsider, he did, but only on condition that the radicals behave and maintain discipline. A brief outward semblance of amity was restored. Under duress, Kussbach agreed to abandon his monolithic leadership in favour of a triumvirate composed of himself, Basch, and Faulstich. Obviously, the plan failed to work.

Just as dangerous to Moderate success was the assimilationist faction led by Pintér. As Director, Pintér had a great deal of power. At *UDV* meetings in Moson County, he alleged that Hungarian minorities should balance privileges and duties. The State should not tolerate any who followed the head of another nation. *Sonntagsblatt* waxed indignant. Hungary ought to prosecute officials who broke the minority laws, not worry about Swabian fidelity. This was the worst type of baiting in twelve years, a tactic designed to persuade the Magyar public that Swabians did not deserve to have their rights fulfilled.

Pintér had his zeal rewarded with an enlarged jurisdiction and an eventually permanent position. Already his authority as organizer of local functions was considerable. He prevented the *völkisch* Árpád Török from delivering a scheduled lecture series in West Hungary. After much wrangling, Pintér permitted two lectures, but took to the rostrum also to warn Burgenlanders not to look to Hitler for inspiration. *Nation und Staat* deemed it an outrage that the government's own man should insult a friendly foreign dignitary's name in such a fashion. Pintér had also brought various pressures to bear upon Török, who had led the Sopron branch through many trials and tribulations. *Nation und Staat* charged that Pintér tried to destroy the chapter by having its dynamic leader eliminated. Kussbach also alleged that Pintér abused his power and position of trust for self-aggrandizement, sharpening the controversy between moderates and radicals, hoping thereby to hasten his own ascendancy.

The government tried to divorce the Swabian problem from Hungarian foreign policy. Kussbach explained why. When Gömbös returned from his 1935 visit with Hitler, he was understandably optimistic and self-confident, having settled the Swabian-Hungarian controversy with Hitler "over our heads." Thereafter, the Swabians sank into insignificance for Gömbös. His sole concession was to offer Kussbach his party's support in the impending elections as a tribute to Bleyer. Kussbach had no idea that Gömbös' visit had nothing to do with Hitler's seeming neglect of the Swabian problem. For reasons of his own, Hitler had ordered his diplomats to safeguard German-Hungarian relations by muting the Swabian issue. Gömbös deluded himself on his persuasive powers with Hitler. Thereafter, even the moderate Swabians were treated with a highhanded contempt which later spilled over into the 1935 elections and irreparably poisoned Magyar-Swabian relations.

In the meantime, the government wearied of growing Swabian dissidence and radicalism. On 5 February 1935, Gratz, Pintér, and Kussbach were hailed before State Secretary Tibor Pataky, the Praesidium's minority expert. Pataky complained of *UDV* officials stepping out of bounds and charges after meetings about insults to the Hungarian nation. Even *Sonntagsblatt* agitated against the state. These outrages would no longer be tolerated. Henceforth, speakers must submit their manuscripts in advance. To the government's chagrin, Pintér was being boycotted by the hierarchy and prevented from investigating activities, as if the *UDV* had something to hide. Henceforward, Pintér would supervise all functions and report regularly to the government. Kussbach would have to consult the elected regional assembly frequently, and stop leading the organization monolithically.

Kussbach protested. Pataky's reorganization scheme would further erode the *UDV*'s already nebulous powers. The *UDV* had nothing to hide, and Pintér was welcome to spend night and day at headquarters. But it would do great harm, because the organization would become discredited as the government's tool. Kussbach had to submit, but demanded that capricious cancellations of scheduled meetings cease. Pataky merely promised to urge the Ministry of the Interior to release uniform guidelines. It was not true, of course, that the *UDV* had nothing to hide. Radical members were deeply submerged in foreign intrigues, and even Kussbach was not blameless. Schnurre warned that if Kussbach's varied contacts with various Reich organizations were to be divulged, it would prove exceedingly embarrassing for the Reich. Kussbach's contact man, Dr. Kohler, should be urged to sift all documents in Kussbach's care.

In January 1935, Kussbach had proposed moderate reform. In addition to various educational measures, he recommended boosting *UDV* prestige. Officials needed untrammeled freedom. German had to be introduced in all Swabian villages and districts. Name-Magyarization abuses had to stop. An independent judiciary must adjudicate minority grievances. Kussbach's proposals were ignored. One month later, Bajcsy-Zsilinszky struck an unexpected blow for the Swabians. In *Szabadság* he deplored Swabian alienation from the Magyar mainstream, yet insisted that they merited concessions, including German middle schools. This was so burning an issue that he would raise it in Parliament. Bajcsy-Zsilinszky defended his about-face on the grounds that the Swabians did not take orders from abroad and hence were patriotic Hungarians after all.

Kussbach was encouraged by Bajcsy-Zsilinszky's change of heart and Gömbös' projected social reforms. He welcomed impending electoral law changes, but condemned the lack of minority reform, when it was clearly of international importance. Should the Magyars not grant the Swabians' cultural demands, Hungary would suffer the consequences. This time, Kussbach went too far, and the government retaliated by proxy. Dr. Martin Richter, a government *UDV* nominee, disciplined Kussbach. Complaints in the name of the Swabians were deplorable, since they had no cause for dissatisfaction. In order to safeguard Magyar patriotic interests, a new method must be devised to elect *UDV* officials. It was insufficient to nominate men the government could trust; henceforth, only untarnished Magyar patriots must be chosen. *Nation und Staat* protested. This would polarize Swabians into assimilants and Pro-Germans. The government would have been more than pleased to isolate the loyal Swabians from the radicals. Gömbös ventured that most Swabians were true to Hungary and had to have their rights; but not Swabians impelled by centrifugal tendencies. *Sonntagsblatt* saw all Swabians as true patriots, neither traitors nor Pan-Germans, because they demanded the execution of existing laws. By all means, annihilate Hungary's Pan-Germans, but also the saboteurs of minority laws.

Internal and external sniping stung Kussbach and he lost patience. This placed him on a collision course with Gömbös. Kussbach imprudently refused Gömbös' offer to become sole Swabian government candidate in a safe riding. All Swabian candidates defected to the opposition, and campaigned for Tibor Eckhardt's Small Landholders' Party. Basch ran in Bonyhád, Kussbach in Soroksár. Furious, Gömbös appointed Dr. Kruger, a close personal friend, to oppose Kussbach. Army detachments and gendarmerie helped Kruger and intimidated the opposition. Kussbach complained and was again tendered a safe riding in Budaörs. When Kussbach demurred, Gömbös was nonplussed rather then angered. He had never experienced anyone refusing a government offer of a safe riding. Despite Gömbös' assurances, electoral terror resumed, and Kussbach was narrowly beaten. So was Basch, and most of the others. Only Gratz was permitted to win.

After his defeat, Kussbach complained to Gömbös that terrorism harmed Magyar-Swabian relations as well as Hungary's revisionist chances. Gömbös treated Kussbach with patronizing condescension. Being the son of a Swabian mother, he was certainly not anti-Swabian, but unconditionally pro-German. In Berlin, he had recently discussed common German-Hungarian problems, but being Hitler's friend entailed difficulties. He could not befriend the Swabians overtly lest he be attacked by the Opposition. Regarding revision, Gömbös chuckled. He knew what he was doing. Kussbach believed that further talks were useless. Apparently Gömbös and Hitler had already settled revisionism and the Swabian problem on the basis of expediency, just as he had feared.[12] Kussbach also observed that Bleyer's nationality policy was dead. Eventually, the Swabians would become radicalized by nationality experts from Berlin, and by young Nazi party functionaries, working through their Swabian confidants in Hungary—Franz Basch and his followers.

Kussbach's courageous but quixotic behaviour cost the Swabians dearly. Within one month, the axe fell on Basch. On 17 April 1935, the Pécs Appeals Court decreed that most citizens in Bátaapáti were *volksbewusst,* rabidly anti-Magyar Swabians. Only German was spoken in offices, and many people hesitated to use Magyar lest they be dubbed "dumb Magyars." In this milieu Basch's statement was inflammatory. On the basis of questionable logic the court sentenced Basch to five months imprisonment and deprived him of his civic rights for three years. Hungary's highest judicial body, the Royal Curia, ratified the verdict on 24 June 1935. After several stays, and a reduction to five months, Basch entered Pécs Penitentiary on 9 September 1936, and was reprieved by Horthy exactly four months later. The loss of his civic rights remained.

The consequences reverberated. Basch raged, the alleged victim of a Kussbach-government conspiracy. The former wished to remove a formidable rival, the latter plotted to ruin his political career. Indeed, the *UDV*'s entire moderate wing demanded his ouster, because in Hungary office holders under a pall generally resigned until vindicated. When the *UDV* met on 14 June 1935, Gratz ordered Basch to resign because he harmed the Swabian cause. Many Magyars in responsible circles wanted the *UDV* dissolved. Thanks to a few irresponsible officials, Gömbös refused to introduce the new school law promised the year before. It followed, therefore, that

> We cannot pursue two contradictory paths any longer. There are fundamental contradictions between the position that wishes to harmonize the preservation of German speech and character with the task of maintaining the spiritual unity between Magyardom and Swabiandom, and the position that wishes to subordinate relations between Magyardom and Swabiandom in the interests of a universal German national idea. Wittingly or unwittingly, radicals risked catapulting the center of gravity of their activities beyond our borders.[13]

Basch refused to resign. Thereupon Gratz, invoking executive privilege, furloughed him. The assembly at once replaced Basch with Pintér. A resolution sustained the primacy of Bleyer's principles, and condemned disruptive activities. Next day, Basch and his comrades bolted. Thereafter the government and an ever-diminishing number of Swabians supported the *UDV,* whereas the pro-German *völkisch* faction, the *Volksdeutsche Kameradschaft,* was persecuted by the regime, but strongly encouraged by Germany. Henceforth the Germans, and indeed more and more Swabians, stigmatized Gratz a traitor. The dissidents wasted no time establishing contacts in Germany. They soon moved in the highest Berlin circles and pursued their *Volkstumspolitik* with the Reich.

Following these events, the Magyars greatly feared growing *völkisch* agitation in Hungary. While Gömbös negotiated with the Reich, Kussbach and Gratz sold the reconstituted *UDV* to the Magyar public. Kussbach explained that Swabian moderates wished to pursue cultural goals only, but in harmony and amity with the Magyars. The *UDV* had but one non-cultural objective: to foster German-Hungarian friendship. Ferenc Rajniss, a Magyar Member of Parliament, accepted Kussbach's assurances on face value. But the twentieth century had intensified nationalism. Until about two years ago, Magyars had been rather tolerant, but Germany's unprecedented growth made them tremble. Rajniss hoped he was wrong, and Germany and Hungary would cooperate to achieve revision. Swabian cultural wishes must therefore be honoured. Rajniss ignored how the Swabians would respond if forced to choose between Germany and Hungary. Kussbach saw Swabian culture resting on four pillars: fidelity, friendship, responsibility, and peace. Swabians were a sensible, religious, and God-fearing people. They obeyed authority and respected the laws: therein lies our strength. Kussbach failed to penetrate the heart of the matter and also ignored nationalism. Obeying authority could become morally fatal. Obedience depended on one's viewpoint. Gratz also ignored realities and behaved as if moralistic appeals and fiat alone would keep Swabians from National Socialism. He declared that henceforth the *UDV* must serve only the government and alluded that many Swabians loved German *Volkstum* better than the Hungarian Fatherland. He hoped this would change. Gratz might have pleased the Magyar public and smoothed his subsequent discussions with Gömbös, but *Sonntagsblatt* resented the totally erroneous notions about the *UDV*'s role. It must serve only Swabians, most of whom were loyal. Both Magyarones and radical extremists harmed the Swabian cause, and would eventually poison Magyar-Swabian relations.[14]

One week later, Gratz emerged from his conversation with Gömbös in an optimistic frame of mind. He had found total understanding for all the cultural aspirations of the Swabians, as well as full benevolence. In Gömbös' view, the recent assembly's expressed loyalty to Hungary had cooled public passions sufficiently to permit the passage of a new school law within a few days. This had become feasible also because certain elements, associated in the public mind with extremism, had now stepped into the background. But the harm done by the radicals' unpolitic behaviour remained. Even now, the government might dissolve the *UDV*, especially if certain recent incidents were not speedily settled. Indeed, the school law was not published until just before Christmas. But the government did not intend to dissolve the thoroughly browbeaten *UDV*. It was needed as a counterfoil against the *Kameradschaft*. Moreover, dissolution at a time when negotiations with Germany were proceeding at Hungary's request would have been monumental folly.

The "certain recent incidents" were explained by a confidential *Kameradschaft* report earmarked for the *VDA*. *Sonntagsblatt*, which had been Bleyer's private property, was bequeathed to his ailing son Franz. Kussbach, who became manager, treated the newspaper as his own, and ignored *Kameradschaft* demands to surrender the publication to them. Three *VDA* secret agents (Berka, Krehl, and Klocke) failed to sway Kussbach, but persuaded König, the managing editor, to defect. They also convinced Franz Bleyer to bequeath *Sonntagsblatt* to an editorial triumvirate composed of *Kameradschaft* stalwarts Basch, Huss, and Faulstich. This was perfectly legal and would have succeeded, but Kussbach discovered the operation and revealed it to Gratz. More, he unraveled the entire confidential fabric of *Kameradschaft* connections with Reich circles, including their receipt of large stipends for *völkisch* agitation. Gratz revealed all in turn to Gömbös and, livid with rage, summoned the *Kameradschaft*. Gömbös knew everything, names and amounts, and intended to dissolve the *UDV* and have all these gentlemen arrested and tried under military statute. Accepting foreign funds for propaganda purposes was espionage, the sentence death. Now Gratz's full fury descended on Basch, Huss, and Faulstich. It was outrageous that German citizens meddled in the internal affairs of Swabians, particularly the *UDV*. He also knew about König's seduction. All this nonsense had to cease and Kussbach must be left alone. The government was not inclined to get rid of him. *Sonntagsblatt* must remain in his care, or be shut down. Finally, Gratz swore that, circumstantial evidence to the contrary, Kussbach was not the informer. The radicals did not believe him. Thereafter, they hated both Kussbach and Gratz. König panicked and returned to the fold. The coup had failed, but it left a legacy of frustration and hate in its wake.[15]

Owing to these disruptions, the Swabian movement lost its homogeneity, most of its leaders, and its traditional spirit of cooperation and compromise. It was *bellum omnium contra omnes*. By the fall, Kussbach's position was precarious. He could not carry out Bleyer's programme. He disagreed both with the government and the *Kameradschaft*. The Magyar public was unsympathetic. Reich circles resented him for destroying Swabian unity. Thereupon Kussbach tendered his resignation. Gratz persuaded him to remain until year's end. In the interim, Kussbach urged *Sonntagsblatt* readers to cherish Bleyer's ideals. On 8 December, the final issue carried Kussbach's farewell message. The period *Nation und Staat* designated as "Kussbach's interregnum" was over. *Sonntagsblatt* was retitled *Neues Sonntagsblatt,* and under the watchful eyes of Gratz and Pintér it became the government's mouthpiece, the only effective forum left to them. The *Kameradschaft* issued its rival *Deutscher Volksbote*. The schism was final.

Henceforward the *VDA* received endless salvoes of repetitive, impassioned complaints and pleas from Basch. The schism was fundamental and irrevocable. The *Kameradschaft* remained the sole *volksdeutsch* group in Hungary. The "official" *UDV* and *Neues Sonntagsblatt* were government stooges. But why would the German press, such as *Berliner Börsenzeitung,* still hail *Neues Sonntagsblatt* as the new publication of the German minority in Hungary? Basch then described Gratz's attempt to subvert the *Kameradschaft.* Gratz told Huss that the government now offered reconciliation, with full amnesty, provided the radicals terminated all contacts with Germany, renounced all further foreign subsidies, and rejoined the *UDV.* The government would even continue the lost subsidies. The alternatives were arrest and prosecution for high treason. Huss accepted, then wavered,[16] and finally stood firm. His comrades followed suit, only to discover that the whole manoeuvre was a government trick to destroy the *volksdeutsch* movement, and to manufacture a legal pretext for the continued existence of the *UDV.* "Now the struggle commences in earnest."

From its power base inside Hungary, the *Kameradschaft* vowed to fight both *UDV* and government. Already, all *volksdeutsch* champions stood firm and a cover organization, *Kultura,* had been established despite last-ditch government opposition. *Kultura* would propagate *völkisch* music, books, lecture series, and concerts. *Neue Heimatblätter,* a scholarly periodical dedicated to Swabian research, supplemented the popular-based *Deutscher Volksbote. Suevia,* for years denied government permission, became the *Jungkameradschaft.* Twenty-two high school students had joined already, whereas Gratz had no youthful following at all. A one-week seminar had been arranged to indoctrinate young women and was attended by selected girls from fifteen communities. A similar programme for young boys was in the planning stages, and another to re-Germanize assimilated Swabian merchants and artisans. Boys and girls journeyed to the mother country to spend time in appropriate homes and camps for reeducation. Basch outlined his alternatives. The *Kameradschaft* might succumb, compromise with Gratz, and abandon all its *völkisch* enterprises, thus committing ethnic suicide and virtual *Volksverrat* (ethnic treason), because the intransigent and nationalistic Gömbös regime had no intentions to deal honourably with the Swabians. The other alternative was a German-Hungarian political compromise at Swabian expense. Basch could not believe that the Reich would ever perpetrate such opportunism. If it did, then the *völkisch* revival in Hungary would crumble.

Basch's reports became more shrill and strident. Gratz harassed Huss to submit, or the money question would be brought to court. The *Kameradschaft* was in dire peril. Dr. Mühl (a *Kameradschaft* stalwart) might lose his physician's license. Every *Neues Sonntagsblatt* issue slurred and threatened.

If only we had more funds, and if only we had more help and understanding in the Reich! We shall endure as long as we can. But we cannot bear the responsibility alone any longer!!!!!

Two weeks later:

> We had to give notice to Albert and Schnitzer [two *Kameradschaft* employees
> the government promised to subsidize if the radicals came to terms]. Our
> money is almost gone. The government has decided to confiscate all issues of
> the *Deutscher Volksbote*. What next? It is bitter to look on helplessly as the
> water rises higher and little hope will dog our steps. But time will vindicate
> us. Do you know what I lose? My work. . .goes to ruin, the purpose of my life.
> Do you know what this means?. . . .Thanks to the Regent's amnesty, the
> process against Muhl was terminated. But the amnesty does not apply to me.[17]

Obviously, the government and Gratz had isolated the Basch group. In
the summer of 1936, the Reich terminated most subsidies, although secret
National Socialist funds continued to trickle in.[18] On the second anniversary
of Bleyer's death, *Sonntagsblatt* blasted certain Swabian leaders for abandoning the deceased leader's path. They must return to "cultural principles."
The *UDV* should not be a political springboard, only serve Swabian culture.
Politicization and the leadership struggle had reached the rank and file.
Even the German press failed to support the *Kameradschaft*. On his October
visit to Germany, Gömbös was hailed as a blood brother. *Germania* lumped
the Swabian question with a few others, and lightly dismissed them all as
certain political vagaries that Hungary engaged in now and then. The
Kameradschaft was cowed but not beaten.

By August 1936, tensions had become acute. Throughout the year, Gratz
had tried to outwit the radicals, but not to accuse them of deliberate treason.
Their approach did, however, serve to exacerbate Magyar-Swabian tensions. Gratz swore to restore and deepen the old Magyar-Swabian harmony.
One month later, he again "praised" Huss and his friends. They were
patriotic, but their views on the December 1935 school law unfortunately
endangered Magyar-Swabian amity. Their deprecation and eschewal of the
new regulation were precisely what many anti-Swabians wished to hear.
Loyal Swabians had been waiting twelve years for this law. Against charges
that he was dictatorial, Gratz maintained he was merely an honest caretaker. The applause of "demagogically bewitched masses," the opinions of
foreign functionaries, were of no account. He did not open his umbrella in
Budapest every time it rained in Berlin.

By late spring, Gratz's patience had evaporated. He desired rapprochement, but not at the cost of Magyar-Swabian harmony. Amity was
unthinkable without settling whether the *UDV* and Swabians would obey

the new direction or cleave to their old, Hungarian traditions. The longer the radicals waited, the more difficult reconciliation would be. The eleventh hour had nearly struck. Should this opportunity be lost, the gulf would widen.

The *Kameradschaft* failed to be reconciled and the struggle continued at the August Assembly. Having foreseen that the radicals planned to capture the *UDV,* Gratz refused to seat those known. But Jakob Brand, a sympathiser, passed a seven-point protest resolution. Only a plenary session quorum could exclude members. The Assembly should be adjourned pending an impartial hearing. Gratz admitted breaking some of the rules, but he remanded the matter to the Minister of the Interior for adjudication. The *Kameradschaft* was stumped. Complaints would be construed as defying Miklós Kozma, one of the power brokers of the Gömbös cabinet.

This crisis overcome, Gratz delivered his opening speech. The *UDV* must arrest Magyar-Swabian spiritual dissonance; defend Swabian interests; and deflect foreign influences. To some extent, this was successful; the Magyar public no longer distrusted the *UDV* as much as before and consequently the obstacles had now largely disappeared. The recent school law was an example. Unfortunately, the price of success was schism. Gratz had failed to heal the rift before the Assembly. But Swabian unity mattered less than Magyar-Swabian amity. Swabians would pay dearly if they forgot this. Gratz granted his opponents sincere concern as patriots who meant well, but whose approach was harmful. It mattered not what he or they believed; what mattered was Magyar public opinion, and how far it would go. Cultural freedom seemed the limit, so Gratz appealed for unity. Troubles were caused by varying phraseology and tactics. Since the greatest obstacle to unity (Kussbach) was gone, Gratz pledged to compromise on all points save one: The *UDV* must remain strictly cultural and not seem a threat in Magyar public opinion.

The *Kameradschaft* rejected Gratz's offer. "Bleyer's spirit has been driven from the *UDV* and the Swabian Volk." Pintér's nomination as Secretary-General mocked Bleyer's memory. In Parliament, Pintér had supported Bajcsy-Zsilinzky against Bleyer. Heckenberger was no better, having been one of Bleyer's sharpest critics. Not one of Bleyer's original collaborators currently officiated in the *UDV.* Gratz's speech was a travesty. He only cared about Magyar-Swabian spiritual unity, not Bleyer's goals. He lied that the new school law would further German education. Having been dragged through so much injury, misery, and humiliation, Swabians would see clearly whom to follow.

Gratz became harsher. The government honestly wished to settle the Swabian problem. For the past fifteen years, each regime had earnestly sought accommodation, but was always prevented more or less by public resistance. Nothing fed this more than the combativeness of radical Swabians. While they were still in the *UDV*, German elementary education could not be realized. Only now, when moderates led the *UDV*, was it possible to introduce the new school law. This was a spurious and simplistic argument. Since 1919 many school regulations had come and gone without making the least imprint on Swabian education.

Next, Gratz stooped to threats. "I do not wish to reveal to the public the real reasons for the obstacle that prevents rapprochement. If Huss and his friends continue their attacks, I may come to it." Gratz meant that unless the radicals capitulated, he would divulge their illegal Reich transactions. When the *Kameradschaft* stood firm, Gratz appealed that the controversy must not injure the *UDV*: In this conflict, poison and gall, insinuations and distrust, should have no place.

Towards the end of the year, Gratz resorted to patriotic ploys. The radicals wished to introduce National Socialism in Hungary, but they did not consider this treason. Thus they became more vulnerable. Gratz conjured an apocalypse: Hitler's system worked for Germany but would not mobilize Hungary, and would fatally injure Swabians. Everyone familiar with the composition and spirit of Magyar society knew that a national socialist system here would be strongly nationalistic, nay, exclusively nationalistic, and would exude to an ultimate level the spirit that had made life so sour for German-Hungarians. The Magyars would suppress all non-Magyar influence, as the Reich smothered non-Aryans. The totalitarian Italians persecuted the insignificant German minority in the Tyrol, where parents could not provide even private German instruction for their children. Could anyone expect that a Hungarian state steeped in national socialist principles would be more tolerant? Anyone believing it greatly deceived himself. Having discredited the *Kameradschaft* with the Swabian public, Gratz now turned to the Magyars. In an interview with *Pesti Napló* Gratz stated that mounting German press attacks against Hungary's Swabian policy related to the internecine Swabian controversy. Germany loathed the *UDV*, but favoured the *Kameradschaft*, hoping to strengthen the latter at the cost of the former.

> But Germany must become quite clear that not all *Auslanddeutschtum* can be treated exactly the same way. German-Hungarians live in a nation having intimate ties with Germany. Hence, existing difficulties and dissatisfactions must be handled soothingly rather than exacerbate the tensions.[19]

The interview pleased the Magyar public but alienated the *Kameradschaft* beyond recall.

Gömbös' death did not change the Swabian controversy or the status of the *UDV*. Basch was amnestied in January 1937, one month ahead of his full sentence—a minor sop to the radicals and the Reich. The Magyars had destroyed Swabian unity, and a polarized and confused rank and file slowly and inexorably moved towards the radicalism hated by the Magyars, and feared by their moderate Swabian fellow travellers.

The School Problem

Hungary's minority education policy always contradicted her public posturing. The dozen years since Trianon had produced scant change in Swabian school conditions. Provincial authorities ignored Budapest's public pronouncements. The largely ecclesiastically-controlled schools claimed immunity from government interference because church autonomy embraced both worship and instruction. Even a determined regime would have faltered before such resistance, and Hungary was far from zealous on minority enforcement. Church autonomy was thus a perfect excuse for inaction, and cited by every postwar regime.

Coincidentally with Gyula Károlyi's departure new ideologies stirred in Europe. National Socialism unleashed integral nationalism, and some Swabian churchmen rallied enthusiastically to the Third Reich. Magyar clergymen panicked. The nationalistic exultation of the former, and the defensive hysteria of the latter, created an oppressive atmosphere for Swabian education. Examples of the schism abound. Edmund Scholtz, the foremost Swabian Protestant leader, exulted when the National Socialists seized power in Germany. He applauded when Hitler forced German Protestants into a single, monolithic ecclesiastic organization and criticized the unsympathetic domestic press, which claimed erroneously that the old Protestant denominations were being replaced forcibly by a new National Socialist Evangelical church. In fact, most Protestants had agreed to unify voluntarily, exuding German patriotism. Swabian Protestants ought to share their enthusiasm.

Scholtz soon became disillusioned with Nazi tactics; but in the meantime, the public associated him with Pan-Germanism. His demand for German education only confirmed the connection between National Socialism and Swabian irredentism. Bleyer's similar clamourings augmented fears of a conspiracy. There were hysterical outbursts in Magyar public life. Bleyer's insistence that the Roman Catholic clergy bore the main responsibility for the failure of Swabian minority education prompted Catholics to counterattack.[20]

Korunk Szava assailed the Swabians indirectly by impugning the honesty of the Hitler Regime's religious motives. Magyars who celebrated National Socialist successes because they hoped to satiate their own romantic visions were in for a shock. Hitler's rise merely signified the return of *Vorkriegsdeutschland*. No degree of Nazi material success would induce us to accept their philosophy. A few months later, *Korunk Szava* accused the Reich of sabotaging the Concordat. Its godless philosophy ranked with Soviet Russia's. It planned to unify and reform the Christian churches at the price of both God and Christianity. National Socialism had reached even Hungary. Clergymen dabbled in it. One was translating Reventlow's advocacy of the new Nazi "non-Christian" Church, which German believers branded as "neo-pagan," into Magyar. Some orders were promoting *Mein Kampf*. Hungarian ecclesiastic authorities must purge this dreadful cancer.

Ethnic discrimination was alien to the Catholic Church and consequently the Swabians could not be attacked on those grounds, or as Germans. *Korunk Szava* distinguished between "German" and "Nazi," and endeavoured to explain the difference between Pan-Germanism and Swabian cultural legitimacy. Bleyer was a good, honest, and true German; he loved but did not idolize his people; he did not deny his Germanhood, nor was he a chauvinist. He claimed for Swabians only what conditions currently demanded. National self-determination was not just a phrase, and Magyar Catholics dared not deprive others of its benefits.

Continuing in the same grudging spirit, *Korunk Szava* warned that the German tidal wave had arrived. But were not Magyar expatriates concerned about their mother country? Why should Germans be different? The Swabians ought to receive German higher education. Just minority demands did not mean Pan-Germanism. A German menace did exist, but the Swabians were blameless. Still, Swabian leaders ought to abandon their own foreign policy; they should not follow (German National Socialist ideologue) Rosenberg, but Vienna's *Ballhausplatz*.

Korunk Szava fooled no one. It planted a row of connected ideas: National Socialists were anti-Christian barbarians; a German menace existed; the Swabians were not Hungarians but Germans; their cultural demands were just, and consequently good Catholics had to dutifully obey their wishes; Swabian leaders toyed dangerously with German National Socialist rather than acceptable Austro-Christian, if not Hungarian, ideas; hence, Swabians were suspect by implication. The Magyar reader, whose anti-German prejudices were already well-cultivated, suspected that for political as well as religious reasons, Magyars could not arrest fundamentally odious German ideas. The impression that the German noose was tightening around their necks caused Magyars to despair and adopt repressive measures against the

Swabians. The Roman Catholic intelligentsia caught the hidden message. *Korunk Szava's* propaganda campaign intensified until by 1937 West Hungary's Swabians were deemed doubtful patriots should Germany lay claim to the region.[21]

The shipwreck of the Swabian minority school system can thus be best understood through Magyar Roman Catholic fear of Pan-Germanism. School laws that were merely guidelines or suggestions meant nothing. As *Sonntagsblatt* summarized, "law and real life are not the same." Government decisions were sabotaged by narrow-minded and evil officials. Whenever a Swabian demanded his rights, he was called "traitor" and "Pan-German." Functionaries believed that resisting the minority laws was their patriotic duty. *Sonntagsblatt* became more strident during Easter Week in response to the hostile government press. The editors considered current minority policy contrary to Swabian aspirations, especially in education.

Pressures on the government mounted not only in Hungary but from abroad. *Nation und Staat* wondered why Hungary refused to improve Swabian education. After all, minority schools were scarcely centrifugal. *Nation und Staat* cited Aegidius Faulstich as the classical example of the new Swabian generation that would not stand idly by and see its own children alienated from traditional *Volkstum*. If Gömbös deemed this a centrifugal tendency, then his policy was no longer Hungarian, but one-sided and racist. The German press noted that even the Magyar papers complained about Swabian mistreatment. Did not Hungary realize that this might damage German-Hungarian relations? Artur Kornhuber of the *Berliner Börsenzeitung* wrote that Gömbös obviously desired closer German-Hungarian commercial relations, but Germans wished to see Bethlen's old school promises honoured. Kornhuber was astounded. The minority problem impeded German-Hungarian friendship, yet Gömbös refused to see the connection between them. Just before Bleyer's May 1933 speech, Gömbös clarified his indifference. A number of speakers in Parliament's Finance Committee feared the Swabians' German sentiments, but feared also denying them cultural freedom. Gömbös argued it was high time to solve the minority problem. A new minority state secretaryship in the Praesidium would be created.[22] A ministerial sinecure was Gömbös' idea of dealing forthrightly with the situation.

In the meantime, Bleyer wearied of delays and unfulfilled promises. His growing frustration generated a desire for a showdown.

> Our immediate aim is to provoke Magyar nationalists to commit themselves
> to an unconcealed attitude, in order for us to be able to turn either to the right
> or to the left. The present situation, which now has lasted for years, is

downright murderous for us. Our nerves are so taut that we cannot endure [the tension] even for another half year.[23]

On 9 May 1933, Bleyer spoke:

Every national minority is entitled to enjoy the most important and at the same time natural right to educate its children in its own language. The only way a cultured people can pass its ethnic legacy and racial characteristics unspoiled and unadulterated from generation to generation is if it has a school system at its disposal.[24]

Bleyer spoke of violations of the minority laws and focused on the school question. The 1868 Nationality Law was the only statute with honest intentions because it had provided the unequivocal right of education in the minority language. Every postwar law was a sham, ambiguous in wording or intent, or crippled by enabling decrees. Bleyer cited that in the fall of 1928, some 390 Swabian localities had 463 so-called minority schools. Of these, 49 were A (10.6%); 98 were B (21.2%); and 316 were C (68.2%) institutions. The same year, Bethlen promised to transform all C schools into B institutions. Only one-teacher schools in mixed Magyar-Swabian communities would be exempted. For one or two years, Bethlen kept his word. Then the execution flagged, and ever since the situation had grown worse. Moreover, only A institutions were genuine minority schools. Swabians might be content with B schools, but never would they or anyone settle for C institutions. These schools offered only two hours of indifferent German instruction weekly, and only from the third or fourth grade onward. Many offered no German instruction at all. The law authorized parents' conferences to demand minority schools, but this was a mere paper decree. Reality contrasted with theory. Hostile teachers, notaries, and priests opposed any type of German instruction. With the possible exception of West Hungary, the situation was similar in kindergartens, continuation schools, and in the *Levente*. Most Roman Catholic schools forbade even the study of religion, not to mention religious services in German. Consequently, Swabian children courted moral and spiritual decay. Seven out of ten Swabian elementary school graduates could not read or write in German, and nine out of ten Swabian high school graduates could not compose a faultless German sentence or write a German letter that would betray their German origin.

Bleyer was interrupted by hecklers, and two deputies of Swabian extraction, Lang and Neuberger, ostentatiously left the Chamber.[25] Bajcsy-Zsilinszky was scandalized at Bleyer's unpatriotic, calumnious speech at a time of national weakness and economic misery. As co-editor of *Nation und Staat* with Rudolf Brandsch, Bleyer consorted with a notorious traitor. Certain minor flaws in minority treatment did exist over the past thousand years, but compared with the Successor States, the Swabians were far better off. They were so well off compared to the poor Magyars that Bleyer's accusations amounted to political extortion. What would the German press say? Bleyer ought to strengthen Hungary's links with Austria and prevent Germany from reaching Hungary's frontiers. Bleyer was possibly even a traitor, having contacted the foreign press. He was the confidential source who slandered Hungary in *Der Auslandsdeutsche*, press organ of the Munich-based *Bund der Auslandsdeutschen*, with which he had long been intimately connected. Bleyer also fed the *Prager Presse* injurious news. Bleyer's pro-Hitler sympathies were well-known. He attempted to re-Germanize mixed villages by stampeding Swabian parents into demanding A schools. Bajcsy-Zsilinszky concluded that many of the prosperous Hungarian middle classes were of Swabian origin. Yet no Magyar ever questioned their right to rise into this milieu, provided they did so as Hungarians. If Swabians insisted on a German education and then aspired to high positions on the basis of nationality, then the Magyars would invoke a quota to protect their own interests. The government must suppress Bleyerite agitation and drive the Swabian movement into acceptable channels, both for their own sake and for the good of the Magyars.[26]

The struggle over Bleyer's speech, a showdown over ethnic education, continued in and out of Parliament. Party members obeyed strict orders not to demonstrate during Bleyer's speech. But party discipline did break down in the tumult generated by Bajcsy-Zsilinszky. There were turbulent scenes in the parliamentary corridors. Bajcsy-Zsilinszky vowed to have Bleyer thrown out of Parliament while many onlookers cheered. University students demonstrated against Bleyer, invaded his home, pelted it with rotten eggs, broke windows, threatened and insulted his wife. The police claimed to be powerless. Two Magyar student associations passed resolutions condemning Bleyer's "insult to the Magyar nation," and demanded his resignation from the university. The dean cancelled Bleyer's classes for safety's sake. *Suevia*, the Swabian student group, resigned en masse from MEFHOSZ (*Magyar Egyetemi és Főiskolai Hallgatók Országos Szövetsége*), the national Hungarian student federation, and clashed with its members in the streets. The Magyar press, with the exception of *Magyarság*, pilloried Bleyer. As *Sonntagsblatt* put it, Catholic, liberal, democratic, and conservative papers alike, spewed their venom and distortions.

Strangely enough, Bleyer's only ray of hope was Gömbös, who suggested in Parliament possible positive developments in the minority impasse.

Gömbös appreciated the parts of Bleyer's speech where he acknowledged Magyar supremacy. Gömbös claimed he had previewed the speech, and warned Bleyer it would loose a storm of indignation, because it seemed to represent centrifugal forces. But student leaders had promised to stop demonstrating. This was a touchy problem, but the government could solve it. Bleyer should provide a written list of all his grievances for negotiation. Gömbös' statement was greeted with stormy applause. Bleyer thanked Gömbös. A list of grievances had already been dispatched on 10 May.

As the initial shock waves abated, Bleyer's calm evaporated. As C.A. Macartney observed, the 'affaire Bleyer' proved, unhappily, a turning point in the relations between Hungary and her German minority. Bleyer had been a moderate, but now he roared in rage against the students, and the inactive university administration. Magyar-Swabian friendship might suffer great injury from his outrages. The sixty-year-old Bleyer even challenged his most persistent heckler, Bajcsy-Zsilinszky, to a saber duel. Bajcsy had dispatched a political opponent twenty-one years earlier and had little trouble with Bleyer. He inflicted several superficial wounds, whereupon the seconds terminated the affair. No reconciliation took place. Undaunted, Bleyer next challenged Miklós Lázár, a deputy who had allegedly flung "traitor!" at him in Parliament. But Lázár denied having meant Bleyer and the case was settled.[27] The duel represented a watershed of a very special kind to Bleyer, whose religious convictions transcended even his loyalty to Hungary and his dedication to the Swabian cause. He had courted excommunication in order to avenge his honour as a German.

The controversy occurred at a time when Hungary had reached economic bottom, and when Germany had almost completely curtailed Hungarian imports. In Parliament, Kánya admitted receiving numerous complaints from the public, protesting the gradual drying up of the German market. This was unfortunate, but a German trade delegation would arrive in Budapest soon.[28] Gömbös chose this moment to deliver a policy statement on the Swabian problem designed for foreign consumption. Gömbös proclaimed his brotherly love toward Hungary's minorities and claimed the Swabians fared materially better than their share in the population suggested. Here he was, son of a Swabian mother, and Prime Minister of Hungary. Was this Swabian oppression? If they had complaints, he would certainly listen. But Hungary needed no new prophets. He would reject all attempts to seek solutions for the minority problem abroad.

Bleyer wondered whether Gömbös had alluded to him as the new prophet. He might be servant, but not prophet. But over foreign aid Bleyer was defiant. Nothing was more natural than for Swabians to maintain cultural contact with Germans. He had been grievously wronged and insulted in Parliament, and demanded satisfaction. Regarding the Swabians' economic condition, it was no longer satisfactory. Swabian peasants were being bankrupted in ever larger numbers, but Magyar peasants also suffered from the Depression.

As the controversy grew, more and more individuals joined in to assail Bleyer. One of the exceptions was Milotay, editor of *Magyarság,* who championed minority rights on practical and ethical grounds, in a tone reminiscent of Deák and Eötvös. Hunyadi and Minister of Agriculture Tibor Kállay sympathized with Bleyer, but Perényi and Pintér flayed him. The Baranya County Council, where Bleyer's earlier nemesis, Keresztes-Fischer officiated, passed a Resolution of Censure. Introducing German in the schools imperiled both Swabians and Magyars. Bleyer's demand of A schools was not minority protection, but anti-Magyar agitation.

Minister of Education Bálint Hóman was somewhat more polite, though equally discouraging. The 1923 school law and subsequent decrees would be obeyed and Bleyer was urged to do likewise. Whether he liked it or not, parents must decide school types, as the Wends and Poles did in Germany. Analysis of ethnic status on the basis of names would create confusion. Further, Bleyer's school statistics were inaccurate. After 1928, the situation had improved. Currently, 376 communities possessed 46 A, 141 B, and 265 C institutions. This certainly proved that Hungary's German schools excelled those in the Successor States. Bleyer replied that school data ought to be published from year to year to avoid misunderstandings. But local officials disobeyed government directives. Furthermore, there were currently nine A schools fewer than previously, and C schools still predominated. Hóman also ignored kindergartens, continuation schools, religious and *Levente* organizations, middle schools, and teacher academies. Regarding Germany's minority school system, Bleyer considered it unfortunate "that we use foreign models to clear up our own minority education." There was a third method. Recent census figures might determine equitably the language of education in a given locality. Bleyer forgot, of course, that using census figures had a fatal flaw. Magyar pollsters would coerce minorities to declare themselves Magyars on pain of reprisals.

The controversy embroiled Bethlen, who argued in *Magyar Szemle* that while Magyars were foolish to deprive Swabians of their rights, these privileges had to have certain limits. He favoured B elementary schools and kindergartens, where Swabians might learn German and Magyar with equal proficiency; but high schools and universities would develop an alienated Swabian intelligentsia and spearhead separatism. Only "certain reichs-deutsch elements" advocated it, while Bleyer and his followers would never consider it. But Magyars had to abandon counterproductive practices and beliefs. The misguided Magyar provincial intelligentsia deemed it patriotic to sabotage German instruction, prohibit German divine services, and eliminate the German spoken word. Bleyer's presentation in Parliament, despite minor mistakes and distortions, was objective and fair. He was unquestionably a Hungarian patriot. Nonetheless, his speech was tactless, ill-advised, ill-timed, and unnecessary. He should have consulted the Prime Minister. But why should a minority leader exercise restraint when chauvinistic Magyars showed neither sense nor forebearance? Performance had lagged in the execution of the school laws over the last two years, but German education must forge ahead again soon, since Gömbös was benevolent and the present situation poor. Bethlen cited statistics that improved Hóman's figures, and partially rectified Bleyer's earlier complaints.

Bleyer responded, defended himself, and analyzed Bethlen's main points. Good; Bethlen desired B schools and kindergartens, but how about continuation schools, the *Levente* movement, and the Church? Did Bethlen mean to ignore them? Bleyer eschewed a Swabian political party, but unless the government fulfilled school promises soon, it would follow soon. Bleyer disagreed that German higher education would harm the Magyar spirit and cause schism. Moreover, Swabian *völkisch* demands were not spawned by *reichsdeutsch* propaganda. Every European minority desired cultural contact with its compatriots. Finally, Bleyer claimed he was not leader of the Germans in Hungary, but champion of a cultural movement. He was faithful to the State, true to the *Volk* [*volkstreu*] and followed in Tisza's and Széchenyi's footsteps. He was ready, as they were, to assume all burdens.

The polemics generated energy which demanded resolution, not more promises. These hopes were dashed in late summer. Bleyer reported a conversation with Gombos as a frank, fundamental talk. Both had been candid and the problem would be solved in both Swabian and Hungarian interests. Privately Bleyer was pessimistic: "It is true that a conversation took place in August between Prime Minister Gömbös and myself, but it had only a preliminary character and led to no concrete steps."[29] Although further talks were scheduled, none were held. Four weeks later, Bleyer was dead.

Sonntagsblatt was noncommittal as it surveyed the first year of Gömbös' minority achievements. Little happened except for several friendly discussions. The reason for *Sonntagsblatt's* leniency was obvious. Gömbös had visited Germany in June and returned glowing over the new regime. Chances for a German-Hungarian accord were good, which might improve the Swabians' situation. Gömbös' pro-German outlook was well-known, wrote the editor, and it did not appear prudent for the Swabians to push the minority issue.

The Bleyer Affair triggered great interest in German education. Thousands of petitions flooded *Sonntagsblatt* and the *UDV* demanding German schools. In some localities panicky Magyar officials allegedly tried to intimidate supplicants. *Sonntagsblatt* relayed the list to the Ministry of Education, where it gathered dust. The new academic year of 1933-1934 brought no improvement. Indeed, as an economy measure, vacation time was extended, the school year shortened. Swabian children suffered doubly, since they received less instruction in their mother tongue than before, and because they were taught by superannuated, incompetent teachers. Young, able instructors increasingly desponded, as the government violated its own laws. How did the government expect citizens to respect the state?

In a similar vein, Franz Rothen denounced the unequal Magyar-Swabian struggle. Bajcsy-Zsilinszky claimed no opposition to minority rights, only objections to radical efforts to hem in the Magyars. Nonsense, said Rothen. The reverse was true. Consider the Magyar official claiming he knew no German, but who charged five Pengő for translations. Clerical teachers knew German imperfectly or not at all. Two-thirds of the institutions designated as minority schools were nothing of the sort. Yet Magyars accused Swabians of exploiting their weakened condition by escalating their demands. Actually, Swabians only wanted the laws obeyed, and would gladly settle for the Nationality Law of 1868.

Rothen's was one of many efforts by Swabian leaders to preserve *Volkstum*. After Bleyer's death, old demands intensified, even as new ones coalesced. The Swabians justified their militancy on the grounds that the Magyars wished to exploit a leaderless people. They were correct. Gömbös was secretly plotting to undermine the Swabian movement. He asserted to Mackensen that the Swabians already lived in a paradise. Nobody desired minority schools except a few politically-minded leaders since the War. Having maligned Bleyer, Gömbös concluded with the ambiguous hope that "progress will be made on the road which I intend to take." That this road was full-fledged Magyarization, nobody doubted.

In this atmosphere of distrust, Gömbös refused to deal with the *UDV* unless Gratz became president. Gratz demanded negotiations on education and other burning issues first. Gömbös eventually bowed to pressure and threats, and on 5 February 1934, ordered negotiations to commence. The meeting led to firmer government control of the *UDV* but school problems received short shrift. In principle, Gömbös favoured transforming all government schools into B institutions within three-four years. Considering the negligible number of government schools, this was a bagatelle. If confessional schools failed to move ahead appreciably within the next two years, appropriate legislation would be introduced. Continuation and middle schools would remain Magyar, and there would be no separate German academies or institutions for the training of kindergarten teachers. Kindergartens might, however, organize along B lines. Parents' conferences would remain. Worse, in future they would have to meet annually by a stipulated date. Concessions governing *Suevia,* the *Levente,* and church services, were peremptorily rejected. The authorities had a "100% duty" to consider Swabian appeals in German; but difficulties were expected in the courts.

Thus government concessions and Swabian demands deviated. But the German-Hungarian trade agreement loomed, and the Magyars had to make a gesture. Gömbös explained to Hitler that he could not overstep the boundaries of a prudent nationality policy. This meant that the Swabians had to become loyal Hungarians and never assume a centrifugal direction. Gömbös pledged to assist the Swabians in the most liberal manner. In communities vaguely designated as possessing German character, bilingual activities would be introduced in kindergartens. The three current minority school types would be maintained, but C institutions would be transformed into B schools in accordance with the wishes and interests of the population in communities with preponderant German character. This promise was nearly worthless. The terms of reference were too vague, and the possibilities of intimidation of Swabian parents by over-zealous local Magyar officials were legion. Concerning teacher training, the weakest link in minority education, Gömbös promised to intensify minority teacher training. Agricultural courses in German would be introduced in Swabian and mixed villages. Gömbös vowed to examine closely complaints voiced to the effect that the German language was not sufficiently used in ecclesiastic life and in the *Levente* movement. This promise fooled no one acquainted with Hungarian conditions. The government had neither the right nor the power to intervene with the churches in matters relating to language of instruction and divine service. Regarding higher education, Gömbös boasted that scarcely another non-German state in Europe cultivated the German language as assiduously as Hungary. Separate German high schools were therefore unnecessary. Besides, graduates of such schools would lack familiarity with the Magyar language. Nothing ever came of most of these plans, and Hitler never replied to this undiplomatic letter.[30]

Gömbös offended the Swabians. He relied on Hungary's strategic importance and on his own self-proclaimed special relationship with Hitler. With the Swabians it was a different matter. Gömbös' reputation as a hard-handed Magyar chauvinist blocked meaningful dialogue. Gratz attempted to justify the government's policy. The economic crisis had arrested the government's attention, but Gömbös would deal forthrightly with the school problem, the key to understanding. Gömbös believed that governments had to honour minorities rights, especially in education. It was slow progress, but nobody's demands could be satisfied overnight. The government was convinced that determining school types was exclusively the parents' job. No system could totally eliminate official influence over parents' groups. Administrators had to have a loyal and honest desire to carry out the law. Yet A and C institutions were faulty. In A schools, children learned no Magyar, in C schools, no German. Bleyer and the government had always favoured B schools, where pupils learned both languages with equal facility. In regions with scattered Swabian populations, C schools still had their place and in Swabian areas kindergartens would become bilingual. If local administrators were as loyal as the government, all problems would evaporate. At least, within the next few months, we shall know where these authorities stand, Gratz thought. But German academies, to satisfy so many different demands, were impracticable, the cost prohibitive, their administration too cumbersome. Special vacation and other courses in existing academies ought to do the job. German middle schools were also impractical. Graduates would find no openings in Hungarian society. But in trade schools, German would be introduced on demand. The government admitted receiving numerous complaints from Swabian parents whose boys served in the *Levente* movement. These youths would no longer have to attend Magyar church services. All this proved that the Swabians could rely on the government's support. Conversely, the government could count on the Swabians, as long as their cultural aspirations were honoured.[31]

This was nothing new, but Gratz wrote with his customary tact. Even so, he disappointed most Swabians. Although it suggested changing the C schools to the better B level, the A institutions would also have to be eliminated. Moreover, Gömbös' vague assurances for the protection of parents' rights seemed insufficient. While most Swabians seriously doubted that such a plan would be satisfactory, the essentially conservative Swabian rural masses were still willing to support Gratz.

It boded ill for the Swabians that as radical forces under Basch and Huss quietly gathered momentum, the moderate leaders disagreed on basic criteria pertaining to minority education. Kussbach rejected the government's veto of German middle schools and teacher academies. Without them, German culture would suffer. But Heckenberger saw nationality in feeling, not language. Kussbach's stand got him in trouble with Gömbös and Gratz, whereas *Sonntagsblatt* and the European minority press blasted Heckenberger as a renegade.[32] In any event, only the government benefited from Swabian disunity. But this advantage evaporated, as more and more

Swabians joined the dynamic, proud, and uncompromising *Kameradschaft*.
The Achilles heel of the Swabian school system was the parents'
conferences. *Nation und Staat* complained that while they "controlled" the
schools there could be no improvement. Only a few communities had
convened and consulted them, but parents were too intimidated to demand
their rights. Under the circumstances, the promise to establish more B
institutions was an empty gesture. Kussbach joined the fray. No parents'
conference had ever successfully introduced a B institution. They were at
the mercy of the antagonistic village intelligentsia, who still believed, as
they had for decades, that patriotism demanded assimilating Swabians.
Despite its sincerity, the government's promise to establish 45-50 B schools
was useless. Consequently, Kussbach's negotiations with Magyar officials in
November 1934 failed. Mackensen observed:

> It is now certain that these negotiations will lead absolutely nowhere. In no
> respect did the Hungarian government make good on its promises given to
> Gratz. . . .[33]

Mackensen, who no longer believed the Swabians would prevail if minority
reform remained in government hands alone, tried to generate high-level
German-Hungarian conversations until his removal early in 1937.

Gömbös owed his success to an uncanny ability to procrastinate, negotiate, obfuscate, and confuse. Whenever the Swabians despaired, he issued
new promises or "solutions." So it was with the floundering school
programme. On 25 August 1935, *Sonntagsblatt* publicized for the first time the
outlines of a new school law that would establish a single, uniform school
type. Gömbös originally planned the change for the 1934-1935 academic
year, but Gratz promised it would be released in a few days, in time for the
current (1935-1936) school season. Gratz had been assured that the law was
ready all along, except that Gömbös desired a few last-minute "improvements." One such revision was that subjects taught only in Magyar would
also be explained in German. Why the one-year delay? Had the Prime
Minister given an explanation? Gratz believed it unnecessary. He already
knew why from previous conversations. The Magyar public had turned so
anti-Swabian that for a time concessions were out of the question. The most
recent *UDV* assembly, which had sworn loyalty to Hungary and eliminated
extremists, had now cooled public passions. If centrifugal forces should
resume agitation, however, the government might change its mind. It is not
certain whether Gratz knew the government did not plan to release the new
school law just yet. Gömbös wished to soothe moderate sensibilities and
silence the radicals on the eve of his impending visit with Hitler.

Of course, the promised school regulation failed to appear in a few days. *Sonntagsblatt* understood the delay. The recent anti-German and anti-Swabian press campaign had hamstrung the government. But fortunately for the Swabians, they never suffered economic or human oppression in Hungary. The press campaign had now abated, and Gömbös would solve the school problem, just as Hitler had dealt with the Poles and Wends.[34]

The *Kameradschaft* had a clear and realistic view of the government's motives and intentions. Its report was secretly submitted to Steinacher. Hostile public and press reactions were deliberately fomented by the government. In Hungary, all cabinet ministers had available slush funds immune from public scrutiny or parliamentary accountability. Recently, such monies had been funneled into the pockets of the Jewish (*i.e.,* liberal) Magyar press. In effect, the government-financed anti-Swabian campaign was used as a pretext for not instituting school reform. The *Kameradschaft* saw the new school law as still another example of government bad faith. The regulation was a fraud. Some radicals discovered this when attending the most recent vacation course for German teachers at Baja. It was an affront to *volksbewusst* Swabians. Its sponsors and most participants rejected German education and favoured C schools. They booed a lecture on correct teaching methods in A and B schools. In fact, only this particular instructor stressed the importance of minority education in the mother tongue. Others declared that the government meant minority schools to capture the Swabian children's loyalties for the Magyar language and spirit, although— to be sure—not by compulsion or through force. When the announcement came that Gombos planned to introduce a new school law that would abolish C institutions once and for all, the overwhelming majority of those present scoffed. For years, school inspectors had told teachers confidentially that the greatly touted transformation of C into B institutions was a mere formality. Undoubtedly, the new regulation would similarly remain a paper law. So much for government promises. It was sad and depressing.[35]

Many of Gömbös' earlier proposals were incorporated into the new school law, when it was finally promulgated on 23 December 1935. It was hailed as a milestone in Hungarian education, designed to simplify administration in the minority school system. Eight school districts were established, each with a regional director, and one uniform school type was created similar to the existing B institution. The old A, B, and C schools were terminated, but the new B institutions were not slated to become mandatory until the beginning of the 1938-1939 academic year. The postponement caused much confusion. Teachers were told that the interim would constitute a transitional period providing experience in the new method by teaching at once in the spirit of the new law. Since the Ministry failed to acquaint teachers with either the new method or the spirit of the law, this directive merely intensified their bewilderment. Yet when the supposedly new curriculum was released on 30 August 1938, only a few days before the beginning of the first mandatory term, it turned out to be an exact copy of the former B curriculum devised in 1923. This confirmed the suspicion that the three-year delay had been simply a device to undermine morale in the minority schools.

Some of the Ministry reforms were insignificant or downright detrimental. For example, the school year was extended to eight months in order to improve comprehension on the part of the pupils, but it was still more than one month shorter than the school year in Magyar institutions. Furthermore, the extra burden of a second language prompted the Ministry to reduce, simplify, or limit a number of important subjects taught to certain age groups. Specific elements of arithmetic were eliminated in the fifth and sixth grades, and teaching first graders to tell the time was discontinued. The most serious limitation of the law was the narrow scope of its jurisdiction and applicability. Officially, it was effective in 346 localities, containing 378 of the 419 Swabian institutions. These consisted of 262 Roman Catholic, 57 Evangelical, 34 state, 17 community, 6 Reformed, and 2 other schools. Nevertheless, only state-controlled schools had to conform to the law. Furthermore, the law was enforceable only in those communities where the *UDV* was permitted to function, and thus could be withdrawn indirectly by arbitrary governmental action against the *UDV*.[36]

The new law had a mixed reception at home and abroad, though most observers approved of it. One thought Hungary had entered a new era of minority reform and now had the right to expect other nations to respect Magyar minorities. Gratz wrote in *Pester Lloyd* that Swabian cultural problems verged on total solution; only suitable teachers were lacking. The *Deutsche Diplomatisch-Politische Korrespondenz* observed that Hungary respected Swabians and permitted them to nurture their cultural heritage. This was excellent timing, since most European states were headed in the opposite direction. *Nation und Staat* believed the law was a giant step in the right direction with a political double-purpose. It established the basic right of Swabian cultural development, and demonstrated to hostile provincials the government's displeasure with their anti-Swabian machinations. Hopefully, they would cease their sabotage once and for all.

But *Wiener Neueste Nachrichten* expressed reservations. The history of Hungarian minority politics suggested the need for great caution. Two preconditions for success were still lacking. There were not enough suitable German, or at least German-speaking, teachers; and provincial obstructions would have to cease. It was doubtful whether Gömbös could overcome the accepted Magyar notion that assimilating Swabians was a patriotic duty. Huss, in *Deutscher Volksbote,* mourned the demise of A schools, though he hailed the disappearance of C institutions. But apparently the new schools first had to be recommended by a school board, or autonomous church authority, or a parents' conference. Hence the law was optimnal, not compulsory. Far from solving the school problem, it inflamed passions between parents and local authorities. How would the government enforce the new schools in confessional establishments? Were they not exempt?[37] Simultaneously, Huss complained to Gömbös in greater detail. His most telling criticism was the hidden provision that virtually rigidified the minority school system. After 1 September 1938, only A, B, and C schools might be transformed into the new type. This meant that in communities where the number of Swabian school children did not reach twenty, parents could never again request the new school type, the new law notwithstanding. It was a clever device to arrest the growth of Swabian culture, at least in mixed areas.[38]

After the promulgation of the 1935 school law, control of the Swabian school system slipped almost completely into the hands of the Magyarized clergy for want of clear administrative guidelines. They exploited the three-year interim period to weaken Swabian education, aided by Gömbös' policy to shirk all responsibility for enforcing any remaining minority school regulation. A Protestant writer saw that the Evangelical Churches in Hungary were overwhelmingly German, yet they were led by Magyars. In the guise of missionary evangelism these leaders were attempting to de-Germanize the Swabian religious communities.

The Roman Catholic clergy's attempt to wreck minority education was at least as effective as the Protestants'. In *Nemzetnevelés,* the Catholic teachers' official organ, a Catholic teacher, currently employed in a C school, urged all minority instructors to rebel. He was not qualified to teach in the complex linguistic spirit the new law prescribed. The children spoke not German but Swabian dialect. Both parents and pupils were quite content with the old law. A Magyar Catholic teacher publicly censured his colleague. *Nation und Staat* exclaimed that whoever defied the multitude on a sensitive issue such as this had courage. A Catholic teacher in Békásmegyer claimed that he and six colleagues had insufficient mastery of German to switch from C to B instruction. The new law confounded him. For thirteen years, he had struggled to Magyarize the children, and now he feared his efforts had been in vain.

Völkisch attitudes were rare in any of the churches. Huber had withdrawn from the Swabian struggle and applied himself to his clerical duties. Under the pressure of the new school law and the resistance it evoked among

Catholic teachers, he emerged from obscurity with a vengeance to take issue with the Magyarone clergy. Exactly one year after the release of the law, the evidence was clear. Hopes had not been fulfilled, despite the government's apparent good will. Regretfully, confessional schools led the struggle against the school regulation, and the government had no direct control over them. Often even religion was no longer taught in German. Swabians were fed up with this charade and demanded their schools, as promised by the government. They would no longer tolerate the ill intentions of unrestrained village potentates. Chauvinistic insanity was a crime when it affected souls. Tens of thousands of children must not be sacrificed, hiding behind the mask of patriotism. In the face of this unjust and un-Christian opposition by minority church officials, Huber maintained, the government could do nothing but wash its hands in good conscience and unctuously declare it could not interfere with autonomous church life.

On rare occasions when clergymen were ordered by their superiors to undertake reforms, they often disregarded them. Béla Kapi issued an order on 17 April 1936, commanding the transformation of all schools in his district into B institutions. Two years later, the order had still to be carried into effect. German had been completely abolished in most C schools, and in any case, the absence of qualified teachers made conversion impossible. In Gyönk, an Evangelical community with a C school, parents decided to adopt the B facility. This was opposed by their minister, and even four months later local school officials had failed to act. Subsequent investigation revealed that the first grade offered no German instruction at all, while the fifth and sixth grades had no German texts. Clergymen trying to help their minority were persecuted. At Baja, the parish priest introduced German instruction in the school. A press campaign forced his transfer and another priest restored the Magyar language.

The desperate situation of the German minority school system was demonstrated by the shortage of teachers. The number of Swabian teachers declined annually after 1933. By 1936, there were only 95 of German mother tongue left in Hungary, and only four taught in minority schools. To be sure, in 1936, eight academies offered special courses to 330 candidates, but they could not meet the rigid requirements because of their poor background. To satisfy the demands of the new schools, the government planned a one-year continuation course for thirty teachers to commence in 1937. But the Swabians required at least 1,400 teachers, and at this rate *Nation und Staat* argued it would take no less than nine years to answer the needs in the minority schools.

When Gömbös died, both the Swabian school system and cultural structure were in shambles. The *UDV* schism between moderates and radicals was final. Name-Magyarization, and other assimilationist devices, intensified. Harassment of uncooperative Swabians by fines, taxations, and petty vexations, grew. Magyar officials became more boldly hostile, the Magyar and Magyarized clergy more uncompromising. German-oriented cultural events were restricted, and the minority schools were in total disarray.[39]

When Kálmán Darányi became Prime Minister, the Swabians hardly knew what to expect. He had no interest in Swabian reform. Would he be any worse than Gömbös? Now the Swabians were back on square one, with about as many minority schools as at the beginning of the Gömbös era. Statistics and reality clashed, however, as *Nation und Staat* pointed out that the letter designation meant very little because an inadequate teaching staff foredoomed German instruction. Nonetheless, in sixty out of the nearly 500 Swabian communities, parents' groups had been consulted, and the overwhelming majority opted for the new B institution. But *Nation und Staat* was not satisfied. The new school would do only as an interim arrangement. The Magyars would not accept bilingual schools for their children in the diaspora either. The government would have to introduce German kindergartens in all Swabian communities and guarantee all such communities the new B facility. German or German-speaking teachers must be made available, impossible without a separate German teacher academy. German middle, continuation, agricultural, and other schools must be gradually established. The *Kameradschaft* demanded more, nothing short of total autonomy in minority education by 1936. But the *UDV* trusted the government, and hoped that with patient perseverance they would gradually win over Magyar public opinion.

Superficially, Gömbös' programme for weakening Swabian culture had apparently worked. Even between 1920 and 1930, the Swabian census based on the mother tongue had decreased by 72,581. This seemed to result from the restrictive minority school system imposed on the Swabians. Children were taught by ill-prepared teachers in overcrowded classrooms, and shifted capriciously from one type of school to another with no apparent regard for their emotional and educational requirements. The teaching of German was suppressed. Textbooks were inadequate. Pupils were not even taught Magyar properly, and in any case the German home environment counteracted its use.

While seemingly contradictory to the aim of Magyarization, such a state of affairs had its desired effects. Realizing that their children might learn German at home, but not the official language, Swabian parents by the mid-1930s frequently voluntarily insisted on Magyar schools for their children to forestall later economic and social handicaps. Moreover, Swabian youngsters desiring a career in the arts and professions had to pursue their studies in Magyar institutes of higher education. As the minority school system was totally unsuitable for this, ambitious Swabian youths usually chose Magyar elementary schools to reach their occupational goals. They also exploited the regulation that permitted children to choose their nationality without parental consent. Although in theory middle and higher education was available to all qualified applicants, in reality most of the graduates were Magyars.[40] At the time of Gömbös' death, therefore, Magyarization had to all appearances made extensive inroads among the Swabians, exactly as Gombos had hoped. In fact however, gathering *völkisch* forces would soon obliterate what was, after all, only a shallow attempt by the Magyars to equate speaking a certain language with the deep and spontaneous passions evoked in association with it, but only in the absence of duress.

The Magyar-German-Swabian Diplomatic Triangle

In the short run, Gömbös' Swabian policy was spectacularly successful. The radical Swabians had nowhere to turn. They pleaded in vain for massive Reich support, but received only marginal moral and financial encouragement. Hungary's strategic location was favourable, and Hitler sought to pacify the Magyars, at least temporarily. The Swabians would have to suffer oppression in silence on behalf of deferred National Socialist imperialism. Gömbös realized dimly that Hitler's puzzling indifference to the Swabians was only a passing phase. Come what may, Hungary had to impose a Magyar solution on the Swabian problem, and create a truly homogeneous Magyar state while she could. Gömbös' proposition to Hitler seemed reasonable. Why should half-million semi-assimilated Swabian peasants block traditional German-Hungarian friendship, when together the two nations might overthrow Versailles and recover their rightful international position among the constellation of world powers?

Gömbös' policy unfortunately rested on faulty premises. Any success flowed more from the accidental configurations of European politics than his astute judgment. Even before Hitler, the Reich never intended to abandon the Swabians, or any other Germans. The Wilhelmstrasse at the end of the Weimar era explained why. The Hungarians were mistaken if they believed that Germany's present aloofness to the German minorities was permanent. Their number and position in postwar Europe made them politically far too valuable to ignore. Since Germany wished to pose as the champion of all ethnic minorities, it would be folly to sacrifice any Germans only because the Reich might derive political advantages from her friendship with the host country. How could Germany convince the world that her minority policy was predicated on ethical rather than political principles? Germany must convince Magyars that the various Swabian organizations were harmless, and prevent recurring persecutions. They must also be persuaded that Germany did not seek to imbue diaspora Germans with anti-Magyar sentiments. Yet no German government could ignore domestic outcries in the face of demands to Magyarize the Swabians.

In mid-December Schön acquainted Gömbös with Germany's position on trade and politics. Gömbös continually interrupted, gushing how much he appreciated the dispatch of Waldeck to resume trade negotiations. He truly valued Germany's friendship, and stressed common German-Hungarian disarmament aims. Gömbös sobered when Schön broached the minority problem, suggesting that Bleyer be received one more time to gain additional information. Gömbös allegedly retorted: "Does it have to be?" Schön thereupon urged that the two governments resume minority negotiations soon. In the meantime, an informal, mixed commission composed of Catholic clergymen might investigate various aspects of minority education. Again, Gömbös balked. He had had no time as yet to grapple with the minority problem, but he would do so shortly. Kánya noted that the domestic minority question was intimately bound with German-Magyar cooperation in the diaspora. No Hungarian government would dream of remedying the former, until it had assurances of some success in the latter.[41] But Gömbös did not intend to make a gesture until a number of his own demands had been met. Notwithstanding Kánya's remark on Magyar-German cooperation, at the time, Hungary's priority with Germany was a favourable trade agreement.

With the advent of Hitler, Germany's posture on expatriate minorities became gradually more uncompromising; but Gombos continued to disregard Swabian rights as if nothing had happened. He granted one concession. In February 1933, Roman Catholic Bishop Berning of Osnabruck arrived in Budapest for discussions with Bleyer and Hungarian church dignitaries, including Cardinal Serédi, Hungary's Primate. The Germans reasoned that as the fate of the Swabians rested primarily in Roman Catholic hands, it might be best to persuade Serédi directly. But German strategy misfired. Serédi, a Magyarized Swabian, had no sympathy for imported *Kultur,* and refused to commit himself. He had to mind the government's and the bishops' sensibilities on the language question. Let the government set an example by transforming C into B institutions. Parents' wishes ought to prevail and many voluntarily desired C schools, consequently, his hands were tied. On German religious services among the youth, the Church had to provide these for the *Levente* in Magyar. All these questions would be examined at the bishops' conference next March, and Berning was invited to submit a detailed brief.

In their private talk, Kánya treated Berning to a lecture in Hungarian diplomatic realities. All Hungarian political personalities saw the Swabian problem not isolated, but part and parcel of the entire minority complex involving the Successor States. This meant that progress on Swabian reform depended on the happy resolution of German-Magyar cooperation in the diaspora. In his conversations with various high church dignitaries, Berning drew a blank. They all stressed, as had Serédi, that Germany must be patient with the Magyars, who were hemmed in between mighty forces of northern and southern Slavs, and feared for their ethnic existence. Consequently, they resented facing the additional burden of German cultural propaganda aimed at alienating the Swabians from Magyardom. With Bleyer, Berning scored success, but then the Swabian leader needed no convincing. Berning stressed the need for a three-point programme that would save Swabian youth for *Volkstum*. A proper German home environment must be buttressed by religious indoctrination and German education. Under no conditions must this circle be broken. He would recommend this approach to the German Foreign Ministry. Bleyer's task was to induce Swabian parents to demand these rights. Berning never saw Gömbös, who was "unavoidably detained" in Parliament, and thus the Bishop had to depart empty handed.[42] Berning's unsuccessful mission underscored the Magyars' tenacity and unity on the one topic on which nearly all of them agreed: the need for national homogeneity and ethnic solidarity against "outsiders."

On the eve of Bethlen's March 1933 Berlin journey, the Wilhelmstrasse reviewed recent unsuccessful efforts by Germany to improve Swabian conditions. Bethlen's November 1930 visit had occasioned a brief flurry on behalf of the minority. Throughout 1931, the two governments exchanged position papers, and finally decided to establish a mixed commission headed by Solf and Teleki. Despite repeated proddings, the Magyars kept procrastinating. In Budapest, Schön had been soliciting Gömbös at least since November. In Germany, Neurath importuned Kánya to activate the question at once. But Berning's Budapest visit was the only tangible result. Gömbös did promise, however, to consult his Minister of Education on further negotiations.

Since all efforts had failed thus far, Germany must enlist Bethlen's aid and sympathy, though even with his help, reform would perforce be very dilatory, owing to Magyar administrative hostility. This vital issue must not be left to drift, because the Swabian position might deteriorate, in view of the de-Germanization mania currently raging in Hungary. Other developments also counseled haste. The National Socialist Party had begun to insinuate itself into foreign affairs. Recently several Party representatives had assured Kánya that the Swabians would never burden good German-

Hungarian relations. Such promises grievously hurt not only Swabians but all Danubian minorities.

The Wilhelmstrasse inadvertently disclosed National Socialist techniques. Hitler believed in pitting two or more kindred agencies or personalities against each other. By year's end, Neurath and Hess engaged in a power struggle over *Auslanddeutschtum*. Foreign nations accustomed to orthodox diplomatic techniques found this confusing. In Hungary, where the government's anti-Swabian policy and the Reich's opportunistic aspirations clashed, the unconventional National Socialist approach was abundantly effective. Bethlen totally misinterpreted the aims, methods, and purposes of the Hitler regime, and concluded that the orderly nature of Germans would soon restore balance. As in Fascist Italy, so in Nazi Germany, the leaders would begin to work in harmony with both internal and external forces.

Overestimating Bethlen's influence and his ability to modify well-entrenched social patterns, the Swabians also supported the former prime minister as their great hope. Kussbach was so encouraged by Bethlen's apparent enthusiasm for Germany that he imprudently revealed his own sympathies for National Socialism. Kussbach announced that the Magyars ought to consider German growth as a good omen for revisionism. More, it would be good if Hungary adopted some of the National Socialist techniques. Hungary had to resign herself to an Austrian *Anschluss,* a clear case of popular self-determination. It was natural for Germany to champion Germans living abroad. Already, the world owed a great debt to Hitler's gifted leadership.[43] Kussbach's rashness destroyed his credibility with the government. Bethlen might flatter Germany in hopes of extracting concessions; but it was imprudent for a Swabian notable to glorify a people and system most Magyars execrated. Kussbach's blunder was compounded a few weeks later when Bleyer delivered his memorable oration in Parliament that set Magyar opinion against Swabian reform in any guise.

Gömbös believed that isolating the Swabian problem from the complex of German-Hungarian concerns would succeed. The Hungarian Foreign Ministry's outline on the occasion of Gömbös' June 1933 visit with Hitler indicates that Gömbös refused to yield an inch, or apologize for Swabian repressions. Gömbös complained that Bleyer's tactlessness had been misinterpreted in Germany, causing vexation, but he would grant an interview and discuss all outstanding issues. Loyal Swabians would gain all the cultural privileges they had the right to expect, thus continuing the policies begun by previous regimes. Gömbös condemned the *VDA* for deeply troubling German-Hungarian relations. Nobody in Hungary understood its rationale that all *Auslanddeutsche* were equally important to the Reich. Why spend more time and energy on the scattered *Donauschwaben* than on the Sudeten

Germans? Why should Germans in the Successor States be incited against
Magyar revisionism? The *VDA* ought to urge Germans to cooperate with
the Magyars, who were offended by their senseless behaviour. The *VDA*
was obviously led by politically naive amateurs obsessed with school
problems. In Hungary, they counted German schools, but considered only
language, not education, and disregarded vast postwar improvements.
Swabians suffered neither political nor economic discrimination, as Gratz
and Bleyer exemplified. Hitler should promote good Magyar-German
relations in the Successor States, and stop German interference with Magyar
revisionism.

Gömbös kept one promise he made to Hitler. On 11 August 1933, he
received Bleyer and grilled him about his recent Munich trip. Bleyer
explained he had visited the Bavarian Academy and the *Institut für Südosteuro-
päische Forschungen,* because he planned to publish German translations of
several Magyar books. He had also met Rudolf Hess to discuss German-
Hungarian relations. The gist of the dialogue was that Hungary and
Germany were historically linked in a common struggle against common
enemies. The Swabians were natural mediators, but first, their status in
Hungary had to be clarified and settled. Gömbös and Hitler were ordained
by destiny to negotiate an equitable solution that would endure for
centuries. Gömbös told Bleyer to consult the government before negotiating in Germany in the future and stop meddling. The Swabian problem was
not Germany's but Hungary's. Gömbös would settle German-Hungarian
questions with Hitler, Magyar-Swabian ones with Bleyer. Hitler had been
told this, and that Gömbös resented German tourists, armed with propaganda pamphlets, overrunning Hungary. He objected that they established
contact with Swabians, and with Germans in the occupied territories, whose
minds they poisoned against the Magyars. Instead, they ought to encourage
cooperation with the Magyar minorities. Bleyer exposed Gömbös' illogic. If
he desired Hitler to influence Germans in the Successor States, then why
insist that the Swabian question was strictly an internal matter? That was
different, Gömbös retorted. Germans living in the Successor States still
resided in historic Hungary, and hence they were technically Hungarian
subjects, as he had told Hitler. Bleyer persisted that the Swabian problem
was internal only in a theoretical sense; practically it was, and would always
remain, an external matter that could never be divorced from German-
Hungarian relations. Gömbös reiterated that he would deal with the
Swabian question in his own way, or not at all. He would not tolerate any
further German propaganda, any secret German financing of the Swabian
movement, nor any anti-Magyar German agitation in the detached territories. He did promise to submit Bleyer's grievances for the Ministerial

Council's consideration. Bleyer would be notified in due time, and then bilateral negotiations would resume.

This crushed Bleyer. Shortly after, he received more discouraging news. Berlin ordered him to avoid henceforth antagonizing the government and the Magyar public. Owing to political considerations, the German government could not exert diplomatic pressure on Hungary. Germany was, however, interested in Swabian cultural aspirations, and would exert friendly persuasion on the Magyars, as in the past. It was small solace, but the Foreign Ministry assured Bleyer of its continued esteem and support. This, together with unremitting attacks by the Magyar public and press, shattered Bleyer. When von Papen visited Hungary in September 1933, he held separate conversations with Bleyer and Gömbös. He warned the former to observe the Foreign Ministry's instructions, whereas from Gömbös he sought assurances that anti-Bleyer student demonstrations would not be tolerated. While Gömbös promised to act, he declared that if Bleyer continued getting instructions from Berlin, he would disown him as Swabian leader.[44] Bleyer's effectiveness thus ended.

On the eve of Bleyer's death, the Swabian movement was in disarray and friendless. On 19 November 1933, Hitler won his greatest electoral victory to-date. This presaged an upsurge in National Socialist influence in all phases of government. Paradoxically, the traditionally-minded German Foreign Ministry showed far greater interest at this time in the fate of the Swabians than the supposedly *völkisch* National Socialists. With the election triumph, Hess' views would prevail over Neurath's, to the temporary detriment of the Swabians. At home, the Swabians were harassed and discredited. *Sonntagsblatt* observed in connection with Bethlen's scheme of full autonomy for returning minorities:

> His declaration would be more effective if the present praxis supported it more. Already during the last two years of Bethlen's premiership, improvements halted completely. . . .By Károlyi's time, the stumbling blocks multiplied every passing day, both with the UDV and the school problem. The same is true this past year, even aside from Bleyer's persecution. We are the most patient minority in Europe, but each year our patience grows thinner.[45]

A few days after Bleyer's death, Mackensen visited Gömbös for what became a monologue on the minority question. Gömbös repeated all the arguments proffered during his June visit with Hitler. Mackensen vowed his government would not dream of interfering in Hungary's Swabian affairs, although "the question still represented a strain on our relations, though less on those between the Governments than on those between the peoples."

Mackensen rejected Gömbös' claim that this was a mere bagatelle. But Gömbös saw the entire minorities question an artificial postwar creation by politically ambitious individuals. Bleyer had been one of them. Then there were the German travellers, *Wandervögel*, and so on, who made Pan-German speeches and stirred up the Swabian citizenry. That was a dangerous game. The entire problem had to be eliminated from the complex of German-Hungarian relations, for which the present moment was auspicious. He would send Hitler exhaustive and objective information about the minorities problem.

Mackensen had loyally defended Bleyer against Gömbös' allegations. Nonetheless, it was an open secret that the more youthful, radical Reich circles considered Bleyer's philosophy passé. The German Catholic Centre, from which Bleyer had always drawn his strength and support, gradually withdrew their patronage. Nazi leaders became more and more disgruntled with moderate policies. As Kussbach observed, in mid-1933, both he and Bleyer sensed that the old guard was rapidly running out of time, as their ideas clashed with those of the young mandarins. These resented Bleyer's Jesuit education, his chair at a Magyar university, and his Christian *Weltanschauung*. Consequently, they launched a whispering campaign against him, which had its effects both at home and abroad.[46] By the time of his death, Bleyer's usefulness was over. The man who had become an embarrassment to the German and Hungarian governments and to the public of both countries chose the perfect time to die.

By the end of 1933, the Wilhelmstrasse began to cooperate with the National Socialist Party on minority matters. By common agreement, Dr. Fricke was commissioned as Hess' confidential agent on German minorities in the Balkans. At year's end, Fricke visited Southeast Europe, including Hungary. Germany's preoccupation with *Volksgenossen* in the diaspora was growing. The Nazis, however, aimed at re-Germanizing in the National Socialist spirit. This was bad news for Gömbös, who had different ideas on the subject of ethnic loyalties.

In an expansive moment, Gömbös had promised Mackensen a personal letter for Hitler, together with an exhaustive dossier on the Swabian minority. In the meantime, the Magyars probed the Foreign Ministry, which refused to respond until the letter had been received and analyzed. Under one suggestion, Hungary proposed to separate the Swabians into two distinct categories. One group would enjoy limited autonomy in designated enclaves. The other would lose its ethnic status and face assimilation. The Wilhelmstrasse considered this would liquidate all Germans living in the East. Magyar-German cooperation in the Successor States as a *sine qua non* for further minority negotiations was still another rejected suggestion because it would make life unbearable for Germans. Nonetheless, the Wilhelmstrasse believed that Hungary wished to revive the stalled Teleki-Solf minority discussions originally scheduled for 1932. Germany would be more than willing to oblige.

German-Hungarian relations had reached an impasse, as neither side wished to yield on substantive issues. The Germans considered the Magyars contumacious on the Swabian problem, an issue vital to *Volkstum* which angered an ally. The Magyars resented the Germans for having thus far refused to support Hungarian agriculture and revisionism, and for stirring up Pan-German, National Socialist agitation in Hungary. The Reich also courted France, Czechoslovakia, and Soviet Russia—Hungary's arch enemies. This generated poor conditions for settling the minority issue, especially since Gömbös had already made up his mind not to give an inch. In time, of course, Gömbös had to yield. Perhaps it was only a coincidence, but ever since he promised to write the letter, Hungarian diplomats encountered nothing but evasions in the Wilhelmstrasse. Evidently, the Germans wanted Hungary to act. Neurath told Masirevich: "I regret that the Hungarian government has not yet devised the means to satisfy the aspirations of the Swabian minority with requisite legislation."[47] Shortly thereafter the Gömbös letter was dispatched.

Gömbös' letter had certain salutary effects on German-Hungarian relations. German diplomatic blocks ceased, and within one week, Germany signed the much-postponed trade agreement. Also, Reich authorities were ordered to prevent the incursion of mostly youthful, irresponsible persons into the Danubian countries, notably Hungary. Unauthorized persons caught in compromising situations would be denied the support of German consular authorities. Most Reich officials and Party functionaries, including Steinacher, assented. Organized groups, especially Hitler Youth, would henceforth be strictly forbidden to enter Hungary without Steinacher's express permission. Hungary reciprocated by moderating her press attacks on Germany, long a sore on German-Hungarian relations. Gratz's speech at the May 1934 *UDV* Assembly on the government's minority programme also soothed the Reich. His report substantially mirrored the Gombos plan. Gratz was far from popular in Germany, yet he might achieve more for the Swabians than a dedicated, though suspect, *volksdeutsch* leader.[48]

The honeymoon did not survive the summer of 1934. The Rome Protocols offended Germany. The Austrian putsch and Dollfuss' murder frightened and dismayed Magyars. Kánya demonstrated Hungary's support of Austria by informing Hitler that "fortunately for Hungary, existing connections with Austria had recently improved considerably, and thus the ring surrounding Hungary had been rent asunder at this point." Afterward,

Germany spurned any Danubian plan not of her own making, and tried to intimidate Hungary by threatening to terminate the trade agreement. In October, Göring visited Southeastern Europe. While in Belgrade and Bucharest, he scorned Hungary's minority policy. It was seconded by Sudeten-German leader Konrad Henlein several days later. Hungary began to fear a new German-led encirclement. Angered, Gömbös summoned Schnurre and raged that Göring had nearly wrecked Hungary's international and domestic position.[49]

As usual, the Swabians invested their time and energy poorly. On 23 July 1934, Kussbach appeared in Berlin, ostensibly to pave the way for Gratz's visit. Gratz wished to explore the degree of support he enjoyed in the Reich. While abroad, Kussbach painted an apocalyptic picture of Swabian misery. There had been no improvements whatever; all the well-known economic and police chicanery continued undiminished. Kussbach's more exhaustive and incriminating report on Magyar repressions reached Steinacher in October. After Bleyer's death, the Magyars had tried unsuccessfully to fragment the leaderless Swabians. Now, the French and the Italians, whose influence had grown noticeably stronger, were urging Hungary to create a homogeneous Magyar state, thereby to resist Germany's *Drang nach Osten*, and block the unification of northern and southern Slavs. Even the spring negotiations produced no agreement because he would not ratify a minority pact with so many hidden disadvantages. Let the government fulfill all its given pledges. Germany might help the Swabian cause by dispatching German travellers to Hungary; by replacing Jewish employees of German firms located in Budapest by qualified Swabians; by supportive articles in the German press; but not yet politically. Of course, Kussbach was unaware of Hitler's orders not to burden German-Hungarian relations by flaunting the Swabian issue. He was unacquainted with Germany's grand designs in Southeastern Europe. Spurned at home, Kussbach was also disliked in Germany. The report was Kussbach's way of restoring his credibility in the Reich. It had no effect whatsoever.

Despite the German-Hungarian chill, conversations on the minority problem took place regularly throughout 1934, but they were getting nowhere. In November, new negotiations between Kussbach and the government achieved nothing. Mackensen knew Kussbach's efforts would fail because the Magyars refused to honour even their earlier commitments to Gratz. Mackensen chafed. Hitler's non-interference directive tied his hands and prevented him from dealing effectively with Swabian problems. Worse still, he could not even confide in the Swabians to explain his predicament. He sympathized with Gömbös and Hitler. Both wished to remove the Swabian dilemma from the roster of German-Hungarian difficulties. But Hitler must respond to the Gömbös letter, otherwise the Swabian problem would become insoluble. Until the two leaders agreed, and until a mixed commission was created, "nothing, but nothing on earth and in heaven, would succeed."[50] Mackensen's advice was not heeded.

As Mackensen had expected, the Swabian position weakened in the new year. Drawing on Kussbach's reports, the German Legation explained that Hungary had stiffened toward the Swabians. During recent negotiations at the Praesidium, Pataky complained bitterly because *UDV* officials were insulting Hungary, whereupon the "reliable" Pintér's position was strengthened. The unmanageable Kussbach was demoted. He was outraged, and since then, the *UDV* and government were far from friendly. Kussbach's tactlessness needlessly endangered the Swabian future. Shortly after Bleyer's death, a Swabian renaissance blossomed, and even normally hostile Magyars urged genuine reform. These intercessions had prompted the Praesidium recently to plan a uniform minority school type. Germany must respond to Gömbös' proposals promptly, lest German-Hungarian relations be imperilled.

Hitler's failure to answer the Gömbös letter was not indecision. He put Hungary's friendship temporarily ahead of the Swabians' welfare. When Kussbach requested the German Legation to subsidize the election expenses of Swabian candidates, he was directed to see Pataky, or else to utilize secret German funds. Also, the Legation refused to exert pressure on Gömbös to nominate Swabian candidates. Kussbach did discuss the subject with Pataky but failed to persuade the government to nominate, let alone finance, the Swabian contenders. Consequently, these bolted to Tibor Eckhardt's Small Landholders' Party, and all but Gratz lost the election. The episode sharpened all the existing tensions.

Gömbös' electoral successes prompted the Wilhelmstrasse to heed Mackensen's unceasing demands for a reply to the Gömbös letter as a means of breaking the deadlock. Swabian-Magyar negotiations in the past year had demonstrated conclusively that no agreement would ever materialize. Indeed, why would Gömbös make concessions after his smashing electoral victory? Swabians could expect no mercy from administrators. Even Minister of the Interior Kozma misunderstood the problem. Magyars felt pressed against the wall and could not comprehend the need for a liberal minority policy, even though failure to act would hurt revisionism. Consequently, only a summit meeting could dispel Magyar fears and resolve the problem. The Reich press was also to blame. German correspondents filed unsubstantiated, wild atrocity stories on the recent election, where Swabian candidates and voters allegedly suffered abuse. Irregularities were not directed against the Swabians *per se,* but against the Opposition. Swabian leaders imprudently joined the Opposition and suffered the consequences. A recent Foreign Ministry memo stated that Magyar electoral abuses had prevented a reply to the Gömbös letter. Obviously the Wilhelmstrasse ignored realities. Moreover, it was an illusion that a Swabian victory would have served the German cause. A Swabian opposition would have been impotent in Parliament. Swabians should have supported Gömbös. Unless Germany acted at once, the Swabian problem would seriously undermine German-Hungarian relations.

The Foreign Ministry took Mackensen's advice seriously and requested Hitler, or possibly Neurath, to respond. Gömbös would be queried on his willingness to negotiate. As inducement, Neurath might personally head the German delegation. The chief topic would be Swabian cultural demands. This was a delicate problem because existing laws were not uniformly applied, and because the Ministry's view of Swabian rights differed from the Magyars'. Swabian youngsters ought to study German, from nursery through technical schools. The training of qualified teaching personnel was essential, hence the need for a college. In "racially German communes" religious instruction, hymns, prayers, and sermons, ought to be given in German, and Swabian cultural organizations left alone. Justified Magyar grievances, such as non-interference in the internal affairs of the Swabians by Reich agencies, were negotiable. In future, these activities must be coordinated more efficiently. Rudolf Hess would have to ensure that all concerned agencies and authorities adhered to any decisions.[51] Indubitably, the Foreign Ministry had in mind subordinating Swabian needs to the requirements of Germany's *Ostpolitik*.

Kussbach and Basch bombarded the Reich with atrocity stories and pleas.[52] But the Foreign Ministry considered Mackensen's plan to negotiate and settle the Swabian difficulty over the heads and without the knowledge of the complainants. It began gingerly to echo Gömbös' sentiments that the Swabian issue should never intrude into, let alone imperil, German-Hungarian relations. Rödiger drafted a plan that not only excluded the Swabians, but would keep the talks strictly secret. The Ministry prepared a brief on the minority question, to be transmitted to Horthy by visiting Field Marshall von Mackensen. This plan was shelved, but other avenues soon opened to expedite the Foreign Ministry's plans to negotiate, although not on the high level originally anticipated.

The most important preliminary exchange was a meeting between Kozma and National Socialist Party representative W. Hasselblatt in Budapest on 7 May 1935. Kozma defensively painted the Swabian picture as very favourable, and Hungary as the only nation that tolerated so many Germans near its capital. Also, the Swabian population grew faster than the

Magyar, as did Swabian land holdings. Nor were Swabians oppressed economically as in other lands. Name-Magyarization was voluntary, never forced, and practiced mainly by urban elements. Hasselblatt demurred. The 1930 census registered severe Swabian population losses; name-Magyarization was not voluntary, as in the universities, the railways, and the military services; and it was both rural and urban.

Kozma thereupon assailed the Swabians' political ineptness. Eckhardt received "intimate feelers" before the government. Even so, Swabian candidates suffered less preelection harassment than any of the Small Landholders' Party. He visited Bonyhád before election week and discovered the Swabians favoured Pekár, not the "radical" Basch. Nonetheless, local administrators and the provincial gentry had undisputably obstructed the minority laws. Henceforth, the Ministry of the Interior would regulate the entire problem, and thus the laws would be obeyed. Kozma cited passages from Field Marshall Mackensen's personal letter to convince Hasselblatt that he and the government were friends of Germany. Magyars had the fullest understanding for National Socialism and for the growing strength of the German people. But in Hungary, National Socialist racial theories were unacceptable. Magyars had sensitive national feelings of their own, accentuated by their constant struggle to survive in a predominantly Slavic and Germanic world. Magyars feared that Reich propaganda endangered the Swabians because it Germanized and alienated them from Hungary. The Swabians were politically "unripe" and impressionable. After exposure to German propaganda, they insisted that *Anschluss* must be hastened, because then Greater Germany would neighbour Hungary and protect the Swabians. Surely it must be more important for Germany to befriend the entire Hungarian people, not just the Swabians. Yet Hungary would solve the minority problem decently, honestly, and permanently, especially in education. But first, Magyar opposition must be overcome, which meant cessation of German propaganda and criticism.

Hasselblatt claimed that in Hungary minority policy must parallel external policy. At every minority congress, the Swabians' position was deemed the worst in Europe, the Magyar minorities' in the Successor States the best. It was difficult to mollify the German public. Other minorities had gained all their rights long ago, the Swabians had none. In the Successor States, Germans considered the Swabians' modest programme inadequate. Their own far more onerous demands had been granted long ago. Nonetheless, there was no danger of Swabian irredentism because Hungary had a powerful symbol—the supranational Crown of St. Stephen—that would always attract the Swabians to their fatherland. Since German-Hungarian relations were also good, the Swabian minority question ought to be the easiest one to solve in all Europe. Kozma was urged to solve the issue as soon as possible. The same day, Hasselblatt discussed minority questions with Pataky and his section chief Oswald. Pataky raised no new viewpoints whatever. Hopefully in the future he would have his work cut out for him by Kozma. Hasselblatt emerged with mixed feelings.

> We will have to wait and see whether Kozma's pledges. . .are more valuable than those of previous Hungarian politicians. . . .At least, the minority problem has been accepted in Hungary officially as a pressing political reality.[53]

Hereafter, Hungarian diplomats frequently raised the minorities problem. The Regent broached it with Mackensen. At the end of May, Pataky called at the German consulate in Geneva and hoped that direct consultations might soon settle further particulars of the course jointly to be pursued. Rödiger believed the Ministry ought to accept Pataky's suggestion promptly, arrange meetings no later than the end of June, and temporarily allow Gömbös' letter to go unanswered.

The question of negotiations soon became so urgent that Neurath personally became involved. He informed Mackensen that although a reply to Gömbös' letter was not to be expected at present, immediate negotiations, in the interests of the German national group in Hungary, must not lapse. Pataky's suggestion might serve as a suitable model, provided the Gömbös regime approved. Now, the diplomatic wheels turned fairly rapidly. In July, Schnurre reported that the Magyars had consented to preliminary conversations. The only problem was that they placed excessive stress on Magyar-German cooperation in the Successor States, as a Hungarian Foreign Ministry Memorandum accompanying his report showed. Consequently, Schnurre requested further instructions. Bülow drafted a three-point programme as a basis for confidential preliminary negotiations. Non-binding consultation would have to cover, as an important and integral item, the Swabian problem in Hungary, which was of special interest. The Hungarians ignored the Swabian problem entirely and stressed German-Magyar efforts in the Successor States. This was only of marginal interest to Germany. Publicity even on future negotiations must be determined by a subsequent bilateral agreement. If all these conditions met with Hungary's approval, Rödiger might arrive in Budapest before the end of August. One week later, the Magyars accepted, and suggested mid-September as the target date. Due to various delays, Rödiger did not commence preliminary talks with Pataky until 7 October, after which they were resumed in Berlin 13-18 January 1936.[54]

It is difficult to see why the Germans desired minority discussions to take place at this time. Germany's advantageous bargaining position evaporated with Bleyer's death and Swabian fragmentation. Under his monolithic leadership, Swabian demands had been so reasonable that an agreement might have pleased most parties, and redounded to the credit of German diplomacy. By the time the ponderous German diplomatic machine swung into action, the situation had completely changed. The Swabian internecine struggle erupted following Gömbös' election victory, thus complicating German-Hungarian negotiations. The question was, which of the Swabian viewpoints should Germany favour? If Kussbach's, then *völkisch* radicals in both countries would cry betrayal. If Basch's, then Swabian moderates and the government would be offended. Indeed, by late 1935, even these two clear-cut alternatives became obscured owing to the radicalization of both. Germany might negotiate an unpopular, strictly political accommodation with Hungary that suited only the Magyars, not the Swabians, for whose benefit these negotiations were ostensibly designed.

Before consultations even began, the Wilhelmstrasse was embarrassed by the Swabian fraternal struggle. Mackensen brought the *UDV* schism to the Ministry's attention. Kussbach played one faction against the other, and opposed Basch's radical direction. There was also the matter of *Deutsch-Ungarische Heimatblätter,* a Swabian scholarly journal established by Bleyer in 1929. After Bleyer's death, Kussbach became the formal owner, Basch the editor. The journal was, however, financed, and thus technically owned, by the *VDA.* Recently, Kussbach terminated further publication claiming that Basch no longer obeyed Bleyer's spirit. The German Legation vainly commanded Kussbach to cease interfering. Early in July, he planned to visit Germany, in order to vindicate himself with the *VDA,* the Party, and the Foreign Ministry. In the meantime, the *VDA* dispatched two "experts" to Budapest to investigate the schism. The Swabians' secret contact in Hungary, Heinrich Köhler, raced to Germany ahead of Kussbach in order to denounce him. Mackensen counseled the Ministry to alert Kussbach that all Reich agencies involved in the Swabian *völkisch* movement condemned his behaviour. Several weeks later, the legation reported that mediation efforts had failed. Kussbach refused to relinquish his ban on the journal, whereupon the *Kameradschaft* founded the *Neue Heimatblatter,* edited by Huss, Schmidt, and Basch. Kussbach also ignored promptings to surrender *Sonntagsblatt* to the radicals, and to resign his position. He could not be forced out until the 20 August assembly. Consequently, the Swabian schism was final.[55]

While German-Hungarian minority talks were being arranged, preparations were also afoot for Gömbös' next meeting with Hitler. September 1935 was poor timing for Hungary. Italy had her hands full in Ethiopia and hence, in the German Foreign Ministry's opinion, Hungary would in future no longer be able to depend on receiving support from Italy on the same scale as before, and consequently would feel the need more than hitherto to seek support from a Germany who was becoming an increasingly important power factor. Germany's lost advantage was thus partially restored. As a result, the Wilhelmstrasse saw little reason to enter into a general commitment on two major Hungarian objectives: German-Magyar cooperation in the Successor States, and cessation of all direct influence on the Swabians from authorities in Germany. These points were to be avoided during the Gombos visit on the pretext that they would be dealt with by the minority experts in October.

In the course of his discussion with Hitler, Gömbös never had the opportunity to discuss the minorities question. But the same afternoon he told Neurath that all possible means would be employed against wild agitators stirring up the peaceful Swabian peasantry. Neurath must stop these people, whatever the flag they might operate under. Aside from this, he reiterated all the well-known stock phrases. Neurath rebuked Gömbös. Germany condemned political agitation among the Swabians. But Magyar chauvinists tried to rob good and faithful Swabians of their ancestral tongue and old customs. This justified Swabian anger and poisoned their minds permanently against Magyars. The Swabians' cultural wishes must be regulated to satisfy all parties. Gömbös retorted that a new school type, resembling the old B institution, was being contemplated. Neurath urged Gömbos to mention this in his forthcoming discussions with Hess and Göbbels. Upon his return, Gömbös misled his Ministerial Council by claiming he had discussed the minority question with everyone, including Hitler, and claimed German interest in the minority problem had waned. He referred to Ribbentrop's vague remark that the question was no longer interesting. Consequently, the government would intensify its measures against German agitators. Hitler later thought that Gömbös' analysis contained totally warped assertions. Göring also swore that Gömbös and Hitler had made no mention of minority problems.[56]

Obviously, neither party acted in good faith. Gömbös wanted to trick Germany into Magyar-German cooperation in the diaspora and abandoning the Swabians to Magyarization in Hungary. In return, Hungary might support Germany in the Balkans. The Germans wanted the Magyars to cease persecuting the Swabians, an instrumental step on the road to Hungary's *Gleichschaltung*. Before preliminary talks on the minority issue had an opportunity to get very far, however, German-Hungarian relations received a rude jolt.

The Reich provided clandestine support for *völkisch* activities abroad.

Gömbös and other Hungarian diplomats had been suspicious for some time, but had no firm proof. A confidential report by Hungary's consul in Munich unmasked elaborate German plottings with Croatian separatists, and revealed the presence of grandiose German plans for a "von Triest bis Riga" imperium that would outflank Hungary and endanger her security. It was in the midst of these worries that Kussbach's controversy with Basch culminated in an irrevocable breach. In a pique, Kussbach divulged to Gratz details of an elaborate, clandestine financing plot of the *Kameradschaft* by Reich circles intimately connected with the German government. Gratz reported to Gombos, and in mid-November, Kánya launched a protest with the German Legation in Budapest.

Dr. Heinrich Köhler was listed as a salaried technical consultant for Pontus G.m.b.H., a Reich business firm domiciled in Budapest. Actually, his position was a subterfuge. He really doubled as contact man for the Swabians with both the Foreign Ministry and the *VDA*. He had at his disposal a ballooning payroll, provided jointly by his two masters. In 1934, he disbursed 35,000 Pengö, the following year, 86,000 Pengö. In contrast, the Hungarian government's total annual *UDV* subsidy seldom exceeded 12,000 Pengö. Köhler also speculated in foreign currencies on the black market, and had absolute powers of disposition over the funds. The *Neue Deutschungarische Heimatblätter, Suevia,* an economic bureau, *völkisch* propaganda in Swabian villages, and organizational and other unusual *UDV* expenses, were all beneficiaries of Köhler's largesse.

Mackensen expressed surprise that in view of the fragmenting of the Swabian movement, Köhler was not unmasked much sooner. Fortunately Hungary did not create a diplomatic scandal. Henceforth, Germany ought to eschew *sub rosa* financing or propaganda work in Hungary. After all, Swabian cultural gains depended on Magyar confidence in Germany's political objectives. At the moment, they were understandably skeptical. Of course, Germany must not cease Swabian subsidies or even propaganda, but funds must be disbursed openly and only with Hungary's blessings. If the Magyars believed that German money was properly used, then Hungary would not block Swabian cultural activities and demands. Pataky should be persuaded of Germany's honourable intentions.

The Ministry followed Mackensen's advice and promised to suspend payments pending a final settlement. It also sounded Hungary on disbursing future funds to either Gratz or any other government designate. Expecting to undercut the *Kameradschaft* with German money, the Magyars accepted the offer. But despite the most intense security surveillance, funds continued to filter into the *Kameradschaft's* coffers through a National Socialist Party branch bureau maintained in Hungary, supposedly for the benefit of

German citizens. The Pataky-Rödiger talks were also unsuccessful. Magyar-German cooperation in the diaspora stagnated. The Germans never entered seriously into these discussions, nor did they expect much in return, beyond a few minor concessions in education. Demands for a German teachers' college, and autonomy for the *UDV,* were merely formalities. The Germans concluded prudently that it was useless to press the Magyars on these highly explosive issues.[57]

Indeed, the only tangible measure dealing with a minority issue that contributed in any way to a diminished tension was Gömbös' much-postponed minority school law of 23 December 1935. For all its faults, it was hailed as a prudent measure, and not only by moderate Swabians, but by nearly everyone in the Reich. Stieve informed Pataky, for example, that the new school law met the Reich's expectation for an adequately comprehensive decree on schools, provided the regulation was loyally applied. The *Kameradschaft,* on the other hand, contemptuously attacked the bill as unequalled political humbuggery perpetrated by a perfidious government on the Swabians. The radicals chafed and fumed under the temporary cessation of copious Reich subsidies, and feared they might become the sacrificial lambs of a German-Hungarian economic-political entente.[58]

Throughout 1936, political events pushed the Swabian problem into the background. In the spring, Germany occupied the Rhineland; an uneasy Austro-German accommodation materialized in mid-year; and Gömbös, while he was still well, was busily creating a Hungarian-inspired Rome-Berlin Axis. During Gömbös' lifetime, the Pataky-Rödiger talks proved inconclusive, yet both sides avoided a deadlock or mutual recriminations. For all intents and purposes, Germany and Hungary pursued what each deemed the most important and potentially fruitful approach to the minority problem. The Magyars played for time. The Swabians must be prevented from becoming too strong numerically, and too faithful ideologically to the Reich. This meant expelling Pan-German agitators from Hungary, and unleashing merciless Magyarization. Germany's objective was exactly the reverse. Hungary, the natural Balkan staging area for Germany, must be secured as a refuge for the Swabians, as it was inconceivable that in all the hostile lands of Europe, Germans should enjoy far greater privileges than the Swabians in ostensibly friendly Hungary. This meant that Swabian radicals would receive secret spiritual and financial support in defiance of Hungarian authorities. It would be an exaggeration to suggest that the two powers agreed to shut a benevolent eye to reciprocal abuses, but certainly the minority issue faded as other, more pressing concerns, began to occupy the attention of both German and Hungarian diplomats.

One major aim the Hungarian government set for itself was to identify and frighten *völkisch* Swabians. In Tolna County, school inspectors distributed a questionnaire among minority school teachers. Did they know of any nationalistic agitation or propaganda in a foreign tongue in their village? Were any children sent abroad to study? What sort of associations functioned in their localities and what were their leaders' names? Another means of identifying Swabian dissidents was an efficient and evidently successful system of censorship. Mackensen asserted that Hungary invariably tracked down and identified senders and recipients of compromising letters and proclamations. Many Swabians courted official disfavour as a consequence. The *Kameradschaft* alerted Reich authorities that a systematic postal censorship system mocked the sanctity of private mail. As evidence, extracts from two letters written by Gratz to Huss were submitted. In one letter, Gratz explained why an article he mailed to *Gazette de Hongrie* had taken two months to publish. It probably "slumbered a while" in the press division of the Praesidium. On his interview with *Magyarország*, which dealt with the *UDV*, the *Kameradschaft*, and Huss, Gratz wrote:

> Whether or not it will appear I do not know. Whenever a topic deals either with you or with me, we have to be always prepared that what we write will languish under quarantine in the Praesidium or the Ministry of the Interior for a long time, and it is not always certain that the quarantine will ever be lifted.[59]

What is revealing here is not that Hungary practiced censorship, but that the government applied it even against a man deemed as loyal as Gratz.

Mackensen's suggestion that Swabians suspected of German sympathies suffered persecution was true. Faulstich complained to the German Legation that radical Swabian leaders were being terrorized by the authorities. At the end of June, they were summoned to police headquarters or court houses and questioned. When were you in Germany last? Who is your contact there? Do you have connections with the *VDA*? Who defrayed your travel funds? Who is your contact in Hungary? Who is the donor for the German movement in Hungary? Whom did you meet outside Hungary? Faulstich claimed he had no idea what the consequences of this war of nerves would be, but he suspected Gratz had brought the authorities down on their heads. Mackensen disagreed. It was Kozma, a surprisingly shortsighted man, who had intensified the anti-Swabian campaign. Mackensen was correct. At the end of April, Kozma had issued orders to the police to interrogate all *völkisch* Swabian leaders. County Chief Lieutenants were directed to issue monthly status reports to his Ministry.

In a confidential report to the *VDA*, the *Kameradschaft* bewailed Hungarian persecutions. On Hungarian soil one immediately felt police surveillance. *Volksbewusst* visitors and their hosts had to expect the gendarmerie with fixed bayonets to burst in and grill the visitor, or even have him dragged to police headquarters. An unusually outrageous case involved fourteen young German female students investigating Swabian folk customs. They were arrested, guarded overnight in a provincial town hall with no privacy, then shipped to Budapest. Some were released, others kept in jail for as many as ten days, in the company of common criminals, including prostitutes, and—as a final insult—inoculated against venereal disease before being expelled from Hungary. This episode caused mild diplomatic waves, but no serious snag in German-Hungarian relations. The situation was so bad, according to the *Kameradschaft,* that Swabian peasants no longer dared offer hospitality to *reichsdeutsch* visitors for fear of reprisals. Fines of up to 100 Pengő—a considerable sum for a poor farmer—were not unusual. If true, the Magyars certainly achieved the stoppage of undesirable alien visitors with a minimum of fuss.

In the *Kameradschaft's* view, these persecutions were psychologically motivated. Magyars wished to make Swabians ashamed of being Germans. Swabian members of the Hungarian Olympic team were forbidden to participate unless they Magyarized their names. Swabians with German-sounding names were denied exit permits even to visit the games. In the army, Swabian recruits were ordered to Magyarize their names. In all Swabian elementary schools, first-graders were introduced to the following motto in their reader: "Begone, German, the Magyars are coming!" A noted Magyar journalist demanded that Swabians should either Magyarize rapidly or else emigrate. Parents were fined up to 10 Pengő if their children were caught singing German songs in public. No wonder these outrages occurred. On his recent visit to Pécs, Kozma had declared that for Hungary the minority problem was no longer a foreign policy problem. From this, the *Kameradschaft* inferred that the Magyars no longer feared German reprisals on account of Swabian persecutions.

But the Magyars believed they were defending themselves against seventy million "friends" and their half-million domestic collaborators. At a meeting also attended by State Secretary Dieckhoff, special German envoy Stieve, and Döme Sztójay, Kozma declaimed the *VDA*'s unseemly German propaganda. He condemned anti-Magyar German minority leaders, including Swabians, such as Basch; and Hungary's inundation by countless Germans, who visited only Swabian settlements.[60] In Hungarian Parliament, a speaker called the government to task for not being sufficiently alert to the dangers of National Socialist propagands. A Reich bureau on Hungarian soil disbursed funds earmarked for anti-Magyar propaganda in

Swabian villages, where daily rows occurred between school authorities and Nazi-infected Swabian parents. In the *UDV* two factions, one dedicated to Hungary and Magyar cultural norms, the other treasonous, imbued with brutal contempt for the allegedly inferior Magyars, waged a life and death struggle. The latter plotted to destroy Magyar culture to accommodate Germany's *Südostraum* aspirations.[61]

But the government was vigilant. In April 1936, Pataky outlined in meticulous detail the *modus operandi* of the National Socialists. The various Reich organizations devoted to *Auslanddeutschtum* had recently come under National Socialist direction. Their agents were increasingly active among the Swabians and hastened their Nazification. The *Kameradschaft* had shifted from Swabian cultural separatism to National Socialism. Members gave Reich authorities mailing lists of Swabians, and Hungary was being flooded with National Socialist propaganda. *Völkisch* and Nazi ideology were now identical. Pataky also ferreted out National Socialist Swabian contacts. He learned that Dr. Hornung, a Swabian lawyer of Pécs, had been commissioned to organize parts of Transdanubia by Aschmann, one of Göbbels' agents.[62]

As the Gömbös era ended, the insoluble minority problem remained. Only German-Hungarian reciprocal economic-political dependencies prevented the irruption of a serious collision. Mackensen saw that the Swabians were attracted by the stirring slogan "ein Volk, ein Reich," and the success of social legislation in the Reich. This is why Swabians flocked to join the *Kameradschaft* in great numbers. Of course, the government knew about the radicals' clandestine financial support by Reich agencies, and thus it considered the *völkisch* group Germany's tool for the destruction of the Hungarian state system. The more the Magyars believed this, the more they would persecute the Swabians. The Reich had to overcome Magyar fear, or all future agreements on the minority issue would be futile.

At the same time, Mackensen believed that Hungary must make concessions. The *UDV* must be granted nothing less than a measure of administrative autonomy. Magyar-German cooperation in the Successor States had to remain a dream while the Swabians were mistreated. Why should Germany intervene with the Germans in the diaspora when Hungary considered similar interference with the Swabians as disloyal? Gömbös' 1935 school law was a satisfactory resolution of a sensitive problem, provided its provisions were loyally implemented, not only in the state schools but in the ecclesiastic institutions as well. Without teacher academies the school law was useless. All the Successor States possessed German academies, why not Hungary? Hungary must also introduce German nursery schools and kindergartens. Indeed, these were the most important institutions from the viewpoint of preserving German *Volkstum*.

Mackensen believed that the Basch affair, and several other similar cases involving *volksdeutsch* Swabians, seriously obstructed a genuine German-Hungarian entente. In future, Hungary must resolve similar incidents in the spirit of reconciliation, not rancour. A so-called "Pan-German map" of Hungary, reputedly published in Germany, was a red herring long kicked about by the Magyar press and another link in the chain of German-Hungarian annoyances. This mythical map, which allegedly showed Germany's borders penetrating purely Magyar-inhabited territory, was never produced, and the German government believed none existed. Unless Hungary enlightened the press, any further mention would be considered an unfriendly act. Finally, Germany insisted that funds for strictly cultural purposes reach requisite Swabian organizations. Hungary must be persuaded that it was not in Germany's interest to stir up anti-government or irredentist sentiments in a nation with which it maintained intimate ties.[63]

Already perturbed by the rapid rise of aggressive National Socialist Germany, Gömbös, and later Darányi, refused to offer the Swabians German language and culture. On the contrary, both intensified their efforts to prevent the development of a native Swabian village intelligentsia, which might become the nucleus and transmitter of both German culture and National Socialist ideology. Under these circumstances, German *Kultur*—indeed, German ethnic survival—seemingly faced eventual extinction in Hungary, since most of the Swabian intelligentsia defected to the Magyar language and ethos, leaving the peasant classes virtually leaderless in the face of hostile government minority policy.

Although official statistics indicated extensive conversions to the Magyar language among Swabians, such figures did not necessarily reflect their true sentiments. Social and psychological pressures, as well as economic necessities, frequently forced Swabians to adopt superficially required Hungarian standards, but as experience has shown, such conversions are seldom permanent. In response to mounting German nationalistic propaganda, particularly after 1935, more and more Swabians deserted the moderate, Magyar-oriented *UDV* for Basch's *völkisch* splinter faction supported covertly by Germany. In 1938, when Germany secured Austria, Hungary's strategic position deteriorated, and Germany's true intentions surfaced. Germany demanded total cultural and political autonomy for the Swabians. On 26 November 1938, the *Volksbund der Deutschen in Ungarn* became the skeleton organization for Swabian self-government under Basch. After Czechoslovakia's demise and Germany's triumphs on the Western Front, the National Socialist tide in Eastern Europe became irresistible. On 30 August 1940, Germany helped Hungary recover parts of Transylvania from

Rumania, but at a heavy price. The *Volksbund* became a *völkisch* state within the Hungarian state. With one stroke of the pen, Hungarian Foreign Minister Csáky abrogated all the anti-German efforts of previous governments. It was poetic justice that Basch, who had suffered most from Magyar persecutions, became the greatest beneficiary of this new turn of events.

NOTES

Chapter I
HUNGARY'S MINORITY POLICY BEFORE WWI

1.) Although these Germans came from every part of South Germany, eventually they acquired the appellation "Swabian" (Schwaben), probably as a jest. F.A. Basch, *Das Deutschtum in Ungarn* (March, 1926), p. 7.

2.) Albert Apponyi, "Historic Mission of Hungary and the States Aggrandized to her Detriment," *Justice for Hungary* (London, 1928), pp. 1-20.

3.)C.A. Macartney, *Hungary and her Successors* (London, 1937), p. 22.

4.)Jakob Bleyer wrote that Swabian fathers were proud of their educated, that is de-Germanized sons, and the uneducated individuals remaining in the villages strove to emulate them. Mathias Annabring, *Volksgeschichte der Deutschen in Ungarn* (Stuttgart, 1954), pp. 32-33.

5.)Macartney, *Hungary and Her Successors,* p. 31.

6.)*Nation und Staat (N&S),* XI (1937-1938), 33. By then, Swabian and Saxon elements in Hungary had merged. Hereafter, they will be cited as German-Hungarians, Swabians, or Germans.

7.)Oscar I. Janowsky, *Nationalities and National Minorities* (New York, 1945), pp. 113-114.

8.)Magyar Királyi Belügyminisztérium, *Magyar statisztikai évkönyv* (Évkönyv) (Budapest, 1910), p. 314.

9.)The Slovak population-school ratio stood at 3,063:1. Jakob Bleyer, "A hazai németség," *Budapesti Szemle* (March 1917), 10-11; "A hazai németség kérdéséhez," *ibid.* (July 1917), 4; "Die deutsche Schulnot in Ungarn," *Alldeutsche Blätter,* 1 December 1917.

10.)Oscar Jászi, *The Dissolution of the Habsburg Monarchy* (Chicago, 1929), p. 440.

11.)C.A. Macartney, *National States and National Minorities* (London, 1934), p. 122.

12.)Gustav Gratz, "Bleyer Jakab," *Magyar Szemle,* XX (1934), 12.

13.)J. Bleyer, "A hazai németség," 6.

14.)R.W. Seton-Watson, *German, Slav, and Magyar. A Study in the Origins of the Great War* (London, 1916), p. 36.

Chapter II
MINORITIES "CONCILIATED"

1.)Mihály Károlyi, *Egy egész világ ellen* (Budapest, 1965), p. 318.

2.)All statistics have been gathered from M.K. Belügyminisztérium, *Magyar statisztikai évkönyv és jelentés 1919-1922* (Budapest, 1925), pp. 162-163 and 165-166.

3.)Until the end of 1919, the area was known as West Hungary, Trans-Danubia, Dunántúl (Magyar). Austrian Chancellor Renner coined the word "Burgenland" to apply specifically to the disputed area.

4.)A Magyar Királyi Központi Statisztikai Hivatal, *Magyar statisztikai közlemények. Az 1920. Évi népszámlálás* (Budapest, 1924), pp. 296-297.

5.)*Wiener Mittag,* 18 November 1918. Also see Johannes Huber, "Ein Mahnruf an die Deutschen in Westungarn," *Neue Post (NP),* 21 November 1918.

6.)Károlyi, *Egy egész világ ellen,* p. 297. Also see Point 4 of Károlyi's Ten-Point Programme, which called for the cessation of the oppression of nationalities. *Ibid.,* p. 319, as well as Károlyi's speech in Parliament on 22 October 1918, in a similar vein. *Ibid.,* pp. 331-333; and *Népszava,* 8 October 1918.

7.)Cited in F. Deak, *Hungary at the Paris Peace Conference* (New York, 1972), p. 18. Even during the war Károlyi denied Magyar oppression of the minorities. *Országgyűlési Napló,* (Naplo) XXXV (1917); debates of 20 March 1917, pp. 237-240.

8.)According to Jászi, the following parties were involved: The Social Democratic Party; Károlyi's own party; and the Radical (Bourgeois) Party. O. Jászi, *Revolution and Counter-Revolution* (New York, 1969), pp. 21-22.

9.)Károlyi, *Egy egész világ ellen,* pp. 352-353.

10.)Jászi, *Revolution,* p. 38.

11.)Jászi subsequently admitted: "The moment we had lost the war I realised that the political integrity of Hungary was beyond saving." Jászi, *Revolution,* p. 57; also see Jászi, *The Dissolution of the Habsburg Monarchy* (Chicago, 1964), p. 342; and Károlyi, *Egy egész világ ellen,* pp. 299-313.

12.)*Österreichisches Staatsarchiv, Neue Politische Abteilung (ÖSA NPA),* Fasc.990. Lu 9/1,3577/1 and 4979/1, 29 December 1918, and 2267/1, 7 December 1928.

13.)*Auswärtiges Amt, Politische Abteilung,* Bonn *(AA PA),* Österreich 92, No. 1, Bd.263.

14.)"Inditványok Nyugat-Magyarország annektálásáról," *Az Ujság,* 15 November 1918; and "Az osztrák szocialisták a magyar vármegyék annektá-lása ellen," *Világ,* 20 November 1918. Otto Bauer conceded that only

Austria's dependency on Hungarian food had prompted his party's cautious approach in West Hungary. *Stenographische Protokolle über die Sitzungen der Konstituierenden Nationalversammlung* (Vienna, 1919), I, 21st session.

15.)"Rendteremtés érdekében," *Vilag,* 20 November 1918.

16.)*ÖSA NPA* Fasc. 990 LU 9/1, 3577/1 and 4979/1, 20 December 1918.

17.)*Ibid.,* 2116/4 and 2319/4, March 1919.

18.)*AA PA,* "Öst. 92, No. 1, Bd. 27. German Legation in Vienna, report of 16 May 1919.

19.)Bleyer, "A hazai németség," 1-14.

20.)Bleyer, "An die Deutschungarn," *NP,* 25 October 1918.

21.)*Der Volksrat der Deutschen diesseits des Königssteigs,* or west of Transylvania.

22.)*NP,* 3 November 1918.

23.)*Ibid.,* 10 November 1918.

24.)*Ibid.,* 12 November 1918.

25.)*Ibid.,* 16, 19, and 20 November 1918.

26.)J. Huber, "Ein Mahnruf an die Deutschen Westungarn," *NP,* 20 November 1918.

27.)*NP,* 21 and 24 November, and 22 December 1918.

28.)László Koncsek, "A bécsi és Sopron megyei ellenforradalom kapcsolatai 1919-ben," *Soproni Szemle,* X (1956), 107. Cf. Macartney, *Hungary and her Successors,* p. 50.

29.)J. Huber, "Was trennt uns von Herrn Brandsch?" *NP,* 9 November 1918, is a good comparison between Bleyer and Brandsch.

30.)*NP,* 11 January 1919.

31.)*Országos Levéltár, Miniszter Tanács, (OL MT),* 27 January 1919, Point 67; *Pester Lloyd (PL),* 4 January 1919; and *NP,* 30 January 1919, for full text of Law VI in German.

32.)"Was sagt Professor Bl.?" *Deutsches Tageblatt,* 13 February 1919; *Budapesti Hirlap,* 25 January 1919.

33.)Macartney erroneously calls Kalmár "Kalmars" and "German." *Hungary and her Successors,* p. 50.

34.)*NP,* 30 January and 1 February 1919.

35.)"Christen, zur Rettung der Kinderseelen," *NP,* 7 March 1919.

36.)*NP,* 12 March 1919.

37.)*ÖSA NPA* Fasc. 990 LU 9/1, 1194/a/4. Report of 27 January 1919; and 899 LU 9/1, 1375/4. Report of 8 February 1919. *OL Külügyminisztérium (Küm.),* res.pol. 1918-1920. Vegyes. 584, 1919.

38.)Béla Kun's article in *Pravda,* 31 October 1918.

39.)Béla Kun, *Válogatott írdsok és beszédek,* Henrik Vass, István Frissné, and Éva Szabó, eds. (2 vols. Budapest, 1966), I, 107.

40.)Kun to Ignác Bogár, Letter of 11 March 1919, *ibid.*, 192. The first such statement was rendered by Kun on 29 March 1919 to the *Neue Freie Presse* (Vienna), and was reproduced in *Vörös Ujság,* 30 March 1919. A. Siklós, "The Hungarian Soviet Republic and the National and Nationality Question," *Acta Historica,* XVII (1971), 74.

41.)Kun, "A Magyar Kerenszky-uralom," *Pravda,* 31 October 1918.

42.)*Vörös Ujság,* 22 March 1919, and "Mindenkihez," *ibid.,* 23 March 1919, more specifically oriented towards non-Magyars.

43.)Julius Deutsch, *Aus Österreichs Revolution. Militärpolitische Erinnerungen* (Vienna, 1920), p. 86. Deutsch was minister of war under Renner.

44.)"Forst Lipót elvtárs Sopronban," *Soproni Vörös Ujság,* 13 April 1919; "Entscheidender Sieg der Grazen Kommunisten," *Der Abend,* 31 March 1919.

45.)Deutsch, *Aus Österreichs Revolution,* pp. 78-79. ÖSA NPA Fasc. 900 LU 9/1, 3145/4, 3675/4, 2 May 1919; 3533/4, 4 May 1919, among others.

46.)*Ibid.,* Fasc. 899 LU 9/1, 434/4 and 880/L/1, 4371/4; 4268/4; 880 LU/I/1 4342; 887 LU 2/3.4776/4; and "Heftige Kämpfe in Westungarn. Eine Denkschrift der Heinzen an den steirischen Landtag," *Reichspost,* 12 June 1919.

47.)"Proletárönrendelkezés," *Vörös Ujság,* 28 March 1919; also cited in S. Gábor, ed., *A magyar munkásmozgalom történetének válogatott dokumentumai* (6 vols. Budapest, 1956-1969), VI, 69 *(MMTVD); "*Az első nemzetközi ezred első zászlóaljának felvonulása," *Vörös Ujság,* 1 April 1919.

48.)Kun, *Válogatott írások,* Speech of 15 May 1919, p. 290.

49.)Paragraph 2 of Law XXVI of Provisional Constitution of 2 Apr. 1919, cited in *MMTVD,* VI, 100-101; and "A nyugat-magyarországi németek a szovjetállamban," *Soproni Vörös Ujság,* 30 April 1919.

50.)*Budapesti Közlöny, (BK),* 24 March 1919.

51.)Law XLI of 7 April 1919, B. Halász, I. Kovács, and V. Peschka, eds., *A Magyar Tanácsköztársaság jogalkotdsa* (Budapest, 1959), p. 86.

52.)See Brandsch's report of Austrian plot in Burgenland; AA PA, Öst. 104, Bd. 16, 12 June 1919.

52.)*Pester Lloyd,* 29 April 1919.

54.)Kun, *Válogatott írások,* Speech of 15 May 1919, I, 290; 20 May, 315; 12-13 June, 356; *Volksstimme,* 18 May 1919.

55.)School nationalization Law XXIV of 1 April; cited in *MMTVD,* VI, 73; school centralization ordinance 10 KN of 18 April, 250-251.

56.)K. Petrák and Gy. Milei, ed., *A M.T.K. szociálpolitikája. Válogatott rendeletek, documentumoks cikkek* (Budapest, 1959), pp. 2 and 31-35; citing Order No. 87039 of 5 May 1919, "Instruction to Insure the Undisturbed

Continuance of Education." Also see "Az uj iskola," *Vörös Ujság*, 3 April 1919.

57.)Order XCI of the Revolutionary Governing Council, 14 May 1919, *MMTVD*, VI, 482.

58.)Jenő Pongrácz, ed., *A Forradalmi Kormányzótanács és a népbiztosok rendeletei* (5 vols. Budapest, 1919), III, 21–23 and 104–105; Order No. 28 of 12 May 1919 by the Commissar of Education.

59.)Law XXIV of 1 April 1919, cited in Petrák and Milei, p. 1, and *MMTVD*, VI, 73.

60.)Vilma Bresztovsky, "A történelem az új iskolában," *Fáklya*, 29 April 1919, and Gyula Krúdy, "Új történelmet kell írni," *Magyarország*, 6 April 1919.

61.)Zs. Kunfi, "A vallás szabad gyakorlása," *Népszava*, 18 April 1919, "A tanítók átképzése," *ibid.*, 1 July 1919. Also see Kun's speech before the National Party Congress, 12–13 June 1919, to the same effect. Kun, *Válogatott írások*, I, 356.

62.)Ordinance of 10 April 1919, cited in *MMTVD*, VI, 179; and Petrák and Milei, *A Magyar Tandácsköztársaság művelődéspolitikája* (Budapest, 1959), p. 12.

63.)*Pester Lloyd*, 13 July 1919.

64.)Halász, *A Magyar Tandácsköztársaság*, p. 71.

65.)F. Eckelt, "The Internal Policies of the Hungarian Soviet Republic," *Hungary in Revolution 1918-1919*, ed. Ivan Volgyes (Lincoln, 1971), p. 101.

66.)"Die Autonomie der Deutschen," *Volksstimme*, 5 August 1919.

67.)*BK*, 15 August 1919, 1 and 16 August, 1-2. Bleyer's appointment was not ratified officially until the end of February 1920.*BK* 29 Feb. 1920, 1-2, citing Law I, Paragraph 6.

68.)"A nemzeti kisebbségek minisztériumának nyilatkozata," *BK*, 17 August 1919, 6.

69.)*OL ME* 1919 XXII, 5768.

70.)See text in *BK*, 19 November 1919, *NP*, 23 November; and *Volksstimme*, 20 November 1919. Delay in publication was due to Rumanian censorship.

71.)*ÖSA NPA* Fasc. 900 LU 9/1, 5682/4.

72.)Deutsch, *Aus Österreichs Revolution*, pp. 79-80.

73.)*NP*, 26 November 1919.

74.)*OL ME* 1919 XXII 5440.

75.)Paragraph 16 of the Nationality Law made this quite plain. *BK*, 19 November 1919.

76.)*OL ME* 1920 XLII/a 8634; Meeting of 2 October 1919.

Chapter III
THE EARLY HORTHY ERA

1.)*Iratok az ellenforradalom történetéhez 1919-1945* (Budapest, 1956), I, 200-207.

2.)E. Ludendorff, *Meine Lebenserinnerungen 1919-1925* (Berlin, 1940), I, 112-142, Letters of 15 May and 19 August 1920 cited in Szinai and Szűcs, "Horthy's Secret Correspondence with Hitler," *New Hungarian Quarterly*, LV (1963), 177.

3.)ÖSA NPA Fasc. 904 Liasse Ungarn. Vienna Legation, report of 29 December 1920; Fasc. 883 Liasse Ungarn II-3, report of 2 August 1922; and Fasc. 905 Liasse Ungarn 9/3, report of 23 March 1921.

4.)Carl Seitz to Gustav Gratz, 29 November 1919, F. Deák and D. Ujváry, *Papers and Documents Relating to the Foreign Relations of Hungary (PDFR)*, (Budapest, 1939), I, Doc. 44. Gratz to Somssich, 29 November 1919, *ibid.;* Somssich to Gratz, 21 December 1919, Doc. 58.

5.)See, for example, "Das letzte Wort werden wir sagen," *NP,* 24 February 1920.

6.)For details, see Deak, *Hungary at the Peace Conference*, pp. 198-203 and 253-290.

7.)"Renner gegen Ungarn," *NP,* 9 January 1920, referring to parliamentary debates of 7 January 1920.

8.)"Westungarn," *Volksstimme,* 17 February 1920; "Aus dem Auslande. Das Burgenland und die Vermögensabgabe," *ibid.,* 24 July 1920; *AA PA,* Abt.IIb, Politik Nr.3, Österreich-Ungarn, Bd.I; Report of German Legation, Vienna, 24 June 1920; and German Legation, Budapest, report of 29 November 1920 and 13 December 1920. *AA PA* IIb, Pol.6, Bd.I.

9.)*Napló,* XII, (1921), 254th Session, 23 August 1921, 616-617.

10.)*PDFR, passim.*

11.)"Nicht alldeutsch sondern deutschungarisch!" *NP,* 8 July 1920.

12.)*AA PA* IIb, Pol.6, Bd.I and III; German Legation, Budapest, report of 30 April 1921 and 17 March 1922.

13.)*Magyarország,* 10 December 1921; and see abstract of article dispatched to the Foreign Ministry (F.M.) by the Budapest Legation. *AA PA* IIb. Pol.6, Bd. III. Also see reports of 21 December 1921 and 17 March 1922, *ibid.*

14.)*E.g., München-Augsburger Abendzeitung, Bayrischer Kurier, Augsburger Postzeitung, Deutsche Tageszeitung.*

15.)Reported in *Ödenburger Zeitung,* 23 January 1921.

16.)*AA PA* Ib, Österreich 92, Bd.XXX, German Legation, report of 21 February 1920. *Ibid.,* IIb, Pol.5, Ungarn, Bd.I, report of 12 April 1920. *Ibid.,* Pol.6, Österreich-Westungarn, Bd.I, report of 15 November 1920. *ÖSA*

NPA Fasc. 904 Liasse Ungarn, telephone conversation of 15 November and report of 13 December 1920.

17.)"Die zweite Einkreisung," *München-Augsburger Abendzeitung*, 15 Feb. 1921.

18.)*ÖSA NPA* Fasc. 904 Liasse Ungarn, report of 17 December and 23 December 1920.

19.)"Nicht alldeutsch, sondern deutschungarisch!" *NP*, 8 July 1920.

20.)*AA PA* IIb, Politik 6, Österreich-Westungarn, Bd. I, report of 19 Jan. 1921.

21.)*Ibid.*, report of 3 March 1921.

22.)"Im Kreuzfeuer der Verdächtigungen," *Tageszeitung*, citied in *Pester Zeitung*, 25 April 1921.

23.)*AA PA* IIb, Pol. 6, Öst.-Westungarn, Bd. I, reports of 12 through 23 Jan.; 2, 12, 13, 23, 24 February; 3 and 20 March; 24 April 1921.

24.)Reports of end of April and 17 May 1919, *MMTVD*, VI, 119-122; 369, and 507.

25.)*PDFR*, Docs. 44, 57, 113, 117, and 125. Also see Lajos Reményi, *Külkereskedelempolitika Magyarországon 1919-1924* (Budapest, 1969), pp. 80-81.

26.)*Ibid.*, pp. 82-83. *OL MT* Jegyzőkönyv, 24 February and 1 August 1921.

27.)*PDFR*, Villáni to Teleki, note of 18 Sept. 1920, Doc. 653.

28.)*Ibid.*, Gratz to Csáky, and Csáky to Gratz, telegrams of 11 and 12 Nov. 1920, Docs. 787 and 788.

29.)*Ibid.*, Docs. 728, 756, 773, 776, 778, 779, 782, 784, 795, 802, 821, 836, 841, 848, 850, 879, 884-886, 889, 890, and 894. Also see, Reményi, *Külkereskedelempolitika*, pp. 94-95, and 155-158; and *OL MT* Jegyzőkönyv, 28 August 1921.

30.)*Deutsches Zentral Archiv*, Potsdam, Auswärtiges Amt (DZA), Abt. II, 40835-1, German Consul, Budapest, report of 18 December 1919.

31.)*OL Küm.* Gazd. pol. Német dosszié, 65. csomó, 1920; *OL* Jogi osztály, törzsszám U70, 24 December 1920; and *DZA* 41278-9.

32.)*Deutscher Reichsanzeiger* and *Preussischer Staatsanzeiger*, 15 April 1921.

33.)*OL FM* 1921-54-20. 242; reports of 20 and 28 January and 27 April 1921, Hungarian Legation, Berlin. *OL FM* 1922-54-72.193, report of 14 Apr. 1922.

34.)*Magyar statisztikai évkönyv 1919-1922, passim.*

Chapter IV
THE EARLY HORTHY ERA

1.)Law 209494-1919.B.II. "A nemzeti kisebbségek népoktatásügye," *BK*, 28 December 1919; *NP*, 11 January 1920.

2.)Hans Eninger, "Die Rechte der nationalen Minderheiten," *NP*, 4 May 1920.

3.)*NP*, 23 January 1920.

4.)*BK*, 11, 14, and 23 January and 28 November 1920.

5.)A typical Swabian argument ran along the following lines: "Just look at Kun, Pogány, and the Jews in general. They all speak perfect Magyar, yet they are traitors to Hungary. Swabians may speak broken Magyar, but at heart they are true Hungarian patriots." Eninger, "Die Rechte. . ."

6.)*OL ME* 1920 XLIII 8634.

7.)B. Bellér, "Az ellenforradalmi rendszer első éveinek nemzetiségi politikája," *Szdzadok*, VI (1963), 1290.

8.)The *Neue Post* blamed "liberal politicians, especially in Budapest County," for spreading malicious rumours about Bleyer and the Ministry of Nationalities. "Die Verdienste des Ministeriums der nationalen Minderheiten," *NP*, 23 October 1920.

9.)For a thorough listing of these protests, see Royal Ministry of Foreign Affairs, *Hungarian Negotiations* (Budapest, 1921), I, Annex 3, 469; and Note XVI, 538, 540.

10.)"Konferenz der nationalen Minderheiten," *NP*, 1 January 1920.

11.)*Ungarländischer Verband der Ungarfreundlichen Nationalen Minderheiten.*

12.)"Ein Memorandum der nationalen Minderheiten," *NP*, 23 January 1920.

13.)*The Hungarian Nation*, I (February 1920), 10-12.

14.)Deak, *Hungary at the Paris Peace Conference,* pp. 539-549; Jászi, *Dissolution,* p. 281; Robert A. Kann, *The Habsburg Empire. A Study in Integration and Disintegration* (New York, 1957), p. 115.

15.)"Ein Protest der westungarischen Abgeordneten," *NP*, 5 Feb. 1920; "Eine ehrliche Nationalitätenpolitik auf christliche Grundlage," *ibid.,* 14 July 1920; "Die Treue der nationalen Minderheiten zum ungarischen Vaterland," *ibid.,* 31 July 1920; "Die Lösung der Nationalitätenfrage. Protest gegen die losreizung Westungarns," *ibid.,* 1 August 1920; "Das Treiben der Gruppe Gündisch und Comp.," *ibid.,* 25 November 1919.

16.)*AA PA* IIb., Pol. 6, Öst.-Westungarn, Bd.I; Fürstenberg to F.M., dispatch of 17 January 1921.

17.)"Vorschlag zur Lösung der westungarischen Frage," *Pester Zeitung,* 9 Nov. 1920.

18.)"Ein Beschluss der *Westungarischen Landsmannschaft,"* *Pester Zeitung,* 12 November 1920; "Die *Westungarische Liga* gegen den Manifest Dr. Hubers," *Pester Zeitung,* 26 November 1920.

19.)*OL ME* 1921 XLIII 523.

20.)*AA PA* IIb. Pol. 6, Öst.-Westungarn, Bd.I, Rosenberg to F.M., letters of 14 and 21 Jan. and 24 April 1921; Bleyer to Zahnbrecher, letter of 19 December 1920.

21.)*OL ME* 1920 XLIII 6218.

22.)"Wir bleiben Deutsche, aber in Ungarn," *NP,* 15 Jan. 1920; "Westungarn will bei Ungarn bleiben," *ibid.,* 20 Jan. 1920; Gratz to Somssich, report of 14 Jan. 1920, *PDFR,* Doc. 75.

23.)"Feindselige Empfang der österreichischen Delegierten in Ödenburg," *NP,* 6 March 1920; "Blutige Tage in der Bácska," *ibid.,* 17 March 1920.

24.)The Swabians welcomed Horthy, because he was a Christian conservative and a monarchist. "Nicholas v. Horthy: Reichsverweser," *NP,* 2 March 1920.

25.)J. Huber, "Die Nationalitätenfrage," *NP,* 17 March 1920.

26.)"Die christliche Partei solidarisch mit der Nationalitätenpolitik Bleyers," *NP,* 9 July 1920; "Ein neuer Erfolg der Deutschungarischen Integritätspartei," *ibid.,* 11 July 1920; "Die Nationalitätenpolitik und Apponyi," *ibid.,* 9 June 1920; "Graf Apponyi über die Nationalitätenpolitik," *ibid.,* 24 October 1920.

27.)"Ministerpräsident Teleki für die Rechte der nationalen Minderheiten," *NP,* 24 July 1920.

28.)*OL ME* 1920 XLIII 6218. Bellér, "Az ellenforradalmi rendszer," 1304-1307; *Napló,* VII, (1920), 136th session, 202-204.

29.)"Die Antwort des Ministers Dr. Jakob Bleyer auf den gegen das Nationalitätenministerium gerichteten Angriff," *NP,* 10 October 1920; "Die Verdienste des Ministeriums der nationalen Minderheiten," *ibid.,* 23 October 1920; "Minister Rubinek gegen christsoziale Abgeordnete," *Pester Zeitung,* 25 November 1920.

30.)"Regierungserklärungen über die Nationalitätenpolitik," and "Altungarische Nationalitätenpolitik," *Pester Zeitung,* 16 November 1920; "Politische Nachrichten," *ibid.,* 28 November 1920.

31.)Bleyer to Zahnbrecher, letter of 19 December 1920.

32.)A. Török, "Jakob Bleyer als Nationalitätenminister," *Ungarische Jahrbücher* (Budapest, 1934), XIV, 42f. Fürstenberg to F.M., letter of 8 January 1921, expressed Bleyer's extreme pessimism. *AA PA* IIb. Pol. 6, Öst.-Westungarn, Bd.I.

33.)*Ibid.,* Bd.II, letter of 2 June 1921. *Napló,* X, (1921), debates of 1 June 1921, 317f.

34.)Nikolaus Degenhardt (Notary of Bakonysarkány), "Braucht das Volk Kultur oder nicht?" *Sonntagsblatt (Sbl.),* 6 November 1921; "Selbsthilfe," *Sbl.,* 30 October 1921; "Wir halten mit deutscher Treue an dem ungarischen Vaterlande und mit derselben Liebe an unseren Muttersprache," *ibid.,* 4 December 1921. For a listing of middle schools in Ödenburg abolished by the government, presumably since 1907, see *AA PA* IIb., Pol. 6, Öst.-

Westungarn, Bd.II, report of 13 October 1921, German Legation, Budapest, to F.M.

35.)For the German viewpoint, see Karl von Loesch and M.H. Boehm, *Grenzdeutschland seit Versailles* (Berlin, 1930), *passim*. For plebiscite results, see *AA PA*, Bd.III, German Legation, Budapest, to F.M., report of 12 December 1921.

Chapter V
"CONCILIATION" DETERIORATES

1.)From 287 to 92.

2.)33,682 out of 83,861.

3.)From 29,460 to 23,965.

4.)Apponyi, "Historic Mission of Hungary," pp. 1-20.

5.)"Vor einer neuen Zukunft," *Sbl.*, 1 October 1921.

6.)"Ein Schwabendeputation beim Ministerpräsidenten Grafen Bethlen," *Sbl.*, 29 January 1922; also see *Pester Lloyd,* 20 January 1922; and *AA PA* IIb, Pol. 6, Westungarische Frage, Bd.III, Fürstenberg to Foreign Ministry, letter of 20 January 1922 and 24 April 1922. Fürstenberg to Rumelin, note of 18 September 1922, *ibid.,* Pol. Beziehungen Ungarn-Deutschland, (PBU-D) Bd.II. J. Bleyer, "In Sachen des Sonntagsblattes," *Sbl.*, 23 July 1922. On Schwartz's acquittal, see "Unsere Rechtfertigungen," *Sbl.*, 31 December 1922.

7.)*Deutsche Allgemeine Zeitung*, 26 July 1922. "Die Zukunft der Deutschen in Ungarn," *Sbl.*, 6 August 1922.

8.)S. Wachtler, "Unsere Volksschulen," *ibid.,* 28 January 1923; J. Bleyer, "Zwei Briefe," *ibid.,* 4 March 1923.

9.)"Zu einer Lehrerwahl," *ibid.,* 18 March 1923; J. Bleyer, "Unsere Sache in der Nationalversammlung." *ibid.,* 4 February 1923; J. Bleyer, "Dr. Gustav Gratz über die Frage der nationalen Minderheiten in Rumpfungarn," *ibid.,* 27 May 1923; G. Gratz, "Nationale Minderheiten," *Pester Lloyd,* 19 May 1923.

10.)*AA PA* IIb, PBU-D, Bd.II; Hungarian verbal note to Wilhelmstrasse, 28 August 1922; F.M. and Fürstenberg, exchange of letters, 8 and 18 September 1922; Fürstenberg to F.M., letter of 13 October 1922; von Stumm to F.M., letter of 22 October 1922; F.M. Internal Memo, 3 January 1923; Welczek to F.M., note of 29 April 1923; Köpke's Report, 6 May 1923. Also see *ibid.,* Büro Reichsminister, Akten betreffend Ungarn, (BR-U), Bd.I, von Mutius to F.M., note of 5 March 1923.

11.)*AA PA* IIb, Pol. 2, PBU-D, Bd.I, Germany's demarche in Budapest, 4 August 1922, and Fürstenberg's telegram and letter of same date, and 18 August 1922; *ibid.,* Bd.II, Hungarian verbal note, 28 August 1922; Fürstenberg to F.M., letters of 8 and 18 September 1922; F.M. Internal Memo, 3 January 1923; and 16 May 1923; Welczek to F.M., letter of 29 April 1923; *ibid.*, BR-U, Bd.I, Fürstenberg to F.M., telegram of 26 August 1922; *ibid.*, Geheimakten, Pol. 2, Ungarn-Deutschland, Maltzan to F.M., 27 May 1923, letter of 3 September 1923.

12.)Law 4800.923 M.E. concerned itself with minority education; decree 110478:1923 VII.a. activated the Law. Minority languages in general were governed by Law II of 1924, which was activated by decree 7500 M.E. of the same year. *Naplo,* XIII, (1923), 143rd session, 22 June 1923. Also see *BK,* 22 June 1923; M.K. Belügyminisztérium, *Statisztikai évkönyv és jelentés 1923-1925* (Budapest, 1928), p. 178. Bleyer's speech in Parliament, 13 May 1927, *Napló,* IV, (1927), 46th session, p. 92.

13.)"Die Regelung der Nationalitätenfrage," *Sbl.,* 24 June 1923. *Budapesti Közlöny* of 22 June 1923, agreed with the viewpoint that the nationality statutes of 1868 and 1919 were still binding. Five years later, however, the official Yearbook wrote that the 1919 Law "in practice resulted in pedagogically faulty language combinations," and that was why the three school types (A, B, and C) came into being. This was a jibe at Bleyer, author of the 1919 Law. *Évkönyv és jelentés 1923-1925,* p. 178.

14.)*Napló,* XXX, (1925), 379th session, 19 February 1925, p. 128; "Unsere wichtigsten Sprachenrechte," *Sbl.,* 1 July 1923.

15.)"Die Muttersprache in den Schulen," *ibid.,* 8 July 1923; "Das Deutsche in Verwaltung," *ibid.,* 5 August 1923, pointed out that with the exception of Sopron and Moson, few communities existed where at least 20% of the population was non-Magyar. "Schlussbericht über die Sprachverordnung," *ibid.,* 2 September 1923.

16.)"Die Zeitungen über die neue Minderheitverordnung," *ibid.,* 1 July; Anton König, "Unsere völkischen Rechte," *ibid.,* 15 July; "Unser Gesetzbuch," *ibid.,* 1 July; J. Bleyer, "An unsere deutschen Gemeinden und an die Eltern schulpflichtiger Kinder," *ibid.,* 9 September 1923; D. Bernstorff, "Die deutsche Minderheit in Ungarn," *ibid.,* 19 Aug. 1923.

17.)J. Bleyer, "Ein Jahr wieder verloren," *ibid.,* 2 September; J. Bleyer, "An unsere deutschen Gemeinden," *ibid.,* 9 September 1923.

18.)J. Bleyer, "Über die Schulverordnung," *ibid.,* 23 September; J. Bleyer, "Offner Brief an den Herrn Regierungskommissar Dr. Georg Steuer," *ibid.,* 8 April 1923. Copy of Steuer's report as *főispán* (#9000-1918, dated 28 August 1918), may be found in *AA PA* IIb, Pol. 2, Ungarn, Bd.II. Franz Ohfolk, "Vor neuen Schuljahr," *Sbl.,* 19 August 1923; A.H. Griesshaber, "Ungarischer Sprachunterricht in deutschsprachigen Volksschulen," *Tolnamegyei Ujsdg,* 20 October 1923 (in Magyar); G. Gratz, "Über die Minoritätenfrage in Ungarn," *Pester Lloyd,* 17 June 1924. As late as in 1934, Gratz believed that

Bethlen's intentions had been sincere, and that chauvinistic local officials foiled him. G. Gratz, "Bethlen külpolitikája és kisebbségi politikája," *Magyar Szemle*, XXII (1934), 133-135.

19.)*Vasvármegye*, 15 January; *Pécsi Est*, 27 June; "Die Durchführung der Sprachverordnungen in den Minderheitenschulen der Diozese Steinamanger," *Sbl.*, 3 February; J. Bleyer, "Eine Hetze gegen Dr. Bleyer und das Sonntagsblatt," *ibid.*, 6 July 1924.

20.)*Napló*, XXI (1924), pp. 74 and 77-78; "Graf Bethlen und die Deutschen in Ungarn," *Siebenbürgisch-Deutsches Tageblatt*, 29 December 1923.

21.)*Napló*, XXI, pp. 77-78.

22.)See the following articles in *Sonntagsblatt:* J. Bleyer, "Hemmungen in der Schulfrage," 21 September; J. Bleyer, "Wie kann die Schulfrage gelöst werden? Ein Vorschlag an die hohe ungarische Regierung," 28 September 1924; Parliamentary debates of 3 February 1925, in "Abgeordneter Dr. Franz Neuberger für die Wünsche des ungarländischen deutschen Volkes," 8 February; J. Bleyer, "Unser Patriotismus," 1 March; Szterényi's speech, admitting "executive violations," in "Baron Josef Szterényi über Nationalitätenfrage in Ungarn," 7 June; J. Bleyer, "Die Schulfrage," 28 June; J. Bleyer, "Die Elternkonferenzen können bis zum 15. August abgehalten werden!" 12 July; J. Bleyer, "Eine neue Schulverordnung," 23 August; J. Bleyer, "Dringende Notwendigkeit deutscher Schulbücher," 27 December, 1925. Also see study plan, decree 62.800/1925 VIII.a., in *BK* 14 August 1925, and *Évkönyv és jelentés 1923-1925*, p. 178. Deadline extension to 15 October, decree 63.348/1925 VIII.a., was published in *BK*, 13 August 1925. Bethlen's speech in Geneva is cited in League of Nations, *Official Journal* (Geneva, 1926), p. 218.

23.)*Pester Lloyd*, 23 June 1923; "Deutsche Vereinwesen in Ungarn," *Sbl.*, 15 July 1923; "Unsere Fest. Die feierliche gründende Generalversammlung des Ungarländischen Deutschen Volksbildungsvereines," *ibid.*, 10 August 1924. Cf. Gratz, "Bethlen külpolitikája," 133-135. The original *UDV* triumvirate consisted of Gratz, Wild, and Bleyer.

24.)"Ungarn," *Der Auslandsdeutsche (DA)*, XIV (1931), 639, editor's comments.

25.)7699/1924 M.E.II, 21 October 1924; "Ein Reskript des Kön.ungar. Ministerpräsidium an den U.D.V.," *Sbl.*, 30 November 1924.

26.)*Sitzungen des U.D.V.*, ed. *U.D.V.*, Budapest, 19 November 1924; J. Bleyer, "Quertreibereien," *Sbl.*, 29 March 1925. See *OL ME* 1926-L-34 (7021) for Pest County assembly. "Die Lage der deutschen Minderheit in Ungarn," *Bleyer Nachlass*, *(BN)*, cited in H. Schwind, *Jakob Bleyer. Ein Vorkämpfer und Erwecker des ungarländischen Deutschtums* (Munich, 1960), p. 125.

27.)OL ME 1925-T-75 and 1925-C-1287; *Pécsi Est*, 27 June 1924; "A máriakeméndi esperesi kör a magyarságért," *Dundntúl,* 25 January 1925.

28.)Bleyer to Gratz, letter of 22 July 1925, *BN,* Schwind, *Bleyer,* p. 128.

29.)F. Bonitz, "Zur Aufklärung," and "Unsere Gegner," *Sbl.,* 5 April 1925.

30.)"Protokoll der Vollzugsausschutzsitzung von U.D.V.," meeting of 1 February 1925, in *BN,* Schwind, *Bleyer,* p. 125. "Die erste Generalversammlung des U.D.V.," *Sbl.,* 30 August 1925.

31.)Meeting of 7 March 1925, *OL ME* 1925-T-147 and 1925-C-1287.

32.)Franz Kussbach, Bleyer's son-in-law, believed the government's minority policy was geared to its foreign policy. *Kussbach Nachlass (KN),* in *Bundesarchiv Koblenz (BAK),* Ostdokument 16 I 79.

33.)Stephen Bethlen, "Hungary in the New Europe," *Foreign Affairs,* III (1925), 445-458. Also see G. Gratz, *Deutschungarische Probleme* (Budapest, 1938), pp. 71ff., and "Verfassung, innere und auswärtige Politik, Verwaltung, Justiz," *Ungarisches Wirtschafts-Jahrbuch (UWJ),* I (1925), 19.

34.)Professor Hoetzsch's speech in Görlitz, cited in "Duetschland für die Auslanddeutschen," *Sbl.,* 12 November 1922.

35.)*AA PA* Büro Reichsminister, Akten betreffend Auslanddeutsche, Bd.I, Foreign Ministry Internal Memo, 7 November 1924. Also see anonymous article authored by Stresemann, in which he declared that Germany must become the "shield of Europe's minorities." *Hamburger Fremdenblatt,* 14 June 1925.

36.)*AA PA* IIb. Pol. 2, PBU-D, Bd.II, Memo of 4 April 1925.

37.)*Ibid.,* Verbal Note of 28 August 1922. Bleyer had also solicited Germany to purchase more Hungarian wine, as this would help Swabian producers. It is not clear whether Bleyer acted for Hungary or as a concerned Swabian, *ibid.,* IIb, Pol. 25 Ungarn, Deutschtum im Ausland, F.M. to Ministry of Food and Agriculture, letter of 27 October 1922. Also see *ibid.,* IIb, Pol. 2, Ungarn, Bd.II, F.M. Internal Memo, 18 September 1922, and Verbal Note of 13 October 1922.

38.)*Ibid.,* 22 October 1922.

39.)*Pesti Hirlap,* 14 January 1923.

40.)13 May 1923.

41.)*AA PA* IIb, Pol, 1, Ungarn, Bd.I, Memo of 12 May 1923. Löbe reiterated his statement to a German reporter, *ibid.,* Pol. 2, Ungarn, Bd.II, 11 December 1922.

42.)*Ibid.,* 20 January 1923; and *ibid.,* BR-U, Bd.I, von Mutius to F.M., Report of 5 March 1923. Also see Nicholas Horthy, *Ein Leben für Ungarn* (Bonn, 1953), pp. 164-165.

43.)*AA PA* Geheimakten, Pol. 2, PBU-D Welczek to F.M., letter of 6 March 1925. Also see H. Beyer, "Die ungarländische Deutschtumsfrage im

Spiegel der diplomatischen Gespräche zwischen Budapest und Berlin," Th.Mayer, ed., *Gedenkschrift für Harold Steinacker (1875-1965)* (Munich, 1966), pp. 310-311.

44.)"Szózat, Aussenpolitik, und ungarländisches Deutschtum," *Sbl.*, 12 July; Karl Czerny, "Deutsch-ungarische Beziehungen," *Pester Lloyd*, 10 July 1925. Also see *AA PA* IIb, Ungarn, Bd.II, Welczek to F.M., letter of 12 July 1925.

45.)*Pesti Hirlap*, 4 September 1925.

46.)*AA PA* (See fn. 44), Welczek to F.M., letter of 4 September 1925.

47.)J. Bleyer, "Deutschland und Ungarn. Eine frohe Botschaft," *Sbl.*, 25 Oct. 1925.

48.)"Politische Wochenschau," *ibid.*, 25 October 1925.

49.)*AA PA* (See fn. 44), Welczek to F.M., letter of 2 November 1925.

50.)*Ibid.*, Horthy to Hindenburg, letter of 22 October, and Hindenburg to Horthy, letter of 10 November 1925. "Der ungarische Kultusminister Graf Klebelsberg in Berlin," *Sbl.*, 1 November 1925.

Chapter VI
HUNGARIAN TRADE AND FOREIGN POLICY

1.)S. Bethlen, *The Treaty of Trianon and European Peace* (London, 1934), pp. 148-149.

2.)The League initiated Hungary's reconstruction on 20 December 1923, and brought it to a successful conclusion in June 1926.

3.)I. Ferenczi, "Der neue autonome Zolltarif," *UWJ*, I (1925), 90-98; *DZA* 41292 and 41278-9; *Köztelek*, 16 October 1927. See Stresemann's statements in *Pester Lloyd*, 17 April 1927, and *Magdeburger Zeitung*, 20 April 1927, promising an agreement with Hungary at some indeterminate future date.

4.)See Stresemann's notes on his Bethlen conversation in Geneva, *DZA* 41279. On Bethlen's Venice sojourn, see *AA PA* BR-U, Bd.I, Neurath to F.M., telegram of 22 December 1927. Hungarian Verbal Note of 9 January 1928, and Schön's report of 17 April 1929, *ibid.*, Pol. 2, PBU-D, Bd.III. On March 1928 cabinet meeting, see *ibid.*, BR-U, Köpke to German Legation, Budapest, telegram of 17 March 1928. See J. Wheeler-Bennett, *Documents on International Affairs. 1928* (London, 1929), pp. 88-94, citing Stresemann's speech in Reichstag, 30 January 1928. One year earlier Schön advised Bethlen that Yugoslavia and Rumania predominated in Germany's economic plans. *AA PA* II, Pol. 2, PBU-D, Bd.III, Schön's report, 17 May 1927.

5.)László Pintér, parliamentary speech, 1 May 1928, cited in L. Pintér, *A politika műhelyéből*, pamphlet II, n.p., n.d., pp. 24-33.

6.)I.E. Nagy, "Rückblick auf die Entwicklung der landwirtschaftlichen Produktion Ungarns," *UWJ*, VI (1930), 46-47; *Honi Ipar,* 15 November 1928.

7.)*AA PA* II, Pol. 2, PBU-D, Bd.III, F.M. Memo of 31 December 1929; *ibid.,* BR-U, Bd.II, F.M. Memo of 15 April 1930; and *OL Küm.* Gazd.Pol. osztály, Német Dosszié 646, 1930.

8.)*AA PA* II, Pol. 2, PBU-D, Bd.III, Schön's Memo of 6 August 1927; letters of 13 and 14 December 1928; memo of 3 April 1929. Also see *Berliner Tageblatt,* 31 March 1929.

9.)*AA PA* BR-U, Bd.I, Schubert's Memo of conversation with Hungarian Minister, 18 April 1929; *ibid.,* with Klebelsberg, 24 April 1929; *ibid.,* Feiffer's Memo of Klebelsberg's conversation with Stresemann, 24 April 1929. According to Schön, the recently adopted slogan of "democratization" in Hungary was a sham designed to attract the favourable attention of the Western Powers. Hungary had neither introduced the secret ballot in rural areas nor amnestied exiled Social Democrats. *Ibid.,* Bd.II, Schön's annual report for 1929, 20 January 1930. *Ibid.,* Schön's Memo on Hungary, 15 Feburary 1930. *Ibid.,* II, Pol. 2, PBU-D, Bd.III. Curtius' Memo on his conversation with Bethlen at Second Hague Conference, 12 January 1930.

10.)*Ibid.,* BR-U, Bd.II, Memo of 16 April 1930. The invitation was formally tendered 11 September 1930 by Curtius. *Ibid.,* Note of 11 September 1930. In between, Klebelsberg turned up in Berlin once more, repeating Bud's earlier pleas. Curtius' response was again evasive. *OL* Küm. Pol. osztály 1504, 6 May 1930, Bessenyei to Walkó, letter of 30 April 1930.

11.)*AA PA* BR-U, Bd.II, Memo of 15, 20 and 25 November 1930; *OL Küm.* Pol. osztály 3893, 24 November 1930.

12.)*AA PA* BR-U, Bd.II, recorded by F.M., 24 December 1930.

13.)*OL Küm.* 17/MK.-res.1928, F.M. Report of 21 January 1928.

14.)*AA PA* BR-U, Bd.III, *passim;* "Handelsvertrag mit Ungarn perfekt," *Berliner Tageblatt,* 23 July 1931; István Görgey's speech, *Napló,* (1932), 68th session, 18 April 1932, p. 437; *Az Est,* 14 May 1932, reporting on trade agreement deception, reported and translated for the F.M. by the German Legation, Budapest. *AA PA* II, Pol. 2, PBU-D, Bd.IV; and Béla Darányi, "Die Verwärtung der neuen Ernte," *Ungarischer Volkswirt (UV),* I (1932), 11-14.

15.)*AA PA* BR-U, Bd.III, *passim;* "Praeferenz über die Hintertreppe," *Deutsche Getreidezeitung,* 11 June 1931. The article, and others like it, offended the Hungarian government, *AA PA* BR-U, Bd.III, F.M. Memo of August 1931.

16.)*Ibid.,* II, Pol. 1, Allgemeine ausw. Politik Ungarn, Bd.II, German Embassy, Paris, to F.M., report of 21 August 1931, and German Legation, Budapest, to F.M., telegram of 20 August 1931; *OL ME Küm.* Pol. oszt, 3667,

25 Aug. 1931, Bessenyei to Gyula Károlyi, note of 22 August 1931.

17.)*AA PA* BR-U, Bd.III, F.M. Memo of August 1931.

18.)*OL Küm.* 5028/1931, Hungarian Legation, Berlin, to Hung F.M., Confidential Report of 21 November 1931; Tibor Kállay, "Ungarns grosses Schicksalsproblem—französische Orientierung?" *UV,* I (June 1932), 3-5. Kállay was Hungarian Minister of Finance.

19.)*AA PA* II, Pol. 2, PBU-D, Bd.IV, Schön to F.M., letter and reports of February 1932.

20.)*Ibid.,* BR-U, Bd.II, F.M. Memo on Hungary, 15 February 1930; Bethlen's statement, 25 November 1930.

21.)*Ibid.,* II, Pol. 2, PBU-D, Bd.III, F.M. position papers of 31 December 1929 and 5 January 1930. Also see *ibid.,* Pol. 2, Geheimakten, PBU-D, Schubert's report, 25 March 1926; and G. Gratz, "Verfassung und Politik," *UWJ,* III (1927), 11-18; also see Stresemann's interview with *Pester Lloyd,* 17 April 1927 ("Reichsminister Dr. Stresemann über die deutschungarischen Beziehungen"), in which he scarcely went beyond polite expressions of sympathy and friendly collaboration; and "Unsere Freundschaft zu Ungarn," *Magdeburger Zeitung,* 20 April 1927, in the same vein. On further developments in German-Hungarian relations, see *AA PA* BR-U, Bd.I, Neurath to F.M., telegram of 25 Jan. 1927; F.M. to Hungarian Legation, telegram of 29 Jan. 1927; *ibid.,* II, Pol. 2, PBU-D, Bd.III, Schön to F.M., report of 17 May and 6 August; Köpke to Schön, note of 1 June; Benzler to F.M., memo of 23 Aug. 1927.

22.)*Ibid.,* BR-U, Bd.I, Stresemann to German Legation, Budapest, telegram of 3 November 1927; Neurath to F.M., telegram of 22 December 1927.

23.)*OL Küm.* Pol. oszt. 197, 18 January 1928, Kánya to F.M., letter of 13 Jan. 1928; *Küm.* 17 MK.-res. 1928, on Schubert-Walkó interchange. See numerous issues of *Sonntagsblatt* on German-Hungarian relations.

24.)*AA PA* II, Pol. 2, PBU-D, Bd.III, Schön to F.M., reports of 29 Feb., 3 and 17, March and 18 April 1928; also see editorial in *Pester Lloyd,* 11 March 1928; "Minister Walkó über auswärtigen Fragen," *Wolff's Telegraphisches Büro,* 19 April 1928; Pintér, *A politika műhelyéből,* parliamentary speech of 18 April 1928, pp. 13-21; *AA PA* BR-U, Bd.I, Memo of 3 May 1928; *ibid.,* II, Pol. 1, Allg.ausw. Pol.Ung., Bd.I, Spring 1928, F.M. Memo; *OL Küm.* Pol. oszt. 1933, 9 May 1928, Kánya to Walkó, letter of 4 May 1928; *ibid.,* 3078, 1 Aug. 1928, Bessenye to Walkó, letter of 27 July 1928.

25.)Mussolini's speech to the Senate, 5 June 1928, in Wheeler-Bennett, *Documents,* pp. 124-149.

26.)*OL Küm.* Pol.oszt. 422, 7 Feb. 1930, Kánya to Walkó, letter of 3 Feb. 1930.

27.)The St. Gotthard affair involved arms smuggling from Italy to

Hungary through Austria. On 1 January 1928, Austrian customs discovered consignment and attempted to seize it. Hungarian officials resisted, the case was brought before the League of Nations, and caused a scandal. Although the League, in its decision of 5 June, minimized the incident, Hungarian prestige suffered a blow. See Gyula Juhász, *Magyarország külpolitikája 1919-1945* (Budapest, 1968), pp. 117-118.

28.)"Graf Bethlen über die ungarisch-deutschen Beziehungen," *Wolff's Telegraphisches Büro,* 15 December 1928.

29.)*AA PA* II, Pol. 2, PBU-D, Bd.III, Schön to F.M., letter and report of 3 April 1929; Zechlin to Editors Theodor Wolff (*Berliner Tageblatt), Georg Bernhard (Vossische Zeitung),* and Dr. Stampfer; identical letters, 4 August 1929; F.M. Memo of 5 January 1930; Curtius' Note of 12 January; *ibid.,* BR-U, Bd.I, Köster (Belgrade) to F.M., telegram of 18 July 1929; *ibid.,* Bd.II, F.M. Annual Report of 20 January 1930. Also see "Die Politik Ungarns," *Neue Preussische Kreuz-Zeitung,* 30 August 1929; Albert Apponyi, "Unsere auswärtige Lage," *Pester Lloyd,* 25 June 1929.

30.)*AA PA* II, Pol. 2, PBU-D, Bd. III, Bülow to German Legations in Budapest, Prague, Belgrade, Bucharest, and Warsaw, simultaneous reports of 13 June 1929; F.M. Memo on Hungary, 5 January 1930; Schön's report of 17 April 1930.

31.)"Graf Bethlen über die auswärtige Politik Ungarns,"*Wolff's Telegraphisches Büro,* 16 January 1929.

32.)*AA PA* II, Pol. 2, PBU-D, Bd.III, Schön to F.M., reports of 3 and 17 April and 29 May 1929; *ibid.,* BR-U, Bd.II, Schön's annual political report, 20 January 1930; *OL Küm.* 324/1930, Baranyai (Geneva) to Walkó, letter of 24 January 1930; *ibid.,* Pol. oszt. 422, 7 February 1930, Kánya to Walkó, letter of February 1930.

33.)Apponyi, "Unsere auswärtige Lage."

34.)*AA PA* II, Pol.2, PBU-D, Bd.III, F.M. Memo on Hungary, 5 January 1930.

35.)*Ibid.,* BR-U, Bd.I, Schubert's report, 22 February 1929.

36.)*Ibid.,* IIb, Pol.25 Ungarn, Bd.I, Schön to F.M., political report, 19 June 1929.

37.)"Fragen der deutschen Aussenpolitik. Dr. Stresemann über das Auslands-Deutschtum," *Deutsches Volksblatt* (Stuttgart), 27 May 1927.

38.)See, for example, "Stresemann an die Auslanddeutschen," *Süddeutsche Zeitung* (Stuttgart), 27 May 1927; "Auslanddeutsche und Wirtschaft," *Schwäbischer Merkur* (Stuttgart), 25 May 1927.

39.)*BAK* R 57 DAI 79. Dr. E. Maurer (representing the *Verein für das Deutschtum im Ausland,* Landesverband Baden) to *Deutsches Ausland-Institut,* letter of 12 Oct. 1924.

40.)*AA PA* BR Auslanddeutsche, Bd.I, Bruns to Reinebeck (Ministry of the Interior), letter of 23 April; Rödiger to Curtius, note of 26 April; F.M. to Curtius, memo of 1 May; and F.M. memo of 11 November 1930.

41.)"Dr. Curtius über das Minderheitenproblem," *Schwäbischer Merkur,* 31 May 1930.

42.)*OL Küm.* res. pol. 1930-23-933, "A Duna völgyében érvényesült német politikáról" (On Projected German Policies in the Danube Valley). This document was unavailable. Excerpts may be found in D. Nemes, *A Bethlen-kormány külpolitikája* (Budapest, 1964), pp. 358-360.

43.)*AA PA* BR-U, Bd.II, Schön's memo on Hungary, 15 February; F.M. memo on Hungarian foreign affairs, 15 November; F.M. memo of Bethlen discussions, 25 November 1930.

44.)*OL Küm.* 4316.1930, 26 November 1930, Walkó to various Hungarian embassies, simultaneous telegrams of 26 November 1930.

45.)*Ibid.,* Pol.oszt.4403, 3 December 1930, Kánya to Walkó, confidential letter of 29 November 1930.

Chapter VII
MAGYARS AND SWABIANS

1.)Magyarones were generally more intolerant than the Magyars. See "Ungarn," *DA,* IX (1926), 218. Also see *KN,* p. 18.

2.)"Die zweite Generalversammlung des U.D.V." *Sbl.,* 29 August 1926.

3.)*AA PA* IIb, Pol. 16, Religion und Kirche in Ungarn, Bd.I, Levetzow (German Legation, Budapest) to F.M., report on *UDV* meeting, 28 August 1926. Also see Gratz, *Deutschungarische Probleme, (DP)* (Budapest, 1938), pp. 88-95.

4.)"Eine Botschaft des Grafen Bethlen an das ungarländische Deutschtum," *Sbl.,* 31 October 1926.

5.)*OL ME* 1926-T-60; 1927-C-9163 and 9797; *Napló,* IV (1927), pp. 158-159.

6.)"Ungarn," *DA,* X (1927), 292-293; "Die vierte Generalversammlung des U.D.V.," *Sbl.,* 28 August 1927; "Allerlei," *Gotthold,* 15 April 1927, 55, citing conference held 29 March 1927.

7.)Gündisch denounced the agreement as a breach of promise by the government. G. Gündisch, "Das Deutschtum Ungarns," *N&S,* I (1927-1928), 43-44.

8.)*OL ME* 1926-C-9248; 1928-C-1989 (2181); 1937-C-15561; J. Bleyer, "Der Lösung der deutsch-ungarischen Frage entgegen," *Sbl.,* 1 July 1928; *N&S,* I(1927-1928), 943-444.

9.)*OL ME* 1929-C-813.

10.)"Nach der Generalversammlung des U.D.V.,"*Sbl.*, 25 August 1929; "Die siebente Generalversammlung des U.D.V.," *ibid.*, 24 August 1930; Gratz, *DP*, citing Gratz's speech at 1930 *UDV* Assembly, pp. 150ff.

11.)"Ungarn," *DA*, XIV (1931), 126-127, and 192.

12.)"Nach der achten Generalversammlung des U.D.V.," *Sbl.*, 30 August 1931.

13.)"Ungarn," *DA*, XV (1932), 425-426; Gratz, *DP*, p. 174; A. Török, "Unsere Minderheitenpolitik in der Wirtschaftsnot," *Sbl.*, 7 February 1932.

14.)Török, "Unsere Minderheitenpolitik."

15.)*OL ME* Nemzetiségi osztály, 27.csomó, C.15135/1934, 17 June 1932; Gratz, *DP*, pp. 16-17; "Nach der IX. Generalversammlung des U.D.V.," *Sbl.*,28 August 1932.

16.)Gratz, *DP*, Bleyer to Gratz, letter of 6 August 1932, pp.17-18.

17.)*Ibid.*, pp. 21-23.

18.)"Als innere Angelegenheit des 'Deutschen Arbeitsgemeinschaft um das Sonntagsblatt'—Vertraulich." Verhandlungsbericht, 20 and 21 August 1932. *BAK*, D.A.I.—Institut, R57 Neu 1155, No. 17. Ironically, while the *UDV*'s position deteriorated nationwide, its position in Baranya improved. Károlyi named former *főispán* Fischer as his Minister of the Interior. The formerly hostile Fischer became the Swabians' grudging defender. "Ungarn," *DA*, XV (1932), 425-426.

19.)For a typical sentiment, see County Notary Association meeting held at Balatonszántó, in which a speaker assailed Germany for fomenting Pan-Germanism among Swabians. *Magyar külpolitika*, X (1929), 7, reprinted from *Magyarság*, 6 July 1929.

20.)Nicholas Kállay, *Hungarian Premier* (New York, 1954), p. 50.

21.)"Gedanken am Ende des Schuljahres," *Sbl.*, 4 July 1926; "Ungarn," *DA*, IX (1926), 41-42; F.A. Basch, *Das Deutschtum in Ungarn* (Munich, 1926), pp. 20-21.

22.)"Die vierte Generalversammlung des U.D.V.," *Sbl.*, 28 August 1927.

23.)*Napló*, III (1927), debates of 5 May 1927, pp. 264-274; "Ungarn,"*DA*, X(1927), 425-426; "Eine Debatte im Abgeordnetenhause über die deutschungarische Minderheit," *Sbl.*, 15 May 1927, citing debate of 5 May.

24.)"Aus der Reichstagrede Dr. Jakob Bleyers zum Kultus- und Unterrichtsetat," *Sbl.*, 22 May 1927; *Napló*, IV (1927), debate of 13 May, pp. 83-93, and 30 May, pp. 419-422.

25.)Guido Gündisch, "Das Deutschtum Ungarns," *N&S*, I (1927-1928), 43-44.

26.)"Ungarn," *DA*, X (1927), 426.

27.)J. Bleyer, "In Sachen der Schulfrage," *Sbl.*, 26 June 1927; Gündisch, "Das Deutschtum."

28.)"Die vierte Generalversammlung."

29.)"Briefe aus dem Ausland. Zur deutschen Schulfrage in Ungarn," *DA*, X (1927), 773-775.

30.)"Ungarn," *DA*, X (1927), 490.

31.)K. Junkersdorff, "Minderheitpolitische Rundschau," *Tägliche Rundschau*, 25 December 1927.

32.)Study plan decree 61.784/1927 VIII.a. may be found in *Gotthold*, 15 September 1927, 128. Also see G. Gündisch, "Vom Deutschtum in Ungarn," *N&S*, I (1927-1928), 115-116.

33.)*Ödenburger Zeitung*, 26 December 1928.

34.)"Stürmische Sitzung im Abgeordnetenhaus," *Sbl.*, 26 Feb.; "Die deutschungarische Frage vor dem Parlament," *ibid.*, 1 April 1928; "Ungarn," *DA*, XI (1928), 170.

35.)"Eine grosse Rede des Ministerpräsidenten Grafen Stefan Bethlen über die deutsche Frage in Ungarn," *Sbl.*, 22 April 1928.

36.)A. König, "Zur Debatte über die Minderheitenfrage im Abgeordnetenhause," *Sbl.*, 29 April 1928.

37.)"Ungarn," *DA*, XI (1928), 306-307.

38.)J. Bleyer, "Der Lösung der deutschungarischen Frage entgegen," *Sbl.*, 1 July 1928; G. Gündisch, "Die Lage. Der Lösung der deutschungarischen Frage entgegen," *N&S*, I (1927-1928), 943-944.

39.)"Die Schulfrage der deutschen Minderheiten," *Gotthold*, 31 July 1928, 100.

40.)J. Bleyer, "Es lichtet am Himmel," *Sbl.*, 14 October 1928; E. Scholtz, "Gedanken am Ende des Schuljahres. Unsere kirchlichen Obrigkeit zur Beachtung empfohlen," *Gotthold*, 15 June 1928, 83. The only serious critique of Swabian education at that time was rendered by *Der Auspandsdeutsche;* see "Ungarn," XI (1928), 777-779.

41.)"Ungarn. Bethlen bei den Deutschen Westungarns. Statistisches über die Volksschultypen," *N&S*, II (1928-1929), 125-126; "Ungarn," *DA*, XI (1928), 704.

42.)*Ibid.*, 777.

43.)Emil Nagy, "Gebiets- und Minderheitenfragen," *Sbl.*, 26 Feb.; F. Hunyadi, "Aufgaben der ungarischen Aussenpolitik," *ibid.*, 11 November; "Grossdeutsche und ungarische Zusammenwirken. Vortrag des Universitatsprofessors Dr. Szekfü in Schandau," *ibid.;* "Das ungarländische Deutschtum als ein Bindeglied zwischen Ungarn und Deutschland," *Deutsche Allgemeine Zeitung*, 7 July 1928.

44.)G. Gündisch, "Ein Wort zu unseren handelspolitischen Verhandlungen mit Deutschland," *Sbl.*, 16 December 1928; "Gespräch mit dem Grafen Bethlen," *ibid.*, 23 December 1928, reporting on 15 December Bethlen interview with the *Neue Freie Presse.*

45.)"Konferenz in der Lage der deutschen Minderheit in Ministerpräsidium," *Sbl.,* 27 January 1929; and *N&S,* II (1928-1929), 482.

46.)A. König, "Ein grosser Tag im Abgeordnetenhaus," *Sbl.,* 2 June; "Eine grosse Rede des Abgeordneten Dr. Jakob Bleyer über die Minderheitenfrage," *ibid.,* 2 June; "Die deutsche Minderheit hat stets die treueste Anhängerschaft an den ungarischen Staatsgedanken bekündet," *ibid.,* 19 May; "Pressestimmen zur Rede des Ministerpräsidenten und des Abg. Dr. Jakob Bleyer über die Minderheitenfrage," *ibid.,* 9 June 1929; *Pester Lloyd,* 25 September 1929.

47.)G. Gratz, "Kis-magyar és Nagy-magyar politika," *Magyar külpolitika,* X (1929), 2-4.

48.)See Zoltán Meskó's demands in Parliament for intensified Magyarization. "Die deutsche Minderheit," *Sbl.,* 19 May 1929; A. König, "Nach der Generalversammlung des U.D.V.," *Sbl.,* 25 August 1929; J. Bleyer, "Hände weg!" *ibid.,* 16 June 1929.

49.)Sárisáp, Dorog, and Annavölgy.

50.)*Napló,* IV (1929), debate of 28 May, pp. 226-228; debate of 11 June, pp. 158-159.

51.)Gratz, *DP* pp. 148-149, covering *UDV* convention, 30 August 1931. Also see "Die Frage der Deutschen in Ungarn vor dem Abgeordnetenhause," *Sbl.,* 15 June 1930, reporting Bleyer's and Bethlen's interchange in Parliament, 5 June 1930, in which Bethlen promised to continue his efforts on behalf of minority education. *Napló,* IV (1930), pp. 116-128.

52.)"Unsere deutschen Volksschulen," *Gotthold,* 31 December 1930, 178-179; "Deutschevangelisches aus dem heutigen Ungarn," *DA,* XIII (1930), 753-754. According to the Wilhelmstrasse, forcible Magyarization in the Protestant churches, and overt violations in the Protestant German schools, were relatively rare. *AA PA BR-U,* Bd.II, F.M. Note of 5 May 1931; *N&S,* V (1931-1932), 186; VI (1932-1933), 101; *Kulturwehr,* II (1926), 270; Hans-Joachim Dahlem, "Die Zwei- und Mehrsprächlichkeit in ihrer Bedeutung und ihren Folgen für die deutschen Volkskirchen Ost- und Südosteuropas," *Auslanddeutschtum und evangelische Kirche Jahrbuch* (Munich, 1935), *passim;* Theodor Grentrup, *Die kirchliche Rechtslage der deutschen Minderheiten katholischer Konfession in Europa* (Berlin, 1928), pp. 131-136. For the parliamentary debates cited by Grentrup, see *Napló,* XXI (1927-1928), p. 74.

53.)"Das Schicksal der deutschen Volksschule in Ungarn," *DA,* XV (1932), 566-568.

54.)I. Bethlen, "Magyarország kisebbségi politikája," *Magyar Szemle,* (1933), 96-98; G. Gratz, "Bethlen külpolitikája és kisebbségi politikája," *ibid.,* (1934), 132-135.

55.)See Table IV.

56.)*Évkönyv* (1919-1922), p. 146; (1928), pp. 248 and 264; "Ungarn," *DA*, XII (1929), 171-172.

57.)Debate of 5 May 1927, *Napló*, III (1927), pp. 263-264.

58.)A. Török, "Das Problem des Deutschtums in Ungarn," *Zeitschrift für Politik*, XXIII (1933), 173.

59.)G. Gündisch, "Das Deutschtum Ungarns," *N&S*, I (1927-1928), 44-45.

60.)"Ungarn," *DA*, X (1927), citing Bethlen's speech in Parliament of 5 May 1927. Also see "Eine Debatte im Abgeordnetenhause über die deutsch-ungarische Minderheit," *Sbl.*, 15 May 1927; *Évkönyv* (1927), p. 205; P. Kleinschmidt, *Auslanddeutschtum und Kirche* (Münster, 1930), I, 195.

61.)"Zur Schulbuchfrage," *Gotthold*, 31 January 1928; and "Zur Schul-buchfrage," *Sbl.*, 5 February 1928.

62.)"Das Deutschtum in Ungarn," *N&S*, I (1927-1928), 943-944, written by Gündisch under a pseudonym; and "Die Schulfrage der deutschen Minderheit," *Gotthold*, 31 July 1928, 100; "Ungarische Fibel für die unga-rische Schulen des Burgenpandes," *Sbl.*, 12 August 1928.

63.)"Ungarn," *DA*, XII (1929), 108-109; *N&S*, II (1928-1929), 483; "Ungarn. Der gegenwärtige Stand der deutschen Sache," *ibid.*, 614-615; "Die Schulfrage," *Sbl.*, 10 March 1929.

64.)The decision was to have similar readers in grades 1 through 6. C schools would begin teaching also in German in the second grade. There would be at least four Magyar books out of a total of eleven. The teacher's guide would contain a section devoted to German literary history and a history of German settlement in Hungary. "Ausschuss für deutsche Schul-bücher," *Sbl.*, 5 May 1929.

65.)Vörösmarty, Petőfi, and Kölcsey for the Magyars; Lenau, Hans Sachs, Goethe, and Grimm for the Germans. J. Bleyer, "Zwei neue deutsche Schulbücher," *Sbl.*, 6 October 1929.

66.)"Ungarn," *DA*, XII (1929), 788-789.

67.)One reader for third and fourth grade A and B schools; one reader for second and third grade C schools; an "excellent" book on nature and economic studies for fifth and sixth grade A and B schools.

68.)Ordinance No. 17 of the Ministry of Education, 1 September 1930; "Deutsche Schulbücher," *Sbl.*, 14 September 1930; Peter Jekel, "Deutsche Schulbücher," *Sbl.*, 28 September and 16 November 1930.

69.)"Neue deutsche Schulbücher," *Gotthold*, 15 September 1930, 124; *N&S*, III (1930-1931), 192; and IV (1931-1932), 270.

70.)Reader for A and B fifth and sixth-grade classes; and fourth, fifth, and sixth-grade reader for C schools; and one more text, a History of Hungary, designed for fourth-grade A schools, was in preparation.

71.)P. Jekel, "Lehrbücher für die deutschen Minderheitenschulen mit A-, B-, und C-Typus," *Sbl.*, 23 November 1930.

72.)P. Jekel, "Die Frage der deutschen Schulbücher," *Sbl.*, 6 December 1931.

73.)*Napló*, IX (1933), Speech of 10 May 1933, pp. 210-215.

74.)In a typical year, out of 103 Swabians enrolled in teacher academies only ten graduated. By no means did all of these situate in the Swabian school system. *N&S*, I (1927-1928), 943-944, obtained this information from *Sbl.*, 1 July 1928. The information is essentially accurate.

75.)*Évkönyv, 1919-1922*, p. 152.

76.)On 15 February 1926, responding to the Bishop's Order 526/VI/1925-26.

77.)E. Scholtz, "Der deutsche Lehrkurs an der Lehrerbildungsanstalt in Ödenburg," *Gotthold*, 31 July 1927, 102; "Ungarn," *DA*, XI (1928), 778.

78.)*Napló*, III (1927), debates of 5 May 1927, p. 271; "Eine Debatte im Abgeordnetenhause," *Sbl.*, 15 May 1927.

79.)J. Bleyer, "Bericht über die Lage der deutschen Minderheit in Ungarn," Gratz, *DP*, pp. 248-250. This report was prepared in 1930. Gratz revised the figures in the light of new, more accurate information.

80.)"Ungarn," *N&S*, I (1927-1928), 943.

81.)*Ibid.*, II (1928-1929), 483; and "Konferenz in der Lage der deutschen Minderheit in Ministerpräsidium," *Sbl.*, 27 January 1929.

82.)E. Scholtz, "Die Ausbildung der Lehrer zu unseren Volksschulen mit deutscher Unterrichtssprache," *Gotthold*, 15 January 1929, 4-5, and *Gotthold*, 31 August 1929, 114-115, mostly reiterating the points of the article written 15 January; E. Scholtz, "Vom deutschen Lehrkurs am evangelischen Lehrer-seminar in Sopron-Ödenburg," *Gotthold*, 31 December 1930, 178-179, citing Point 40 of Kapi's report *Volksschulangelegenheiten;* Also see "Ungarn," *DA*, XII (1929), 108-109.

83.)*Évkönyv*, (1931), p. 9; "Ungarn," *DA*, XIV (1931), 553-554; "Der Lehrerfortbildungskurs in Baja," *Sbl.*, 4 September 1932.

84.)E. Scholtz, "Landeskirche und Minderheitenfrage," *Gotthold*, 30 June 1931, 90-91; Johann Neubauer, "Die günstige Auswirkung der Fortbildungs-kurse für Lehrer, die an deutschen Minderheitenschulen wirken," *Sbl.*, 18 September 1932; and "Ungarn," *N&S*, VI (1932-1933), 100-101, both citing a contemporary issue of *Gotthold*.

85.)*Napló*, IX (1933), speech of 10 May 1933, pp. 210-215; I. Bethlen, "Magyarország kisebbségi politikája," *Magyar Szemle* (1933), 89-104.

86.)*N&S X* (1936-1937), 167; *Évkönyv* (923-1925), ffc. 230 and 232; and *ibid.*, (1929), fc., 239.

87.)Bleyer ran in Villany, Gündisch in Bonyhád, and Faul-Farkas in

Soroksár.

88.)Neuberger in Magyaróvár; Klein in Tolna; Schwindt in Törökbálint; Perlaki in Pécsvárad; Weichert in Pilisvörösvár; Marschall in Jánoshalma; Pintér in Surány; Wachtler in Nezsider. Some of these candidates were branded Magyarones by Swabian public opinion.

89.)In Baranya County Swabians represented 34.7% of the population.

90.)"Ugran," *DA*, X (1927), 21-23; "Der Siegeszug Dr. Jakob Bleyers in dem Villányer Bezirk," *Sbl.*, 28 November 1926.

91.)*OL ME* 1926-T-241; "Umschwung in Ungarns Minderheitenpolitik?" *Kölnische Volkszeitung*, 6 November 1926; and "Die ungarischen Parteien und das Deutschtum," *Tägliche Rundschau*, 17 September 1926.

92.)"Brief aus Rumänien," *Sbl.*, 10 May 1931.

93.)The *Bleyer Nachlass (BN)* contains information on Bleyer's activities in this regard. See, for example, his draft, "Deutschungarische Volkspartei," and letters of 13 June 1927 and 29 May 1931 to Karl von Loesch.

94.)Jekel, Hufnägel, Kussbach, König, and Faul-Farkas, besides himself.

95.)Bleyer to von Loesch, letter, n.d., cited in *BN*; J. Bleyer, "Nach den Wahlen," *Sbl.*, 12 July 1931; and "Ungarn," *DA*, XIV (1931), 496.

96.)"Sieg Dr. Bleyers im Villányer Bezirk," "Nach den Wahlen," *Sbl.*, 5 July 1931; "Die achte Jahreshauptversammlung der U.D.V.," *Sbl.*, 30 Aug. 1931.

97.)"Honvédminister Gömbös wünscht, dass die Offiziere einen magyarischen Namen annehmen," *Sbl.*, 10 August 1930.

98.)"Ungarn," *DA*, XV (1932), 203; "Von der Namenmagyarisierung," *Sbl.*, 24 May 1931.

99.)Cf. J. Bleyer, "Ein ungarischer Mello-Franco," *Sbl.*, 15 January 1933; Bethlen, "Magyar kisebbségi politika," 101-102. Also see A. Rónai, "A nemzetek számszerű csökkenése csonka-magyarországon," *Magyar Szemle* (1938), 74-78, in a similar vein.

Chapter VIII
GOMBOS' TRIUMPHS

1.)*OL Küm.* pol. 132.1933. Hóry to Gömbös, letter of 14 January 1933; *Documents on German Foreign Policy, Series C (DGFP-C)* (London, 1957), I, Report of 1 December 1932, 35; *AA PA* II, Pol. 2, PBU-D, Bd.IV. A number of the succeeding documents were consulted in the original (*AA PA*), others in the English translation (*DGFP-C*).

2.)*AA PA* II, Pol.2, PBU-D, Bd.IV, Schön to F.M., Report of 26 Nov. and 10 Dec. 1932; and Neurath to Hassell, 27 Feb. 1933; *DGFP-C*, I, 233-235.

3.)*Ibid.*, Gömbös to Hitler, Memo of 6 Feb. 1933, delivered verbally by Kánya on 7 Feb. 1933, 34-35; and *AA PA* II, Pol. 2, PBU-D, Bd.IV, Memo of

6 February 1933. Also see Gömbös' report of his meeting with Hitler. Cabinet meeting of 18 March 1933, attended by Horthy. M. Szinai and L. Szűcs, *The Confidential Papers of Admiral Horthy* (Budapest, 1965), 61–63; OL *Küm.* pol. 1933-21/7-400; and 361/pol.-1933, Wettstein to F.M., letter of 8 Feb. 1933, on Kánya-von Papen conversation of 4 February.

4.)*DGFP-C*, I, 168ff.; Ol *Küm.*res.pol.1933-20-178, Gömbös' letter of 28 Feb.; *ibid.*, 1933-20, Hungarian F.M. Memo on Bethlen's trip; *AA PA* BR-U, Bd.III, Memo of 6 March 1933.

5.)*DGFP-C*, I, Gömbös to Hitler, letter of 22 April 1933, 327–328; *AA PA* IIb, Pol. 2, PBU-D, Bd.IV, Hitler to Gömbös, letter of 28 April 1933.

6.)Bethlen suggested this possibility the following year. G. Gratz, "Bethlen külpolitikája. . ." 126.

7.)Visit of 17-21 June 1933. For a draft of the agenda by the Hungarian F.M., see OL *Küm.*res.pol.1933-21-303(284) of 16 June 1933; *AA PA* BR-U, BD.III, F.M. Memo of 19 June 1933, on Heeren's talk with Masirevich.

8.)"Was wir dazu sagen," *Der Angriff*, 19 June 1933.

9.)OL *Küm.*2510 pol./1933; *DGFP-C*, I, Hassell to F.M., Report of 30 June 1933, 615–616; *Documents of British Foreign Policy, Second Series* (London, 1946), V, British Ambassador's report from Vienna, 29 June 1933, Doc. 397.

10.)*AA PA* II, Pol.3, Beziehungen Ungarn-Österreich, Bd.II, F.M. Memo, drawn by Köpke, 14 July 1933; German Ambassador, Vienna, to F.M., Report of 15 July 1933.

11.)*DGFP-C*, I, Hassell's report of his conversation with Gömbös and Kánya in Rome, 28 July 1933, 691–693. Also see Hassell)s subsequent report on his talk with the Italian Foreign Office concerning the Gömbös visit. The Italians stressed the importance of the Four Power Pact and its repercussions on Italian-Hungarian relations, *ibid.*, Report of 30 July 1933, 702–704; and Köster (Paris) to F.M., Report of 18 Sept. 1933, referring to Kánya's conversations with French Foreign Minister Paul-Boncour and Prime Minister Daladier, *ibid.*, 808.

12.)*AA PA* BR-U, Bd.III, Bülow's Memo of 20 September 1933; also cited in *DGFP-C*, I, 825–826; Rödiger to German Legation (Budapest), 11 Aug. 1933, *ibid.*, 737.

13.)*Ibid.*, II, Köpke to F.M., Memo of 1 Dec. 1933, 164–166, and footnote 5, 166.

14.)*DGFP-C*, II, Bülow's Memo of 11 Jan. 1934, 335–337. The Wilhelmstrasse appeared determined not to conclude agreements with the Magyars, at least until receipt of the Gömbös letter. See *AA PA* IIb, Pol. 25 Ung. Deutschtum in Ungarn, Bd.I, Rödiger to Neurath, Memo of 8 Jan. 1934. While Hungary was notified officially a few days later that trade talks would commence the following week (*ibid.*, II, Pol.2, PBU-D, Bd.IV,

Neurath to Kánya, Letter of 13 Jan. 1934), on 24 January Masirevich was informed that "there could be no question" of a political alliance. See *ibid.*, Geheimakten, Pol.2, Ungarn, PBU-D, no volume. The Foreign Ministry thought it would be embarrassing for Germany to refuse Hungary's demands outright. See Renthe-Fink to Mackensen, at the request of Köpke, letter of 13 Jan. 1934. This letter also shows the Foreign Ministry's mystification about Hungary's motives in pursuing the idea of a consultative pact. Mackensen was told to investigate and report. In Mackensen's view, Gömbös had nothing to do with the idea, it was "hatched" by Masirevich. *Ibid.*, Renthe-Fink's Memo to F.M., 23 Jan. 1934.

15.)*Ibid.*, and *DGFP-C*, II, Neurath's Memo of 18 Jan. 1934, 379-380. Also see Bülow's Memo of 24 Jan. 1934 in a similar vein. *Ibid.*, 417-419.

16.)*Ibid.*, Mackensen's report of 14 Dec. 1933, 229 and 233. Masirevich reiterated to Neurath that on the question of the Swabian minority a letter from Gömbös to Hitler was imminent. *Ibid.*, 18 Jan. 1934, 379-380.

17.)*Ibid.*, Gömbös to Hitler, Letter of 14 Feb. 1934, 478-481. Presumably on Hitler's orders, State Secretary Lammers wrote on 11 May 1934 that "the letter was not to be answered for the time being. Submit again on June 1." On June 17 a decision was made that "a reply to the letter will now no longer be considered." *Ibid.*, 693-694.

18.)*Ibid.*, I, Neurath to Hugenberg, Letter of 17 May 1933, 455-456.

19.)*OL Küm.*gaz.pol.oszt. Német dosszié 640.I/3. Winchkler's Memo of 11 Oct. 1933.

19.)*DGFP-C*, II, Neurath to Kánya, Letter of 13 Jan. 1934, 353-354; and *AA PA* II, Pol. 2, PBU-D, Bd.IV.

21.)*Ibid.*

22.)*DGFP-C*, II, Reich Chancellery minute of 17 Jan. 1934, 371-373. For details of the agreement, see 604-607. In 1929, Hungary obtained from Germany merchandise valued at 212,500,000 Pengő, or 20% of her total import. In the same year, Hungary exported to Germany produce worth only 121,197,000 Pengő, or 11.7% of her total export. *Évkönyv* (1930), p. 129. By 1936, Germany was Hungary's most important trading partner, absorbing 23.1% of Hungary export. *Magyar Statisztikai Szemle*, XV (1937), *passim*. The low point had been 11.2% in 1933.

23.)*DGFP-C*, II, Bülow's confidential enclosure on the pact, 13 Mar. 1934, 605-607; Mackensen's Report of 28 Feb. 1934, 544-547; and *AA PA* Geheimakten, Pol.2, Ung. PBU-D.

24.)*DGFP-C*, II, Köpke's Memo, 9 March 1934, 580-582; and Bülow's Memo, 10 March 1934, 583-584. Neurath added the following marginal note: "Entirely in agreement. v.N., Mar. 10."

25.)*AA PA* Geheimakten, Pol.2, PBU-D. Bülow referred to Masirevich somewhat contemptuously as "der Ungar." Also see Bülow to German Legation, Budapest, letter of 15 March 1934, *ibid.,* and DGFP-C, II, 613-614.

26.)*OL Küm.* res.pol. 1933-23-310, letter of 1 July 1933. Also see Mussolini to Dollfuss, letter of 1 July 1933. J. Braunthal, *The Tragedy of Austria* (London, 1948), pp. 184-187. DGFP-C, I, F.M. Memo of 14 July 1933, 653-654; *ibid.,* Hassell's report of conversation with Gömbös and Kánya in Rome, 27 July 1933, 691-693. Hassell's report of 30 July contained the Italian version of the conference. It was substantively identical with Gömbös' and Kánya's reports. *Ibid.,* 702-704.

27.)*OL Küm.* 629/pol.-1934, Masirevich to F.M. letter of 21 February 1934.

28.)Gömbös' notes on his meeting with Mussolini and Suvich in Rome, 13 Mar. 1934, *OL Küm.*res.pol. 1934-23-103, cited in L. Kerekes, ed., *Allianz Hitler-Horthy-Mussolini. Dokumente zur ungarischen Aussenpolitik (1933-1944) (Allianz).* (Budapest, 1966), pp. 115-117.

29.)DGFP-C, II, Bülow to German Legation in Vienna, Note of 19 March 1934, 636-637. F.M. to Vienna, Note of 15 March 1934, 614-615. Also see Bülow to Lammers, Note of 20 March 1934, in the same spirit. *Ibid.,* 648-649. This contradicts Mackensen's Memo of 18 March 1934. According to Mackensen, Kánya was "visibly glad" after receiving a telegram from Masirevich, who had just been advised by the Wilhelmstrasse that "Hungary's diplomacy enjoyed (Germany's) full confidence." *AA PA* Geheimakten, Pol.2, PBU-D.

30.)*DGFP-C,* II, Mackensen to F.M., Memo of 20 Mar. 1934, 645-647; Neurath's Memo of 21 Mar., 649-650; Mackensen to F.M., Report of 21 Mar., 651-653; Mackensen to Neurath, Letter and Memo from Kánya, 10 May, 809-813; and Neurath to Mackensen, Letter of 18 May 1934, 825-826.

31.)*AA PA* II, Pol.3, Österreich-Ungarn, Bd.III, Gömbös' speech of 7 May 1934.

32.)*Ibid.,* II, Pol.2, PBU-D, Bd.IV, Mackensen to F.M., Report of 14 May 1934, and Bülow'report, 25 May 1934.

33.)*OL* Küm.pol.oszt.1834.VI.6.1823; László Vélics to Kánya, Secret Dispatch of 4 June 1934.

34.)*Ibid.,* VI.18.1984; Masirevich to Kánya, Secret Report of 11 June 1934. Also see *AA PA* II, Pol.2, PBU-D, Bd.IV, German F.M. to Budapest Legation, Report of 11 June 1934, and F.M. Memo of 21 June 1934.

35.)*Ibid.,* Bd.V, Mackensen to F.M., Report of 26 June 1934.

36.)*OL Küm.* Kabinet res.1934.14, Mackensen to Kánya, Note of 29 May 1934. Also see Colonna's report to Gömbös, *ibid.,* res.pol.1934.23.320.

37.)*AA PA* II, Pol.2, PBU-D, Bd.V, Hassell to F.M., Telegram of 31 July 1934.

38.)*DGFP-C*, III, Lammers to Neurath, Note of 7 August 1934,295. Memorandum of conversation between Kánya and Hitler, 6 Aug.1934, *ibid.*, 295-299.

39.)Kurt Schuschnigg, *Ein Requiem in Rot-Weiss-Rot* (Zurich, 1946), pp. 211-214 and 233-238.

40.)*AA PA* II, Pol.2, PBU-D, Bd.V, F.M. Memo, drawn by Köpke, 14 Sept. 1934, with Annex.

41.)*Ibid.*, Mackensen to F.M., Report of 5 October 1934.

42.)*Ibid.*, Mackensen to F.M., Report of 16 Oct. 1934. For Gömbös' conversation with von Papen, see document listed as II Oe 2807, 9 Oct. 1934. *OL Küm.* 3302/Pol.-1934; Daily report of 8 Oct. 1934. Also see A. Hóry, *A kulisszák mögött* (Vienna, 1965), 20ff. On France's policy, see M. Ormos, *Franciaország és a keleti biztonság 1931-1936* (Budapest, 1969), pp. 346ff.

43.)Göring attended King Alexander's funeral. While in Yugoslavia, he expressed the hope that Yugoslavia would grow in power, and stated that the German minority was better treated in Yugoslavia than in Hungary. *DGFP-C*, III, 583, Schnurre to Köpke, letter of 6 Nov. 1934. Also see Hassell to F.M., Telegram of 8 Nov., on his talks with Gömbös in Rome, *ibid.*, 596-598. On 17 November, Masirevich complained to Neurath, and was rebuffed. *AA PA* BR-U, Bd.III, 17 November. One week later, Masirevich informed Bülow that Hungary had not meant to take Germany to task, nor to accuse it of "defection into the camp of the Little Entente." When informed of this meeting, Neurath was annoyed, and resolved not to receive Masirevich again, for the time being. *DGFP-C*, III, 23 Nov.1934, 665.

44.)*AA PA* II, Pol.2, PBU-D, Bd.V, Hassell to F.M., Telegram of 22 Oct.1934. Plainly, the Magyars greatly resented friendly Yugoslav-German relations, although Neurath assured Masirevich that Hungary and Italy had nothing to fear. Neurath's Memo, 25 Oct.1934, in *DGFP-C*, III, 530-531, reiterated the next day, *ibid.*, 534-535.

45.)*BAK*, Aussenpolitisches Amt der NSDAP, NS 43/Band 44, Fol.1. Abteilung Sud-Öst (1-c), 27 October 1934.

46.)*OL Küm.* 6391 Pol.-1934, László Vélics to Hung.F.M., Report of 1 Nov. 1934; Mackensen to Stieve, Letter of 30 Nov. 1934, cited in L. Kerekes, *Anschluss 1938* (Budapest, 1968), p.90. Also see *Donau-Zeitung* (Passau), #256, 7 Nov. 1933.

47.)*DGFP-C*, III, Bülow's Memo of 4 Jan. 1935, 772-773; and 774-775. No doubt Bülow referred to von Papen's statement to Bethlen at the end of November 1934. The National Socialists desired gradual amnesty for the culprits of 25 July, Nazi participation in the *Vaterländische Front,* and eventual representation in government. In return, Germany would renounce intervening in Austria and would recognize Austrian independence. Kerekes,

Anschluss, pp. 158-159.

48.)*DGFP*-C, III, Bülow's Memo of 5 Jan. 1935, 775-776.

49.)*OL Küm.*res.pol.1935-23-1; Schuschnigg, *Ein Requiem,* pp. 264-290.

50.)*OL Küm.* pol.oszt.1935-I/24-290.

51.)*Ibid., Küm.*res.pol.1935-23-295; 1935-21-51; and *ibid.,* The Horthy Papers, II.C.5. Letter of 13 May 1935, cited in Szinai and Szűcs, "Horthy's Secret Correspondence with Hitler," *New Hungarian Quarterly,* IV (1963), 180-181; and Szinai and Szűcs, *The Confidential Papers of Admiral Horthy* (Budapest, 1965), pp. 81-82.

52.)*OL Küm.*res.pol.1935-21-354; or 1935-21-352, cited by Szinai and Szűcs, *supra.*

53.)*DGFP*-C, IV, Renthe-Fink to Hösch, Memo of 19 Feb.1936, 293, note 4; and *ibid.,* Mackensen to Neurath, Letter of 12 June 1935, 291-293.

54.)*AA PA* II, Pol.1, Allgemeine auswärtige Politik Ungarns, Bd.III, Mackensen to F.M., Letter of 29 May 1935.

55.)*DGFP*-C, IV, unsigned memorandum, with covering letter by Renthe-Fink, of 27 Sept.1935, 657-660.

56.)*Ibid.*

57.)*AA PA* BR-U, Bd.III, Schacht to Göring, Renthe-Fink, and State Secretary Posse of the Ministry of Trade, Note of 30 Sept. 1935. Also see *DGFP*-C, IV, Schacht to Lammers, Letter of 28 Sept.1935, 663-664.

58.)*AA PA* BR-U, Bd.III, Neurath's Memo, 29 Sept. 1935. Also see *DGFP*-C, IV, 667-668. The minorities question was discussed the following day (671-672).

59.)*Ibid.* Indeed, the large German-Hungarian armaments transaction depended on the Hungarian-Yugoslav settlement. Such a rapprochement remained a keystone of Germany's plans, at least until the 1936 German-Italian reconciliation; 774-775; Mackensen's Report, 7 Oct. 1935, with Enclosure, *ibid.,* 708-711. *AA PA* BR-U, Bd.III, Mackensen's personal letter to Neurath, no date (probably 11 Oct. 1935). Also see his Report of 10 October 1935, *DGFP*-C, IV, 717-718, and 11 Oct., 719.

60.)See the reaction of the Czechoslovak press, particularly to the Gömbös visit. *OL Küm.*pol.oszt.1935-X/4-3002, Bessenyei (Prague) to Kánya, Letter of 30 Sept. 1935.

61.)*AA PA* BR-U, Bd.III, unsigned F.M. memo of 4 Oct. 1935; Gömbös to Kánya, Memo of 5 October 1935, *Allianz,* p. 117.

62.)Debate of 13 Nov.1935, *Napló,* III, (1935), 33-35.

63.)*AA PA* II, Pol.3, Ungarn-Österreich, Bd.III, Mackensen to F.M., Telegram of 29 Nov. 1935; and *OL Küm.*res.pol.1935-20-749.

64.)*AA PA* II, Pol.3, Ungarn-Öst., Bd.III, von Papen to Hitler, Secret Report from Vienna, 10 Jan.1936. Kánya discussed some of the same points with Colonna in Budapest on 18 January, and requested Mussolini to clarify Italy's intentions in Central Europe. L. Kerekes, "Akten des ungarischen Ministeriums des Äusseren zur Vorgeschichte der Annexion Österreichs," *Acta Historica,* VII (1960), 368.

65.)*Der Hochverratsprozess gegen Dr. Guido Schmidt vor dem Wiener Volksgericht* (Vienna, 1947), pp. 439-440.

66.)Kerekes, "Akten," Villáni to the Hung. F.M., Report of 15 Jan.1936, 366-367.

67.)*OL Küm.*res.pol.1936-23-80; 1936-23/27-581; 1936-20/25-607; *AA PA* II, Pol.3, Ung.-Öst., Bd.III, von Papen to Hitler, Secret Report, 28 Jan. and 8 Feb. 1936. Also see *Hochverratsprozess,* pp. 398-401.

68.)*OL Küm.*res.pol.1936-20-511. Also see Kerekes, *Anschluss,* pp. 182-183, and *DGFP*-C, IV, Renthe-Fink's report of conversation with Sztójay, 8 Feb. 1936, 1116.

69.)*Ibid.,* Instructions of 13 Feb.1936, 1132-1133; also see Busse (Official of Dept.II), Memo of 21 Feb.1936, 1168; *AA PA* II, Pol.3, Ung.-Öst., Bd.III, Mackensen's Report, 17 Feb, 1936.

70.)*DGFP*-C, IV, Bülow's Memo, 21 Feb. 1936, 1166-1168; Neurath's Memo, 28 Feb. 1936, *ibid.,* 1210-1211.

71.)*Ibid.,* V, Circular of the German F.M., 6 Mar.1936, 22-23; *ibid.,* 60, note 3; Mackensen to F.M., Telegram of 9 March 1936, 60-61. Also see notes 9 and 10, *ibid.,* 61. H. Fillunger, an official of the S.A. Sammelstelle, reported that recently the Magyar press had grown more pro-German. Even the "Jewish-liberal *Az Est* had stated editorially that Hitler's occupation of the Rhineland did not endanger the peace". See *AA PA* II, Pol. 2, PBU-D, Bd. VI, report of 11 March 1936.

72.)*Allianz,* Gömbös, Kánya, Schuschnigg, and Berger, meeting of 13 March, pp. 119-123.

73.)Schuschnigg's negotiations with Czechoslovakia were strictly economic. This was corroborated by Hodža. M. Hodža, *Federation in Central Europe* (London, 1942), p. 128.

74.)Gy.Ránki, *et al.,* eds., *A Wilhelmstrasse és Magyarország. Német diplomáciai iratok Magyarországról 1933-1944 (Wilhelmstrasse)* (Budapest, 1968), Schnurre to F.M., Report of 17 March 1936, Doc. 51; and *Allianz,* pp. 129-133.

75.)*Ibid.,* pp.123-127; and *ibid.,* Kánya and Hassell conversation, Daily Report of 24 March 1936, p. 127.

76.)*DGFP*-C, V, Bülow's Memo, 20 March 1936, 222-223; Renthe-Fink's Memo, 31 March 1936, *ibid.,* 346; Bülow's Memo, 3 April 1936, *ibid.,* 383-384, and 25 April 1936, 473-476; *ibid.,* note 6, p. 502; *AA PA* II, Pol.2, PBU-D, Bd.VI, Neurath's Memo, 4 May 1936.

77.)Kerekes, *Anschluss,* pp. 188-189.

78.)*DGFP-C*, V, Wiedemann to Reschny, Letter of 25 April 1936, 476; Neurath's Memo, 13 May 1936, *ibid.*, 537.

79.)Kerekes, *Anschluss*, pp. 200-201; *Hochverratsprozess*, pp. 475, 483, and 511-512; and Schuschnigg, *Requiem*, p. 246. See Wodianer to Ápor, Letter of 28 July 1936, Kerekes, "Akten des ungarischen Ministeriums," Doc.5

80.)*DGFP-C*, V, Neurath's Memo, 30 June 1936, 704-705.

81.)The visit materialized at Horthy's initiative about five weeks earlier, immediately after the conclusion of the Austro-German agreement. In the absence of the ailing Gömbös, the Regent no doubt wished to put the finishing touches to the Rome-Berlin Axis, and lay the groundwork for future joint action in Eastern Europe. See Szinai and Szűcs, *Confidential Papers*, pp. 82-83.

82.)"*GDFP-C*, V, Neurath's Memo, 24 August 1936, 925-926; also see *Wilhelmstrasse*, pp. 138-139; and G. Ciano, *Ciano's Diplomatic Papers* (London, 1948), conversation with Villani, 7 Sept. 1936, pp. 35-38.

83.)*Allianz*, Memo of Kánya-Göring conversation, 11 Oct.1936, pp. 130-131.

84.)*Wilhelmstrasse*, Mackensen to F.M., Report of 13 Oct.1936, Doc. 62. Also see Werkmeister to F.M., Report of 22 Oct.1936, Doc.64; *OL Küm.pol.* 1936-21/27-3560.

Chapter IX
THE GERMAN-MAGYAR-SWABIAN TRIANGLE

1.)Bleyer to Hans Otto Roth, Letter of 17 Mar.1933, *BN*, Schwind, *Bleyer*, p. 147.

2.)"Die Sozialdemokraten in den deutschen Gemeinden auf dem Vormarsch," *Sbl.*, 15 Jan. 1933.

3.)Johann Faul-Farkas, Johann Dengl, Franz Kussbach, Laurenz Landgraf, Franz Basch, Peter Jekel, and Franz Rothen. See "Ungarn," *N&S*, VII (1933-1934), 249-250, on *UDV* struggle after Bleyer's death.

4.)*Wilhelmstrasse*, Report of 8 February 1936, with Annex of 6 Feb, Docs. 18 and 18-1; G. Gratz, "A magyarországi németség ügye," *Magyar Szemle* (1938), 360, and Gömbös to Gratz, Letter of 2 May 1934, 361. The *Kameradschaft's* version differed from Kussbach's. Basch and Faulstich allegedly "pushed Kussbach into a corner" and tried to induce him to form a triumvirate composed of the three of them. At first Kussbach agreed, then reneged, and still later denied ever having heard of the incident. See *KN*, p. 35.

5.)A. König, "Die Krise unserer Nationalitätenpolitik," *Sbl.*, 5 Feb.1933; *DA*, XVI (1933), 124-125; "Für Recht und Wahrheit," *Sbl.*, 8 April 1934; A.

Török, "Hitlerpropaganda und Minderheitenrechte," *ibid.*, 18 Mar. 1934; G.C. Paikert, *The Danube Swabians* (The Hague, 1967), p. 115.

6.)See I. Bethlen, "Magyarország kisebbségi politikája," 89-104; *Öden-burger Zeitung,* 19 April 1933, interview with Tibor Eckhardt; "Wir müssen die kulturellen Rechte der ungarländischen Deutschtums sichern. Eine grosse Rede des Abgeordneten Stefan Milotay über aussenpolitische Fragen," *Sbl.*, 6 May 1934; "Rumänien," *N&S,* VII (1933-1934), 167-168, on the 5 November elections in Transylvania.

7.)Examples have been gathered from the following sources: "1925-1933. Der U.D.V. im Pester Komitat," 6 April 1933; "Gendarmerie und Volksbildungsabend—Legitimierung in Deutschboy," 18 Feb. 1934; "Das Singen und Spielen der Nationalhymne verboten!" 18 March 1934; "Der Musikwettstreit verboten," 18 June 1933; "Nachrichten des U.D.V." 2 Dec. 1934; "Bedauerliche Szenen bei der Versammlung in Nagymányok," 30 Dec. 1934; Aegidius Faulstich, "Betreibt der U.D.V. Politik?" 17 February 1935; "Graf Bethlen über aussenpolitische Fragen. Das Verhältnis des nationalen Ungarn zu seinen Nachbaarstaaten," 8 April 1934; various articles in 11 February, 11 and 18 March 1934 issues, all in *Sbl.; DA,* XVI (1933), 124-125; "Ungarn," *N&S,* VII, 26-28, 128, and 167; VIII, 122-124, 192, and 326-327; *BAK,* Ministerium des Innern, R18-3329 and 3330; Report of 31 May 1935.

8.)"Generalsekretär Dr. Franz Basch zu 3 Monaten Gefangnis verurteilt," *Sbl.,* 7 October 1934.

9.)"Ungarn," *N&S,* VII (1933-1934), 702-703; VIII (1934-1935), 22-27; G. Gratz, "Die Regierung und die deutsche Minderheit," *Sbl.,* 13 May 1934; "Die zehnte Generalversammlung des U.D.V.," *Sbl.,* 13 May 1934; "Die elfte Generalversammlung des U.D.V.," *ibid.,* 26 Aug. 1934.

10.)It took over a year for the final verdict. The court found Méhely innocent on the grounds that Bleyer had indeed encouraged the spread of German culture in Hungary, and thereby drove a wedge between the Swabians and Magyars. To this extent he was unwittingly unpatriotic. "Ungarn," *N&S,* IX (1935-1936), 251-253; also see *ibid.,* VIII (1934-1935), 191-192, and 273-274.

11.)*Ibid.,* 237; Willman, "Unsere bisherige Arbeit und unsere Aufgaben in der Zukunft," *Sbl.,* 27 Jan. 1935; *Wilhelmstrasse,* Schnurre to F.M., Report of 12 Feb. 1935, Doc. 31; *KN,* pp. 44-48.

12.)"Abg.Ladislaus Pintér über das ungarländische Deutschtum. Warum immer über Hexen sprechen, die es nicht gibt?" *Sbl.,* 24 Feb.; "Ministerpräsident Gömbös uber das ungarländische Deutschtum," *ibid.,* 2 June; "Allem Terror zum Trotze stimmen wir auf Dr. Kussbach," and "Die Regierung gegen die Terrorakte im Soroksárer Bezirk," *ibid.,* 24 Mar. 1935; "Ungarn,"

N&S, VIII (1934-1935), 326, 399-401, and 597-598; *BAK*, Ministerium des Innern. R18-3329, Report of 22 Feb. 1935, based on Kussbach's secret communication to the *VDA*. The other Swabians defeated in the election were Török, Faulstich, Faul-Farkas, Sauerborn, Brandt, and Lang.

13.)"Dr. Franz Basch: fünf Monate Gefängnis. Urteil der königlichen Tafel Fünfkirchen," *Sbl.*, 21 April; "Ungarn," *N&S*, IX (1935-1936), 707-709. Horthy amnestied only Basch's prison sentence; his civic rights were not restored, *ibid.*, X (1936-1937), 322; *BAK*, D.A.I. Elaborat. Juli 1935. Three years later Gratz wrote that one of these irresponsible officials was Basch. Gratz objected to his behaviour during the recent election campaign. "He pursued such extremist propaganda that it upset Tolna County's traditional Magyar-Swabian amity." Gratz, "A magyarországi németség ügye," 362. All see Gratz, "Deutschtum und Ungartum," *Sbl.*, 23 June 1935.

14.)"Treu zu Dr. Jakob Bleyer über das Grab hinaus," *Sbl.*, 23 June 1935. According to the *Kameradschaft*, Richard Huss, on behalf of the radicals, passed a resolution of solidarity with Basch. It was signed by everyone except Gratz, Kussbach, König, and Faul-Farkas. Gratz thereupon furloughed Basch by virtue of his executive powers. *BAK*, R57. Elaborat.Juli 1935; *Kulturwehr*, XI (1935), 585-586. According to the *Kameradschaft*, Gratz's "treason" and "coup d'etat" resulted in a split into two camps: The *Kameradschaft*, embracing all unreservedly *volksdeutsch* Swabians and true champions of *Volkstum*, as well as several "silent" fellow-travellers. Spokesmen in the countryside belonged without exception to this group; and the opposition camp, represented by "yesmen" named by the government to the *UDV*; assimilants; renegades; Magyars—even one Slovak;—and Kussbach. *BAK*, R57 Elaborat. July 1935; F. Kussbach, "Was wir wollen," *Sbl.*, 14 July; F. Rajniss, "Was wir verlangen," *ibid.*, 21 July; F. Kussbach, "Wie können wir vorwärtskommen?" *ibid.*, 25 Aug.; G. Gratz, "Die Gegensätze im ungarländischen Deutschtum," *Pester Lloyd*, 8 Aug. 1935; and same title, *Sbl.*, 15 Sept. 1935.

15.)Gratz's interview with *Sonntagsblatt* on his 17 August audience with Gömbös: "Vor der neuen Schulverordnung. Exzellenz Dr. Gustav Gratz über seine Aussprache mit dem Ministerpräsidenten," *Sbl.*, 25 Aug. 1935; *Wilhelmstrasse*, Schnurre's Memo, 6 Mar. 1935, Doc. 32; *BAK*, D.A.I. R57 Neu 1155. Bd.26, Unsigned, undated *Kameradschaft* report. For Gratz's account of the subsidies, see Gratz, "A magyarországi németség ügye," 363, and Gratz, *DP*, p. 205.

16.)*Wilhelmstrasse*, Mackensen to F.M., Report of 26 June 1935, Doc. 35; "Ungarn," *N&S*, IX (1935-1936), 248-253; See Gratz's letter of 17 December 1935 to Huss, which bears out Basch's claim. *BAK*, D.A.I., R57 1299. Also see Huss' letter to Gratz, of 21 Dec. 1935, *ibid.*

17.)*Ibid.*, Zusammenfassung. Dr. Basch. Dezember 1935; Zwischenberichte der volksdeutschen Kameradschaft in Ungarn, Report of 22 Dec. 1935; and Reports of 9, 10, and 14 Jan. 1936, in a similar vein.

18.)Gratz's comment in 1938. Gratz, *DP*, p. 233, note 2; and Gratz, "A magyarországi németség ügye," 365.

19.)Wilhelm Bäuml, "Um Sonntagsblatt und U.D.V.," *Sbl.*, 8 Dec. 1935; *Neues Sonntagsblatt (N.Sbl.)*, 12 April 1936; 5, 24 May 1936; 13 Sept.; 1, 22 Nov., 27 Dec. 1936; *BAK*, D.A.I. R57 1299, see *Kameradschaft* report to *VDA*, Resolutions of 20 and 31 Aug. 1936; Gratz's speech to the Plenary *UDV* Assembly, 20 Aug. 1936, see Gratz, *DP*, pp. 230-233. Also see "Ungarn," *N&S*, X (1936-1937), 324-325; *Pesti Napló* interview of 10 Jan. 1937, cited in *BAK*, Ministerium des Innern, R18-3330.

20.)E. Scholtz, "Evangelische 'Reichskirche' in Deutschland," *Gotthold,* 1 June 1933, 90; "Kundgebung zur kirchlichen Lage in Deutschland," *ibid.,* 1 Aug. 1934, 114; "Ungarn," *N&S*, IX (1935-1936), 198-199.

21.)*Korunk Szava,* III, 1 Feb. 1933, title page; György Széchenyi, "A vajudó Németország," *ibid.,* 15 Dec. 1933, 392-393 and 404; IV, 1 Feb. 1934, 44; "Az idő sodrában," *ibid.,* 15 Apr. 1934, front page; *Nemzeti Ujság,* the Roman Catholic daily, reinforced the messages contained in *Korunk Szava.* *DA*, XVI (1933), 505. M. Szabados, "Védekezzünk a germán veszély ellen!" *Korunk Szava,* VII (1937), 133-134.

22.)"Minderheitenpolitik in der Provinz," *Sbl.,* 2 April 1933; "Die Osterpresse und die Minderheitenfrage in Ungarn," *ibid.,* 23 April 1933; "Graf Bethlen verkündet in Berlin die deutsche und ungarische Interessengemeinschaft," *ibid.,* 12 March 1933; "Die deutsch-ungarische Beziehungen. Eine Unterredung mit dem Ministerpräsidenten Gömbös," *ibid.,* 23 April 1933; "Für und gegen die deutsche Minderheitenfrage in Ungarn. Ministerpräsident Julius Gömbös uber das Siedlungsproblem," *ibid.,* 7 May 1933; "Ungarn," *N&S*, VI (1932-1933), 100.

23.)*BN*, Schwind, p. 148.

24.)*Napló*, XV (1933), Bleyer's speech, 9 May 1933, 210-215. For German text, see J. Weidlein, *Geschichte der Ungardeutschen in Dokumenten 1930-1950* (Schorndorf, 1959), pp. 79-80.

25.)*Napló*, XV (1933), 223.

26.)*Ibid.,* Bajcsy-Zsilinszky's speech, 9 May 1933, 221-224, and 10 May, 276-277.

27.)Gömbös' speech of 17 May, "Ministerpräsident Julius Gömbös über die deutsche Minderheitfrage in Ungarn," *Sbl.,* 21 May 1933; "Eine Erklärung des Abgeordneten Dr. Jakob Bleyer. Dankan den Ministerpräsidenten," *ibid.,* 21 May 1933; J. Bleyer, "Was ich zu sagen habe," *ibid.,* 28 May 1933. The duel took place on 20 May. "Förderungen Dr. Bleyers zum

Zweikampf," *ibid.*, 28 May 1933.

28.)"Aussenminister v. Kánya über die ungarische Aussenpolitik. Ungarn und Deutschland, *ibid.*, 28 May 1933.

29.)J. Bleyer, "Weitere Erklärung des Ministerpräsidenten Gömbös über die Minderheitenfrage," *ibid.*, 28 May 1933; "Ein glückliches, gesegnetes Neujahr!" *ibid.*, 1 Jan. 1933; "Eine grosse Rede des Abgeordneten Stefan Milotay über die Minderheitenfrage in Ungarn," *ibid.*, 4 June 1933 (speech of 30 May); J. Bleyer, "Zur Demonstration der Generalversammlung des Munizipalrates des Komitates Baranya," *ibid.*, 4 June 1933; J. Bleyer, Erklärungen des Kultus- und Unterrichtsministers Valentin Hóman über die deutsche Schulfrage in ungarischen Reichstag," *ibid.*, 4 June 1933; I. Bethlen, "Magyarország kisebbségi politikája," 89-104; J. Bleyer, "Graf Bethlen über die Frage der deutschen Minderheit in Ungarn," *Sbl.*, 11 June 1933; "Aussprache zwischen dem Ministerpräsidenten Julius Gömbös und Dr. Bleyer. Offenheit und Vertrauen," *ibid.*, 20 Aug. 1933, on 11 August conversation; Bleyer to Deutsche Akademie, Letter of 8 Nov. 1933, *BN*, Schwind, p. 164.

30.)"Ein Jahr Gömbös," *Sbl.*, 15 October 1933; "Die deutschen Dörfer wünschen deutsche Schulen. Tausende von Unterschriften," *ibid.*, 21 May 1933; Franz Rothen, "Das Sonntagsblatt und Szabadság," *ibid.*, 28 Jan. 1934; Richard Huss, "Kultur, Vaterland und Nationalität im Staat," *Sbl.*, 25 Feb. 1934; *DA*, XVI (1933), 469, citing an observer from the Budapest area; *DGFP-C*, II, Mackensen to F.M., Report of 14 Dec. 1933, 229-233; *Wilhelmstrasse*, Mackensen to F.M., Report of 8 Feb., with Annex of 6 Feb. 1934, Docs. 18 and 18-1.

31.)G. Gratz, "Die Regierung und die deutsche Minderheit in Ungarn," *Sbl.*, 13 May 1934. Also see *Pester Lloyd*, same date.

32.)"Ungarn," *N&S*, VII (1933-1934), 583-584.

33.)Reported in *N&S*, VIII (1934-1935), 192 and 272; *Wilhelmstrasse*, Mackensen to Stieve, Letter of 30 Nov. 1934, Doc. 29.

34.)Schnurre mentioned in his report of 12 February 1935 that negotiations on a single school type had been in progress for some time. *Wilhelmstrasse*, Doc. 31. Also see Kussbach's corroboration, Kussbach to *VDA*, Report of 22 Feb. 1935. *BAK*, Ministerium des Innern. R18/3329; "Vor der neuen Schulordnung. Exzellenz Dr. Gustav Gratz über seine Ausprache mit dem Ministerpräsidenten," *Sbl.*, 25 Aug. 1935; "Zur bevorstehenden Schulverordnung," *Sbl.*, 1 Sept. 1935.

35.)*BAK*, Ministerium des Innern. R18/3329. *Kameradschaft* report transmitted from the *VDA* to the Ministry of the Interior, 30 Sept. 1935.

36.)Law 11.000/1935.M.E., announced in Parliament 20 May 1936 by Bálint Hóman, Minister of Education. *Napló*, VIII (1936), 63ff.; *Évkönyv és jelentés* (1936), pp. 94-95. Ordinances No. 110000-1935, No. 760-1936, No. 115084.1937X, No. 111110.1938VKM; *Magyarországi rendeletek gyüjteménye 1919-1939. Vallás- és közoktatásügyi miniszteri rendeletek* (Budapest, 1942), XVIII, 952-954.

37.)"Ungarn," *N&S,* IX (1935-1936), 323-327.

38.)Cited in J. Weidlein, *Geschichte der Ungardeutschen,* pp. 152-153. Also see *DA,* XIX (1936), 494ff. The *Kameradschaft's* critique was couched in even stronger language in a report to the *VDA.* Undated, unsigned report, probably of January 1936, *BAK,* D.A.I. R57/1299. Also see *ibid.,* Ministerium des Innern. R18/3329, *Kameradschaft* report, relayed to the Ministry by Dr. Steyer.

39.)"Ungarn," *N&S,* IX (1935-1936), 397; X (1936-1937), 140-141, 163, 193, 231-233 and 785-786; No. 18699.1937 VKM, cited in *Évkönyv és jelentés,* (1935), p.100; various *Kameradschaft* reports, *BAK,* Ministerium des Innern. R18/3329 and R57/1299. One way to judge the effects of the 1935 School Law is to study its influence on the numerical growth of the Swabian elementary school population. The number of Swabian pupils, which had increased each year since the 1925-1926 school year until 1932, began to decline thereafter. From its highest point of 59,751 in 1931-1932, the number decreased to 50,633 by 1937-1938, a decline of 15%.

40.)See list of grievances drawn by the Wilhelmstrasse in preparation for German-Hungarian negotiations. *Wilhelmstrasse,* Memoranda of 29 Nov. 1936, Docs. 73-1 and 73-2. Although between 1930 and 1941, the number of those who claimed to be of Swabian descent declined only be 1,573, as many as 173,638 of the total of 477,057 Swabians now maintained that they were Magyars according to nationality. *Évkönyv* (1930), p. 22; A központi statisztikai hivatal, *Az 1941. évi népszámlálás—demográfiai adatok* (Budapest, 1947), pp. 8-9; Árpád Török, "Das Problem des Deutschtums in Ungarn," *Zeitschrift für Politik,* XXIII (1933), 167-168; *Évkönyv és jelentés* (1935), pp. 295, 313 and 319; (1936), pp. 277, 295, and 301.

41.)*AA PA* II, Pol.2, PBU-D, Bd.IV, German Legation, Budapest, to F.M., Position paper, n.d., received 30 Nov. 1932; Schön to F.M., Political report, *ibid.,* 10 December 1932.

42.)Berning was vatican representative commissioned to look after the spiritual welfare of Germans in Eastern Europe. See *AA PA* BR-U, Bd.III, and *ibid.,* IIb, Pol.16, Religion und Kirche in Ungarn, Bd.I, Schön to F.M., Report of 24 Feb. 1933.

43.)*Ibid.,* BR-U, Bd.III, F.M. Memo for the Foreign Minister, 6 March 1936; *DGFP-C,* II, Docs., 31, 60, 74, and 140; "Ungarn und Deutschland. Graf Bethlen über seine Eindrücke in Deutschland," *Sbl.,* 23 April 1933; Árpád Török, "Graf Bethlen fährt nach Deutschland," *Ödenburger Zeitung,* 1

Jan. 1933; "Für und gegen den Nationalsozialismus. Eine lebhafte Debatte über den Hitlerismus," *Sbl.,* 30 April 1933.

44.)*Allianz,* Hungarian Foreign Ministry Outline for Gömbös-Hitler discussion, 16 June 1933, Doc. 3. Also see Wilhelmstrasse Memo, drawn by Heeren, 19 June 1933. *AA PA* BR-U, Bd.III. *Wilhelmstrasse,* Bleyer's Report to the German Legation, 11 Aug. 1933, Doc. 13. Next month, Masirevich repeated some of the same Magyar complaints to Hitler. See Bülow's Memo of Masirevich-Hitler interview, 20 Sept. 1933, *AA PA* BR-U, Bd.III. Masirevich declared: "A political entente between Germany and Hungary must be infinitely more important than the re-Germanization of a few hundred or even thousand Magyarized Swabians." For other complaints, see Schlimpert's Report to F.M., 29 Aug. 1933, commenting on Kánya's grievance against Friedrich Hussong's "Ein deutsches Stadtschicksal in Westungarn," *Der Montag,* 21 Aug. 1933. The article assailed the attempted de-Germanization of Ödenburg, Kánya's native town. Kánya also voiced other, familiar Magyar grievances, expressed by Gömbös earlier. In his *Nachlass,* Kussbach reminisced that German agents, briefed by the National Socialist Party, descended in droves on Hungary's Swabian regions. Both he and Bleyer condemned their unsavoury influence. *KN,* p.28. *DGFP-C,* I, Rödiger's instructions for the Budapest Legation, 11 August 1933, Doc. 400; *Wilhelmstrasse,* Doc. 12; *OL Kum.pol.168.cs.* 21/7 tetel, 2776/1933, cited in L. Tilkovszky, "A Német irredenta és Magyarország," *Történelmi Szemle,* XIII (1970), 379-380.

45.)Anton König, "Graf Bethlen über die Minderheitenfrage," *Sbl.,* 19 Nov., 1933.

46.)*DGFP-C,* II, Mackensen to F.M., Report of 14 December 1933, 229-233; *KN,* p. 29.

47.)*AA PA* IIb, Pol.25.Deutschtum in Ungarn, Bd.I, F.M. Memo, 8 Jan. 1934; *Wilhelmstrasse,* Neurath's Memo, 18 Jan. 1934, Doc. 17; *BAK,* D.A.I. R57 551, Confidential NSDAP Summary of Report Nr.4/34.Hamburg., by Ehrich.

48.)*AA PA* II, Pol. 2, PBU-D, Bd. IV, F.M. Memo, 22 and 25 May 1934, and 11 June 1934; and *ibid., IIb, Pol.25, Deutschtum in Ungarn, Bd.I, F.M. Memo, 24 July 1934.*

49.)*Wilhelmstrasse,* F.M. Memo of Hitler-Kánya conversation, 6 Aug. 1934, Doc. 25. See *ibid.,* Docs. 27, 27-1, 27-2, and 28, 2-17 Nov. 1934, on various conversations involving Schnurre, Neurath, Gömbös, and Masirevich.

50.)*AA PA* IIb, Pol.25, Deutschtum in Ungarn, Bd.I, F.M. Memo, 24 July 1934; *BAK,* Ministerium des Innern. R18 3329, Kussbach's report to Steinacher; Confidential Status Report on the Germans in Hungary; with covering letter, Steinacher to Ministry of the Interior, 24 October 1934; *Wilhelmstrasse,* Mackensen to Stieve, Letter of 30 Nov. 1934, Doc. 29.

51.)*BAK,* Ministerium des Innern. R18 3329; Mackensen's report to F.M., based on information provided by Kussbach on the proceedings of Gömbös' ministerial council. Kussbach also sent a copy to the Reich Ministry of the Interior through Steinacher. *Wilhelmstrasse,* Schnurre to F.M., Report of 12 Feb. 1935, Doc. 31; Schnurre's Report of conversation with Kussbach, 6 March 1935, Doc. 32; Mackensen to Stieve, Letter of 6 April 1935, Doc. 33; *DGFP*-C, IV, Unsigned Memo, 17 Apr. 1935, Doc. 38.

52.)See, for example, group of letters addressed to Steinacher and relayed to the Ministry of the Interior. *BAK,* Ministerium des Innern. R18 3329, 31 May 1935 and 30 Sept. 1935.

53.)*Ibid.,* R18 3330. Hasselblatt's Report, 7 May 1935.

54.)*DGFP*-C, IV, Rödiger's Memo, 6 June 1935, 274-276; Neurath to Mackensen, Letter of 27 June 1935, 370-371; Schnurre to F.M., with Enclosure, 27 July 1935, 502-505; Bülow to Budapest Legation, Telegram of 20 Aug. 1935, 567-568; Mackensen to F.M., Telegram of 27 Aug. 1935, 586.

55.)*Wilhelmstrasse,* Mackensen to F.M., Report of 26 June 1935, Doc. 35, and note 1, referring to Mackensen's 17 June 1935 Report to the F.M.; Schnurre to F.M., Report of 6 Aug. 1935, p. 103, note 2. Kussbach successfully resisted resignation proceedings from nearly every quarter until 1 January 1936.

56.)*DGFP*-C, IV, F.M. Memo, 27 Sept. 1935, 667-670; *AA PA* BR-U, Bd.III, Neurath's Report of Gömbös-Hitler conversation, 29 Sept. 1935; Neurath's Memo of 30 Sept. 1935; Lorenz's Memo, 25 Oct. 1935, 774-775; *Wilhelmstrasse,* Mackensen's Report, 7 Oct. 1935, Doc. 43, and note 1, p. 112.

57.)*OL Küm.*3352/pol.1935. György Szabó to Hungarian F.M., Report of 6 Nov. 1935; *DGFP*-C, IV, Mackensen to F.M., Report of 21 Nov. 1935, 842-847. Mackensen continually urged moderation and caution as the only means of allaying Magyar suspicions, and creating tolerable conditions for the Swabians. Mackensen to F.M., Report of 15 Feb. 1936, *Wilhelmstrasse,* Doc. 50; Stieve to Budapest Legation, Report of 30 Jan. 1936, Doc. 49.

58.)*DGFP*-C, IV, Stieve to Budapest Legation, Report on Pataky talks, 1046-1049. See the voluminous *Kameradschaft* literature transmitted to the NSDAP Foreign Office through Dr. Steyer, requesting that pressure be exerted on the then visiting Pataky by high Party authorities. *BAK,* Aussenpolit. Amt der NSDAP, Letter and enclosure of 19 Dec. 1935; also see *ibid.,* D.A.I. R57 1299, Reports of 22 Dec. 1935 through 14 Jan. 1936; and *ibid.,* Ministerium des Innern, R18 3329, Steyer to Tiedje, Letter and Annex of 22 Feb. 1936.

59.)*Ibid.,* R18 3330, Staatspolizei, Berlin, to Ministry of the Interior,

Letter and Attachment, 30 Nov. 1936: *ibid.*, Steyer to Ministry of the Interior, Letter of 31 Dec. 1936, with Enclosures: Gratz to Huss, letters of 5 and 8 Dec. 1936; *Wilhelmstrasse,* Mackensen to F.M., Report of 15 Feb. 1936, Doc. 50.

60.)*BAK*, Ministerium des Innern, R18 3330, Strictly Confidential Report, *Kameradschaft* (signed *Spectator*) to Steinacher, n.d., covering letter, Steinacher to Ministry of the Interior, 1 Oct. 1936; Twardowski to Min. of the Int., Note of 15 Dec. 1936, with Enclosure. Pataky's notation of 27 April 1936 is cited in Tilkovszky, "A német irredenta," 386, note 81.

61.)*Napló,* VIII (1936), Anna Kethly, Speech of 19 May 1936, pp. 35-37.

62.)Pataky's Mamorandum, "A csonkahazai németségnél észlelhető visszás jelenségek," *OL ME.* Nemzetiségi osztály, 35.csomó. C15501/1936, cited in Tilkovszky, "A német irredenta, 386; *ibid., Küm.*1045 pol., Pataky to F.M., Report of 26 March 1937.

63.)*Wilhelmstrasse,* Mackensen to F.M., Letter of 29 Nov. 1936, Docs. 73-1 and 73-2.

APPENDIXES

APPENDIX I

NATIONALITY CENSUS, 1880-1910

NATIONALITY	YEAR 1880	% OF TOTAL	YEAR 1890	% OF TOTAL	YEAR 1900	% OF TOTAL	YEAR 1910	% OF TOTAL
Magyars	6,403,687	46.7	7,356,874	48.7	8,651,520	51.4	9,345,000	54.5
Germans	1,869,877	13.6	1,988,589	13.1	1,999,060	11.9	1,817,000	10.4
Slovaks	1,845,442	13.5	1,896,641	12.5	2,002,165	11.9	1,970,000	10.7
Rumanians	2,463,035	17.5	2,589,066	17.1	2,798,559	16.6	2,950,000	16.1
Serbs & Croats	631,995	4.6	678,747	4.4	629,169	3.7	650,000	3.6
Ruthenes	353,226	2.6	379,782	2.5	424,774	2.5	460,000	2.5
Others	211,366	1.5	243,795	1.6	333,008	2.0	398,000	2.2
TOTAL	13,778,628	100.0	15,133,494	100.0	16,838,255	100.0	17,590,000	100.0

Magyar statisztikai évkönyv, passim; Nation und Staat, XI, No. 3 (1937), 33;

H.W. V. Temperley, ed., A History of the Peace Conference, London, 1921, Vol. V,
p. 151.

APPENDIX II

Diminution of Germans in Trianon Hungary

YEAR	TOTAL NO. OF GERMANS	% OF POPULATION	GERMANS IN RURAL AREAS	% OF GERMANS	GERMANS IN URBAN AREAS	% OF GERMANS
1880	607,505	11.4	427,156	70.5	180,429	29.5
1910	554,237	7.3	441,729	81.5	109,482	18.5
1930	478,630	5.5	397,246	83.0	81,384	17.0

Nation und Staat, XI, No. 3 (1937), p. 166.

APPENDIX III

HIGHER EDUCATION CENSUS BEFORE WORLD WAR I

NATIONALITY	% OF POP. 1910	% OF GYMN. GRADS 1912-13	% OF UNIVERSITY GRAD. 1910-11
Magyars	54.5	82.0	89.4
Germans	10.4	7.8	4.3
Slovaks	10.7	2.1	0.6
Rumanians	16.1	5.7	3.8
Ruthenes	2.5	0.1	0.0
Croats	1.1	0.2	0.4
Serbs	2.5	1.6	1.1

Robert A. Kann, The Habsburg Empire. A Study in Integration and Disintegration, (New York, 1957), pp. 108 and 115; Oscar Jászi, The Dissolution of the Habsburg Monarchy, (Chicago, 1964), p. 281.

APPENDIX IV -1

Survey of Magyar and German Minority Elementary Schools, Teachers, and Pupils, 1918-1938

MAGYAR SCHOOLS

	NUMBER OF MAGYAR SCHOOLS	NUMBER OF MAGYAR PUPILS	NUMBER OF TEACHERS IN MAGYAR SCHOOLS	PUPIL TEACHER RATIO
1918-19	5,247	734,935	13,753	54:1
1919-20	5,561	770,914	15,615	49:1
1920-21	5,776	801,170	16,668	48:1
1921-22	5,946	853,640	17,438	49:1
1922-23	6,003	728,809	16,734	44:1
1923-24	6,017	654,672	16,515	40:1
1924-25	5,969	Unkn.	15,594	Unkn.
1925-26	5,842	Unkn.	Unkn.	Unkn.
1926-27	5,948	628,003	15,540	41:1
1927-28	6,035	682,647	16,122	42:1
1928-29	6,109	757,696	16,811	45:1
1929-30	6,217	828,151	17,505	47:1
1930-31	6,284	880,191	17,695	49:1
1931-32	6,288	913,932	17,783	51:1
1932-33	6,310	909,149	17,832	51:1
1933-34	6,369	901,844	17,862	50:1
1934-35	6,312	884,599	18,039	49:1
1935-36	6,318	880,231	18,188	48:1
1936-37	6,332	880,045	18,260	48:1
1937-38	6,346	882,323	18,576	47:1

APPENDIX IV -2

Survey of Magyar and German Minority Elementary Schools, Teachers, and Pupils
1918-1938

	PURELY GERMAN NUMBER OF SCHOOLS	PURELY GERMAN NUMBER PUPILS	MIXED MAGYAR-GERMAN NUMBER OF SCHOOLS	MIXED MAGYAR-GERMAN NUMBER PUPILS	MIXED GERMAN-MAGYAR NUMBER OF SCHOOLS	MIXED GERMAN-MAGYAR NUMBER PUPILS	MIXED GERMAN-SLAV NUMBER OF SCHOOLS	MIXED GERMAN-SLAV NUMBER PUPILS	NO. OF TEACHERS IN GERMAN MIN. SCHOOLS	NO. OF SWABIAN TEACHERS IN ALL OF HUNGARY	PUPIL-TEACHER RATIO IN GERMAN MIN. SCHOOLS
1918-19	281	32,827	None	None	--	--	--	--	543	273*	--
1919-20	287	33,682	None	None	--	--	--	--	571	305*	--
1920-21	92	11,610	192	29,499	--	--	--	--	719	150*	--
1921-22	58	7,506	201	29,460	--	--	--	--	657	150*	--
1922-23	53	825	183	23,965	16	5,380	--	--	619	101	49:1
1923-24	9	239	214	24,603	36	4,458	--	--	674	96	43:1
1924-25	4	UNKN.	244	Unkn.	43	Unkn.	--	--	720	84	Unkn.
1925-26	48	"	396	"	Unkn.	"	18	Unkn.	Unkn.	88	"
1926-27	48	4,115	397	43,419	--	--	18	2,251	1,162	83	43:1
1927-28	49	4,640	386	46,088	--	--	18	2,451	1,187	74	45:1
1928-29	49	,355	393	53,602	--	--	16	2,533	Unkn.	Unkn.	Unkn.
1929-30	47	5,870	387	56,308	--	--	19	3,809	1,242	"	53:1
1930-31	46	6,296	386	60,961	--	--	19	4,037	1,260	"	56:1
1931-32	46	6,579	387	60,398	--	--	19	4,056	1,268	"	58:1
1932-33	46	6,420	382	61,690	--	--	19	3,900	1,243	"	58:1
1933-34	47	6,468	380	61,042	--	--	19	3,844	1,247	"	57:1
1934-35	47	6,259	378	53,050	--	--	19	3,796	1,239	"	56:1
1935-36	47	6,169	373	56,756	--	--	19	3,768	1,208	"	56:1
1936-37	47	6,211	373	56,878	--	--	19	3,743	1,209	"	55:1
1937-38	47	6,146	372	56,351	--	--	19	3,682	1,227	"	54:1

* Includes Urban and Trade School Instructors

Magyar Királyi belügyminisztérium, Magyar Statisztikai évkönyv és jelentés,

(1919-1922), pp. 162-163, 165 and 166; (1927), p. 205; (1929), p. 239; (1933), p. 287; (1937), p. 289;
(1923-1925), pp. 230-232; (1928), p. 248; (1930), p. 256; (1934), p. 289; (1938), p. 277.
(1926), pp. 220-222; (1931), p. 256; (1935), p. 299;
(1932), p. 264; (1936), p. 281;

APPENDIX IV -3 (Concluded)

Breakdown of Number of Teachers, and of Pupil-Teacher Ratio in Elementary Minority Schools

Number of Elementary School Pupils with German Mother Tongue

YEAR	GERMAN MINORITY SCHOOL		MIXED MINORITY SCHOOL		Number of Elementary School Pupils with German Mother Tongue
	# OF TEACH.	PUPIL-TEACH. RATIO	# OF TEACH.	PUPIL-TEACH. RATIO	
1918-19	543	61:1	NONE	NONE	81,851
1919-20	571	59:1	"	"	83,861
1920-21	193	60:1	526	56:1	63,003
1921-22	129	58:1	528	56:1	61,577
1922-23	26	32:1	500	48:1	54,788
1923-24	19	12:1	655	37:1	48,596
1924-25	6	UNKN.	714	UNKN.	UNKN.
1925-26	UNKN.	"	UNKN.	"	39,084
1926-27	104	39:1	1,058	41:1	40,825
1927-28	109	42:1	1,078	43:1	44,231
1928-29	UNKN.	UNKN.	UNKN.	UNKN.	50,112
1929-30	113	52:1	1,129	50:1	54,964
1930-31	114	55:1	1,146	53:1	58,010
1931-32	116	57:1	1,152	55:1	59,751
1932-33	111	58:1	1,132	54:1	58,149
1933-34	116	58:1	1,131	54:1	56,558
1934-35	116	54:1	1,123	53:1	54,228
1935-36	117	53:1	1,091	52:1	52,843
1936-37	116	53:1	1,093	52:1	51,945
1937-38	116	53:1	1,111	51:1	50,633

SELECTED BIBLIOGRAPHY

I. UNPUBLISHED DOCUMENTS

Auswärtiges Amt. Politische Abteilung. Bonn.

Bundesarchiv. Koblenz.

Deutsches Zentralarchiv. Potsdam.

Országos Levéltár. Budapest.

Österreichisches Staatsarchiv. Neue Politische Abteilung. Vienna.

II. PUBLICATIONS OF DOCUMENTS, SPEECHES, MEMOIRS AND AUTOBIOGRAPHIES

Bethlen, István, *Bethlen István gróf beszédei és írásai,* Budapest, 1933, Vol. I

Curtius, Julius, *Sechs Jahre Minister der Deutschen Republik,* Heidelberg, 1948.

Geheimer Briefwechsel Mussolini-Dollfuss, Vienna, n.d.

Hivatalos Közlöny, Budapest.

Der Hochverratsprozess gegen Dr. Guido Schmidt vor dem Wiener Volksgericht, Vienna, 1947.

The Hungarian Question and the British Parliament. Speeches, Questions, and Answers thereto in the House of Lords and the House of Commons from 1919 to 1930, London, 1933.

Karsai, Elek, *Iratok a Gömbös-Hitler találkozó (1933. június 17-18.) történetéhez,* Budapest, 1962.

Kőte, S., *A Tanácsköztársság közoktatási rendeletei,* Budapest, 1957.

League of Nations, *Protection of Lingual, Racial or Religious Minorities by the League of Nations,* Geneva, 1931, 2nd ed.

M.T.A. Intézet, ed., *A Magyar Tanácsköztársaság jogalkotása,* Budapest, 1959.

Magyarországi Rendeletek Gyüjteménye. Vallás és közoktatásügyi miniszteri rendeletek, Budapest, 1942, 42 vols.

Nemzetgyülési Almanach, Budapest, 1920-1940.

Stresemann, Gustav, *Vermächtnis* (ed. Henry Bernhard), Berlin, 1932, 3 vols.

Térfi, Gyula, ed., *Magyar törvénytár,* Budapest, 1925.

Zsigmond, L. ed., *Diplomáciai iratok Magyarország külpolitikájához 1936-1945,* Vol. I, 1936-1938, Budapest, 1962.

SECONDARY WORKS
BOOKS

Ádám, M. *et al., Magyarország és a Második Vildgháború,* Budapest, 1966.

Andresen, Karsten, *Die deutschungarischen Wirtschaftsbeziehungen und das Problem ihrer engeren Ausgestaltung,* Rostock, 1935.

Andics, Erzsébet, *Ellenforradalom és bethleni konszoliddció,* Budapest, 1948, 2nd ed.

Apponyi, Albert, *A nemzetiségi kérdés multja és jövője Magyarországon,* Budapest, 1926.

Auerhan, Jan, *Die sprachlichen Minderheiten in Europa,* Berlin, 1926.

Bahr, Richard, *Deutsches Schicksal im Südosten,* Hamburg, 1936.

Balogh, Arthur von, *Der internationale Schutz der Minderheiten,* Munich, 1928.

Beller, Bela, *Az ellenforradalom nemzetisegi politikajanak kialakulasa,* Budapest, 1975.

Beneš, Edvard, *Five Years of Czechoslovak Foreign Policy,* Prague, 1924.

Berend, I. and Ránki, Gy., *Magyarország gazdasága az első világháború után 1919-1929,* Budapest, 1966.

Bethlen, I., *The Treaty of Trianon and European Peace,* London, 1934.

Boehm, M.H., *Die deutsche Grenzlande,* Berlin, 1925.

Bölitz, Otto, *Das Grenz und Auslanddeutschtum - Seine Geschichte und Bedeutung,* Berlin, 1930.

Borsody, Stephen, *The Triumph of Tyranny. The Nazi and Soviet Conquest of Central europe,* London, 1960.

Bretton, Henry L., *Stresemann and the Revision of Versailles. A Fight for Reason,* Stanford, 1969, (1953).

Chmelář, Joseph, *National Minorities in Central Europe,* Prague, 1937.

Das Deutschtum des Südostens im Jahre 1928, Gratz, 1929.

Dreisziger, Nándor, A. F., *Hungary's Way to World War II,* Astor Park, 1968.

Erbe, Rene, *Die nationalsozialistische Wirtschaftspolitik 1933-1939 im Lichte der modernen Theorie,* Zurich, 1958.

Feledy, Jules, *Hungaro-German Economic Relations,* Unpublished Ph.D. diss., McGill, 1970.

Flach, P., *Dichtung und Wahrheit,* Munich, 1956.

Flachbarth, Ernst, *The History of Hungary's Nationalities,* Budapest, 1944.

Flachbarth, Ernst, *System des internationalen Minderheitenrechtes,* Budapest, 1937.

Gasztony, Endre Béla, *Revisionist Hungarian Foreign Policy and the Third Reich's*

Advance to the East, 1933-1939, Univ. of Oregon, Ph.D. diss., 1970.

Göttling, Hans, ed., *Aus Vergangenheit und Gegenwart des deutschungarischen Volkes Heimatbuch*, Budapest, 1930.

Hartmann, R. and Riedl, F., *Deutsches Bauernleben in Ungarn*, Berlin, 1938.

Hillinger, Michael, George, *The German National Movement in Interwar Hungary*, unpublished Ph.D. diss., Columbia Univ., 1973.

Incze, M., *Az 1929-1933. Évi világgazdasági válság hatása Magyarországon*, Budapest, 1955.

Irinyi, Károly, *A Naumann-féle Mitteleuropa-tervezet és a magyar politikai közvélemény*, Budapest, 1963.

Jacobsen, Hans-Adolf, *Hans Steinacher, Bundesleiter des VDA 1933-1937 - Erinnerungen und Dokumente*, Boppard a/Rh., 1970.

Jacobsen, H-A., *Nazionalsozialistische Aussenpolitik 1933-1938*, Frankfurt, 1968.

Jánossy, Dennis A., *Public Instruction in Hungary*, Budapest, 1929.

Junghann, Otto, *National Minorities in Europe*, New York, 1931.

Kis, Aladár, *Magyarország külpolitikája a második világháború előestején*, Budapest, 1963.

Klocke, H., *Deutsches und madjarisches Dorf in Ungarn*, Leipzig, 1937.

Kónya, Sándor, *Gömbös kísérlete totális fasiszta diktatúra megteremtésére*, Budapest, 1968.

Kornis, Gyula, *Magyarország közoktatásügye a világháború óta*, Budapest, 1932, 2nd ed.

Kornis, Julius, *Ungarns Unterrichtswesen seit dem Weltkriege*, Leipzig, 1930.

Kovács, Alajos, *Magyarország népe és népesedésének kérdése*, Budapest, 1941.

Kovács, Alajos, *A németek helyzete csonkamagyarországon a statisztika megvilágosításában*, Budapest, 1936.

Kraus, Herbert, *Das Recht der Minderheiten*, Berlin, 1927.

Lackó, Miklós, *Arrow-cross Men, National Socialists 1935-1944*, Budapest, 1969.

Lackó, M, *Nyilasok, Nemzetiszocialisták 1935-44*, Budapest, 1966.

Macartney, C. A., *Problems of the Danube Basin*, Cambridge, 1942.

Márkus, L., *A Károlyi Gyula-kormány bel és külpolitikája*, Budapest, 1968.

Moravek, Endre, *Magyarország nemzetiségei - mult és jelen*, Budapest, 1934.

Nemes, D., ed., *Az ellenforradalom története Magyarországon 1919-1921*, Budapest, 1962.

Olay, Ferenc, *Kisebbségi népoktatás*, Budapest, 1935.

Paikert, G. C., *The Danube Swabians, German Populations in Hungary, Rumania and Yugoslavia and Hitler's Impact on their Patterns*, The Hague, 1967.

Riedl, Franz H., *Das Südostdeutschtum in den Jahren 1918-1945*, Munich, 1962.

Robinson, Jacob, et al., *Were the Minorities Treaties a Failure?* New York, 1939.

Rosenberg, Alfred, *Der Zukunftweg einer deutschen Aussenpoltik*, Munich, 1927.

Royal Institute of International Affairs, *Nationalism - A Report*, London, 1939.

Schmidt, H. et al., *Das Deutschtum in Rumpfungarn*, Budapest, 1928.

Schmidt, R. and Boehm, M., eds., *Materialen der deutschen Gesellschaft für Nationalitätenrecht*, Berlin, n.d.

Schmidt-Pauli, E. von, *Graf Stefan Bethlen*, Berlin, 1931.

Schmidt-Wulffen, W-D., *Deutschland-Ungarn 1918-1933. Eine Analyse der politischen Beziehungen*, unpublished Ph.D. diss., Univ. of Vienna, 1969, 2 vols.

Schnee, H. and Draeger, H., eds., *Zehn Jahre Versailles*, Berlin, 1929, 2 vols.

Seton-Watson, Hugh, *Eastern Europe between the Wars 1918-1941*, Cambridge, 1946.

Sforza, Carlo, *Diplomatic Europe Since the Treaty of Versailles*, New Haven, 1928.

Soós, Katalin, *Burgenland az európai politikában 1918-1921*, Budapest, 1971.

Soós, G. K., *A nyugat-magyarorszdgi kérdés (1918-1919)*, Budapest, 1962.

Steinacker, Harald, *Austro-Hungarica*, Munich, 1963.

Sveton, Jan, *Statistische Madjarisierung*, Bratislava, 1944.

Sziklay, János, ed., *A magyar revizió 1920-1941*, Budapest, 1942.

Teleki, Paul, *The Evolution of Hungary and its Place in European History*, New York, 1923.

Temperley, H.W.V., ed., *A History of the Peace Conference*, London, 1921, 6 vols.

Toynbee, Arnold, ed., *Survey of International Affairs*, Oxford, 1927-1937, 15 vols.

Truhart, Herbert von, ed., *Völkerbund und Minderheitenpetitionen*, Leipzig, 1931.

Türcke, Kurt E. von, *Das Schulrecht der deutschen Volksgruppen in Ost und Südosteuropa*, Berlin, 1938.

Weinberg, Gerhard L., *The foreign Policy of Hitler's Germany. Diplomatic Revolution in Europe, 1933-36*, Chicago, 1970.

Winkler, Wilhelm, *Die Bedeutung der Statistik für den Schutz der nationalen Minderheiten*, Leipzig, 1926.

Wlassics, Gyula, *The Territorial Integrity of Hungary and the League of Nations*, Budapest, 1919.

Wolzendorff, Kurt, *Grundlagen des Rechts der nationalen Minderheiten*, Berlin, 1921.

Zimmermann, L., *Deutsche Aussenpolitk in der Ära der Weimarer Republik*, Göttingen, 1958.

Zsigmond, László, *A német imperializmus és militarizmus ujjáéledésének gazdasági és nemzetközi tényezői (1918-1923)*, Budapest, 1961.

IV SECONDARY WORKS
ARTICLES

Ádám, Magda, "Az ellenforradalmi rendszer reviziós külpolitikájához," Andics, E., ed., *A Magyar nacionalizmus kialakulása és története*, Budapest, 1964.

Balogh, Sándor, "A bethleni konszolidáció és a magyar 'neonacionalizmus', Andics, E., ed., *A Magyar nacionalizmus kialakulása és története*, Budapest, 1964.

Bellér, Béla, "A nemzetiségi iskolapolitika története Magyarországon 1918-ig," *Magyar pedagógia*, No. 1 (1964).

Bende, I., "Mezőgazdasági kivitelünk helyzete," *Magyar szemle* (1933).

Berend, I. and Ránki, Gy, "German-Hungarian Relations Following Hitler's Rise to Power (1933-1934)," *Acta Historica*, VIII (1961).

Bigler, Robert M., "Heil Hitler und Heil Horthy! The Nature of Hungarian Racist Nationalism and its Impact on German-Hungarian Relations 1919-1945," *East European Quarterly*, VIII, No. 3 (1974).

Eckelt, Frank, "The Internal Policies of the Hungarian Soviet Repbulic," *Hungary in Revolution, 1918-1919*, ed., Ivan Volgyes, Lincoln, 1971.

Ferenczi, I., "Der neue autonome Zolltarif," *Ungarisches Wirtschafts-Jahrbuch*, I (1925).

Fukász, György, "A polgári radikálisok nacionalizmusa (Jászi Oszkár és a nemzetiségi kérdés)," Andics, E., ed., *A Magyar nacionalizmus kialakulása és története*, Budapest, 1964.

Gergely, E., "A M.T.K. nemzetiségi politikája," *Jogtudományi közlemeny*, (1959).

Gratz, Gustav, "Állami közösség és népközösség," *Magyar szemle*, No. 4 (60), (1932).

Gratz, Gustav, "Verfassung und Politik," *Ungarisches Wirtschafts-Jahrbuch*, III (1927).

Hillgruber, A., "Deutschland und Ungarn 1933-1944," *Wehrwissenschaftliche Rundschau*, IX (1959).

Hoeft, K-D., "Die Agrarpolitik des deutschen Faschismus," *Zeitschrift für Geschichtswissenschaft*, VII, No. 6 (1959).

Karsai, Elek, "Documents. Meeting of Gömbös and Hitler in 1933," *New Hungarian Quarterly*, III (1962).

Kerekes, L., "Akten des ungarischen Ministeriums des Äusseren zur Vorgeschichte der Annexion Österreichs," *Acta Historica*, VII (1960).

Kis, Aladár, "Az ellenforradalmi rendszer reviziós külpolitikájának kialakulása," Andics, E., ed., *A Magyar nacionalizmus kialakulása és története*, Budapest, 1964.

König, A., "A hazai németség két frontja," *Magyar szemle,* No. 3 (127), (1938).

Kónya, Sándor, "A fasiszta kormánypolitika Gömböstöl Telekiig," Andics, E., ed., *A Magyar nacionalizmus kialakulása és története,* Budapest, 1964.

Kővágó, L., "Államszövetségi tervek a Tanácsköztársaság idején," *Történelmi szemle,* IX (1966).

Kühl, J., "Das ungarländische Deutschtum zwischen Horthy und Hitler," *Südostdeutsche Heimatblätter,* IV (1955).

Low, Alfred D., "The First Austrian Republic and Soviet Hungary,"*Journal of Central European Affairs,* XX, No. 2 (1960).

Pethő, T., "Contradictory Trends in Policies of the Horthy Era," *New Hungarian Quarterly,* IV, No. 12 (1963).

Rónai, A., "A németek számszerű csökkenése csonka-Magyarországon," *Magyar szemle,* No. 1 (133) (1938).

Sachse, H., "Die Verluste des ungarischen Deutschtums," *Schriften zur Volkswissenschaft,* (1937).

Schwind, Hedwig, "Jakob Bleyers Eintritt in den Kampf für das ungarländische Deutschtum," *Südostdeutsche Forschungen,* I (1936).

"La situation de la Hongrie en 1938,"*Journal de la Societé hongrois de Statistique,* (Budapest, 1939).

Spira, Thomas, "Connections between Trianon Hungary and National Socialist Germany, and the Swabian Minority School Problem," *Internationales Jahrbuch für Geschichts- und Geographie- Unterricht,* XV (1974).

Spira, Thomas, "Connections between Trianon Hungary and the Weimar Republic, and the Swabian Minority School Problem," *Internationales Jahrbuch für Geschichts- und Geographie- Unterricht,* XIII (1970-71).

Szász, Zs., "Egy kisebbségi folyóirat," *Magyar szemle,* No. 3 (131), (1938).

Szigeti, József, "A szellemtörténeti nacionalizmus," Andics, E., ed., *A Magyar nacionalizmus kialakulása és története,* Budapest, 1964.

Windisch, Éva, "Die Entstehung der Voraussetzungen für die deutsche Nationalitätenbewegung in Ungarn in der zweiten Hälfte des 19. Jahrhunderts," *Acta Historica,* XI, No. 1-4 (1965).

Windisch, Éva, "A magyarországi német nemzetiségi mozgalom előtörténete (1867-1900)," *Századok,* No. 4-6 (1964).

Wirthoven, A., "Die deutsche Bevölkerungsfrage in Ungarn," *Neue Heimatblätter,* III, No. 1 (1938).

INDEX

EAST EUROPEAN MONOGRAPHS

The *East European Monographs* comprise scholarly books on the history and civilization of Eastern Europe. They are published by the *East European Quarterly* in the belief that these studies contribute substantially to the knowledge of the area and serve to stimulate scholarship and research.

1. *Political Ideas and the Enlightenment in the Romanian Principalities, 1750-1831.* By Vlad Georgescu. 1971.

2. *America, Italy and the Birth of Yugoslavia, 1917-1919.* By Dragan R. Zivojinovic. 1972.

3. *Jewish Nobles and Geniuses in Modern Hungary.* By William O. McCagg, Jr.

4. *Mixail Soloxov in Yugoslavia: Reception and Literary Impact.* By Robert F. Price. 1973.

5. *The Historical and Nationalistic Thought of Nicolae Iorga.* By William O. Oldson. 1973.

6. *Guide to Polish Libraries and Archives.* By Richard C. Lewanski. 1974.

7. *Vienna Broadcasts to Slovakia, 1938-1939: A Case Study in Subversion.* By Henry Delfiner. 1974.

8. *The 1917 Revolution in Latvia.* By Andrew Ezergailis. 1974.

9. *The Ukraine in the United Nations Organization: A Study in Soviet Foreign Policy, 1944-1950.* By Konstantin Sawczuk. 1975.

10. *The Bosnian Church: A New Interpretation.* By John V. A. Fine, Jr. 1975.

11. *Intellectual and Social Developments in the Hapsburg Empire from Maria Theresa to World War I.* Edited by Stanley B. Winters and Joseph Held. 1975.

12. *Ljudevit Gaj and the Illyrian Movement.* By Elinor Murray Despalatovic. 1975.

13. *Tolerance and Movements of Religious Dissent in Eastern Europe.* Edited by Bela K. Kiraly. 1975.

14. *The Parish Republic: Hlinka's Slovak People's Party, 1939-1945.* By Yeshayahu Jelinek. 1976.

15. *The Russian Annexation of Bessarabia, 1774-1828.* By George F. Jewsbury. 1976.

16. *Modern Hungarian Historiography.* By Steven Bela Vardy. 1976.

17. *Values and Community in Multi-National Yugoslavia.* By Gary K. Bertsch. 1976.

18. *The Greek Socialist Movement and the First World War: The Road to Unity.* By George B. Leon. 1976.

19. *The Radical Left in the Hungarian Revolution of 1848.* By Laslo Deme. 1976.

20. *Hungary Between Wilson and Lenin: The Hungarian Revolution of 1918-1919 and the Big Three.* By Peter Pastor. 1976.

21. *The Crises of France's East-Central European Diplomacy, 1933-1938.* By Anthony J. Komjathy. 1976.

22. *Polish Politics and National Reform, 1775-1788.* By Daniel Stone. 1976.

23. *The Habsburg Empire in World War I.* Robert A. Kann, Bela K. Kirily, and Paula S. Fichtner, eds. 1977.

24. *The Slovenes and Yugoslavism, 1890-1914.* By Carole Rogel. 1977.

25. *German-Hungarian Relations and the Swabian Problem.* By Thomas Spira. 1977.

26. *The Metamorphosis of a Social Class in Hungary during the Reign of Young Franz Joseph.* By Peter I. Hidas. 1977.

27. *Tax Reform in Eighteenth-Century Lombardy.* By Daniel M. Klang. 1977.